Henry Adams

The Middle Years

Henry Adams

The Middle Years

BY

Ernest Samuels

THE BELKNAP PRESS OF
HARVARD UNIVERSITY PRESS
Cambridge, Massachusetts
London, England

Third printing 1979

Library of Congress Catalog Card Number 58–12975

ISBN 0–674–38753–8

Printed in the United States of America

TO MY WIFE

Preface

THIS volume is a biographical and critical study of the main portion of that period of his existence which Henry Adams jestingly deprecated as his life. "Education had ended in 1871," he declared in *The Education of Henry Adams;* "life was complete in 1890." Thereafter, with life safely on the shelf, he adopted the pose of a posthumous existence and carried it off with unexampled vigor until his death in 1918. The wry paradox summarily dismissed from the record twenty of the most interesting and active years of his career. It was this twenty-year period that embraced the first great productive season of his literary genius and the most significant years of his emotional life. Within it lay the secret of his subsequent pilgrimages of mind and spirit.

In the present book, as in my preceding volume, *The Young Henry Adams,* the ironic mystifications and personal symbolism of *The Education* have been set to one side in order to see the maturing of a powerful and independent mind, not under the aspect of a cosmic theory, but as the product of its time and place in the afterglitter of The Gilded Age. The one-time private secretary in the London legation had long since given way to the ambitious journalist filled with the passion of political reform and he in turn had been transformed into the learned don at Harvard and the autocrat of the *North American Review.* Along the way the confirmed bachelor of thirty-four submitted with ironic grace to the congenial bondage of matrimony. In the present narrative we follow Adams and his wife, Marian, to Washington to inaugurate the middle phase of his career, the thirteen crowded, vivid, and, at the last, tragic years, which were to place a solid array of more than fifteen volumes bearing his name upon the shelves of his library. The period opened on the highest note of expectation; it closed with his desperate flight to the South Seas in 1890, a divided and lonely Faust.

Only recently has it become possible to recreate this portion of his buried life in all its uninhibited exuberance, passion, and despair. When, years ago, his friend Worthington Chauncey Ford published two volumes of Adams's letters, he adopted much of the reticence of *The Education* and by judicious selection and abridgment edited out clue after clue to Adams's private life. Some of the obscurity was dispelled by the collection assembled by Harold Dean Cater, but the crucial letters did not become available until some years later. Early in 1954 through the kindness and interest of Mr. Thomas B. Adams, Trustee of the Adams Manuscript Trust, I was granted access to the enormous treasure of family papers deposited with the Massachusetts Historical Society, the unique record of four successive generations of the most historically important family in America. In April 1956 these papers, faithfully kept intact for half a century, were conveyed to the Society by a historic deed of gift. This great collection is being edited by Lyman Butterfield for the publication project authorized by the Adams Manuscript Trust and carried on jointly by the Massachusetts Historical Society and The Belknap Press of Harvard University Press. A microfilm edition of the Adams Papers has been distributed to important library centers in the United States.

The Henry Adams papers constitute one of the most significant collections of the fourth generation. The thousands of closely written sheets that fill the rows of letter boxes in that collection contain much of the ephemera of the tea table and the club, but intermingled in rich profusion are the profound and often anguished self-searchings of the study. A distinguished biographer himself, Adams knew that nothing could be safely discarded. At long intervals he winnowed his papers, anticipating as he said the work of his literary executor; in the end the destructive impulse spent itself, for the riddle of human personality, especially his own, increasingly absorbed him. Every man, he once remarked, had at least two or three personalities and sometimes a dozen. If the immensely enlarged record reveals a brilliant mind in the grip of many prejudices and contradictions, it also shows a terrifyingly honest one, which more than ever defies a simple formula to explain it.

Confronted by the overwhelming mass of fresh source materials, which include also the extensive Adams collections at the Houghton Library and elsewhere, one may say *amen* to Adams's own comment that "a great mass of material is almost as troublesome to a biography as a short allowance." The embarrassment of riches has had very great compensations. For example, the carefully filed sheaves of letters from correspondents around the world admit one to the other side of the enormous dialogue which Adams carried on with the members of his circle: John Hay, Clarence King, Cecil Spring Rice, Elizabeth Cameron, Margaret Chanler, Charles Milnes Gaskell, Sir Robert Cunliffe, Brooks Adams, Charles Francis Adams, Jr., Oliver Wendell Holmes, Jr., Henry James, John La Farge, Augustus Saint-Gaudens, Stanford White, Raphael Pumpelly, Edith Wharton, Bernard Berenson, Tati Salmon, Queen Marau, Baron Kaneko, Henri Hubert, and scores of others. Certain finds have yielded invaluable sidelights: a striking fragment of Henry Adams's Diary for 1888–1889; Charles Francis Adams's long lost *Memorabilia;* a sheaf of Henry Adams's sonnets to Elizabeth Cameron; the unpublished remainder of his letters to his wife; and a group of 130 letters of Mrs. Henry Adams to her father and other correspondents which fill the vital gaps in the Ward Thoron edition. Much untouched material has also come to light in newspapers, magazines, public archives, court records, memoirs, and biographies.

The biographical aspect of this volume has necessarily received an increased emphasis. The interconnection between his life and writings grows richer and more complex as his literary artistry rises to mature expression. It is that process which is the central concern of this book. In the interval which has passed since the earlier volume appeared, Adams's major writings have had the benefit of able and perceptive expositors. In this work I have sought to show, for the writings of 1877 to 1890, their genesis, growth, and final form as part of the total fabric of his thought and feeling.

Northwestern University   Ernest Samuels

Acknowledgments

For their generous assistance in the gathering of materials for this volume, I wish to thank the directors and staff members of the following libraries, institutions, and archives: Boston Athenaeum, Boston Public Library, British Foreign Office Archives, Corcoran Gallery of Art, Harvard College Library, Houghton Library, Johns Hopkins University Library, Library of Congress, Massachusetts Historical Society, Newberry Library, New York Historical Society, New York Public Library, Northwestern University Libraries, Princeton University Library, Spanish Historical Archives, University of Chicago Libraries, Western Reserve University Library, Thomas Crane Public Library.

It is particularly pleasant to acknowledge my obligations to the many persons who shared some of their reminiscences of Henry Adams with me, made available private records and correspondence, and responded to a wide variety of inquiries: Mr. Bernard Berenson, Mr. Irving Brant, Mr. Harry Crosby, Miss Ruth Draper, Mrs. E. T. Gough, Mrs. Frank E. Harris, Mrs. Robert Homans, Mr. Henry Cabot Lodge, Jr., Mr. Mark De Wolfe Howe, Mr. Donald Marshall, Mr. Stewart Mitchell, Mrs. Rosalie Myers, Dr. Palfrey Perkins, Mr. Charles Scribner, Mrs. Ward Thoron, Miss Aileen Tone. I am especially grateful to Mr. Stephen Riley, Director of the Massachusetts Historical Society, for the many kindnesses which have made it a joy to use the facilities of the Society. My dependence upon fellow scholars is suggested in the Bibliography and specifically indicated in the notes. My thanks go also to my colleagues at Northwestern University and elsewhere who were never too busy to answer questions within their special disciplines, from history to geology, from anthropology to systematic theology.

To the Adams Manuscript Trust and in particular to Mr. Thomas B. Adams, I am indebted for the privilege of access to the Adams family papers prior to the launching late in 1954 of the edition of *The Adams Papers* by the Massachusetts Historical Society. Since that edition, which is being edited by Lyman Butterfield and is to be published by The Belknap Press of Harvard University Press, has been in progress, the papers on which it is based have been closed to investigators, though a microfilm edition of the entire body of family manuscripts through the year 1889 is currently being produced by the Society and may be used subject only to the restrictions of copyright. Grateful acknowledgment is also made to Mr. William A. Jackson, Director of Houghton Library, for permission to quote from the Godkin Papers; to the New York Historical Society for permission to quote from the Gallatin Papers; to Charles Scribner's Sons for permission to quote from the correspondence relating to the publication of Adams's *History;* to Houghton Mifflin Company for permission to quote from *A Cycle of Adams Letters, Letters of Henry Adams, 1858–1891,* and *1892–1918,* edited by Worthington C. Ford, and *Henry Adams and His Friends,* edited by Harold Dean Cater.

I am grateful to the Trustees of the John Simon Guggenheim Memorial Foundation for the Fellowship which helped provide an uninterrupted year for completing the manuscript of this volume and to the Administration of Northwestern University for leaves of absence and liberal grants-in-aid which have fostered the entire project from its inception.

CONTENTS

Henry Adams

The Middle Years

Chapter One

The Return of the Native

1 Flowering Judas and Laissez Faire

WASHINGTON, 1877. The great day had come to an end for which the bugles had blown reveille in 1861. Wakened to the morning's work of civil war and crusade, the nation had embraced large hopes, heroic concerns, and the epic mood. Now in the faded twilight of Reconstruction, dimly flickering over betrayed ideals and cynical evasions, the glory of that dawn was forgotten, its noble promise settled for political cash. No reveille signalled the new day, for the time of little men and little issues had come again.

Eight months had passed since the March morning when Rutherford B. Hayes had been shoved and hustled into the Executive Mansion with the reluctant last-minute blessing of a wrangling Congress. The passions of the "stolen" election still eddied about the cloakrooms and flared in recriminations through the press when Henry Adams and his wife arrived in Washington on November 10, joyously self-exiled from Boston. Stale conspiracies hung in the air, but Grantism, which had driven Adams into political opposition, was dying. The indulgent and gullible host at the Great Barbecue had taken his salute of twenty-one guns from the frigate "Constitution" at Philadelphia and set off in mid-May for a tour of the world, to admire and be admired as the ex-president of the newest world power, glad to be free of the bewildering exasperations of public office.[1]

For seven years Adams had profitably bided his time in Boston and Cambridge waiting the turn of the wheel, intermittently fretting at his self-imposed exile. Harvard gave him, as his father had pointed out, a dignified refuge during the Republican proscription, "a stepping stone in another career." There had been no stronger reason for giving up a career as an influential Washington journalist. Through all his successes as assistant professor of history at Harvard and as editor of the *North American Review* the desire to return to Washington never left him. The aura of political corruption, like an exotic and immodest perfume, excited more than it disgusted him. Cavillers might scorn the city of magnificent distances, so much of its splendors still on the engineers' drawing boards, but to Adams the broad outward thrusting avenues were more congenial than the meagre provincial lanes of Beacon Hill. He thought of it as his adopted city. The softer climate promised a wider margin to life and surcease for rheumatic bone and muscle tormented by New England winters. Nor could the elegant propriety of Marlborough Street in the Back Bay offer anything to beguile the passer-by as exotic as the lemon scent of magnolia that floated across President's Square and swirled about Andy Jackson's monument.[2]

On the surface Adams's coming to Washington was an "experiment," merely "searching archives," in his deprecatory phrase. But when he made his farewells in Quincy, he and his wife more pleasantly relaxed than was their wont, his father sensed the truth. "I feel," wrote Charles Francis Adams in his diary, "as if he was now taking a direction which will separate us from him gradually forever." With his intimates Henry did not conceal his own relief. He felt the elation of a Whitman: "I gravitate to a capital by a primary law of nature." He and his ambitious wife could occupy "the niches which ought to be filled." Once as a young man he had countered his mother's dread of moving to Washington as a Congressman's wife by the tempting picture of making "your 'salon' the first in Washington." The callow ambition of 1858 for a social center in Washington, a "family joint stock affair," had expired in the doubtful eminence of the London legation. Time and changing fortunes had dissolved the family partnership, but the vision of a Washington house as a center of influence, and possibly of power, remained.[3]

His decision to resign his post at Harvard puzzled and a little annoyed President Eliot even if it did not surprise the brilliant intimates of Adams's academic and social circle who heard his sardonic tirades at The Club. Adams made no secret of his contempt for a college system in which "the teacher assumes that teaching is his end in life, and that he has no time to work for original results." Yet his Harvard circle included some of the most original minds in America, men who were to leave their stamp upon broad areas of American thought and life: John Fiske, Oliver Wendell Holmes, Jr., Henry and William James, Raphael Pumpelly, H. H. Richardson, John La Farge, William Dean Howells, Chauncey Wright, Thomas Sergeant Perry. Perhaps only his equally hypersensitive friend Henry James, who just a year before had begun his own permanent exile in London, could have fully sympathized with Adams's discontent and sensed its hidden springs.[4]

The Albert Gallatin manuscripts had just been entrusted to him. He was to edit them and write the official biography. President Eliot would obviously have been glad to indulge him in almost any arrangement to give him freedom for his new task, especially since the burdens of the *North American Review* had already been liquidated by a political spat with the publishers. But one temptation Eliot omitted, the offer of a full professorship with an accompanying doubling of salary. It would have been a mark of consideration which

Adams had richly earned. Although his private income and that of his wife already made him independent of his salary, he was much too practical in his calculations to be impressed for long by empty honors. On any absolute scale he would gladly concede, as he had once said, his immense shortcomings; but relatively to the mass of men, that was another matter. It always irked him to be undervalued by his fellows. After all, Eliot had turned to Adams only after failing to entice E. L. Godkin, editor of the *Nation* and close friend of Adams, with an offer of twice the salary paid Adams and the rank of full professor. Adams's decision to accept the Gallatin project was sudden and characteristically impulsive. On March 2, 1877, he submitted a scheme to President Eliot for setting up a rival course to his own under his disciple Henry Cabot Lodge to "combat the inert atmosphere which now pervades the college." Six weeks later he had already grasped the providential deliverance from a career of "mere railing at the idiocies of a university education." [5]

Increasingly, teaching boys seemed mean work and depressingly repetitious, whatever the illusory charm of perpetually renewed youth asprawl in classroom chairs. When he ran down to Baltimore a week after his arrival in Washington in order to see President Gilman's new type of university on the German style, he was not tempted to change his mind and firmly resisted Gilman's offer. In his revulsion he was not even willing to lecture on his experience as a teacher. His thoughts ran to outrage, as when he wrote an English friend, "Such swarms of prigs as we are turning out, all formed by prigs and all suffering under a surfeit of useless information." More important than all was his deepening dislike for the tense social ritual of the little world compressed between Harvard Yard and Beacon Hill. His friend James Russell Lowell, after twenty years' distinguished service at Harvard, had made his escape only a few weeks be-

fore, welcoming President Hayes's offer of the Madrid legation with eloquent understatement. "I *should* like to see a
play of Calderon." [6]

The fixed footstool of creation, honored by the Autocrat,
was already receding to some alien shore, a curiously fit pun-
ishment for the State Street that tried to forget the Hartford
Convention. Decay — and new life — were in the air, but the
new life had a vulgar glow. Commercial and industrial Boston, more than ever, looked askance at an Adams. On the
eve of Henry Adams's departure from Boston two of his
brothers suffered defeat: in the winter of 1877 John Quincy
II failed of election to the state senate and Brooks by the
closest of margins lost his bid for a seat in the lower house.[7]

In the new Boston there was no room for the abstract
statesmanship nourished in the Quincy homestead. There was
also a want of occupation for the descendants of sea-ranging
merchant princes, like the Sturgises, his wife's cousins. Marian
Adams's grandfather, Captain William Sturgis, had dominated
the China trade for nearly half a century before the Civil
War. Some of the Sturgis sons had helped officer part of the
family empire in Canton and Manila. Now an economic revolution was underway. George Santayana, himself a Sturgis
connection, felt "the failure of nerve, the sense of spent mo-
mentum" among his privileged yet dispossessed cousins. The
Brahmin class began to close ranks against the outsider, to
turn inward and become defiantly parochial, and cultivated
their genealogies. The process fostered a desiccation of spirit
and a mandarinism that Adams found increasingly repellent
as he recognized his own large share of the symptoms.

From the vantage point of his home on Marlborough Street
in the new Back Bay, where the rational gridiron of broad
streets gave illusory promise of a revitalized Boston, he saw
signs of an even more striking change. In his long walks he
heard the blurred falsetto brogue of the Irish immigrants who

flourished and multiplied despite the decades-long disapproval of the Puritan families. Boston was already a half-Irish city and year after year Roman Catholic churches sprang up in new and old neighborhoods with the rapidity of military outposts, heralding the passing of Brahmin control.[8]

The election of a Republican governor of Massachusetts in 1877 led the *Nation* to hope that there might soon be "a restoration of the city government to the hands of the better classes." Gamaliel Bradford in the Boston *Advertiser* reported wholesale political jobbery and inspired the cry for limitation of the suffrage. There were even deceptive moments of hope. A "conservative" victory cheered the historian Francis Parkman. "Fortunately the low and socialistic elements — for we have them thanks to the emigration of 200,000 Irish to Boston — have suffered a defeat." [9]

The dedication of H. H. Richardson's Romanesque masterpiece, Trinity Church, in nearby Copley Square, on February 9, 1877, must have stirred Adams's sense of irony. His college classmate had built for permanence; the massive granite piers and lofty vaulting had provided an object lesson in church architecture for Adams and the members of his medieval history seminar. His friend and colleague John La Farge, an intimate of Adams's brother-in-law, Harvard treasurer Edward Hooper, had given a medieval splendor to the walls with his murals. Standing beside his two towering friends as he shrewdly estimated their work, he could hardly escape the sense of anachronism. In his sceptic's eye, as his novel *Esther* would hint, Trinity already seemed a monument to the religious past of Boston. As the words of the historical sermon of his Harvard college mate, Phillips Brooks, filled the great nave at the consecration service, he heard the past speak and not the future.

If Boston trembled for the future, the Washington of 1877 hurried to embrace it. One of the earliest planned cities, it was a chant democratic in brick and stone, celebrating the new order for the ages. There were a few blemishes. The unfinished shaft of the Washington monument, upon which work had been suspended since the beginning of the Civil War, hinted the disproportion between reach and grasp. But Governor Alexander Shepherd's remarkable transformation of the cluttered and overgrown Civil War city, reflected a Napoleonic daring — and knowledge of the power of "honest graft." Fine new paving and spacious sidewalks met the eye; the open sewers had disappeared, and sixty thousand new trees lined miles of streets. Every sign pointed to a brilliant future. The one-time Southern lethargy had succumbed to the War and Reconstruction. There was a refreshing hint in the air — at least to transplanted New Englanders — of Yankee bustle and enterprise. Modern horse cars glided swiftly along Pennsylvania Avenue where a few years before omnibuses and hackney coaches had lurched through clouds of dust and quagmires of mud. The first telephone had begun its impertinent clamor in the White House.[10]

To his English friend Charles Milnes Gaskell, Adams prophesied, "One of these days this will be a very great city if nothing happens to it. Even now it is a beautiful one, and its situation is superb." Three weeks after his arrival the *Nation* carried a lyrical tribute to the city that should have silenced most criticism of his move. The city, it said, offered a remarkable union of society and politics. There had been an extraordinary growth of libraries, museums, and art galleries and the "opportunities for literary and scientific study [were] almost, if not quite unsurpassed on the continent." The winter climate was suited to "cultivated persons whose health is delicate." With 150,000 people, Washington was scarcely half as populous as Boston, but the city had a spaciousness and monumental aspect absent from the quaintly huddled web of streets that pressed upon Boston Common.

Only a short canter from President's Square lay the lovely
wooded ravines of Rock Creek, still an almost primitive wilderness, which lent the city an idyllic aspect unique among
world capitals. For the nature lover, dogwood and flowering
Judas, rhododendron and hepatica lavished their beauty upon
the seasons.[11]

For all its bustling progress Washington still bore the mark
of the South. One third of its people were emancipated Negroes, thousands of these hidden away in noisome shacks in
the notorious "alley system" that threaded its squalid way
behind the deep lots of the town. The white population, made
up mainly of clerks and functionaries, represented every state
of the Union, the down East nasalities mingling with the soft
furry drawl of Texas. No other city presented such a mixture
of the older American strains. There were no factories or
large mercantile businesses and hence few recent European
immigrants.

Unlike Boston, the religious climate of Washington was
overwhelmingly Protestant. Different also was the strange
mobility of the population. The last great exodus had taken
place eight years ago when Grant came into office. In high
society the velocity of turnover seemed greater because of
the frequent changes in the diplomatic corps. Change was
the law of life and it gave Washington society something of
the fevered quality of a fashionable casino with its mysterious
entrances and exits, its dazzling stakes and disappointed ambitions. Family connections were duly honored but no long-
established families dominated the municipal life or reproduced the inbred provinciality of Boston. An emancipated
world, it was also a highly artificial one, without a significant
local politics of its own, and yet excessively charged with
the politics of the rest of the nation and swept by crises
from the corners of the earth. The separation of the capital
from the great financial and political centers made the op-

eration of party government more awkward than in London, Paris and Berlin but the length of the strings gave the reassuring illusion that the puppets had a life of their own. In this intensely political ambient Adams was destined to spend the remaining forty years of his life, as Lafayette Square's "longest resident." [12] There were to be many absences and the invariable summer flight, but wherever he would travel he would carry Lafayette Square on his back.

With a fine sense of the drama of their situation, Henry Adams and his wife Marian established their comfortable menage in one of William W. Corcoran's notable properties, the "yellow house" at 1501 H Street, a short block from President's Square, the elm bordered little park occupying two city blocks whose official name became Lafayette Square in the following year, 1878, the Republican City Administrator quietly ignoring Andrew Jackson whose statue dominated the square. After two winters there, out of sight of the White House but with a fine glimpse of the Square from the H Street windows, they moved down the street to another Corcoran property, "the little White House" at 1607 H Street where Adams could train the quick-firing guns of his wit directly upon the front door of 1600 Pennsylvania Avenue, a scant three-hundred yards away across the lawns and flower beds. At a safe distance from family counsels of prudence, Adams and his wife shopped with a touch of defiant extravagance. Fine paintings and water colors hung from the walls. Their baggage of oriental rugs made an impressive show. A fashionable clutter of Japanese vases and bronzes lent a special emphasis. Looking about their charming parlor from which the "dreary Congressional look" had been exorcized the two happy refugees from Boston felt pure bliss. "We strut around as if we were millionaires," said Marian. "Henry says for the first time in his life he feels like a gentleman." [13]

Each day as he crossed the square on his way to the State Department where his friend William Evarts, the new Secretary of State, had given him carte blanche to the great collection of Jefferson papers, he passed the heroic equestrian statue of Jackson, the Virginian thoroughbred rampant, the cocked hat outstretched in a triumphant and permanent salute. It always seemed to Adams a piece of private satire that this ancestral enemy of the family should mar his view of the White House, that seat of power so tantalizingly close and yet separated from him by the whole world of Jacksonian democracy.

A few steps beyond the intersection of H Street and Connecticut lay the "modest squarish dwelling" where old George Bancroft labored over his vast history. A block and a half farther down Jackson Place and he was abreast of "The President's Palace" itself, that storm center of ancestral memory. Here the irascible John Adams had briefly camped in the last year of his term and Abigail had hung her laundry to dry in the unfinished East Room while the soiled linen of her husband's party flapped in the sunshine for Jeffersonians to rejoice. Here from 1825 to 1829 John Quincy Adams had found himself thwarted at almost every turn by the venomous opposition of Andrew Jackson's partisans, lacking the one thing needful for success, the common touch. Here his father had come in 1861 for his disconcerting interview with the rough-hewn Lincoln. It was a place of troubling memories, memories of vulgarity, of spite, of coarse canards and bitter frustrations. To a patriot grandson the implications ran deep. They bore directly on the researches for the Albert Gallatin biography that took him to the third floor office in the new State Department building through the winter of 1877–78. Gallatin, the irreproachably scrupulous Secretary of the Treasury under Jefferson, had seen his conservative principles flouted again and again as the popular movement swept past him.

The State Department, "magnificently hospitable" in its new quarters, installed him at a private desk with space for his personal copyist and gave unlimited access to the restricted archives. From the library windows there was a fine open view across the Ellipse. Directly south were two small lagoons adjoining the vaguely edged tidal swamplands. The report of a fowling piece occasionally startled the reflections of statesmen — and historians, for the low ground of "Foggy Bottom" was still favored by duckhunters. The great South Front, completed in 1875, presented to an awed nation the most extensive and colossal version of a French chateau yet seen on the continent, a baroque kaleidoscope of pavilions, porticoes, porches, colonnades and chimneys, topped with a mansard roof, the effect French neoclassical or Italian renaissance, depending on the tourist's mood. Grant, after the tutoring of world travel, thought it the most curious structure he had seen. Marian Adams, eager to be pleased with her new surroundings, considered it beautiful. After twenty-five years of irritated contemplation, Henry Adams was to call it "Mr. Mullet's architectural infant asylum." [14]

Preoccupied with his first large scale literary work, Adams had little time for the sort of activity that had moved him like a tongue of flame early in the centennial year when he had made an abortive attempt to get back into politics. Even more remote were those exciting days of '69 and '70 when he had haunted the cloakrooms of Congress, hobnobbed with the brilliant group of Washington journalists, and used his eloquent pen to aid Congressman James Abram Garfield in tracking down the Gold Conspiracy. He had leagued himself with men like Charles Nordhoff of the New York *Post*, Murat Halstead, editor of the Cincinnati *Commercial*, "Marse"

Henry Watterson of the Louisville *Courier-Journal,* and Sam Bowles, editor of the Springfield *Republican.*

In the years away from Washington, Adams had closely watched the pattern of ineptitude, corruption, and political jobbery and had tried to make the *North American Review* an instrument of reform. Rejecting the economic determinism of the Boston businessman and tariff reformer, Edward Atkinson, Adams had followed the *Nation* line that the corruption in government was a purely political phenomenon. The seven years had provided rich but confusing materials for the social philosopher: the scandal of the Gold Conspiracy was followed by that of the Credit Mobilier, which mired the whole Congress in Oakes Ames's scheme for promoting western railroads at public expense. Even the irreproachable Garfield had been unable to resist the cut-rate stock offer to insiders. For a season, public business seemed an unlicensed hunting preserve. Through the headlines of that Gilded Age ran the stories of the "Salary Grab"; the wholesale bribes to Federal tax collectors, the sale of trading posts in the Indian territories, the graft in the collection of customs duties, the exposure of Orville Babcock, President Grant's private secretary, as an active member of the Whiskey Ring. Secretary of War Belknap had escaped impeachment for taking bribes only by handing Grant his resignation. Even the highest levels of the diplomatic service had its swindling business promoters. As for the Freedman's Bureau at the heart of the Reconstruction machinery, it was an independent realm of corruption.

Adams and his friends in the Liberal Republican movement of 1872 and 1876 had hopefully tried to reform the Republican party from within, but without control of the party machinery they were helpless. The Democrats squeezed as much partisan advantage as possible from the endless series of exposures, but not even a majority of the popular votes could win them the election of 1876 against the determined resistance of the party in power. Now, Hayes victorious, thanks to a single dubious vote in the Electoral College, was determined to conciliate public opinion, especially the crusading newspapers. He avoided Grant's mistake of seeking a millionaire cabinet and showed his respect for the influence of the liberal Republicans by appointing William Evarts to State and Carl Schurz to the Interior; with the latter especially Adams was on the friendliest terms.[15]

These coadjutors who survived Grant promptly rallied to Adams's convivial little dinners of six and eight. In spite of his resolution to "keep clear of politics" and listen to the "monkey-show," he found himself once again helping to manage the affairs of the Liberal Republican clique and becoming involved in their feuds. Schurz's efforts in the Cabinet to reform the civil service drew the fire of Senator Blaine's loyal secretary, Gail Hamilton [Mary Abigail Dodge] in the New York *Tribune*. Her line, as she was soon to write to Blaine, was that "all outcry against the machine is useless; that the first thing its most violent opposers do is to make another. This country is too large to be carried on by hand-sewing." Adams promptly tried to get Charles Nordhoff of the New York *Herald* to "sass" her. This maneuver failed, but on another front Adams and his wife won a total victory. As social representatives of the independent reform group, they systematically excluded Senator Blaine from their society and won his lasting ill will.[16]

Henry Cabot Lodge continued to look to Adams for advice. He had taken over Adams's classes at Harvard, but ambitious for a political career kept a very active hand in Massachusetts and national politics. In 1878 he joined John T. Morse as co-editor of the influential *International Review*. Since the *Review* had supported civil service reform, Lodge considered the attacks on Schurz to be meant for him as well. He blustered countermeasures. Adams dissuaded him, sensing the fatally weak point in Lodge's make-up, and in the process he asserted the relation of politics to history. "Your danger is a very simple one, and no one can hurt you but you yourself. It is that of adopting the view of one side of a question. No man whose mind will not work on its own independent pivot, can escape being drawn into the whirl-pool of party prejudices. Unless you can find some basis of faith in general principles, some theory of the progress of civilization which is outside and above all temporary ques-tions of policy, you must infallibly think and act under the control of the man or men whose thought, in the times you deal with, coincides most nearly with your prejudices. This is the fault with almost every English historian. Very few of them have had scientific minds, and still fewer have hon-estly tried to keep themselves clear of personal feeling."

Hayes had recently shown his moral integrity by standing up for sound money against the popular clamor for green-backs. Adams cautioned Lodge that the Independents would do well not to "bother" Hayes but to "mind our own busi-ness, and make money if we can." The Democratic Congress had done enough to jostle the cart by passing, over Hayes's veto, the "swindling" Bland-Allison Act, partially remonetiz-ing silver. A few months later, he advised Lodge to put the quietus on premature talk by Boston leaders of reform candi-dates for the next campaign, two years distant. "I should tell Wilson squarely that more harm than good will be done by stirring now." [17]

With power so precariously divided between a Republican President and a Democratic House and the parties them-selves uncertain what policies to adopt in a post-war world, Adams felt an unaccustomed uncertainty. Living so close to the political center, where the currency debate tended to obscure every deeper issue, he followed his old bent toward finance, but found the old dogmas no longer easy to apply. He turned as always to the literature of the subject, resolutely tackling Francis Walker's just-published book *Money*. Baffled, he wrote to the author, his former associate, "We are all talking silver here, and no one understands it. [The book] asks our own questions back again in a rather Sphynxian accent. . . . I have found myself obliged here to resort to questionings and silence. . . . I suppose ten years will solve the silver question as ten years solved the bank problem, but I am anxious to know how." [18]

He was shocked to learn that one of his former allies in the civil service reform movement, one-time Secretary of the Interior Jacob Dolson Cox, had come out in support of the "silver mania." Cox, a Representative from the "Western" state of Ohio, had been obliged to take account of the seething resentment of his constituents against the eastern money monopoly. To Adams this was proof that Westerners were no better in their commercial morals than they were in their social manners. The opinions aired at the Adams's table found their way into Godkin's editorials. The *Nation* declared that "advocacy of a change in the coinage not in order to make the standard of value steadier, but in order to make the payment of debts easier . . . [is] . . . *prima-facie* evidence of dishonesty. . . ." Henry's brother Brooks took a similar position in his article in the *International Review*, picking up the question where Henry left off ten years earlier.[19]

Except for this obsessive interest in the currency question, Adams was singularly untouched by the social and economic disorder of the time. The intimates of his circle denounced political and commercial fraud, but they were even more hostile to radical labor agitation. There was reason enough for conservative alarm over the violence of the labor disputes of 1877. To historians it was to be one of the "blackest" years in American history. Railroad rate wars had led to wage cuts;

these in turn provoked an epidemic of bloody strikes throughout the nation. At Pittsburgh at least 20 strikers and militiamen were killed, scores wounded, and in the ensuing tumult
$3,000,000 worth of railroad property was destroyed by what
the historian Rhodes has called "the dregs of society . . .
tramps, communists, criminals and outcasts." There was desperate fighting in Chicago, where in a single clash between
the police and "a mob of the dangerous classes" 10 rioters were
killed and 45 wounded. At one time in New York State alone
16,000 militiamen were under arms. Regular army troops put
down mob violence in Wilkes Barre, Scranton, and Easton.

The suppression of the railroad strikes did not end agitation. Labor union mass meetings continued to attract large
and militant crowds. There were frequent meetings in the
quiet city of Washington itself, denunciations of want in the
midst of plenty, resolutions demanding the eight-hour day
and recognition of the right to strike, outcries against defla-
tionary monetary policies. Western notables like the Hon.
Carter H. Harrison of Illinois addressed the joint labor unions but did not deter them from drawing up resolutions on
the "deadly conflict between labor and capital." [20]

The stories of these happenings came to Adams each day
in his copy of the Washington *Star*, but they touched him
only as vague reverberations from some kind of half world,
if not underworld of American experience. The *Nation* was
doubtless right when it declared that the noisy schemes of
labor reform were the sort "conceived by a tramp by his
evening fire, when full of stolen chicken and whiskey," and
no better than the proposals of the Communists who deluded
their victims with schemes for public works and factories. As
a practical realist Godkin warned that fostering such ideas
was "a great cruelty to the ignorant and unthinking" because
"Property, when really alarmed, is a terrible antagonist . . .
and it has no bowels of compassion." Admittedly the roar of

discontent could be heard "all over the Western World from the Urals to the Rocky Mountains," but, said Godkin, no means had been discovered of coming to terms with the "Red Spectre." The principles of laissez faire were immutable, he added. "Hospitals, almshouses, and asylums for the poor and infirm are among the marks of a superior civilization . . . but it cannot be said that society owes even these to its weaker members." The threats of the poorer classes must be met by substantial increases in the Federal army. The religious press was no more temperate in its denunciations of the trade-unions, the *Christian Advocate* declaring that "the worst doctrines of Communism are involved in these unions." These ideas, so intimately a part of Adams's social philosophy, were to be given scientific form a few years later by the Reverend William Graham Sumner, in his essay *What Social Classes Owe to Each Other*. Like his forerunner, the Reverend Thomas Robert Malthus, he asserted that they owed absolutely nothing. "A drunkard in the gutter is exactly where he ought to be." Christian ethics were valid so far as they did not conflict with Herbert Spencer's commandment, "the survival of the fittest." [21]

"To the man caught on a stool high enough to see over the crowd," Adams airily wrote to Walker, "the spectacle is not without entertainment. But this process of elevation requires that one's head should be in the clouds; that is, a trifle solitary and cool. I am used to it and 'rather like it,' but it does not suit everyone." The only conceivable remedy was, as the *Nation* put it, "the ordinary and rather vague one of individual prudence." Business statistics — or at any rate his offhand impression of them — indicated that the worst was over. A degree of patriotic optimism colored his report to Gaskell at Wenlock Abbey. "As nine-tenths of our people, or thereabouts have passed through bankruptcy in the last five years, we are quite free of debt. Everyone is about as well off as before. I think on the whole we are fairly prosperous." [22]

A later age may indeed be shocked by Adams's profound detachment from the less respectable classes of society. Yet he was undeviatingly consistent. Only sentimental reformers or mistaken humanitarians would fly in the face of irresistible logic and the laws of political economy. All of Adams's associations were fixed within an élite society of educated, able, and wealthy men who shared the same respect for economic necessity and obeyed the imperatives of *l'égoisme à deux, à trois,* or *à quatre.*[23] Only here and there on the fringes of that aristocratic society were there men like William Dean Howells and Samuel Clemens whose humble origin gave them a sympathy for the underdog. Howells had already drifted out of Adams's orbit and maintained only literary relations with the equally detached Henry James. His realistic novels of undistinguished common life were bound to be as distasteful to Adams's sensibilities, mild as the realism was, as Zola's more lurid French version of the new literary mode.

Somehow Adams managed never to meet Clemens, though they shared many friends. Perhaps the gaucheries that disturbed the wife of Richard Watson Gilder when the editor of the *Century* brought Clemens to dinner uninvited suggested the value of distance to the Adams salon. But if their paths did not cross, Clemens was to learn enough about Adams, no doubt through Hay, to write a broad travesty on his exclusiveness in "The £1,000,000 Bank-Note." Yet there was no lack of generous impulses, warm affection, and sympathy within the Adams circle, but these were lavished upon the elect and withheld on principle as well as preference from the outsider. The anti-labor union bias of John Hay's novel *Breadwinners,* a best seller of the early eighties, it has been said, had its germ not so much in the railroad strike of 1877 but in the comfortable study of Henry Adams. The two friends shared with the rest of their cultivated circle a passionate belief in political democracy joined to an equally passionate disapproval of economic democracy, a fatal division as the late Irwin Edman has remarked. As the gap steadily widened between labor and capital toward the end of the century, the unresolvable contradictions of this tradition were to drive Adams and his fellow travelers into the blind alleys of desperate pessimism.

2 The Social Vortex

If the world outside Lafayette Square with its well-tended lawns and flowerbeds and great sheltering elms was disorderly and uncouth, ravaged by bloody strikes or by devastating yellow fever epidemics, within its proximity lay a world pleasurably reminiscent of the Mayfair and Belgravia which had so charmed the Adamses during their delightful wedding visit five years before. Lafayette Square offered the nearest thing in the United States to compare with the charming purlieus of Grosvenor Place with its view of Queen Victoria's palace. It needed no daring imagination to see the nation's capital as a new London, a London improved and methodized, shorn of the vast residential and business purgatories of the English capital. Having tasted the best of the old world, Henry Adams and his resourceful wife set about to reproduce a center of culture and politics, of cosmopolitanism, of literature, art, and learning, of wit and inspired table talk.

There was much to do for he was "at the beginning of a frightful wrestle over a new house and the preparations for an entirely new career." There was but one cloud on the horizon of their new felicity. They keenly felt their child-

lessness. A certain philosophical resignation colored his reflection. "One consequence of having no children is that
husband and wife become very dependent upon each other
and live very much together. This is our case, but we both
like society and try to conciliate it." [24]

Their Boston salon had had serious limitations. The ad-
mixture of academic figures had been excessive. Interests
were unavoidably provincial and almost unbearably familial.
The prevalence of Adamses was especially trying for Marian,
and she too had been eager for emancipation. Except for
Henry they all dominated their womenfolk. Marian was not
happy at the influence that Charles Francis, Jr. continued
to exert upon Henry's career. Undoubtedly she had come
between the two brothers who had been such close collab-
orators.

Charles was well on the way to becoming a man of large
business affairs and a kind of public oracle, as the newspaper files indicate. Marian took Charles's measure fairly
early and he soon learned to respect — and a little fear —
her satirical wit. It was no easy task for her to hold her own
among the opinionated Adamses. Not a submissive type nor
given to demure self-effacement Marian could be as censorious as her husband. Henry's family had accepted his
wife into the "family concern" with a trace of reserve. Brooks,
it is said, had doubted the wisdom of the marriage, mindful
of the idle talk about the eccentric Hoopers. Henry had
countered that affection and care would protect his wife.
His engagement to "Clover" Hooper had come as a surprise
to his father, when the news reached him in Geneva in the
midst of the *Alabama* arbitration. The elder Adams knew
little of her, but her good reputation among their friends
reassured him and the old man wrote in his journal, "I trust
that the issue may be propitious." Afterwards, the one thing
that troubled his prudent nature was the scale of living that

Henry and his wife adopted. Shortly after the pair removed
to Washington, he sent an admonition which he felt Henry
"will not relish." [25]

A plain woman alongside her handsome sisters-in-law,
Marian had her own kind of distinction. Petite, no more than
five feet two, she was still only an inch shorter than her distinguished and scholarly looking husband, who walked beside
her with a certain emphasis of stride as if to make up for
his short stature. Marian reflected in her exquisite bearing
and restrained but elegant dress a kind of perfection of
Boston society. Her family had a colonial lineage at least
as old as the Adamses. The Hoopers and the Sturgises had
helped create the aristocracy of Massachusetts. An ancestry
of successful bankers and merchants, teachers and doctors
conspired to endow her with poise, intelligence, wit, and the
means to display them to best advantage. There was more
than a touch of her grandfather Sturgis's venturesomeness
that chimed with Henry Adams's own restless spirit. [26]

In her unfailingly regular Sunday letters to her long-
widowed father, Dr. Robert William Hooper, a wealthy retired oculist, she kept up unbroken the close communion of
the Boston years, when as the last to marry of the three
children, she had become the favorite and most indulged of
them all. Her father's Sunday letters to her also had the regularity of a devoted ritual. In her "hebdomadal drivel" —
"my diary" — she shared the excitements of her new and
emancipated life, bringing to view with extraordinary im-
mediacy the Washington milieu. She gaily threatened to
inflict her reports unless she were "ill in bed or dead." From
the almost masculine energy of these letters one senses something of the way in which she mothered Henry Adams,
supplying that domination at the hands of women which he
craved. There runs through them a forceful energy, a decorous
and yet ebullient high spirit, a patter of quick nervous charac-

terizations, serving the week's social adventures hot on the skewer.

In these incessant budgets of news there is no perilous self-study, no hints of moods, no depths to worry her "dear Pater." She had little taste for the inquisitorial self-analysis that her good friend Henry James imposed upon his heroines but enchanted him nonetheless with her intellectual vivacity. Like her husband she had a gossip columnist's instinct for diverting morsels and knew the value of exaggeration as a cure for dullness.[27]

The early letters to Dr. Hooper set the pace for the hundreds that were to follow in the ensuing eight years. "I have instituted 5 o'clk tea every day, thereby escaping morning visitors & it's very cosy — I forgot to say in telling of the dinner how nice the Sewards are — He is charming & his black skull cap which he can never leave off very picturesque — His wound of 1865 was never closed. . . ." Graphic vignettes of celebrities and snatches of political small talk regularly floated in a stream of domestic trifles. "Sherman thinks Plevna will prove a second Metz — says the Turks must go down. . . . We all adjourned to pay our respects to Mr. and Mrs. Hayes. . . . She is quite nice-looking — dark with smooth black hair combed low over her ears — and a high comb behind — her dress a plain untrimmed black silk a broad white Smyrna lace tie round her neck — no jewelry. . . . The new Minister to Russia was introduced to me — he looks like a handsome unprincipled old white buffalo. . . . The Hayes suffer much from rats in the White House who run over their bed and nibble the President's toes. . . . Henry is writing home today so you can swap letters with Mrs. Adams. . . ." Scandals in high places shared the page with Pepysian glimpses of Washington culture. "General Buchanan was a colonel in the regular army many

years ago when a young lieutenant rode drunk into the mess
and tried to get on the table. The colonel naturally requested
the dismissal of that lieutenant whose name was Ulysses S.
Grant — the wheel went round and somehow or other General
Buchanan didn't get to the top. . . . One item of last night's
amusement I reserve as 'unfit for print' but it's the best. . . .
We went to a 'Literary club,' a 'Washington' literary club.
Pickwick pales beside it — I thought I had seen fools — but
not until I had seen & heard Judge Drake of the Court of
Claims did I know what an ass was & is — he must be self-
made — it would be blasphemy to attribute him to any
other creator." The kaleidoscopic show fascinated her. She
preferred "humans" as she said, but occasionally Henry
would "sigh for his pines" and the seclusion of their summer
place near the sea at Beverly Farms.[28]

Each spring Dr. Hooper would come down to Washington
to visit the Adamses for a few weeks at their "charming old
ranch house at 1501 H Street," a house which his generous
Christmas checks had helped to furnish. Several superb
rose trees blossomed in front and a wisteria vine that Marian
planted became her special signature across the façade. Her
father continued to spoil her with attention and to lavish
presents upon her. With one check she bought a piece of
woodland between her father's place and theirs at Beverly
Farms, gaily forestalling Henry's gift of it.[29] In the summers
at Beverly Farms father and daughter renewed the old intimacy of Boston while Henry Adams kept faithfully to his
desk.

Marian took command of their Washington social life
from the beginning. Her small stature belied her driving
energy and ability as a manager. Henry submitted with
affectionate docility to her management. Henry James once
remarked, "We never knew how delightful Henry was till

he lost her; he was so proud of her that he let her shine as
he sat back and enjoyed listening to what she said and what
others let her say." [30]

Ruefully the Adamses surrendered to the calling card evil,
distributing their social largess with extreme care, however,
as it became more and more coveted by the social climbers
of the capital. As they did "not hanker for a large circle of
congressional friends," they found the rules of etiquette "a
delightful hedge." Swamped by official invitations, they increasingly begged off from the "kettle drums" and "Germans,"
in spite of Henry's passion for dancing. Marian detested late
functions and insisted on a reasonable curfew at their own
dinner parties. "Clover and I," Henry commented, "find our
own house more agreeable than most others." Still social
crises recurred. For example, their friend Charles Nordhoff,
"green as a gosling," sponsored one aspirant who turned out
to be a "female lobbyist of shady repute." Lobbyists particularly were tempted by the procession of inner circle
political leaders who came to the Adamses, people like
Secretary Evarts, Attorney-General Devens, Secretary of the
Interior Carl Schurz, Congressman Abram Hewitt and the
influential E. L. Godkin. Sometimes Henry had to be called
on to decline an invitation where the situation called for
special diplomacy. It was, as Marian wrote, a "process of
picking off burrs, which is not pleasant." When Congressman Fernando Wood, one time Mayor of New York, "con-
descended" to call first, Marian was not to be so easily
placated. "I may be squeamish but I do prefer the hospitality
of gentlemen who have not forged." An old acquaintance,
Kate Chase Sprague, whose declining beauty "puffy and
painted" seemed the just reward for her social sins, also
applied in vain. On occasion Marian found that it "takes
two to make a snub." A young miss notorious for her flirta-
tion with the Vice-President ignored the cut direct of the

etiquette books and made a speedy call, putting the Adamses to their frostiest mettle.[31]

In the "social vortex" of Washington they had "to steer gingerly, tack, reef, and at times scuttle one's ship." Marian's antipathies were perhaps more violent than her husband's and seconded his passion for exclusiveness. Her witticisms even more than her husband's went daily from mouth to mouth. At times Marian felt a little constraint in writing to her father because he insisted on circulating her vivid diary among at least a dozen relatives and friends, all the while protesting his innocence. She warned "Papa Ananias" that if he could be really trusted "you don't know how many spicy things I should put in." Even as it was, she had to caution him repeatedly that some of her choicest bits had come back "twisted and sharpened."[32] The Adamses succeeded in protecting the quiet of their Sundays from the importunities of their church-going neighbors. Irritated by the officious piety of political circles in keeping Lent they defiantly set out to make that season a time of special gaiety for their friends, obeying the same impulse that provoked Mark Twain to "hunt up," as he said, "new and troublesome ways to dishonor" the Sabbath-day.[33]

One of the few houses at which they became habitués during their first season was the Schurz's. There on Sunday evenings Carl Schurz would improvise with exquisite feeling at the piano. He, in turn, became one of the regulars at their tea table, appearing three times a week to add his authoritative voice to the cheerful clamor. Even more devoted was General Richard Taylor, son of President Zachary Taylor, who would come every day at "the stroke of five and stay till six." He was one of their contingent of Southern admirers, a group which included the gallant Senator Lucius Q. C. Lamar of Mississippi, then beginning his service in the Senate. There was also William H. Trescott, a former slave holder and Southern spokesman, who not long before had helped Adams out with an article on the "Southern Question" in the *North American Review*. General Taylor usually played devil's advocate. He "disbelieves in democracy and universal suffrage as firmly as Mr. Frank Parkman," said Henry's recording angel, "but is too much a man of the world to wail over the inevitable, like our friend Trescott." Lamar pleased them with his honesty and intelligence, but "in common with almost all southerners" persisted in the delusion that slavery had been "a delightful status for the Negro." To a little friendly baiting by Adams he once parried, "Ah, there, Mr. Adams, you ask me to look at myself in perspective." [34]

Already a connoisseur of Japanese art, then increasingly in fashion, Adams became fast friends with the Japanese minister Yoshida, who also shared Adams's lively interest in archaic law. Yoshida converted him from whist to Go-Bang, to the accompaniment of heroic collations of oysters and champagne. Adams promptly began teaching the game to friends like Aristarchi Bey, the Turkish minister, and set a fashion for the season. As Marian did not have her husband's sturdy constitution and tired more quickly than he, Henry accommodated himself to her gait. Besides he was now forty and "the grave was yawning for him." In Boston he used to be "frivolous" and "flicker out to a ball," alone if need be, while Marian sat by the fire. She had long since given up waltzing, much to the disgust of Henry's mother. "I think it's not in my line," she once wrote. In Washington he grew more sedate, though not quite willingly as one of Marian's latest entries in her "diary" was to hint. "Thursday to bed early and made Henry take my regrets to a young dance . . . where my frisky husband even danced." [35]

His wife ran their household with the aid of a staff of four regular servants, including an "indoors man," a staff that was soon to grow to six. In the spring of 1878 they began their habitual rides together, prowling through the woods to Georgetown, "finding about as much country life as in Beverly," and returning laden with white "bloodroot and other flowers." They were usually accompanied by two scampering skye terriers, Boojum and Pollywog. If the dogs strayed, it was the resolute Marian who did the necessary detective work, for on such occasions Henry became as she said "hopeless and useless with grief." [36]

For a number of weeks during their first season in Washington "Clover" was delighted to collate manuscripts with him in the comfort of the new State Department building, the two of them looking, she said, like "Cruikshank's illustrations to *Old Curiosity Shop*, Sampson and Sally Brass on opposite stools." The household ran on with agreeable and efficient smoothness. To save time they would sometimes have a guest to breakfast to talk, for Henry was "economical of hours" and one hour was lost "anyway in eating and feeding dogs." Zealously, she protected him from unwelcome interruptions. "Henry meantime being a man works hard, eats, sleeps, has no social scruples, but divides all my pleasures and doubles my burdens. He and the four dogs lead a life of Arcadian simplicity." [37]

Fond of entertaining, Adams and his wife had the means to make an art of it. Their joint income had now grown to twenty or twenty-five thousand a year.[38] The guests were always skillfully paired off as for a play. Sometimes a sample of a particularly successful dish like terrapin would be expressed to Boston to delight Dr. Hooper, with the precious recipe attached in case of spoilage. Although across the way Mrs. Hayes would not serve wine, deferring to the prohibitionists, at the Adams table the members of the diplomatic corps found the ritual of fine vintages faithfully respected.

Once the German Minister, quite carried away by the cuisine, exclaimed to his wife, "Oh, Lilly! Dass wir immer so essen konnten!"

The fame of their salon rapidly spread through the social circles of Washington, New York, and Boston, and admission to it became the brevet to fame — and a certain envy — among outsiders. Society columnists, ruthlessly held at bay, were not easily placated and bided their time. The twenty wax tapers in the chandelier would "light up to great advantage" the superb oriental Worth gown of Mrs. Bigelow Lawrence, the New York social leader, or their glow would fall upon the peripatetic Jack Gardners of Boston, she, as their friend Nick Anderson once noted, "homelier than ever in person" but the "same generous hospitable, cheery little body as of yore," and already famed for her objets d'art. John Hay, still exiled to Cleveland where he was serving his strangely congenial apprenticeship to his father-in-law, one of the chief financial and railway barons of Cleveland, began his visits. Started at last on the Lincoln history, Hay came in for a fortnight's work with Nicolay. Marian thought Mrs. Hay a "handsome woman, very — but never speaks." As for Hay, "he chats for two." William James, visiting Washington for the first time, seemed "a wee bit hypochondriac" but roused them agreeably with his combative talk.[39]

For science Adams could count on another favorite, Professor Simon Newcomb, the astronomer and mathematician, now in charge of the great new telescope at the Washington observatory. When he and Clarence King would come together, only the most valiant survived the abstruse talk of "curves of heat" and "catastrophic environment." The Adamses thrilled with vicarious excitement when King bounded into the house bringing the improbable horizons of the Far West close with his mountaineer anecdotes. He was an intermittent house guest from the beginning. A debonair little man, no taller than his host, with "blithe blue eyes and fresh tint" and close cropped hair that "early grew sparser and sparser," his carefully trimmed Vandyke belying the athlete, King frankly relished the paradoxes of his own career and enjoyed mystifying his hosts with sudden arrivals and as sudden departures to investigate gold and silver strikes all over the continent. There was a dashing versatility in the way he played his role as their "Byron" of the sage brush and the drawing room. He would show up with a Piute basket or send an antelope head as a New Year's greeting, each gift accompanied by an Othello-like tale.[40]

The politicoes were the most frequent visitors, coming in occasionally like Hewitt, after a rough handling in the House, to be comforted by one of Senator Lamar's inexpressibly funny stories. At an impromptu caucus on the silver purchase bill, the "Bland Swindle," as Adams regarded it, David A. Wells dinned into their ears the distasteful jargon of the silverite. Then Horace White, former editor of the Chicago *Tribune,* would come in to counter with the gospel of the "gold bug" and "bloated bond holder." Adams and Godkin severely lectured Congressman Jacob Dolson Cox for his wild talk of social upheaval if the silver bill were defeated. At another session they prodded Attorney General Devens on the danger of the silver legislation until he assured them that President Hayes would do "the proper thing" if the bill passed. At this time also Adams's acquaintance began with Wayne MacVeagh, former Minister to Turkey, who, though a son-in-law of the boss Simon Cameron, rejected the "family's principles or want of principles" and made common cause with the reform wing of the Republican party. The suave and knowledgeable Aristarchi Bey, Minister from Turkey, also swam early into their orbit, without waiting for them to call, but they at once recognized him as useful "for filling in at a dinner." [41]

President Hayes was the first of a long line of Presidents
with whom Adams was to endure an intimacy of sorts. Adams
thought him a nonentity. The President, for his part, was
equally unimpressed. During the winter of 1878 he dropped
in at the Schurz's, where Lamar, Godkin and Adams were
relaxing over cigars. The trio hardly looked up. Baffled,
Hayes left after twenty minutes. Encountering Nordhoff at
the White House, he grumbled, "Nordhoff, I've just met
two of your reformed Democrats at Schurz's — Godkin and
Henry Adams. What dull owls they are!" Nordhoff, in ecstasy,
hurried across the Square to share the Presidential *mot*.[42]

As Adams looked back on the experimental first winter
in Washington he was able to call it an unqualified success.
He had "worked hard and with good effect." His wife "had
a house always amusing and interesting." For her part, the
drama of Washington life was so agreeable that she looked
ahead to their continued residence with avid anticipation.
When they had first moved into Marlborough Street four
years before, she had exclaimed, "Life is so pleasant I wish
death and old age were only myths."[43] After a season in
Washington, there was even stronger reason for such a wish.

Yet death and old age were visibly not myths. In Washington death had its picturesque side. The white and gold
hearses in the frequent processions to St. Johns Church looked
to Marian "just like bon bons on wheels." All too often they
had to endure the clichés of the Episcopal ritual that ended
the chapter for friends and acquaintances. Unbidden, there
would rise to the surface Marian's horror — and fear — of
a lingering death and her brief comments regularly expressed
a kind of *absit omen*. "He was a pleasant courteous old man,"
she wrote of one of their departed friends, "and had a happy
life until his wife died, and is to be envied for having laid
it down so easily — I cannot understand why the Episco-
palians pray to be delivered from 'sudden death.' Henry

and I have made up our minds that where we die there we will be buried and not expressed to Boston like canned terrapin." Not long after, when their friend General Taylor died after a long, painful illness, the offending prayer made her positively wrathful.[44]

In their summer place at Beverly Farms in August, 1878, when Henry Adams began to think about going to Europe to collect source materials for a great historical project to follow the Gallatin biography, he could hardly avoid stretching himself with a luxurious yawn. "Every now and then, in my bourgeois ease and uniformity, my soul rebels against it all, and I want to be on my wandering again, in the Rocky Mountains, on the Nile, the Lord knows where. But I humbly confess that it is vanity and foolishness. I really prefer comfort and repose. . . . It is ludicrous to play Ulysses. There is not in this wide continent of respectable mediocrity a greasier citizen, or one more contented in his oily ooze, than myself." He almost regretted the unimpeachable domestic morality of their circle of friends, smugly complaining, "We do not even talk scandal."

3   Science and Politics

Adams's vision of Washington as the future cultural and intellectual center of the nation, the London or Paris of the New World, was the common dream of the large number of scientists who had been drawn to Washington by the exigencies of the Civil War and had stayed on to man the many new bureaus and departments that had sprung into being. One of the most active spirits in that scientific renaissance was Clarence King.

King had been graduated from the Sheffield Scientific School of Yale College in 1862. Resisting the lure of military glory, he had gone out to California with an emigrant train to join the California State Survey under Josiah D. Whitney. Stirred by the race to complete the transcontinental railroad, King descended upon Congress in 1867 with a grandiose scheme for a survey of a one hundred mile belt along the new railroad to the Rockies from the Front Range to the Sierra Nevadas, to illustrate "the leading natural resources of the country contiguous to the railroad and for purely scientific research." An irresistible empire builder of twenty-five, he got his appropriation almost single-handed. He promptly summoned his Yale classmates to assist him in the epochal task.[45]

For several years King had now been busy publishing the reports of the Geological Exploration of the Fortieth Parallel and writing his major contribution to it, *The Systematic Geology*, of the region. From time to time he would descend upon Congress from his headquarters in Newport, Rhode Island, with requests for more money for the massive quarto volumes. Adams had seen part of the far flung field work of the expedition in the summer of 1871 when as a guest of his one time Quincy neighbor, the geologist Frank Emmons, he joined the Survey in western Wyoming. Its magnitude and daring excited Adams's imagination. Not since the exploration of Siberia a hundred years earlier, under orders from Catherine the Great, had any government undertaken such an ambitious scientific inquiry into its domain. Adams had spent a month with the outfit of Arnold Hague, one of the principal geologists of the group, in the Medicine Bow country, and then seeking more dramatic scenery, he had joined Emmons's party farther west in the canyons of the Green River in the Uintah Range. He ran into Clarence King, who was the geologist in charge of the Survey, in Estes Park and the famous friendship began. The two men felt themselves to be fellow scientists, working in complementary fields. Adams thought of his work in history as scientific; King thought of his geology as historical — the Survey was "an epitome of geological history." In both men their professional interest was coupled with intense literary ambition, King having originally aimed at being a novelist. King, like Adams, loved to play with the paradoxes and enigmas of his science. Dazzled by the wilderness of hypotheses of King's science, Adams had returned to Harvard and his historical studies somewhat more willing to accept the limitations of his own field.[46]

Now Adams was once more on intimate terms with the extraordinary coterie of men surrounding King and his chief associate, John Wesley Powell, the explorer of the Colorado River, and on easy terms with the scientists of the Smithsonian. The grand reconnaissance in the geological history of the new empire of the American West anticipated the movement of Adams's own studies toward establishing a scientific cross section in American history. He followed with the closest interest the series of seven reports as they were brought out under King's direction. In 1877 as the scientific capstone and introduction to the whole series, King published his *Systematic Geology* of the region. Three other lesser surveys, each independent of the other — Hayden's, Wheeler's, and Powell's — brought their own contingents of scientists to Washington. Washington was also a center of invention and as privileged insiders Adams and his wife visited the laboratory of the Signal Corps to try out the first long distance telephone circuit.[47]

Inevitably Henry Adams became involved in the rivalries arising from the overlapping of the surveys and the differences in their methods. There were differences also over the political and economic implications of their work, especially over Powell's revolutionary proposals for conservation of the Western lands. The clash of rival ambitions erupted into violent public controversy, the most bitter being the long drawn out and tragi-comic feud between Professor Edward Cope and Othniel Marsh. Marsh, sponsored by King and Powell, had just succeeded Joseph Henry as President of the National Academy of Science and Adams was drawn into his camp in opposition to Ferdinand Hayden, geologist-in-charge of the Territorial Survey, who coveted a leading role. Scientists leagued with their chiefs until the behind-the-scene activities in the clubs of Washington resembled rival conspiracies, as they jockeyed for control of the proposed reorganization of the Surveys.

It was natural that King and his allies should gravitate into a scientific and social organization of their own, especially when it became obvious that their group would carry the day. In mid-November of 1878, a new club was founded, appropriately called the Cosmos Club. Its purpose was "to bind the scientific men of Washington by a social tie and thus promote that solidarity which is important to their proper work and influence." Major Powell, the initial organizer, became the first President.

Henry Adams joined the original promoters as an "author" at the founding meeting on January 6, 1879, and was made a member of the first Committee on Admissions. Among the many notable founders, besides King and Powell, were men like Spencer Baird, Secretary of the Smithsonian, Daniel Coit Gilman, President of Johns Hopkins, William Harkness, the Navy mathematician, Lester Frank Ward, a professional pale-ontologist with Powell's Survey, and Theodore F. Dwight, Librarian at the State Department. The first club rooms, opposite the Treasury on Pennsylvania Avenue, were only a short walk from Adams's home. In 1882 the club took the house at 23 Lafayette Square and by 1886 was settled permanently in the cluster of houses running to the corner of H Street.[48]

The excitement over the impending consolidation grew fiercer from day to day with Hayden's "spies" reportedly tracking down every rumor. King hurried in and out of town at frequent intervals, making his headquarters at the Adamses. On March 3, 1879, the bill passed setting up the consolidated United States Geological Survey in Schurz's Department of the Interior and King thought his work finished. Powell took himself out of the running for the Directorship by going into the new Bureau of Ethnology and he proposed King's candidacy in spite of King's known distaste for office routine. His desperate summons "I beg you to come and help me pull through" caught King in Los Angeles and toppled his defenses. The Senate confirmed King's appointment early in April in the face of Hayden's wild charge that King was corrupt. To the Adamses it was a "Waterloo victory," for they knew King's royal tastes. The six thousand dollar salary might well ruin him as he would be barred from the private practice of mining engineering.[49]

For a time the new bureau almost monopolized the Cosmos Club; however, leaders in many other fields soon leavened the geology with a cross section of intellectual Washington. Year by year the roster came to include many other distinguished friends and acquaintances of Henry Adams: Francis Walker, Superintendent of the Census, Alexander Graham Bell, Samuel Pierpont Langley, and Simon Newcomb; Horace Gray of the Supreme Court, Levi Leiter, the Chicago capitalist, James Lowndes, Adams's personal lawyer, Richard Hovey, Thomas Nelson Page, Raphael Pumpelly, the noted explorer of Mongolia, and Ward Thoron, the investment banker and scholar. The Cosmos Club became a place for convivial gatherings on Monday night for the exchange of the vital small talk of politics and history, science and art.[50]

Adams's interest in the new directions of science took, therefore, a great leap forward when he came to Washington.

Clarence King's arresting lecture at the Sheffield Scientific School on "Catastrophism and Evolution" reopened for Adams the old argument between Agassiz and Lyell. Adams dashed off a brief notice for the *Nation* to call attention to the epochal nature of King's theory. "In the face of the facts of our geology the uniformitarian theory breaks down and must be abandoned; . . . the existence of geological catastrophes must be accepted as part of the science, and must be allowed to have had a considerable, if not a principal, effect on the evolution of species." In an environment of violent change only the most "plastic species" could survive. Nature, plainly, "did proceed by what amounted to leaps" and these leaps corresponded with the alleged "gaps" in the geological record. Inherent in the idea was an escape from a deterministic universe, a crack in the iron fabric through which the romantic sceptic might defy science through science itself. In those "leaps" of nature was foreshadowed the possibility of a creative, emergent, evolution which would restore to life its immemorial mystery and wonder. The matter called for close watching.[51]

When the *Systematic Geology* appeared, Adams continued his scientific reflections in a two-column review in the *Nation.* King's effort to grapple with the great "riddle" of the cause of the giant displacement of strata in the Rockies seemed to him the most significant aspect of the work. Once the "laws" could be enunciated geology would become "a science in a new sense, and many of the most serious difficulties in studying past and even future changes of the earth's history might be overcome." King's theory of volcanic agencies rested in turn on William Thomson's [Lord Kelvin] thermodynamic analysis of the cooling of the earth's crust, Thomson being one of King's favorite authorities. The principle of entropy, dissipation of energy, expressed in the Second Law of Thermodynamics, had been long familiar to geologists, but Adams's allusion here is his earliest mention of the law that would later engross him. He was obviously impressed with the daring way in which the imaginative King differed with his friend, the cautiously scientific Powell, who theorized that erosion had kept pace with the slow upheaval of the mountain masses. King, himself, was later to regret the extreme features of his hypothesis, but by that time Adams was moving on to fresher scepticisms.[52]

The popular interest in science and the conditions for social progress matched that of the learned societies. The Chautauqua Literary and Scientific Circle helped to slake some of the universal thirst for knowledge. Washington newspapers loaded their inside pages with long excerpts from the scientific and learned journals, especially of a sensational turn, such as on the conflict between religion and science, on monetary theory, and on the perennially terrifying question of the age of the sun and its ultimate death. The most controversial subject was the women's rights question and the future of the family. The *Star* asked, "Are We Dying Out?" above an excerpt from the *Journal of Psychological Medicine.* The medical expert warned of the growing physical degeneracy of American women, the increase of nervous diseases, the loss of muscle, the dying out of the maternal instinct caused by modern fashions like the corset and the "temptations of too great prosperity." This was the line also taken by Dr. S. Weir Mitchell, the favorite neurologist of Washington and Baltimore society.

The news columns carried even graver matter to alarm the conservative masculine social philosophers of Adams's circle. In the "etiolated" society of Washington, as John Hay was to call it, the Anglo-Saxon woman, gentled by a few generations of good breeding and wealth, stood high upon her pedestal above the vulgar strife of the market place and the ordure of men's desires, a useful icon to compensate for

the sins of a man's world. But at the local conventions of
the women's suffrage movement a new feminine ideal was
emerging. Militant speakers clamored immodestly for emancipation in politics and society to match the compulsory
equality of factory labor. It was an ominous sign of the
times. Adams had not yet read Nietzsche's dictum addressed
to the élite of the Western world, "The happiness of man is,
'I will.' The happiness of woman is, 'He will.'" But acutely
feeling the currents of the time, Adams unconsciously concurred in it. In the artificial and feverish high society of the
Gilded Age in Washington the Woman Question showed
every promise of becoming a momentous one for the social
philosopher. One of the authorities on Adams's bookshelves,
Horace Bushnell, *Women's Suffrage: the Reform against Nature*, forecast an alarming evolutionary change; not only
would woman grow taller and more brawny as a result of
entering politics but an "immense moral transformation" would
come to pass when her prestige vanished and she became a
miserable failure. That spectre, like the Red Spectre, also
ranged as far as the Urals, for Tolstoy in his recent *War and
Peace* noted of 1812 that "there were then as now conversations and discussions about women's rights, the relation of
husband and wife and their freedom and rights." Americans
had long basked in de Tocqueville's praise that the prosperity
and strength of America were owing "to the superiority of
their women"; now they wrestled with the far-reaching
implications of that dogma.[53]

Not since the great days in the London of the 1860's had
Adams lived in so vital and intoxicating an atmosphere, one
surcharged with the most extravagant hopes and fears. The
grand visions of the possibilities of science which had so
excited his imagination fifteen years before were now being
realized on the largest scale under the aegis of Federal
government. His grandfather's dream of lighthouses in the

sky, of a frontier transformed by science, came daily closer to fulfilment. No wonder that he exulted to his English friend that here he and his "fellow *gelehrte*" might help bring in an American century which would say in its turn "the last word of civilisation." Here a science of society was at last within the grasp of mankind; here theory and practice might learn to run toward the future on both feet.

Chapter Two

The Admirable Alien

1 The Better Part of Valor

WHEN Albert Rolaz Gallatin, Gallatin's only surviving son, invited Henry Adams to write the biography of his father, he did so, as he said later, because since his father's death in 1849, he "had not been able to find anyone competent to write his history and with whom I was willing to trust his papers. Your name of Adams was all sufficient for me to place the most implicit confidence in your discretion, integrity and talents." For Adams, eager to make a reputation as a historian, the long delay was a stroke of luck. The figure of the elder Albert Gallatin, Secretary of the Treasury under Jefferson, had already begun to emerge in his thinking as the type of the ideal statesman. On such a subject the labor would be itself ample reward. He gladly agreed to accept only out of pocket expenses for research and copying.[1]

One of Adams's financial articles, "The Legal Tender Act," had had a special interest for the Gallatins. The hero of that article was the New York banker, James Gallatin, Albert Gallatin's eldest son, who in 1862, true to his father's economic orthodoxy, had advised Secretary of the Treasury Chase to borrow money for the war on the open market rather than issue fiat currency. The Gallatin name, in turn, was a household word to the Adamses. Gallatin figured importantly in the diary of John Quincy Adams, especially as a fellow negotiator of the Treaty of Ghent and one of the few persons to whose judgment J. Q. Adams willingly deferred. In 1837, when Henry Adams's father had called for a prompt return to "rigid settlement in coin," it was Albert Gallatin who had dared to accept the challenge. Under his leadership the New York banks had been the first to resume payment in specie. In 1844 the aged John Quincy Adams came down to New York to a banquet honoring his old comrade in diplomacy, irresistibly summoned by Gallatin's wish "to shake hands with you once more in this world." Recalling their long and disputatious friendship, Adams told the gathering, "Whether agreeing or differing in opinion with him, I have always found him to be an honest and honorable man." It was the highest praise one incorruptible statesman could pay another.[2]

The Gallatin papers fell into Adams's hands soon after he had begun his lectures on the history of the United States from 1789–1840, precisely the period within which Albert Gallatin's active career lay. Adams had espoused a quasi-Jeffersonian position in his lectures, leaving to his assistant Henry Cabot Lodge the eulogy of Hamilton. With the mass of Gallatin's letters and papers before him, he could now see the onset of the War of 1812, from the point of view of a Pennsylvanian. The papers supported the dicta which he had thrown off in his recent review of von Holst's *Constitutional and Political History*, that a centralizing tendency inhered in the Constitution; that "the precedents established by the Federalist administrations were accepted and enlarged by the Republican administrations" and that the War of 1812 created a distinctively American sense of nationality, superior to section and party. One of his first reactions was an impulse to look at the arguments for the States-rights' position. He picked up Calhoun's much-touted *Disquisition on Government* to see what the master theoretician of the South had to say on the great constitutional issues which had racked

Gallatin's party, carefully noting "Begun, May 1, 1877"; but the work inspired nothing but contempt and the margins bristled with angry jottings. It was no more than the "crude vagary of a South Carolina planter, half-educated and half-trained," based on the antiquated and "wretched" premise that government is of divine origin. "Reason," Adams noted, "has no place in Calhoun's conception of society." On the most vital point he was the complete antithesis of his contemporary Albert Gallatin.

The project grew rapidly under Adams's hands. Reams of transcripts rose on his study table at Beverly Farms. At first he had thought that only "a little more copying" would be necessary from the official archives, but when he got to Washington he struck "rich soil" in the Jefferson papers. Nonetheless, as a result of "six months of steady application" the editing of the documents was practically complete and he could turn to the biography as more transcripts continued to come in from New York, most notably of notes and letters from Voltaire to Gallatin's grandmother.[3]

On Christmas Eve, 1877, he sent off for approval the draft of the first three chapters, attaching an explanation which, had he included it in his preface, might have forestalled some of the criticism that came to him. "I have not attempted to translate the French letters. My reasons for doing so are: that it is always a little impertinent to suggest that one's readers are ignorant of French, and the American reader has a good deal of pride in such matters; that as a matter of fact most of the readers of this class do understand it; that a translation requires a great deal of labor and will occupy much space; finally, that as regards M. de Voltaire, I have my doubts whether the man who thinks he can translate him, is not a little of a fool." The draft had proceeded with gratifying speed, but Adams gave notice that the "real labor" lay ahead and that henceforth "progress must be slow and difficult." [4]

Avid as always for anecdotes he went to Baltimore to interview the picturesque and waspish old Madame Patterson-Bonaparte, living alone with her raffish memories of the Emperor's family and of the ruthless decree which had annulled her marriage to Jerome, Napoleon's youngest brother. She had once been on the closest terms with Gallatin and his wife. Henry's vivid impressions were promptly relayed to his father-in-law. "She is ninety-three years old and a miser. Henry was shown into a squalid room high up in a boarding house, no carpet on the floor, no anything anywhere, but a bedstead and a trundle bed for her attendant. Madame Bonaparte was dressed in old calico duds, sitting in her armchair. Henry says very handsome still if she would wear lace and diamonds and black velvet. She talked a great deal, had no criticism for Gallatin. As her tongue is a very sharp one that was rather surprising. She predicts that there will not be a sovereign in Europe in twenty years from now. She expresses great contempt for life in America, told Henry her memoirs are all prepared ready to be published, at her death of course she meant." The piquant reminiscences with which he had hoped to enliven the biography did not materialize and Adams had to content himself with the meagre personalities of the Gallatin papers.[5]

The writing of the background story of revolutionary Virginia inspired Adams to visit the localities where that history had been made. One focus of interest lay at Mt. Vernon. Twenty-seven years had passed since as a boy of twelve he had trudged along the mazy paths of that national shrine at the side of his father. His wife had never visited the place. Together they went down by steamer and "moused" about like all other tourists, reverently pausing at the deathbed, yet not overlooking the quaint touch of the opening in the bedroom door for the use of the cat. The visit deeply impressed Henry Adams for now every facet of the place was drenched with historical significance. In the same way Adams arranged early in May for a two day visit to Monticello with Jefferson's granddaughter Sarah Randolph. The Adamses did not head north for their annual visit to Beverly Farms until they had made a swing through western Pennsylvania visiting the backwoods locale of Gallatin's early career and the scene of the "Whiskey Rebellion." The most dramatic incident of Gallatin's life occurred at Brownsville (Redstone Old Fort) near Uniontown when he outfaced the irate riflemen of the Whiskey Rebellion. By June 7, 1878, Adams wrote from Beverly Farms to old George Bancroft, "We are at the end of our wandering for the present and I am at work again, to my great joy." [6]

Adams called on a number of experts for help, gracefully acknowledging his chief debts in the Preface. He owed most to his venerable neighbor and "friendly adviser," George Bancroft, who met his "numerous and troublesome demands" with "unfailing generosity." Though no disciple of Bancroft, Adams had in him the congenial model of a historian who celebrated the rise of American nationality with a patriotic fervor rivalling that of the German professors of history from whose pages a unified Germany had arisen. Adams confronted his historical task with like devotion, concerning himself with the crucial period when the nation created by the Constitution had to undergo the test of success, of the transition from ringing theory to the daily friction of party and sectional politics. He thus made common cause with Bancroft who was then working on his *History of the Formation of the Constitution* and passed on to him some of his finds among the Jefferson papers and other sources along with successive batches of proofs as they came from the printer.[7]

He profited especially from Bancroft's critical reading of the proof sheets as the following letter testifies:

April 25, 1879

My Dear Mr. Bancroft

"Absolutely cowed" is extremely strong; — meant so. Is it incorrect or unwarranted? If so I will change it.

If not, I know nothing in their expressions in regard to Mr. Jefferson's predecessor that should entitle Mr. Jef. to more than simple justice — at least from me. As my judgment may, however, be warped, I hesitate.

My own opinion is that J. *was* a coward, as he proved by resigning his governorship of Virginia in the face of a British invasion. C'était son seul défaut.

Ought I to say less than I have done? With my conviction on this subject, I thought this single word "cowed" essential. But I will defer to you.

Thanks for your kind encouragement. I have adopted your amendments in every case but one. That the Federalists wanted real war with France in 1799, I must maintain; all their letters openly say so, though I only quoted Cabot, thinking him authority enough.

Ever truly Yrs   Henry Adams

Bancroft evidently did not choose to press his gentle remonstrance so "cowed" stayed in though shorn of the scornful modifier. To get the woman's point of view, besides that of his own fireside critic, he enlisted two notable Boston blues. Writing to one of them, Mrs. Samuel Parkman, a Beverly Farms intimate, he gallantly exaggerated, "My two readers are you and Mrs. George Bancroft. If I shall have no more, but these two are enough to satisfy my ambition." [8]

The biography gave Henry Adams as agreeable a problem as a philosopher historian might wish. He could be as objective and detached as he ever was in his essays on British finance and yet point a moral for the times with even more stunning force. The issues which had stirred the country since the Civil War had all had their counterparts in Gallatin's time: currency and government financing, tariff revision, naval expansion, the spoils system, taxation, retirement of the public debt, public improvements, relations with England, the power of the Executive and the role of the Cabinet. Gallatin's career was a touchstone that might expose the political hacks who under Grant had debauched the government and whose influence still darkened national councils.

As a historian and literary artist Adams had a multiple problem — to bring Gallatin out of Jefferson's shadow, to rehabilitate his character from the Federalist calumnies that had gathered about it and to show that if his public career ended ultimately in failure, it was the failure of a tragic hero confronted by a hostile destiny. Like the Adamses he achieved leadership "by the sheer force of ability and character without ostentation and without the tricks of popularity," but in one vital trait he excelled them: "His temper was under almost perfect control." His power, like theirs, "lay in courage, honesty of purpose, and thoroughness of study." [9]

Courage is the bright thread upon which the narrative is strung, personal and moral courage, courage in the face of physical danger, courage united to forthright speech. Again and again Adams contrasts this courage with the supposed lack of it in Jefferson. At the time of the Whiskey Rebellion Gallatin went in person to urge acceptance of the Federal government's peace terms. "A word from Bradford, the old, personal enemy of Gallatin, would have sent scores of bullets" at him. Singlehanded he "had won the battle." Jefferson, on the other hand, when faced with dangerous crises, seemed always to flee. The Federalist taunt of the boy-poet Bryant still had bite.

Poor servile thing! derision of the brave!
Who erst from Tarleton fled to Carter's cave.

More charitable historians have since dismissed the ignomini-
ous escape from Cornwallis's raiders as a clumsy misadventure, but the romantic idealist in Adams demanded gallantry
before prudence even though he sensed its impracticality.
When editing Lodge's article on Hamilton for the *North
American,* he had rallied him, "Your abuse of Jefferson is
a trifle crude and wants delicacy of touch, but it is always
safe to abuse Jefferson and much easier than to defend him."
Perhaps the artistic need — and wish — to exalt Gallatin at
Jefferson's expense now tempted him. Perhaps he could not
rid himself of ancestral feelings. A quarter of a century later,
looking across at the White House on the eve of Theodore
Roosevelt's inauguration, he still nursed the old grievance.
"It is just a hundred years since [Jefferson] turned my harm-
less ancestor into the street at midnight." Perhaps even more
important in shaping his attitude was his wish to identify
himself with Gallatin, seeing in Jefferson the mirror of his
own weaknesses, his aversion to rough combat, his love of
abstract generalizations, and his own Hamlet-like indecision.
He would allow no one to impugn the physical courage of
Gallatin, least of all Jefferson. That Jefferson once did so,
even though without malice, affected Adams like a personal
affront. "If Mr. Jefferson thought that his Secretary of the
Treasury wanted the moral courage to speak out [against the
notorious duellist, Randolph] at the risk of personal danger,
there is no more to be said so far as concerns Mr. Jefferson."
Perhaps the singular violence of Adams's reaction stemmed
from his own obscure sense of guilt at having failed to prove
his own mettle on the field of battle during the Civil War.[10]

Gallatin was no doctrinaire statesman like Jefferson. He
had been one of the signers of the 1792 Pennsylvania resolution condemning sumptuary taxes by the federal government,
but by 1796 he came to see the unwisdom of that stand and

refused to recommend repeal. The "supple" Jefferson on the other hand curried favor with the frontiersmen by securing repeal upon his accession to the Presidency. In the matter of removals from office, Gallatin pressed Jefferson in 1801 to make a firm statement that "so far as respects subordinate officers, talent and integrity are to be the only qualifications for office." Jefferson drew back from a forthright commitment, the first of a long series of similar evasions, in Adams's stern appraisal.

Foreseeing the mischievous consequences of the Embargo Act, Gallatin warned that war was preferable to a "permanent embargo." Adams agreed it was the only "respectable policy, — war, immediate and irrespective of cost," but the overwhelming question was, obviously, with whom? England or France? Jefferson overruled the bold logic of his cabinet minister. Gallatin opposed Jefferson's feeble scheme for a cheap gunboat navy. Again "Mr. Jefferson did not take the advice, and, as usual, Mr. Gallatin was the one to suffer for the mistakes of his chief." The gunboat program proved a costly failure. In his message of 1806 Jefferson dreamed of a vast scheme of internal improvements — a national university, great highways and canals, "his last bequest to mankind," but his vision stopped short of practical measures and he irresolutely talked of a constitutional amendment. Gallatin immediately drafted a comprehensive plan and submitted it to the Senate, in the meantime having initiated the Cumberland Road — all without a constitutional amendment. While Jefferson doubted and temporized like Irving's Dutch governor, Gallatin found the money for the Louisiana Purchase and pushed through the plan for a national bank.[11]

The crucial test of the two men came in the last year of Jefferson's administration with the passage of the dreaded Enforcement Act which Gallatin, charged with the direction of the embargo, had demanded, though it violated his theo-

retical principles as a Republican. By bowing to the logic of
events he drove the Federalists to the now empty refuge of
the States' rights position which had once been the basic
plank of his own party. Gallatin had accepted the terrifying
lesson that "circumstances must by their nature be stronger
and more permanent than men." But not so Jefferson.

"Brought at last face to face with this new political fact
which gave the lie to all his theories and hopes, even the
sanguine and supple Jefferson felt the solid earth reel under
him, and his courage fled." His scrupulous neutrality toward
France and England had purchased no more respect than
the despised Federalists had been able to command. "He
abandoned his hope of balancing one belligerent against another; he abandoned even the embargo; he laid down the
sceptre of party leadership." He did "what no president has
a constitutional right to do; he abdicated the duties of his
office the moment the election was decided," throwing the
"burden of responsibility" upon his successor Madison and
upon Gallatin, who agreed to continue in the Treasury. "Mr.
Gallatin was made of different stuff. In his youth almost as
sanguine as Mr. Jefferson, he knew better how to accept defeat and adapt himself to circumstances, how to abandon
theory and move with his generation. . . . Facts not theories
were all that survived in the wreck of Mr. Jefferson's Administration." [12]

2 The Failure of a Hero

From the dramatic contrasts of the biography there emerges
Adams's ideal of the modern statesman, one able to "move
with his generation" and still to lead it. The book was both
testament and prophecy; it epitomized the political morality
of which all of the Adamses were trustees and it warned of

the dangers that lay ahead of the Hayes Administration and its successors if the lessons of the past were ignored. He conceived the underlying political movement as a dynamic process, but was not yet ready to translate that movement into scientific terms. He came no nearer to a philosophy of history than the general notion that politics is governed by a dark necessity and that the true art of politics and government is to discover that necessity and to take it into one's calculations. Gallatin "learned to recognize in the fullest extent the omnipotence of circumstance." He was politically educable; Jefferson was not. Yet, as the event proved, the education of Albert Gallatin was an education in the irony of existence; the age-old lesson of Greek tragedy, and of all folk wisdom. Jefferson's placating inaugural statement, "We are all Republicans; we are all Federalists" was translated by circumstances, into "Whether we are Republicans or Federalists in our aspirations, we are all Federalists in practice." By 1814 Gallatin had outgrown the dogmas which had been the original strength of his party. He was "riper, wiser, and infinitely more experienced than in 1800"; "the tone of his mind had remained as pure as when he began life"; but he had lost "that sublime confidence in human nature which had given to Mr. Jefferson and his party their single irresistible claim to public devotion." His statesmanship had become what practical statesmanship must always become — "a mere struggle to deal with concrete facts at the cost of philosophical and a priori principles." The great dream was lost; "there was no longer any great unrealized conviction on which to build enthusiasm." [13]

In the public arena, fate regularly took her revenges. Gallatin had fought to renew the charter of the Bank of the United States, realizing the immense value of a central bank to the Treasury. The bill was lost on the casting vote merely because Congressmen disliked President Madison. Four years later when "the government was bankrupt, the currency in frightful disorder, and loans impracticable," the Bank was restored. High as the price for public education had been, the lesson did not stick and the bank died under Jackson, because, as Adams, an advocate of central banking, moralized: "The popular fear of its hostility to our liberties was one of those delusions which characterize ignorant stages of society." [14]

This "delusion" significantly put him in mind of a contemporary one, the common fear that the great corporations were above the law. With *Munn vs. Illinois* in mind, the case in which the Supreme Court approved state regulation, he scoffed at the old "prejudice," one which he and his brother Charles had in fact shared in their *Chapters of Erie.* Now he leaped to the conclusion, prematurely as he would one day discover, that "The people of the United States have learned . . . that they hold all corporations at their mercy, and that if there is any danger to liberty, it is quite as likely to be the liberties of the corporations as those of the people who suffer." He forecast that similar irrationalities would probably settle the current silver question. In spite of such negative perturbations, his nascent theory of historical determinism recognized the presence of a mysterious energy or power at work in society which resembled one of the primary forces of nature. "There are moments in politics when great results can be reached only by small men. . . . Especially in a democracy the people are apt to become impatient of rule, and will at times obstinately refuse to move at the call of a leader, when, if left to themselves, they will blunder through all obstacles, blindly enough, it is true, but effectually." [15]

In Gallatin's management of the Treasury Adams found the true secret of power of the ideal statesman. Like his friend Godkin, he had long admired the British system of giving parliamentary status to the treasury and had impressed that ideal upon his students. "There are [wrote Adams] to the present time, in all American history only two examples of practical statesmanship which can serve as perfect models, not perhaps in all respects for imitation, but for study, to persons who wish to understand what practical statesmanship has been under an American system. . . . Only two had at once the breadth of mind to grapple with the machine of government as a whole, and the authority necessary to make it work efficiently for a given object; the practical knowledge of affairs and of politics that enabled them to foresee every movement; the long apprenticeship which had allowed them to educate and discipline their parties; and finally the good fortune to enjoy power when government was still plastic and capable of receiving a new impulse. The conditions of the highest practical statesmanship require that its models should be financiers; the conditions of our history have hitherto limited their appearance and activity to its earlier days. . . . The Treasury is the natural point of control. . . . The highest type of practical statesmanship must always take this direction. Washington and Jefferson doubtless stand pre-eminent as the representatives of what is best in our national character or its aspirations, but Washington depended mainly upon Hamilton, and without Gallatin Mr. Jefferson would have been helpless." [16]

Though in Adams's view Gallatin was superior to Jefferson both as a statesman and a man, his career was as much a tragic failure as Jefferson's. Jefferson's administration had "fixed beyond question the republicanism of national character, established a political system purely American, and sealed this result by reducing the national debt until its ultimate extinction was in full view." There but remained the grand strategy of directing the future course of the republican system by a scheme of "moral and economical development." In the heightened style which Adams reserved for the climaxes of his narrative, he wrote: "For this result Mr. Gallatin, in the ripened wisdom of his full manhood, might fairly say that his life had been well spent. For a time he saw the prize within his grasp; then almost in an instant it was dashed away, and the whole fabric he had so laboriously constructed fell in ruins before his eyes." England, determined to destroy American commercial competition for world markets, dismissed American diplomatic efforts with contempt. Napoleon, though more devious, had treated them with equal contempt.[17]

Adams, rewriting history in the clearer light after the event, believed that the United States might have improved her position by immediately going to war with France at the initial provocation, as the Hamiltonian Federalists had advocated before John Adams had intervened. England would then have been compelled to abandon her policy of suffocating American trade. But neither Jefferson nor his opponents had sufficient freedom of action to accept the principle of either a preventive or an offensive war. The disaster that finally overwhelmed them, war with England, was neither Gallatin's "fault nor that of Mr. Jefferson; it was the result of forces which neither he nor any other man or combination of men, neither his policy nor any other policy or resource of human wisdom, could control." Beneath this somber estimate there lurked a certain detached aestheticism, a faint hint of an ultimate reading of human experience. That so much hope, aspiration and popular faith should fail without the possibility of revival gave to the Administration "into which Mr. Gallatin had woven the very web of his life" "a certain indefinable popular charm, like old-fashioned music."[18]

3   *Problems in Political Biography*

Into the writing of the book, his first major literary under-taking, Adams poured so much of his personal conviction and so thoroughly made himself a partisan of his hero that he always looked back upon it with special affection. Blemishes he willingly conceded, but these sank from view before the image he had evoked. Out of the past and the stream of time he had drawn the perfected and idealized father-states-man and he turned to him with a warmth of attachment that temperament and custom had always prevented in his re-spectful relations to his own father. "To do justice to Gal-latin," he later wrote to Samuel J. Tilden, "was a labor of love. After long study of the prominent figures in our his-tory, I am more than ever convinced that for combination of ability, integrity, knowledge, unselfishness, and social fit-ness, Mr. Gallatin has no equal." Eager for a symbol to which his political ideals might cleave, he had at last found it in Gallatin.[19]

The biography does much to clarify what Adams meant when in the spring of 1877 he wrote to President Eliot of Harvard that his views, unlike Lodge's, tended to "democ-racy and radicalism." He was indeed hostile to Hamilton, but not so much for his principles as for his character as an adventurer and an *arriviste*. If he followed Jeffersonian de-mocracy, it was only as far as Gallatin might lead him. The algebra of political means and ends ultimately rested upon the simple arithmetic of character. In his scheme character was principle; principle was character. Adams's democracy was one purged of doctrinaire social theory; his radicalism one purged of Jacobinism. Jefferson might complacently aver that "the tree of liberty must be refreshed from time to time with the blood of patriots and tyrants," seeing a certain wholesomeness in occasional rebellions; but such was not Adams's view of the social order. He assayed Jeffersonian democracy not in the radiance of the Rights of Man but in the steadier light of the *Wealth of Nations*.[20]

The "positive characteristics" of Jefferson's administration, he asserted, were "financial," meaning "economic." For a brief moment he laid his hand upon the clue which, as Parrington has written, "old John Adams had followed so tenaciously," the clue to be found in "the economic springs of action." "The philanthropic or humanitarian doctrines which had been the theme of Mr. Jefferson's philosophy . . . when reduced to their simplest elements amount merely to this: that America, standing outside the political movement of Europe, could afford to follow a political development of her own; that she might safely disregard remote dangers; that her armaments might be reduced to a point little above mere police necessities; that she might rely on natural self-interest for her foreign commerce; that she might depend on average common sense for her internal prosperity and order; and that her capital was safest in the hands of her own citizens."

So far as Gallatin succumbed to the doctrinaire notions of his party he was mistaken and gave himself needless anxiety as, most notably, in his acceptance of "the great dogma of the Democratic principle" that a national debt was a danger to the nation. The fact was, said Adams, that "republicanism, and even democracy had been long antecedent to the discharge of the debt." "The Federalists made the debt a subordinate, Mr. Gallatin made it a paramount consideration in politics. . . . The war of 1812 was a practical demonstration of at least momentary failure of Mr. Gallatin's principle, and the failure occurred in dealing with precisely those difficulties which the Federalists had foreseen and tried to provide for. . . . The United States naturally and safely gravitated back to Mr. Gallatin's system after the war of 1812, and has consistently followed it to the present time. The debt has been repeatedly discharged. Neither the army nor the navy has been increased over the proportions set by Mr. Gallatin and Mr. Jefferson. Commerce protects itself not by arms nor even by the fear of arms, but by the interests it creates. America has pursued in fact an American system — the system of Mr. Gallatin." [21]

If Adams reduced the area of disagreement between the Federalists and their opponents, he readily admitted that what remained was chasm deep. He protested that the current tendency to blur the differences between the two factions was a serious mistake. "They were in deadly earnest," he declared, "and no compromise between them ever was or ever will be possible. . . . Mr. Jefferson meant that the American system should be a democracy, and he would rather let the world perish than that principle, which represented all that man was worth, should fail. Mr. Hamilton considered democracy a fatal curse, and meant to stop its progress." Had Adams's analysis gone on to make this a controlling theme, the inconsistencies between strategy and principle, however interesting from the point of view of dramatic irony, might have been seen in a truer perspective. No matter how much the great adversaries were obliged to change — and exchange — tactics as they went in and out of office, neither, as Adams emphasized, lost sight of the controlling ends. Since for the Jeffersonians political democracy was largely extra-Constitutional, child of the Declaration of Independence rather than of the Constitution, their strategy required that they strive steadily to redress the advantages which that document gave to the Federalists without impairing their own vital stake in it. For each it became a tool to be hammered into usefulness, at no matter what cost to doctrinal consistency. [22]

Outwardly the massive *Life* resembled the conventional

and still popular "life and letters" biography, but Adams
superimposed upon the form an artistic and dramatic tension
that was new. The interaction of the chief actor with the
secondary personages gave rise to a succession of dramatic
moments. The action leading up to these tableaux he developed with a novelist's feeling for intrigue and narrative
complication, as for example in the treatment of the Whiskey
Rebellion, the working out of Randolph's charges against
Madison, the fateful progress of the Embargo, and the struggles of the Ghent negotiation. The whole career is dramatically conceived, with an almost Sophoclean irony in its
reversals of fortune. Gallatin's land speculations proved nothing but a burden and a disappointment. Yielding to his
romantic feelings he attempted to retire to the lonely isolation of his frontier estate only to discover he was unfitted
for such a Rousseauistic existence. He deliberately threw
away all the advantages of aristocratic birth and education
and yet succeeded far beyond every reasonable expectation.
His pronunciation of his adopted tongue exposed him to
ridicule; the ridicule redounded to his credit. What a con-
catenation of circumstances had made him great! His career
teased his biographer by its succession of mischances. How
much it illustrated the play of fortune and fate, of free will
and necessity, of chance and prevision.

The emphasis was frankly placed upon Gallatin's "political
and public career." That, as Adams said, was "the main
object" of the work. The personal aspects of Gallatin's life,
its varied interior drama was little more than hinted at. The
separation between the public and private man was rather
stiffly maintained: "The story of his private life shall be carried a few steps further to a convenient halting place." Nevertheless he was aware of the biographer's responsibility, re-
gretting at one point that for the period of greatest interest,
from 1801 on, "Of his social life, his private impressions, and

his intimate conversation with the persons most in his confidence at this time, not a trace can now be recovered." There is little indication that Adams made a very serious effort to recover these traces. The literary theory to which he gave allegiance hardly warranted exhaustive search. Committed by his method to quoting a large number of letters in full, he had little space for developing the linking narrative with any degree of artistic fullness. The method was at least as old as Mason's pioneer life of Gray, published a century earlier, in which he "allowed the letters to tell their own story" so that Gray became "his own biographer." Its most impressive current exemplar was George Trevelyan's brilliantly successful *Life and Letters of Lord Macaulay* which appeared the year before Adams started work on the *Gallatin*. Adams never forgot the satisfaction that his English friend's book gave him. A quarter of a century later it rose up in his mind as he wrote the Preface of the *Mont-Saint-Michel and Chartres* as a nephew's model tribute. In the case of the *Gallatin*, his misfortune was that the letters had little of the charm and allusiveness of Macaulay's.[23]

Some of his difficulty arose from his sense of obligation to his craft. "A large part of the following biography," the Preface began, "relates to a period of American history as yet unwritten, and is intended to supply historians with material which, except in such form, would be little likely to see the light." His young colleague, Lodge, had made a similar avowal in the Preface of his *Life and Letters of George Cabot* in 1877: "I have printed everything which seemed to me of any historical value; and I have given the letters exactly as they are written." In his praise of the book Adams ignored the young scholar's disclaimer that the nature of the materials prevented the "writing of a suitable biography." Mr. Lodge, said Adams, "as a rule, is disposed to let his characters speak for themselves, which is a great virtue in a biographer."[24]

The congenial emphasis on politics produced a rather curious disproportion. Gallatin retired from public life in 1827 at the age of sixty-six. "Intellectually," said Adams, "the next fifteen years were the most fruitful of his life." He devoted himself to science, especially Indian ethnology, with such success that he came to be recognized as the "Father of American Ethnology." Having corresponded with his authoritative friend Lewis Henry Morgan on the subject, he ventured the judgment, "Perhaps one might not wander very far from the truth if one added that these [scientific] pursuits were, on the whole, his most permanent claim to distinction." Yet of the nearly seven hundred pages of the biography Adams devoted only two to these pursuits.[25]

The style of the work cost him much trouble, for he had not yet achieved a sure idiom though he knew what he wanted. "The historian," he had once observed, "must be an artist. He must know how to develop the leading ideas of the subject he has chosen, how to keep the thread of the narrative always in hand, how to subordinate details, and how to accentuate principles." The materials resisted the form. "The most difficult thing to me is to vary the length of my sentences so as to relieve the attention," he wrote Lodge. "In the struggle to do this, I have sometimes found myself doing very clumsy things." More than this, he was still the captive of his old favorites, Gibbon and Junius, Burke and Macaulay. It was still his habit to re-read his Macaulay to "whet" his style. The result was that the book was studded with bravura passages of a somewhat old-fashioned eloquence, massive periodic sentences artfully wrought and sustained, often ending in an exuberant flourish: ". . . and held Congress down to its contemptible and crouching attitude of impotent gesticulation and rant." It is almost as if he were parodying the florid oratory of his statesmen. The demands of a style that still bordered upon the grandiloquent often led to fine-sounding but vague generalizations, exciting to the imagination but a little baffling to the understanding. In a fine peroration to the section on the Treasury he wrote that "except those theories of government which are popularly represented by the names of Hamilton and Jefferson, no solution of the great problems of American politics has ever been offered to the American people. Since the day when foreign violence and domestic faction prostrated Mr. Gallatin and his two friends, no statesman has appeared with the strength to bend their bow, — to finish their uncompleted task." [26]

The *Gallatin* and the three volumes of *Writings* were a formidable assault in force upon the reviewers. The *Writings* appeared first, the Preface being dated January, 1879; the Preface of the biography carried the date, May, 1879. Adams and Marian left for Europe immediately afterward, the reviews following them in their travels. Practically all of them put him lastingly on the defensive. The *North American Review* dismissed it with the briefest of mention: "a valuable repository of information for the real student of history" but "too voluminous, and has too much of the character of a digest of material, to be attractive to the general reader." That was all, an insultingly brief squib, to notice a monumental achievement; certainly a poor requital by his successor, Allen Thorndike Rice, for Adams's distinguished service as editor from 1870 to 1876. If he had any claims upon an American magazine for a fair hearing, it was upon the *North American,* still the foremost serious review in the country. The slight was not the kind that he could easily forgive, as his reactions to other notices of the book suggest.[27]

He had in fact made too little concession to the "general reader," having so far yielded to scholarly scruple as to quote document after document in full and many long letters in the original French. The *Saturday Review* condemned him for having "monstrously . . . enlarged his work," provoking his

annoyed comment that the magazine had always been "idiotic"
on "everything American." The London *Athenaeum* also de-
plored its length, but conceded that the book offered "much
instruction" if the reader had the necessary "patience and
perseverance." Lodge privately suggested that the biography
should have been cut. Adams agreed. "Pruning would improve
it. I think fifty pages might come out, to great advantage, and
perhaps a hundred could be spared. My only excuse is the
great difficulty of judging these things in manuscript." Lodge
judiciously praised it in a long article in the *International
Review*. "Patient investigation is everywhere apparent," he
declared, "and is supplemented by a firm historical grasp, and
by vigor and originality of thought and opinion." He acknowledged that because of Gallatin's character the narrative was
"too uniformly sombre — a defect which Mr. Adams does not
always overcome." Gratefully, Adams told him it was "the
best by far of the reviews I have seen," save that like the rest
it sinned in staying too close to the book. "They all are de-
ficient on illustration, comparison, in short — criticism in the
true sense; all are obnoxious to the complaint they mostly
bring against Gallatin, that of being dull, and with no excuse,
for there is ample material for a very spicy review." That
such criticism was denied the *Gallatin* must have seemed a
foretaste of what he must steel himself to expect and have
deepened his contempt for the ordinary reviewer.[28]

The defense of his attitude gave him an opportunity to press
upon Lodge the ultimate implications of the book. "To my
mind the moral of his life lies a little deeper than party politics and I have tried here and there rather to suggest than
assert it. The inevitable isolation and disillusionment of a
really strong mind — one that combines force with elevation
— is to me the romance and tragedy of statesmanship. The
politician who goes to his grave without suspecting his own
limitations, is not a picturesque figure, he is only an animal."

Here summed up was not only his judgment upon Gallatin, but upon his great and lonely forbears and — by a spiritual extension — upon himself. To Lodge it was another veiled warning, which he would not — or could not — heed, as Adams found out to his deep distress.[29]

Adams was also let down, and even more disappointingly than in the case of the *North American,* by the *Nation.* Its review, a long two-part unsigned article, attacked the work with a strangely personal violence. The anonymous critic charged that in make-up "this volume falls little short of being an outrage both on Albert Gallatin and on everyone who wishes to know anything about him." Not only did the book have "the appearance of ponderosity," it had "sunk the author in the editor," and set itself against the current fashion which allowed the "artistic biographer" to bring his subjects "before us as the central figures in the events they helped shape." The author of the *Gallatin* had "sinned knowingly, and is accordingly entitled to no mercy." The reviewer's perceptive comment in the second part hardly atoned for the slashing condemnation of the "clumsy volume": "In reality it is the story of [Gallatin's] failure that Mr. Adams tells us, and he tells it with great spirit and ability, interspersed at times with a controlled eloquence — which is made doubly attractive by its admirable taste." If Adams resented the fact that Godkin, his good friend and political ally, should have published such an equivocal review of his first major writing, he did not demean himself to give any sign, and later when Godkin pressed him on the subject, he rather maddeningly insisted that he "never dreamed of taking offense at it." After all, the reviewer obviously brought no expert knowledge of his own and what he said was "the most commonplace newspaper comment, which did not rise to criticism." [30]

Too full of a piquant secret to realize his tactlessness, Godkin had hurried to inquire of Mrs. Adams whether Henry had taken offense. With ironic aplomb, Marian had replied, "If as you say a genial and suave notice of the Life of Gallatin was intended to 'do Henry good,' I've no doubt it will and that future works will be full of what Mary Mapes Dodge calls 'Sparkling Sallies.' " Henry himself declined to rise to the bait. Unable to endure the uncertainty Godkin tried again after the lapse of a year. Adams reproached him with such forceful dignity that Godkin did not dare play out the rather cruel jest. Godkin was saying in effect, "It was not my fault; it was the man around the corner who made me do it because he said it would do you good." Adams turned the tables on Godkin. He had been "a little hurt" to see that in the annual literary review the *Nation* had "coolly remarked that in the field of American history, the only book worth noticing which had appeared in the course of the year was *the American translation* of von Holst's second volume." Less easy to forgive was the fact, which he had just learned, that Godkin had almost given away to their friends the secret of Adams's authorship of the novel *Democracy.* That reproach must have brought Godkin up sharp. The author of the review of *Gallatin* was none other than Henry's elder brother, Charles Francis Adams, Jr. Godkin had been on the verge of showing that he could keep the secret of neither brother, something that would surely have cost him Henry's friendship.[31]

In his review Charles took all too literally Henry's longstanding invitation to him: "I shall be pleased to have you kick my tail whenever you see the necessity. If one saw the occasion oneself, of course, one could kick one's own tail." The occasion had come, but now Charles's motives were a little diluted with jealousy. "You know perfectly well," ran his somewhat disingenuous justification to Godkin, "that my article was very complimentary on its substance, merely criticizing sharply certain defects in details." "If Henry and his wife can't stand that, but insist on pure and solid taffy, he'd better stop writing. My good sister-in-law don't favor me much now, and if she finds it is I who dared criticize her adored Henry, my goose will be finally cooked. That's a trifle; but unfortunately the medicine will cease to work. My sole object in writing the review was to induce Henry not to treat any audience at all as a thing beneath an author's consideration. From what you tell me I do not think I labored in vain. It will, however, be worse than in vain if he hears it is I who labored." [32]

Henry apparently did not learn the identity of his *Nation* critic, though a version of the story was afloat in Washington ten years later when young Cecil Spring Rice of the British embassy, then forming a friendship with Adams, picked it up. One is tempted to believe that supreme ironist that he was, Adams hit upon the secret and decided to relish the cream of the jest by never letting on. A past master at both sharing and keeping secrets, he would have been thoroughly in character. As for Charles, he was to have the satisfaction of seeing most of his "medicine" work: the make-up of his books became a matter of almost finicking concern to Henry, and his handling of quotations became a fine art, though he did not give up his basic preference for the life-and-letters genre of biography.[33]

His friend John T. Morse in his *Atlantic* article was chiefly concerned to show that Gallatin was unworthy of so large a book, being "questionably of the first importance." He also thought its value impaired by the "occasional slurs upon Mr. Hamilton, and a dark background of profound antipathy to Mr. Jefferson." All of which, Mrs. Adams reported to her father, "amused" Henry "extremely." Morse had evidently read the book "between daylight and dark, and perhaps upside down." Still another friend, young J. Laurence Laughlin, like Lodge one of Adams's "batch" of doctors of philosophy at Harvard, helped launch the book with a favorable article in the Boston *Literary World* calling it "a most serious and important study . . . broad, masterly, and with a dignity quite its own." An earlier highly laudatory article in the same periodical on the three volumes of *Writings* called them "the most important contribution to documentary history of the United States we have had for a number of years." The authoritative *Magazine of American History* saw few blemishes in the biography. Adams deserved "highest praise." He rose "above partisanship to the true plane of impartial history." To this hospitable reviewer it was a "compact volume," and a work fittingly entrusted to the grandson of Gallatin's "able coadjutor." [34]

Strangely mixed as its initial reception was the biography surmounted the early detractions and ultimately established itself as a definitive work among professional historians. Bernard Fäy wrote, "The great work of Henry Adams is still a sufficient summing-up of Gallatin's activities." To the distinguished authors of *The Growth of the American Republic* it stands as "one of the best Republican biographies." Only after three quarters of a century has it had to surrender its title of "definitive" to Raymond Walters' scholarly and comprehensive biography which at last meets the challenge of Henry's brother Charles for a biography in the "modern" fashion. But though it adds flesh and far more of the color of life to the irreproachable Gallatin and his times it reveals no serious flaw in Adams's scholarship and leaves unaltered Adams's high estimate of this ideal statesman.[35]

Chapter Three

The Great American Mystery

1 The Education of Madeleine Lee

ALTHOUGH the prefaces of the Gallatin volumes were dated 1879, the writing and compiling were finished well before the end of 1878. By the first of August, Adams was "straining . . . weary muscles to put four bulky volumes onto the tired world next year." That done, he would "hurl the whole batch at the head of an unconscious public," and cross the Atlantic again in order to "grub in the foreign office papers in London, Paris, Madrid, perhaps even St. Petersburg." Late in November the presswork was finished on two of the four volumes. Already he had found a more engrossing occupation, a project far less imposing in mass, but calculated to have an infinitely greater impact upon the public. It was the novel *Democracy*.[1]

That Adams had another missile that he was going to hurl anonymously at the public was kept a profound secret from all but his most intimate friends, at first only Godkin and Clarence King, in addition of course to the publisher Henry Holt. After the book was published and he had returned from Europe in 1880, he included John Hay and his wife, and Raphael Pumpelly (if Holt's recollection was correct), the adventurous mineralogist whom King brought into the Geological Survey in 1879. Hay, appointed Assistant Secretary of State, November 1, 1879, did not come on to live in Washington until five months after the Adamses left for Europe. Few literary secrets have been better kept from the public. As late as 1915 even William Roscoe Thayer, in his *Life of John Hay,* felt obliged to state as a conjecture "only Mr. Adams possessed the substance, and style, and the gift of Voltairean raillery which distinguish it." In a footnote explaining a joke, however, he flatly stated, "Mr. Adams wrote *Democracy.*" By that time, however, his authorship was the common and jealously guarded property of the inner circle of "nieces." Librarians continued their attributions to Clarence King and John Hay until the fact of Adams's authorship was confirmed by Holt in 1920, two years after Adams's death. One of the most curious aspects of the "mystery" was that it had been publicly solved in 1909 in *A Manual of American Literature,* edited by Theodore Stanton of Cornell. The *Manual* described *Democracy* as "an anonymous novel the authorship of which has hitherto baffled the critics, and which the present writer can now announce definitely to have been the work of the historian Henry Adams." The scholarly text soon dropped out of sight and with it the fact of Adams's authorship of the novel.[2]

Anonymity was no new thing to Adams. All of his early newspaper work had been unsigned and some kept even from his father's knowledge. Similarly anonymous were almost all of his contributions to the *Nation* and the *Post.* Several of his weighty magazine contributions here and in England were unsigned in compliance with the current publishing practice, the authorship commonly becoming an open secret. Holt who received the manuscript in the spring of 1879 "with the most strenuous injunctions regarding secrecy," recalled that Adams had explained that it wasn't that he feared unpopularity so much as that "some of the characters were carefully drawn from prominent living persons who were his friends, and some of these he had touched humorously and ironically."[3]

In the person of the heroine, Adams drew not only the portrait of his wife Marian but also more tellingly the portrait of himself. Mrs. Lightfoot Lee, a sophisticated, wealthy, and high-principled widow, comes to Washington "to see with her own eyes the action of primary forces; to touch with her own hand the massive machinery of society; to measure with her own mind the capacity of the motive power. She was bent upon getting to the heart of the great American mystery of democracy and government." She wanted desperately to know "whether America is right or wrong." In its imaginative way her investigation is the very modest forerunner of *The Education,* a kind of interim report preceding by a quarter of a century the definitive one. The education of Madeleine Lee in national politics gives her a pretty grim picture and in the end she runs away in horror and disgust to Europe quite as her creator sought a moral bath in 1870, after a year of Grant's administration, flight being the only apparent way out of the impasse.[4]

In *Democracy* Adams gave shape to his long standing interest in fiction. As a youth, living in Berlin, he had toyed with the idea of writing a novel. Discarded then, the idea lurked in his mind, cropping up momentarily again in a design to write a novel about a consumptive girl with whom he was lightly flirting in 1870. He felt a "delicious thrill of horror," fancying himself de Musset whispering sentiment and literary quotations into ears of an imminent corpse. "Is not this delightfully morbid," he teased his friend Gaskell. "I have marked it for a point in my novel, which is to appear in 1880." He hit the date, but the *frisson* of horror proved largely political. Politics and literature had a tendency to go together in his mind. But he knew his own powers well enough to realize that he must wait until his subject had got him "as well as I the subject." Octave Feuillet's immensely popular *Histoire de Sybille* in the *Revue des Deux Mondes* had been an early enthusiasm in England. Delighted by Feuillet's technique, his approach, and the intensely psychological style, he bought seven volumes of the complete novels. The finely discriminating portraits of accomplished women of the world evoked a rustling world of taste and dignity in which Adams's reveries of ideal femininity could float as in a native atmosphere. On the almost bare stage of the *roman démeublé*, the drama of sensitive consciences played itself out in a pattern highly suitable for borrowing. The psychological insights of George Eliot also challenged him to probe his own inner world. He felt a vivid sense of identification with fictional creations like Casaubon in *Middlemarch*.[5]

Of all the literary influences that played upon him none could have been more congenial than the novels of Disraeli, the highest type of the statesman artist. In countless ways these novels spoke directly to him. Wasn't he like Egremont in *Sybil* who "yielded himself to the delicate and profitable authority of women"? Had not Disraeli written *Coningsby* "to elevate the tone of public life" and put into the mouth of his hero the Adams creed: "Let us think of principles and not of parties"? Madeleine's quest to get at the heart of "the great American mystery of democracy and government" had its parallel in the quest of one of Adams's favorite Disraelian heroes, *Tancred*, Lord Montacute, who, oppressed by social and political problems of his day, set out for the Holy Land to get at the heart of the great "Asian Mystery." Tancred too had known disillusionment.[6]

Not only was the novel an outlet for a long pent up literary impulse, it erupted out of his disgust with such folk heroes as Ulysses S. Grant and the silver-tongued James G. Blaine and their cronies in the "kitchen Cabinets" of ill-fame. Blundering as Jefferson had been, he was a demi-god beside the President whose strings were pulled by Conkling and Butler and their like. In the contrast between the large-minded early years of the Republic and the moral chaos of the post-Civil War era, lay the seeds of profound disillusionment. The polarities of the novel and its Voltairean ironies imaginatively parallel those of the *Gallatin*. The heroine bred to the old-fashioned ideal that public office is a public trust, scrupulously sensitive to the morality of ends and means, committed to the ideal of philosophical statesmanship, runs head on into the vulgar necessities of practical politics and practical statesmanship. She witnesses the conflict between theory and practice, the conflict from which Jefferson fled and which Gallatin faced, though at the cost of surrendering his dream of a new society. It was a paralyzing dilemma. Adams had confronted it as a political journalist and as a historian. In the *Gallatin* fate, political and economic determinism, was the over-arching force that thwarted moral idealism. The idealistic Madeleine trapped in the center of warring motives is driven at last to admit that "life is more complicated than I thought" and clearly more sordid.[7]

Late in March, 1880, the New York *Tribune*'s "Literary Notes" carried a brief item:

The Leisure Hour Series is to have added to it the first novel by an American author. Its scene is laid in New York and Washington, and its author would appear to be a resident of one place or the other. It is intimated that many readers will imagine they see portraits in the book.

The sly hint "fetched" them. Before the end of April, a second printing was called for. In all there were nine printings of the 1880 edition. Word of its scandalous success winged across the ocean. The appetite whetted by such critics of democracy as Carlyle, Dickens, Ruskin, and Matthew Arnold snapped hungrily at this domestic confession of failure. Whitman had had his say in *Democratic Vistas* but that turgid diatribe lacked the vivid cases and the drama of the novel. Besides it still breathed defiant hope. The new book, though a little critical of English snobbery and bad taste in women's clothes, allowed a cultivated Englishman to glow with pleasurable complacency. Prime Minister Gladstone recommended it highly. Mrs. Ward in her review said that everyone was talking about it in England.[8]

The English edition came out in June, 1882, being immediately followed by a paper-back edition at a shilling. In October at Adams's suggestion Holt brought out a cheap American edition that quickly went through five printings, Adams selecting choice excerpts from the earlier reviews for an inserted flyleaf so that "wretches may open on it, and know what they ought to think before they begin." In 1885, having had his amusement, appropriately Adams made a gift of the copyright to the National Civil Service Reform League. A 1902 edition went to three printings. The nominal copyright continued to stand in Holt's name as shown in the 1908 edition, identified as the 16th printing. This was reprinted in 1925, 1926, and 1933, the 1925 printing being the first to carry Adams's name as the author with Holt's recollections as a Foreword. The most recent edition came out in 1952. In 1901 Holt offered to issue the book as a play but Adams declined. As an old man Adams gleefully recalled for Brooks's improvement: "The wholesale piracy of *Democracy* was the single real triumph of my life." A Tauchnitz edition and a French version carried its vogue to the continent in 1882.[9]

Slight as the plot is and economical of intrigue, it achieves a unity of tone and effect not unworthy of Adams's good friend Henry James. Far less the dedicated artist than James, however, Adams allowed his political thesis to drive him into caricature. It is notable that at the very time when James was creating Isabel Archer, with all her charm and Puritan rectitude, submitting her to the moral ambiguities of European life, Adams was fashioning a sister figure, much less fully realized it is true, but one equally avid of experience who is forced to confront the evil of the world in somewhat the same terms, but without Isabel Archer's ultimate courage. Adams too places the center of interest in the consciousness of the heroine Madeleine Lee who had "the most extravagant notions about self-sacrifice and duty." [10]

Left a widow with a fortune of $20,000 a year Madeleine, still very attractive at thirty, finds herself bored with her sophisticated existence in New York. She had yielded to the current vogue of Schopenhauer and his fellow pessimists, but "Philosophy in the original German" led to "nothing — nothing." Schopenhauer assured his readers that optimism was not merely absurd but "a really *wicked* way of thinking." Only through the denial of the will to live could man — or woman — attain Nirvana. Practical philanthropy "seemed to lead nowhere." Adams put his favorite Carlylean queries into her mind. "What gave peculiar sanctity to numbers? Why were a million people, who all resembled each other, any way more interesting than one person? What aspiration could she help to put into the mind of this great million-armed monster that would make it worth her love or respect?" She was "eating her heart out because she could find no one object worth a sacrifice," for she had "aspirations for the infinite." She knew enough of Malthusian economic theory to feel that charity did "harm as well as good." New York society seemed to her as sterile as Boston; wealth and the opportunities of culture produced no genuine intellectual élite. She was unimpressed by the "Brobdingnagian doctrine" that "two blades of grass" were better than one. What she wished was that "the grass should be of improved quality." Her complaint dramatically recapitulated the idealism of Adams's Class Day oration twenty years before at Harvard. [11]

She was uncertain whether her ennui was "real ambition" or "mere restlessness," the doubt that always perplexed her creator. In order to find out she would have to spend a season in Washington. "What she wished to know, she thought, was the clash of interests, the interests of forty million people. . . .

What she wanted was Power." To the reader who now has the advantage of Adams's letters and those of his wife for the period, what follows is little more than veiled autobiography, the life and opinions of Henry Adams and his Washington circle in 1878–79.[12]

Settling herself in Lafayette Square with her younger sister Sybil Ross, in a house which she tastefully civilizes with European bibelots, Mrs. Lee becomes the protégé of a high-minded Southern lawyer, John Carrington, a distant cousin of her late husband, himself a Lee of Virginia. Through Carrington she meets the party dictator, Senator Silas P. Ratcliffe of Illinois, worshipped by the press as the Prairie Giant from Peonia. An aspirant to the presidency he had just missed the nomination by three votes. He is obviously the man best qualified to show her to the heart of the mystery.

Madeleine established a brilliant and exclusive salon to which is attracted a representative company of politicians and diplomats who had learned "the art of finding its mistress at home." Ratcliffe, a widower of fifty, is immediately drawn to the cultured aristocrat, and soon preempts a place in her drawing room at her Sunday evening at-homes. From him and from her other callers like the witty and cynically forthright Baron Jacobi, the self-appreciative Massachusetts poet-historian Nathan Gore, eager to be reinstated to the Spanish mission, the protective tariff lobbyist and rich dilettante Mr. Hartbeest Schneidkoupon, the opinionated young congressman Mr. French with a gentlemanly interest in reform politics, she begins to piece together the variegated mosaic of Washington politics and society. At a dinner the great Ratcliffe warmed by Mrs. Lee's presence completely disconcerts the lightweight reformer French by attacking civil service reform as just another "Yankee notion," related to the wooden nutmegs of Connecticut. When Mrs. Lee earnestly queries "What is to become of us if corruption is allowed to go unchecked?" Ratcliffe replies, "No representative government can long be much better or much worse than the society it represents." Disarmed by his candor and his confidences about the struggle for power between the new president and himself, Mrs. Lee begins to lose her faith in the practical worth of the principle that a political leader should do "whatever is most for the public good." Her education takes a great stride forward when she asks Ratcliffe, "Is nothing more powerful than party allegiance?" "Nothing, except national allegiance," he replied. When challenged, Ratcliffe boldly admits he ordered the falsifying of election returns as Governor of Illinois in order to win the presidency for his party and thus save the Union.[13]

As the season wore on, "the dance of democracy round the President now began with wilder energy," the sordid jubilation that Carlyle had pre-figured in the carmagnole dance of the French Revolution. To escape it for a day, Ratcliffe joins an excursion to Mount Vernon arranged by Lord Skye, the British Minister, to entertain a fortune hunting Irish peer Lord Dunbeg. He is soon paired off with the irrepressible and highly eligible Victoria Dare. In the shadow of Mount Vernon the members of the group naturally fall to discussing the significance of George Washington. The estimates range from Lord Skye's manly tribute to the statesman to Carrington's disenchanted eulogy of Washington as the squirearch of a vanished society. The realistic Ratcliffe, irritated by the worshipful tributes, breaks out, "If Washington were President now, he would have to learn our ways or lose the next election." He has already admitted, however, that "the West is a poor school for Reverence." The one New Englander, Gore, declares that in spite of the traditional hostility of New England toward Virginia, "We idolize him. To us he is Morality, Justice, Duty, Truth; half a dozen Roman gods with capital letters." [14]

Moved by the beauty of the Potomac, Lord Skye expresses the European's disappointment in the American character: "Your national mind has no eyelids. It requires a broad glare and a beaten road. It doesn't know the beauty of this Virginia winter softness." Mrs. Lee loyally rejects the charge. "America still had her story to tell; she was waiting for her Burns and Scott, her Wordsworth and Byron, her Hogarth and Turner." "You want peaches in spring," said she. "Give us our thousand years of summer, and then complain, if you please, that our peach is not as mellow as yours." [15]

Washington emerges not only as a shared symbol of American unity, but also as a sign of something irreparably lost. While the steamer draws away from the peaceful shrine, Mrs. Lee asks herself bitterly, "Why was it that everything Washington touched, he purified, even down to the associations of his house? and why is it that everything we touch seems soiled? Why do I feel unclean when I look at Mount Vernon? In spite of Mr. Ratcliffe, is it not better to be a child and to cry for the moon and stars?" At such a moment the personal parable rises perilously close to the surface. And it is in this scene that Mrs. Lee — and thus Adams — unconsciously anticipates in a remark about Washington's tomb Adams's artistic scruples about the memorial that St. Gaudens was one day to build for him. Madeleine Lee "insisted that the tomb, as it stood, was the only restless spot about the quiet landscape, and that it contradicted all her ideas about repose in the grave. Ratcliffe wondered what she meant." His was the wonderment of all barbarians — especially from the West.[16]

Into this idyllic setting comes the first intimation of the evil that lurks below the surface, the glimpse of the serpent in the Garden of American politics. One of the members of the party is a pretty young widow, Mrs. Sam Baker, whose late husband's estate is being administered by Carrington, the attorney. When Ratcliffe learns her identity, he becomes significantly

"absorbed in his own thoughts," as well he might, for he had
had dealings with Baker. Baker had been a notorious lobbyist
who had made full use of his wife and her "showy" charms
in his corrupt profession, all of which Mrs. Baker later described quite artlessly to Madeleine Lee in a scene which
advanced the latter's education another violent step down-
ward. Since as executor Carrington has access to Baker's in-
criminating records, Ratcliffe must now look to his defenses.[17]

The new President had come from Indiana naively determined to free himself from the domination of Ratcliffe, the
party dictator, and to apply the principle of civil service reform. The well-intentioned President, a shrewd amalgam of
Grant and Hayes, tries to immobilize Ratcliffe by luring him
into a hostile cabinet as Secretary of the Treasury. But the
President, ignorant of the really fine art of political management, is himself outmaneuvered. Ratcliffe takes the Treasury
knowing its strategic value. The President, deafened by the
clamor for patronage and overwhelmed by the difficulties of
composing his inaugural address, turns panic-stricken for help
to the astute Ratcliffe. Given a free hand Ratcliffe extracts a
Cabinet post for one of his own men. The President's enfeebled
principles succumb and he at last asks Ratcliffe to make room
for a few "friends of mine. . . . Just stuff 'em in somewhere." That ended civil service reform and "Ratcliffe's friends
did come into their fair share of the public money." [18]

Adams follows this noisome episode of political intrigue with
another idyllic interlude, a visit to Arlington cemetery and
the home of Robert E. Lee. This time it is Mrs. Lee's sister
Sybil and Carrington who ride back into the gracious past on
the bridle path westward along the Potomac to the Chain
Bridge, a favorite ride for Henry Adams and his wife. Sybil,
unlike Madeleine, was not given to analyzing her feelings,
but even she was sobered by the vast graveyard. "Here was
something new to her. This was war — wounds, disease, death."

And Carrington had been a rebel soldier, "a traitor." Here was the center of another complex dimension of the American experience, a center from which the present must somehow be measured. "They looked across the superb river to the raw and incoherent ugliness of the city, idealized into dreamy beauty by the atmosphere, and the soft background of the purple hills behind. Opposite them, with its crude 'thus saith the law' stamped on white dome and fortresslike walls, rose the Capitol." A mystic symbol of the developing life of the American democracy, the river opens out to embrace the city — on the one side the heroic values, traditions, and aspirations of the past, of Mount Vernon and Arlington, on the other the city built on the edge of a swamp, a kind of parody of the great dream.[19]

The intuitive Sybil senses her sister's peril. The intellectual and unrealistic Madeleine has deluded herself into thinking that if she marries Ratcliffe, she can reform him and through him Washington politics. Sybil and Carrington decide to prevent the marriage. Ratcliffe, knowing the danger he faces from Carrington as executor of the lobbyist Baker, gets him out of the way by arranging his appointment to the Mexican Claims Commission in Mexico City, an appointment that the unsuspecting Carrington is not in a position to refuse. Before leaving, Carrington, who has been hopelessly in love with Madeleine, declares his love to her but she gently refuses him. "You would wake up some day, and find the universe dust and ashes." When, however, he warns her to run away from Ratcliffe, she flares up, "I will not be dictated to!" One resource remains. On a last ride with Sybil, whose feelings toward Carrington now verge upon love, he gives her a letter to be used only if all else fails to stop the impending marriage.

Ratcliffe was now ready for the final assault. His opportunity came at a colossal ball given in the middle of April by Lord Skye in honor of the Grand Duke and Duchess of Saxe-Baden-

Hombourg. For Adams, the ball provided a canvas for his liveliest satire, satire as fresh and apt as when it was written more than three-quarters of a century ago. "Everyone hastened to show this august couple the respect which all republicans who have a large income derived from business, feel for English royalty." Millionaires from all over the country, persons from the North Pole to the Isthmus of Panama clamored for cards. "It is astonishing," Adams dryly observed, "what efforts freemen will make in a just cause." The snobbery, the rivalry in dress, the clamor over precedence, the toadying to aristocracy, the social hypocrisy and gaucherie of social climbing Americans are unsparingly lampooned. Even the heroine and her sister do not escape. Sybil's dress specially ordered from the "Master," Worth of Paris, is a duplicate of the gorgeous confection created for "the reigning favorite of the King of Dahomey." [21]

With mock-heroic bravura the book describes the night of sublime inspiration in which the idea for the gown was conceived. It is this passage which Adams conceded to his wife, and her knowledgeable touch is plainly visible. "An imperious order brought to his private room every silk, satin, and gauze within the range of pale pink, pale crocus, pale green, silver and azure. Then came chromatic scales of color; combinations meant to vulgarise the rainbow; sinfonies and fugues; the twittering of birds and the great peace of dewy nature; maidenhood in her awakening innocence; 'The Dawn in June.' The Master rested content." An unconsciously ironic commentary on this spoofing passage occurs in a letter which Marian Adams wrote to her father about five months later from Paris. "Henry and I were presented in great form to the great Mr. Worth . . . and I so far yielded to Henry's wishes as to order a duplicate gown to one making for the Grand Duchess of Würtemberg." [22]

Ratcliffe now appears as a genuinely impressive figure,

"what with Mrs. Lee's influence [On a mere overheard hint from her he had begun to take a cold bath every morning], and what with his emancipation from the Senate chamber with its code of bad manners and worse morals." With careful calculation he addresses an elevated appeal to Mrs. Lee's nobility of mind — and ambition. Before she can give her answer, Sybil rushes in to her rescue. That night, before a log fire, Sybil plays her trump card. In a scene strongly reminiscent of Becky Sharp's theatrical gesture when she flung before Amelia the guilty billet of George Osborne, Sybil shows her Carrington's letter. It tells how Sam Baker as a lobbyist for a steamship company had bribed Senator Ratcliffe with $100,000 in bearer bonds to insure the passage of a ship subsidy bill. The letters, in cipher code, had turned up in Baker's papers. It was a key identification and no informed reader could miss the author's quarry, Senator James G. Blaine, the central figure in the Mulligan letters scandal of 1876. Adams's satiric net was characteristically wide, fusing a number of shady transactions. The charge against Blaine had arisen out of the railroad land grant of 1869; only afterwards in 1878 did he figure in an ocean subsidy bill. The letters in cipher code recalled the scandal which came to light in the 1877 Congressional investigation of the Louisiana vote frauds of the Hayes-Tilden election, a scandal which tarred both parties. As a Liberal Republican Adams bestowed his satire with Swiftian impartiality.[23]

The sordid disclosure had its anticipated effect upon Madeleine. But in her anguished vigil before the fire, so like that of James's heroine, Isabel Archer, her thoughts went far beyond the sordidness of Ratcliffe's conduct. Dissecting her own motives she saw in herself bewildering ambiguities that compromised her own moral pretensions: "ambition, thirst for power, restless eagerness to meddle in what did not concern her, blind longing to escape from the torture of watching other women with full lives and satisfied instincts, while her own life was hungry and sad." Thus emerges the latent theme of the novel, the role of the educated woman in politics and society, a subject of increasing concern to all of the Adamses. The good that Madeleine might have hoped to accomplish could only be at the cost of her womanly nature and instincts. Disillusioned, she cries out "with a gesture of helpless rage and despair, 'Oh, how I wish I were dead! how I wish the universe were annihilated!' " When one perceives how much of Marian Adams's personality is interwoven with Adams's own in the character of Madeleine Lee, the cry suggests, in the light of subsequent events, an almost frightening clairvoyance.[24]

It was a profoundly true insight that a person in whom the emotional springs of life have been imperilled should wish for death, but one wonders whether Adams, the literary artist, ever sensed from what inner depths the impulse for that portrait came. Madeleine Lee foreshadowed her tormented successor Esther, in Adams's second novel, and her painful soul-searching must have left a vaguely disturbing image in the mind of Adams's wife, an image to be deepened by Esther's struggle. The reader can hardly avoid the surmise that Adams must have felt a secret sense of guilt for the critical overtones of the portraits, a remorse that after his wife's death led him into a long career of self-punishment and expiation.

The final act of the drama, Madeleine's confrontation of Ratcliffe, and her explicit rejection of him, has its chief interest in Adams's estimate of contemporary political morality. Ratcliffe admits his venality, but defends it on the casuistical ground that the ends justify the means. When the contested election was thrown into the House, the Republican Party managers solicited funds to insure victory. So, in the fictionized account, Ratcliffe argued that he was honor bound to support the party. The *quid pro quo* was passage of the ship subsidy bill. The government had to be kept out of the "blood-stained hands of the rebels." So Blaine, in the campaign of 1876, had waved the "bloody shirt." [25]

The heart of the great American mystery lay bare before her and it was cankered with disease. This leading statesman "talked about virtue and vice as a man who is color-blind talks about red and green." He was nothing more than a "moral lunatic." Madeleine cannot find her way back through the thicket of her own motives, but she is unyielding: "I will not share the profits of vice." Honest in his passion for her, if in nothing else, Ratcliffe denounces her as a coquette. As he stormed down the stairs he encountered Baron Jacobi, the man who from the first had taken his measure, and who now "with diabolic malignity" offered felicitations. Ratcliffe brutally thrust him aside and at the same instant Jacobi struck him in the face with his cane. Sobered by the shock Ratcliffe hurried away. The climactic scene was a skillful adaptation of a parallel episode in Thackeray's *Vanity Fair*, and in Ratcliffe one glimpses the moral corruption of old Lord Steyne. When the outraged Rawdon Crawley drove the lovesick old reprobate out of his violated home, he struck him in the forehead with his own jeweled gift.[26]

The education of Madeleine Lee in the workings of democracy, at least so much of it as was visible in Washington, led to a blind alley. But her experiment of a winter in Washington was not wholly a failure. In the course of her quest she had discovered her own flaw. Her unruly will to power had betrayed her: existence was really a vanity. "I want to go to Egypt," is her final remark to Sybil; "democracy has shaken my nerves to pieces. Oh, what a rest it would be to live in the Great Pyramid and look out for ever at the polar star." Not in action, not even as a passive observer of life, could the spirit find repose but only in the abdication of life and of the will to live, only in Schopenhauer's non-human absolute of Nirvana. For the reader interested in more mundane matters and a happy ending for true love, Adams has Sybil Ross write a report to Carrington: "If I were in your place I would try again after she comes back." Only an inattentive reader could take the conclusion seriously. Not only the political but the personal theme is basically tragic. Mrs. Lee's "great grievance" was human nature itself, the same human nature that had betrayed Albert Gallatin and his chief, Thomas Jefferson.[27]

2 A Gallery of Odds and Ends

The spirit in which the novel was conceived was kin to the fierce idealism that had moved him ten years before to write the "Session" articles. Here was another hard "blow at democracy," the blow of the parent who in stern desperation resorts to the woodshed. Violent as the satire was, it reflected a mind eager to amend democracy. To the philosophic reader the tone was by no means hopeless. Adams was careful to remark that "underneath the scum floating on the surface of politics, Madeleine felt there was a sort of healthy current of honest principle, which swept the scum before it and kept the mass pure." She was asserting no less than Whitman an almost mystical faith in the dogma of democracy. The wife of John Richard Green wrote a keenly perceptive letter to Marian Adams. "I hope you enjoyed *Democracy* as much as we did. Mr. [Henry] James looked very severe and grave over it, but I am not sure whether it was on patriotic or artistic grounds. I don't understand the patriotic objection, for the author seemed to me profoundly convinced that America had made the only solution worth having of the problem of government." [28]

Clarence King brooded over the novel as unhappily as James, but with the added provocation that he knew the identity of the author. To Adams he seems to have held his peace, but he unburdened himself in "moral lectures" to their mutual friend Hay and even made some progress on a sequel, titled *Monarchy*, which would expose the shabby moral of *Democracy*. He complained to Hay that Henry's novel confirmed the "cruelest suspicions" of the English reader, but, he said, "the Briton will not see, as the Adamses cannot see, that only a woman from Boston (which is more cockney than London) could make such pitiable social blunders as Mrs. L[ee]. Poor woman, she knew how to manage Beacon Street . . . but when she met the world on another basis, where of necessity the fences are all down, she made a silly, blundering, blind failure of a campaign, infinitely more lamentable than anything the woman from Peonia, who knew not bric-a-brac, could possibly make."[29]

The book did achieve a kind of symposium on democratic government. Like a symposium it sought to explore all sides of the question with intelligent scepticism rather than to answer it. When Ratcliffe declared that "this particular government was the highest expression of political thought," though he may not have believed it or, equally bad, did not understand the maxim, he was uttering the compliment that vice usually pays to virtue. To the Massachusetts aspirant to the Spanish mission, Gore, Adams assigned his most cogent affirmation of faith. It was Gore's view that Mrs. Green took to be the author's. "Democracy asserts the fact that the masses are now raised to a higher intelligence than formerly. All our civilization aims at this mark. . . . I grant it is an experiment, but it is the only direction society can take that is worth taking; the only conception of its duty large enough to satisfy its instincts; the only result that is worth an effort or a risk. Every other step is backward and I do not care to repeat the past. . . ." At which point Mrs. Lee interposes the idealist's logic, "Suppose society destroys itself with universal suffrage, corruption, and communism." Gore answers stoically, "Did you ever make the acquaintance of a fixed star? . . . Suppose you see one of these fixed stars suddenly increase in brightness, and are told that a satellite has fallen into it and is burning up, its career finished, its capacities exhausted? . . . what does it matter?" Such an Olympian detachment made Madeleine shudder that she was "finite." Gore did not falter. "But I have faith; not perhaps in the old dogmas, but in the new ones; faith in human nature; faith in science; faith in the survival of the fittest. Let us be true to our time, Mrs. Lee! If our age is to be beaten, let us die in the ranks. If it is to be victorious let us be first to lead the column. Anyway, let us not be skulkers and grumblers." It is a personal confession, his "catechism" Gore calls it with something of a Brahmin's shyness, but conscience had made him brave. There can be little doubt that the "catechism" came from the depths of Adams's heart, that it spoke the irreducible dogmas of his proud inheritance.[30]

The book provoked an angry and baffled clamor from American reviewers, and an occasional grudging admission that it hit the mark, but in general they played down the sensational implications. Said the New York *Tribune:* "The book contains enough truth to be wholesome rebuke, and also it contains enough falsehood to be a cruel libel." The *Nation* hopefully declared that its effect would "probably be slight on account of the obviousness of its bias and misrepresentation." It was a "most deceptive book" in the opinion of the *Atlantic*; it "misrepresented and misunderstood the people" it portrayed. On the other hand, the Louisville *Courier*, "Marse" Henry Watterson's paper, obviously pleased with the depiction of Carrington as a virtuous Southern gentleman, serenely observed: "All will find in it meat for reflection and some for repentance. . . . *Democracy* is a good book; we hope it may be a popular one." Much of the annoyance spent itself in scornful attacks upon the anonymous author. One can imagine the hilarity with which some of these press clippings went from hand to hand among the little group of conspirators. The author had obviously not "mingled in what is really, in the true sense, the best society of the Capital" (Boston *Transcript*). "In spite of its aristocratic air of cosmopolitanism, ease, and man-of-the-world experience, there is more than a suspicion of callowness about it — of that state of mind which it has become popular to characterize as provincial. . . . lack of opportunity for personal comparisons . . . lack of acquaintance with historical facts" (*Appleton's*). *Harper's* barely noticed the volume and the *North American Review* patriotically ignored it.[31]

In England the success of the novel was nothing short of sensational, appetites having been fully whetted by a few American copies which had passed around London the preceding season and made the book the talk of the town. All the periodicals treated it as a major literary event and devoted column after column to praise the force of its satire and its literary artistry. For the moment the author ranked at least on a par with Howells and James. Critics willingly overlooked the satirical thrusts at the vulgarity and dowdiness of English duchesses where there was so much to flatter British vanity in really important matters. It was a pleasure to have the trans-Atlantic democracy dragged into the dock for trial again like a disheveled harridan. A wave of self-righteousness surged through the press: "most damaging impeachment," *Edinburgh Review*; "hideous system of corruption," *Westminster Review*; "the leaden monotony, the vulgar self-interest," *Spectator*; "so shamelessly corrupt and so completely vulgar," *Graphic*; "not

only big but coarse, and its politics venal," *Saturday Review.*
Blackwoods pronounced the definitive epitaph.

If this is what government comes to when the favor of the masses
is manipulated by the vulgar and unscrupulous intellect . . . we
cease to wonder at and can scarcely condemn the flight of the
elegant exiles disgusted by a system so hopeless. . . . The curious separation of elegant Pharisees standing aloof and watching
contemptuously and mournfully . . . is one of the most extraordinary spectacles ever presented to the world.

Of course *Blackwoods* said little more than Whitman had
ten years before: "It is the fashion among dilettantes and
fops (perhaps I am not guiltless) to decry the whole formulation of the active politics of America, as beyond redemption,
and to be carefully kept away from." And nearly ten years
later Lowell would warn that "a yielding to this repulsion
by the intelligent and refined is a mainly efficient cause of
the evil, and must be overcome, at whatever cost of selfish
ease and aesthetic comfort." Hypnotized by surface phenomena, friend and foe met on the common ground of ignorance of the great social and economic revolution transforming
their society, unwilling to surrender faith in the dogmas of
laissez-faire economics. Among Adams's acquaintances in
Washington, only Lester Frank Ward of the Geological Survey
had cut through to a new theory of democratic society. In
London, Adams's friend, James Bryce, took the novel as a
text for an article defending democracy and urged his readers
not to be misled by such exaggerations. Adams himself had
already begun to have misgivings about his own dogmas; he
had voiced the opinion, years before in fact, that "fatal"
changes in the Constitution had taken place which "were not
the result of the war, but of deeper social causes." But the
deeper "social causes" still eluded him and he dismissed Henry
George as an alarmist. Like his heroine, Adams could not
embrace the millions in his sympathies. Emotionally sensitive,

he had tended to draw back from the "rough and tumble" of life to which his brother constantly invited him. Yet he felt himself inwardly tugged by it, challenged, tantalized. Like Madeleine he had been horrified by his education in the price of Power, but he would have had to admit that the fault lay in part in himself, in the violent contradictions of his nature, in the habitual excesses of his temperament. If Charles seemed to "like the strife of the world," Henry habitually clung to his instinct to "detest it and despise it." The novel justified to himself his choice. As he said to Brooks, many years later, "I bade politics good-bye when I published *Democracy*."[32]

As a *roman à clef* the novel was thoroughly searched for clues to the identity of the originals. This seems to have been its chief attraction in political circles. Newspapers sensitive to possible libel suits and political repercussions generally named no names. With a certain pious disingenuousness the New York *Times* cautioned eager hunters, "Doubtless all these fictitious politicians are compounded of odds and ends, features borrowed from many models." Loving a secret that teased so many persons, Adams never spoiled his private mirth by identifying the originals of his satire and through his letters, Marian's, and those of John Hay eddy and swirl, in a cloud of high spirited badinage, the guesses and surmises made by friends and enemies of the identity of the characters and of the author.

The portrait of James G. Blaine as Ratcliffe was the most easily recognized. Blaine publicly cut Clarence King, supposing him to be the author of the novel. Adams's contempt for Blaine went back many years before Blaine's exposure before Congress in 1876. Twice he had blocked the nomination of Adams's father for the Presidency. Pretending interest in civil service and revenue reform, Blaine had flirted with the Liberal Republican group in 1870. When in 1875 Blaine deliberately tricked the Liberal Republicans, Adams regarded him as dishonorable. The masterly speech 'in which Blaine managed to extricate himself from the Mulligan letters simply indicated, as Adams said, that he could "squeal louder than all the other pigs." His attacks upon their friend Carl Schurz's civil service program closed the book. From then on Blaine became "our pet enmity" and they "refused even social recognition," deliberately cutting him and his wife even after he became Secretary of State under Garfield.[33]

The physical description of him by Mrs. Lee fitted closely, especially the steely glint of the eyes, the special mark which Gamaliel Bradford also seized upon. But the thinly disguised political history made the identification certain. In spite of the savage features of the portrait, Adams allowed certain attractive qualities to the adversary, not merely in his appearance and personality, but in his character as well, the qualities that had made him the "plumed knight" of Ingersoll's nominating speech and the hero of the man on the street. Mrs. Adams was habitually unable to allude to Blaine without disgust, yet she had to concede that his oration on Garfield was a superb performance. "What a pity," she remarked to her father, "that so much ability should be unsupported by enough moral sense to make him an honest servant." Adams himself glimpsed hidden depths in the man. He showed Ratcliffe capable of being "filled with disgust and cynical contempt for every form of politics. During long years he had done his best for his party . . . and all for what?"[34]

As an Adams, Henry had been brought up to despise the fetish of party loyalty. It was the sacrifice of personal honor and integrity on that altar that most deeply shocked Mrs. Lee. Yet in condemning Ratcliffe — and Blaine — with such uncompromising rigor, Adams was preparing an untenable position for himself that could end only in complete political

cynicism. Hay, soon to become his closest friend, campaigned
for the Republican ticket in September of 1879, acting on the
practical hint of Secretary Evarts. He not only supported
Blaine but developed an affection for him, as for that matter
had the idealistic Howells. Learning of Blaine's re-election
he congratulated him, "Pass greatly on! Thou hast overcome."
Adams had to close his eyes to Hay's moral eccentricity
while the moralist in him would grow more sardonic at the
world — and at himself. One eccentricity he had already
allowed himself, a friendly truce with his neighbor General
Beale whose house was a rallying place for the Grant crowd
of "Stalwarts," and this for the sake of the irrepressible and
charming young gossip Emily Beale who was already a
privileged habitué of the Adams tea table. Soon another exception would have to be made for the notorious Pennsylvania politician, Senator James Donald Cameron, whose
lovely young second wife, Elizabeth, was destined to trans-
form the social life of Lafayette Square. What could be
made of a world that divided a man against himself and
compelled morality to be selective? Madeleine Lee found
the answer in flight.[35]

More than Blaine hovered behind the Mephistophelian
figure of Ratcliffe. There lurked also shabbily grandiloquent
Roscoe Conkling, the "beast Conkling" of Mrs. Adams's letters,
"asinine and offensive" and similarly to be avoided in public.
In this malignant composite portrait of a United States senator,
Adams symbolized every hateful trait of the breed of men
who had thwarted Adamses as far as memory ran. "Democracy, rightly understood," went one of the gibes in the novel,
"is the government of the people, by the people, for the
benefit of senators." "By and with the advice and consent of
the Senate" was the talisman of evil fortune. Gallatin had
succumbed to it. The State Department lived in terror of
it. Adams once remembered the simple expressiveness of a

Cabinet officer's remark: "A Congressman is a hog." The animal suggested to him by senators like Blaine and Conkling he honored in the name of Ratcliffe. "A wiser generation," said the author of *Democracy*, "will employ them in manual labor." [36]

Both Blaine and Conkling had tried to dictate Cabinet appointments to Hayes as they had formerly done to Grant, but Hayes successfully resisted them. But Hayes's difficulties had not ended there and from the inside story of his struggle with the powerful Senator Oliver Morton of Indiana who had been his rival for the nomination Adams took the materials for the ironic episode of the President's effort to immobilize Ratcliffe in a hostile Cabinet. Morton similiarly tempted by Hayes had replied with great astuteness that he would "never put himself in a place from which he could be dismissed by any man" and submitted a list of candidates acceptable to him, in effect imposing his own choice on the President. [37]

The identification of Nathan Gore as John Lothrop Motley, the historian and former Minister to London, posed no great puzzle to the politically literate. Gore explained his recall from London in these words, "The President . . . objects to the cut of my overcoat, which is unfortunately an English one. He also objects to the cut of my hair." It was common knowledge as Secretary Fish once told Adams that "Grant took a dislike to Motley because he parted his hair in the middle." At the time the New York *World* proposed this advertisement: "Wanted: A respectable man willing to be minister to England. He must smoke, must not part his hair in the middle or write books, and must have contributed to the saviour of the republic, either a house, a farm, a cottage, a span of fast horses, or a pair of shirt studs." [38]

As for the fictional President and his wife, they were obviously "composite" portraits. Reviewers recognized that Lincoln, Grant, and Hayes were all levied upon — there was the Western uncouthness of Lincoln, the grossness of taste of Grant, and the nightmare mediocrity of Hayes. The new President "had begun his career as a stone-cutter in a quarry, and was, not unreasonably, proud of the fact." The wary reader could surmise that the stone was granite and at once make the necessary substitution. In portraying the President as a bewildered and semi-literate figure who could not complete his inaugural address, Adams aimed at Grant, but the episode may well have been grounded in the private knowledge that his friend George Bancroft had written President Johnson's first message to Congress. Hayes's feebleness and good intentions lie close to the surface of the sketch as befitted the "third-rate nonentity" of Adams's original estimate. In more questionable taste were the patronizing allusions to Mrs. Hayes's provincial morality. As a religious enthusiast she barred wine, billiards, and cards from the White House and insisted on high necked gowns and long sleeves, all of which of course amused Mrs. Lee at the Presidential reception. Adams must have repented the satire a little when, shortly after their return from Europe, they received "a quantity of cut flowers with Mrs. Hayes's compliments." They soon formed a somewhat more gracious private estimate. Marian Adams conceded, "She's a kind, simple-minded woman; a touch of the country schoolmistress about her, but not a bit of nonsense or vulgarity."

The formal models of Mrs. Madeleine Lee and her sister Sybil were the elegant Mrs. Bigelow Lawrence, one of the favorite Beverly Farms neighbors of the Adamses, and her sister Fanny Chapman. Blaine's platonic devotion to Mrs. Lawrence once inspired Marian Adams to comment, "If Blaine were a widower, she would not long be a widow." Mrs. Lawrence recognized the tell-tale touches, but Adams never let on. More than twenty years later he could still chuckle over his escapade. Holt hankered to make a play of the novel. "I thought my old — five-and-twenty-year old sins were long dead and buried," Adams wrote to Mrs. Cameron, "but they rise like Mrs. Bigelow Lawrence who will die convinced that she was meant as the heroine of that scandalous work. I saw it in her eye at Bayreuth." [39]

Emily Beale quickly recognized herself in the *enfant terrible* gaiety of Victoria Dare. Miss Beale's unconventionalities were the talk of Washington, so much so that Marian Adams hesitated to have her introduced to her Boston connections. General Beale, a bonanza miner and his California-bred daughters, had opened their Washington home, the Decatur House on Lafayette Square, with a banquet whose opulence at one hundred and fifty dollars a plate stupefied the press. Miss Beale was wont to stroll about with a gigantic staghound on a leash. She was too good a piece of local color to omit from the scene of *Democracy*. She was a perpetual resource of artlessly devastating remarks. One that went posthaste to Dr. Hooper was her reply to a recently displaced politician who asked her, as the General's daughter, if she knew of a permanent place for him. "Without forethought or afterthought," as Marian commented, "she replied, 'Why you know the penitentiary has been yawning for you for years!' At which point, according to Miss Emily, Senator Allison who was sitting nearby 'gave me the most vulgar wink I ever received from a Western Senator.' " [40]

In the figure of Baron Jacobi, Adams drew upon another regular of their salon, Grégoire Aristarchi Bey, the Turkish Minister at Washington since 1873. An immensely popular figure in Washington society, he apparently had little official business to distract him. Adams developed a very great respect for his knowledge of European and Latin American affairs and came to rely on him as an oracle. When he was recalled in 1883, Adams, who had become one of his confidants, urged the editor of the *Post* to hire him as a correspondent. "The State Department would cower at your feet." The scheme

fell through and Aristarchi Bey, discredited at home, became
a political adventurer in Paris. It is his old world cynicism
that Adams puts into the mouth of old Jacobi: "You Americans believe yourselves to be excepted from the operation of
general laws. You care not for experience. . . . Well, I declare to you that in all my experience I have found no society
which has had elements of corruption like the United States.
The children in the street are corrupt, and know how to cheat
me. The cities are all corrupt, and also the towns and the
counties and the States' legislatures and the judges. Everywhere men betray trusts both public and private, steal money,
run away with public funds. . . . I do much regret that I
have not yet one hundred years to live. . . . The United States
will then be more corrupt than Rome under Caligula; more
corrupt than the Church under Leo X; more corrupt than
France under the regent." Under such tutelage Mrs. Lee comes
to see that democratic government "was nothing more than
government of any other kind." [41]

The social graces and sophisticated externals of Mrs. Lee
may have been borrowed from Mrs. Lawrence, but the mind
and temperament was that of Henry Adams and to a degree
that of his wife Marian. She is the only woman in New York
who knows American history. Like her creator she was incurably restless, "tortured by ennui," sceptical, indifferent to
religion, scornful of preachers and transcendentalists, eager to
know "men who cast a shadow" and disgusted with the mediocrity of Boston life. She is endowed with the traits admired
by the Adamses — a preoccupation with good manners, good
breeding, *savoir faire,* a restrained but elegant taste in the
arts, scorn of the vulgar and commonplace. Her intellectual
interests reflect his own: Swift, Ruskin, Taine, John Stuart
Mill, Swinburne, Dante, Voltaire, Molière, Aesop, Macaulay,
the Arabian Nights, and — Gustave Droz, a currently popular
French novelist. She appreciates the ironies of Southey's "Bat-

tle of Blenheim" and of *Vanity Fair.* She accepts Darwin with
an ironic kind of pleasure especially because the ignorant
Ratcliffe resents the imputation that men are descended from
monkeys. "After all," she tells the irate Ratcliffe, "we ought to
be grateful to them, for what would men do in this melancholy world if they had not inherited gaiety from the monkeys
— as well as oratory." But her intellectual identity with her
creator is most apparent in her habits of mind. She was
haunted with a passion for "discussing things and hunting
first principles." She had a certain doubleness of vision, a habit
of impersonal curiosity about her mind, an inveterate impul-
sion to take off her "mental clothing, as she might take off a
dress, and looking at it as though it belonged to some one
else, and as though sensations were manufactured like clothes."
It was an accurate self-characterization of one who liked to
sit on a high stool. Ed Howe of Kansas described the trait
in his homespun way when he "once said that Henry Adams
was the only man in America who could sit on a fence and
watch himself go by." [42]

In his characterization of her as purely a woman, Adams
gave voice to ideas which he shared with Marian, and some
obviously inspired by his admiration of her. Like his well-bred
friends he acknowledged the moral and cultural superiority
of women, but he also saw in Madeleine "a woman's natural
tendency towards asceticism, self-extinction, and self-abnega-
tion." Denied maternity as an outlet, the fulfillment of the
instinctual side of her nature, Mrs. Lee cries out in a kind of
despair, "Was the family all that life had to offer?" One can
only surmise from what depths of private feeling, depths which
no letter could confess, this cry rose up to hint of the anguish
of childlessness in their lives. [43]

The social fastidiousness of Adams and his wife, the product
of a common heritage, found sharpest expression in the condemnation of western manners. Nothing shocked Mrs. Lee so

much as western crudity. The President's wife, a native of
Indiana, is "a coarse washerwoman." One western Congressman comes appropriately from "Yahoo City." One of Sybil's
greatest fears for her sister if she should marry Ratcliffe is
that she would die of inanition in Ratcliffe's home in Peonia
with its horsehair sofas and chromo lithographs on the walls
and a "strong smell of cooking everywhere." Sybil's prejudice
extended to "western men and women, western towns and
prairies, and, in short, everything western down to western
politics and western politicians, whom she perversely asserted
to be the lowest of all western products." It was a provincial
view and Adams himself could see the humor in its excess;
nevertheless it reflected "common sense." After all, as John
Stuart Mill had written to Godkin, the "mental type formed
by the positions and habits of the pioneers" was the least attractive side of "American social existence." [44]

3 Critics and Hoaxes

The genuine excellence of the novel was widely appreciated
despite the patriotic reservations. It was obviously the work
of no literary novice, as both American and English reviewers
discerned. Some saw similarities to Henry James in the use of
the technique of psychological self-examination (the interior
monologue as it is now called) and the rejection of elaborate
and realistic setting. A few thought the idea stemmed from
Daudet's *Nabob,* one of the successes of 1877. It was compared favorably with Trollope's political novels. Mrs. Humphrey Ward in the *Fortnightly* rated it with the best of Lord
Beaconsfield. Almost everyone conceded that the novel was
"clever," but there was wide divergence of opinion on its other
qualities. William Cary Brownell in the *Nation* thought the
love interest and political interest poorly blended; whereas the

reviewer in the London *Spectator* believed that in "grafting political interests on a romance" the author surpassed Lord Beaconsfield and showed "the touch of a master hand." The undoubted power of Ratcliffe's characterization drew much praise. "Nothing in its way so good in our literature," said the . *Atlantic.* The *Saturday Review* called it a "masterpiece" and characterized Sybil as the most pleasing young woman in American fiction. The New York *Tribune* gave the most judicious explanation of the success of the novel in England:

> There is a certain fine workmanship, a polished style, a brightness and finish, of which Englishmen have learned to look for better examples in American fiction than in their own. . . . It is distinguished by an ease and smartness in which English fiction is apt to be especially deficient. But its chief attraction was the piquancy of its subject. . . . the picture of social and political life at the American capital for which the Old World has been looking — a mob of coarse, ignorant, smart, and dishonest people, with only the British minister moving among them as a superior person.[45]

These varied estimates suggest the astonishing assimilative powers of Adams's memory, a memory which he always underrated. Most striking are the complex echoes from Thackeray, whose novels were long-standing favorites — the array of Morality names, the satire of snobbery and vulgarity, the unscrupulousness of Baron Steyne, the hint of Becky Sharp in Victoria Dare, and the reminiscence of "Mrs. Lightfoot" from *Pendennis.* Arlington Cemetery puts Sybil in mind of George Osborne lying dead at Waterloo, for she was then reading *Vanity Fair.* In short Adams's intellectual associations were inveterately literary and he habitually dramatized political life in terms of fiction. When Garfield was shot, his first thought was of Thackeray and Balzac. They "never invented anything so lurid as Garfield, Guiteau and Blaine. . . . Arthur is a creature for whose skin the romanticist ought to go with a carving-knife." His own half-serious self-criticism suggests how far his artistic reach exceeded his grasp. His novel, he said, was "a failure because it undertook to describe the workings of power in this city, and spoiled a great tragic subject such as Aeschylus might have made what it should be, but what it never in our time will be. . . . I hate to see it mangled à la Daudet in a tame cat way." [46]

There is a temptation to see in Adams's choice of a woman as a protagonist a characteristic symbol, "a lack of the male principle" such as is said to be exhibited also by Henry James. On the other hand, had he made the principal character a man the key would have been in full view. The great vogue of the novel was paralleled by an intense interest in the authorship, and the guessing game went merrily on for several years to the vast entertainment of Adams and the elect few in on the secret. Only one person ever nominated Henry Adams as the author, one of his English friends, Mrs. Humphrey Ward, the novelist, who in her long and favorable review, shrewdly conjectured that he might well be the author as the novel seemed "to have almost exactly followed the lines laid down" in Adams's article "Civil Service Reform" in the *North American Review* for 1869. It was variously conjectured that the author was an Englishman, a Southern sympathizer, a member of an antebellum Washington family, a Washington society woman. In their letters Adams and his wife tossed about the names of nominees in a flood of badinage and raillery at each new flurry of public interest.[47]

"I am glad the secret is coming out," Adams chaffed Hay on the score of a news item naming him as author. "I was always confident that you wrote the book or at any rate that you knew who did. . . . I wrote to King to have your name put on the title page of an English edition, with Jim Bludso

and Little Breeches in a neat appendix." Six months later
the pot being stirred again, he added another dash of spoofing. "I understand from my sister-in-law, Ellen Gurney, that
Hon. J. G. Blaine at a dinner party in New York said that
Mrs. H.[enry] A.[dams] 'acknowledged' to have written
Democracy. You know how I have always admired Mr.
Blaine's power of invention! The *Republican* in a list of
reputed authors puts J.G.B.'s name first, with Gail [Hamilton
(Mary Abigail Dodge)] as collaborateur." "I am much
amused but not surprised at your suggesting me of having
written *Democracy,*" Marian wrote her father, "as I find
myself on the 'black list' here with Miss Loring, Arthur
Sedgewick, Manton Marble, Clarence King, and John
Hay. . . . All I *know* is that I did not write it. Deny it from
me if anyone defames me absent, and say to them, as Pickering Dodge of his parrot: 'If she couldn't *write* better than
that I'd cut her —— head off.'" Indeed the secret *had* to
be kept if the Adamses were to hold up their heads in Washington. Only a short time later two women novelists satirized
Washington society and paid the extreme penalty. *American
Court Gossip* reported that Mrs. Dahlgren was "snubbed by
some of the grande dames without mercy" for *A Washington
Winter,* and Frances Burnett was "sneered at behind her
back" for her *Through One Administration.* Mrs. Adams anticipated the unfavorable judgment by a few years as she
"never returned" Mrs. Burnett's social call.[48]

Godkin had almost set the cat free at the moment he was
trying to stifle the impulse to spill the secret of the *Nation*
review of the *Gallatin.* Late in 1880 Marian's sister Ellen,
the wife of Dean Gurney of Harvard, seems to have shared
a morsel of news with Marian: Godkin was letting on that
he knew who wrote the novel but was pledged not to tell.
Adams sternly tasked him, "Are we wrong in thinking . . .

that this remark might have seriously embarrassed us? You
can relieve my mind too of a considerable weight by telling
me whether the Gurneys have not obtained either through
you or through their own perspicacity, a clue or suspicion
as to the authorship of that book." Marian's postscript somewhat blunted the sting. "I only want to say that old friends
must not come to make mountains out of molehills. As one
grows old mountains are hard to climb." Godkin somehow
wriggled to safety. The legend that Adams read the manuscript aloud to the members of their little group in Lafayette
Square during the winter of 1878–79 must be in part apoc-
ryphal as Hay was apparently not yet in on the secret and
the "Five of Hearts" had not yet been constituted. As late as
November of 1880 Adams reproached Godkin saying that
when he confided the secret to him he had "almost decided
not to print." His "annoyance was due only to the fact that,
had my other confidant, King, also said as much, my secret
was gone." [49]

If this episode had its moments of painful uneasiness,
there was another one that inspired unalloyed joy among
these lovers of a hoax. Strangely enough, Henry's public-
spirited brother Charles, who had so long collaborated with
Henry, did not suspect him and ultimately came to believe
that Hay was the chief author. Immediately after publication,
Charles wrote to him: "The book I sent you was the very
'coarse' novel — Democracy. I send you another copy, not
that I admire it, but I was rather pleased with the leading
character — Randolph — in which the author seemed to me
to show some insight into the mixed ability, cant, vulgarity
and shrewdness of our Western statesmen. The idea of the
final retirement to Peonia is good. Poor Grant! Think of
finishing at Galena at 55 after his career! No wonder he
wants a third term." "Coarse" and "Randolph" to boot! It

was a little slip of recollection, but Henry must have felt
that it would be just as well to leave his brother in the dark
for the present, and give Marian a laugh.[50]

How the hilarious brew was doubly distilled appears in
the following exchange of letters, which immediately followed the anonymous publication of John Hay's anti-labor-
union novel, *The Breadwinners,* in the winter of 1883. Charles
Francis Adams, Jr. took pen in hand again and addressed
himself to the editor of the *Nation:*

> I have just been reading the "Breadwinners," that book which
> has created recently so much comment. I do not know whether
> you have seen it, nor do I think a great deal of it. Meanwhile
> there is some curiosity as to who the author is. I am sure I do
> not know; but one thing is to me very plain. It is written by
> the same hand that wrote the novel "Democracy" some years ago,
> which had so large a circulation in England. It has the same
> coarse, half-educated touch; and the Nast-like style of its portrait
> and painting is unmistakable. . . .
>
> Could you have a short paragraph written for the "notes" of
> the "Nation" suggesting this idea? . . .

At the bottom Godkin succinctly queried — "What shall I say
to this?" — and dispatched it to Henry Adams. Godkin, of
course, did not yet know that Hay was the author of *The
Breadwinners.*[51]

Delirious with joy, Henry dashed off a letter to "Colonel
John Hay," enclosing the one from Godkin.

> I want to roll on the floor; to howl, kick and sneeze; to weep
> silent tears of thankfulness to a beneficent providence which has
> permitted me to see this day. I want to drown my joy in oceans
> of Champagne and lemonade. Never, No, never, since Cain wrote
> his last newspaper letter about Abel was there anything so
> droll. . . .
>
> I am going to have it cut in gold letters on the front of our
> new houses. I would not part with this autograph of my beloved
> brother for all his cattle-yard stock. Poor though I be, I am richer
> than common men can dream of, so long as I have the whole
> Arabian Nights, the Odyssey, and Alice in the Looking Glass, all
> crowded into one small page of fraternal writing.

He enjoined the strictest secrecy upon his "Dear Heart," saying that he would urge Godkin "to get the 'Note' if possible, and print it with the author's initials. . . ." He signed himself "Ever your poor, coarse and half-educated friend, Henry Adams," and added, "My coarse and half-educated wife has had a fit over her brother-in-law's Nast-like touch."

The scheme succeeded. The unsuspecting Charles rose like a trout to the fly. His letter to the editor duly appeared over a modest "A," dated February 8, from Boston. Content with his earlier characterization, he repeated it. Both novels he said had "the same strong, coarse, Nast-like drawing of aspect and character." He went on to add, however, a mixture of sense and nonsense that ought to have tempered Henry's merriment a little bit with a slight shadow of uneasiness.

The work is crude and there are few fine touches to it. It is always provokingly near the verge of being very good. In "Democracy," as in "Breadwinners" we are conscious of the same keen, observant eye, working through a hand which is quite lacking in training, and which also, either naturally or from indolence, is unequal to a sustained effort. I fancy it would be safe to guess that the author had worked on a newspaper. He certainly has seen a good deal of politics, and was never a man of business. That he was once in the army is plain. Who he is I have not the remotest idea.[52]

Something about those novels obviously had a puzzling familiarity to Charles, a mystery to which he felt he ought to have the key and yet one that unaccountably eluded him — or, perhaps, he *did* have his suspicions. After all, Charles had himself played the game of secrets with great zest. The criticism of the style seems a curiously pointed — mayhap unconscious — addition to his anonymous criticisms of Henry's *Gallatin*. The gibe about the man of business had its satirical relevance to both his brother and Hay. The allusion to army service, if an intentional thrust, neatly took off both "Colonel" Hay and his brother, neither of whom had smelled powder, whereas he had earned his colonelcy in the field. In any case, whatever the private surmises on either side, the incident was closed with gentlemanly finality, never to be reopened in spite of the gossip that continued dimly to float about the Square.

4 A Riot of Interests

In the second autumn in Washington, the Adamses settled into the accustomed grooves with almost audible sighs of pleasure. Henry now had a "charming little bay mare, Daisy" and his wife was breaking in the "frisky" Prince to the accompaniment of sundry bruises. Their "establishment" was "set afloat à la Noah's ark," said his wife. "Henry and I, 2, 2 dogs, (Polly [last of a new litter] is given to Mr. Brown?), 2 horses, 2 women servants, 2 men servants." Each morning at nine, except when the ice became treacherous, they would clatter off along the back streets to avoid the crush of horsecars and provision wagons into the countryside. A favorite run took them along the laurel-margined road up the Potomac to the Chain Bridge and they relished the "glorious glimpses of the distant city." Entranced by the autumn colors edging the country roads, they wished "the days were twice as long." Usually back at the Square by eleven, Henry had six hours at his desk at the State Department before dinner. Life was inordinately full as his head buzzed with projects, the *Gallatin* rapidly finishing, a much more grandiose historical project beckoning in the distance, and his first novel burgeoning, the germ having probably been planted on the visit to Mount Vernon that spring.[53]

Henry did not need to dissemble when with a touch of complacency he fretted, "Life is going so fast that I hardly know whether the remnant is worth exerting oneself about."

The "riot of interests and individualities" almost stunned the pair, yet the ceaseless dance that began with five o'clock tea so fed his restless cravings that at the slightest let-up in the round of dinners and receptions, he felt neglected and abandoned. In the brief lull after Christmas, he reassured his father-in-law, who tended to worry about their pace, "we are quiet as mice here. . . . We hardly ever go out, and no one invites us anywhere." Marian's more reliable reports must have evoked an understanding smile. What had happened was that Professor von Holst and General Taylor had been obliged to miss Christmas dinner with them and they had languished at home for the day.[54]

A more typical week brought Congressman Cox and von Holst on a Sunday with "good talk until midnight." On Tuesday a small party at Madame Outrey's, the wife of the French Minister, "mostly diplomates — counts and barons and marquises thick as blackberries." Thursday they had to miss a "game" party at the Schurz's when an unexpected guest dropped in. As for the circle round their new Japanese tea-table, all the "regulars" were back in attendance, reinforced by numerous birds of passage from the legations. During the doldrums of the Christmas week, Clarence King, Schurz, and Henry Cabot Lodge joined the court. King, ever their favorite guest, agog with the "politics" of the Survey, captivated Marian with his bright chatter, whether "raving" about the latest New York fashions in silk turbans or joking about his California escapades. "No one was so good company" in the drawing room or on a shopping trip to beguile the hours until Henry got back from his desk. Secretary Evarts came in to clot the air with his habitual oratory, and to pass on a venomous tidbit from the grandson of Hamilton, "The Adams family grow viler in each generation." Adams could afford to smile, knowing that as a historian he would have the last word.[55]

The Liberal Republican remnant came so incessantly as to mark theirs as a "political house." The good-natured wrangling would leap from currency to the recent Southern outrages or to Schurz's efforts to protect the Indians. Even the ambitious Garfield put in an appearance, risking the suspicions of the orthodox Republicans. Notably absent that winter and spring was John Hay, busy with his part of the Lincoln biography and too ill to visit Washington. And in the intervals there were always "our eminent Boston constituents" to entertain and lobbying friends like their New York lawyer friend Sam Barlow. In mock anguish Marian declared, "I am going to put a sign out 'Railroad Hotel. Meals served at all hours.' " At least they were growing skillful at dodging receiving lines. Adams contrived some spare moments to begin forehandedly brushing up on his French in anticipation of a research trip abroad. Marian gave up early because their tutor, a "nasty little Jesuit," too obviously shunned soap and water.[56]

One experience of the winter made a profound impression upon Adams. Leaving King as guest in residence, he and Marian accompanied the British Minister Sir Edward Thornton and his distinguished entourage for a ten day trip to Niagara Falls. Snugly quartered at Prospect House on the Canadian side, they sang English ballads and looked out at the enormous icicles that glittered from the lip of the Falls. While Marian nursed a sore throat, Henry joined the rest in a wild sleighride in a snowstorm, "shinnied" up icicles, and "lunched on mince pie and pickles in some squalid restaurant." Ignoring their solemn promise to King, they scampered across the crevasses of the ice-bridge to the American side, because Henry had brooded over the dazzling vista until he could not resist the attraction. Utterly care-free they passed the time with whist and poker and singing the irresistible lyrics of "Give my chewing gum to sister, I shall never want it more." Thriftily, Adams noted the eerie beauty of the scene and the camaraderie, storing them away for the right literary moment.

The tuneful evenings about the fire inspired Marian to rent a piano and order all her music sent down from Marlborough Street and her German lieder from her father's home. Washington could now be home to them without reservation. In the spring, Dr. Hooper made his headquarters with them for several weeks, in what had become a regular custom. The days went by, as Adams told Gaskell, "like a dream of the golden age." Only a single comic misadventure disturbed the even tenor. The Washington dog-catcher carried off Adams's favorite dog "Boojum," in spite of Marian's outcry. The incident elicited a long punning *jeu d'esprit* from Marian. Henry went off to bail the dog out. " 'We sat in the cart in dogged silence,' said Boojum. Then he heard Henry's voice, 'My poor Boojum, it's all right now.' They rode home on a horse-car and his mistress 'hugged me and kissed me and fed me and then did it all over again.' She sailed out to scold 'the very wicked man who ruled this city' and 'came home for tea at five o'clock looking quite happy.' His mistress, said Boojum, thought his story 'moves about too much' but he explained that after all 'dog's tales always do.' " [57]

As usual Adams was unable to avoid continued involvement in the affairs of his friends. Lodge enlisted him to dragoon contributors for the *International Review*, a task which he went at so vigorously among his acquaintances that it was mistakenly assumed that he was a co-editor with Lodge and John T. Morse. But if his position was not official, he clearly exercised some of its prerogatives as Washington agent. Young Lodge, then just making the transition from scholar to politician, gratefully accepted his mentor's suggestions. Adams persuaded the ever-reluctant J. D. Cox to do an article on the Indian question, and put Simon Newcomb to work on the Silver question. Unable to tackle the tempting Cipher scandal himself, he pressed Lodge to get a young man to expose it, promising to be on the lookout also for a candidate.[58]

Crowded as the season was with literary projects, the surmise has been offered that still another anonymous work poured from his pen, the "Diary of a Public Man," the authorship of which has mystified Civil War historians for three quarters of a century. The *Diary*, which ran in the *North American Review* from August to November of 1879, was probably the most sensational editorial coup of Adams's successor, Allen Thorndike Rice. It purports to be an eye-witness account of a strategically placed political figure in Washington during the crucial days of the Great Secession Winter of 1860–61, by a man who moved freely in the highest political circles, a confidant of some of the leading actors in the drama, including Seward and Lincoln. The pseudo-diarist had access to confidential information from almost every clique, North and South. He had a Boswellian memory for pungent conversations and a raconteur's ear for Lincoln anecdotes.[59]

The effort to attribute it to Henry Adams can hardly be more than agreeable academic daydreaming. One of the most incongruous and improbable touches is the admiration, even hero worship, expressed by the Diarist toward Stephen A. Douglas, who figures as his friend and confidant. Adams's own feeling toward Douglas was one of bottomless contempt. In his 1861 letters he had stormed that Douglas was "gross, vulgar, demagogic; a drunkard, ruined as a politician." In his unpublished article "The Great Secession Winter" he scored Douglas as "a coarse politician. . . . No man in the whole nation has done so much as he to degrade the stand-ard of political morality." There are in fact so many discrepancies between the *Diary* and Adams's own experience and opinions, contemporaneously recorded in his letters and his contributions to the Boston *Advertiser,* that only the most determined imagination can entertain the farfetched hypothesis. To have concocted a fifty-five page serial which transformed and concealed his personality and attitudes in elaborately complex ways would indeed have been an extraordinary tour de force, but as completely pointless as it is incredible. Motiveless malignity was not one of his traits.[60]

As one reviews the pell-mell rush of activities of that season, a forge full of irons kept busily glowing, one can accept Adams's defense to his friends that he had little time for letter-writing that year. All his projects were moving better than he had dared hope in this wonderfully productive period, the *Gallatin* was lumbering through the press, *Democracy* was off to Holt. Eager for another lark he snatched at General Miles's offer of a trip to the Yellowstone, but Dr. Hooper, fearful for Marian's strength, dissuaded them. Unwilling to "dawdle about Beverly Farms" for the summer, they promptly booked passage on the *Gallia* for May 28, 1879. If there was time to reflect on their two-year "experiment" in Washington, they could term it an unqualified success. Prudently, they gave up the house at 1501 H Street with its wisteria and the "superb rose trees" coming into bloom, amenities which a new owner, to their disgust, would dispense with. Their letters gave no slightest hint, however, of any intention of returning to reside in Boston. Five days after he reported to Albert Rolaz Gallatin that publication was complete Adams was aboard ship, where Mr. Gallatin's appreciative note caught him. "You have performed this task in a manner which is perfectly satisfactory and meets my warmest approbation; indeed I know not how sufficiently to thank you for all your zeal and labor." Before embarkation there was time for a characteristic act of prudence and one that revealed the maturing of their mutual respect and affection. Just before their marriage in 1872 Adams and his wife had made out reciprocal wills. Now Marian executed a codicil, doubtless also reciprocal, changing the provision for a life estate to a complete and unlimited bequest to her husband.[61]

Chapter Four

European Orbit

1 Searching Archives

Six years had passed since Henry Adams and his wife had last visited England and the Continent on the wedding journey that took them as far as Philae, above the First Cataract of the Nile. Just past forty he light-heartedly donned his "cloak of historian" with a sardonic flourish, the "grave yawning" for him, and set out to enjoy the agreeably flattering cachet that his work had inspired in scholarly circles. The sprinkling of American and British reviews of the *Gallatin* circulated usefully among his English acquaintances. James Russell Lowell wrote from Madrid to compliment his one-time student, and, being a scholar, judiciously noted an error in a quotation. Too much the gentleman to submit tamely to praise, Adams responded with his usual stammer of self-depreciation. "No one has ever read it, or ever will, but perhaps, some centuries hence, antiquaries will use it." [1]

Adams's intention to go abroad had crystallized in August of 1878. He needed "a winter in Spain and Paris, and a spring in London . . . to study the diplomatic correspondence of the three governments, in regard to America, during the time of Napoleon, from 1800 to 1812." Just thinking of the ocean voyage made him queasy and he wished for a "flying machine." Working in the records of the State Department, he had very quickly seen that he lacked the counterparts of the illuminating reports sent home by American envoys from foreign listening posts. As secretary to his father in London for seven years, he had learned the importance of secret diplomatic dispatches. A more immediate incitement was the example of his eminent friend and neighbor, George Bancroft, who had spent a fortune in exploring foreign archives and making transcripts for his monumental *History of the United States* [to 1789].[2]

In September of 1879, several months after his arrival in England, he wrote a more detailed scheme of what he was seeking to Lowell, as he desired his help with the Spanish archives. "The papers I want from the Spanish government belong wholly to the time of the first Napoleon. That brigand, as you know, swindled Spain out of Louisiana, and then sold us that province in violation of his contract with Spain. The more I have studied the matter, the less I am impressed with the dignity of our own government in this transaction. . . . I want to tell the whole truth, in regard to England, France and Spain, in a 'History of the United States from 1801 to 1815,' which I have been for years collecting material for." The allusion suggests that he now regarded his 1877 compilation, *Documents Relating to New England Federalism, 1800–1815*, as the first step toward his *magnum opus*. That work published in part to refute von Holst's imputations against John Quincy Adams and in part as a companion work to Henry Cabot Lodge's *George Cabot* had plunged Adams deep into the unpublished state papers of the period.[3]

For nearly a month after their arrival on June 5, the Adamses surrendered to the long-anticipated pleasures of London. It felt good to get back to the cosmopolitan bustle, for they agreed with Dr. Johnson that "he who is tired of London is tired of life." They took lodgings in Half Moon Street in Piccadilly, but one street away from their good friend Henry James. Henry's good companions, Sir Robert Cunliffe and Charles Milnes Gaskell, royally welcomed them and they were soon embarked on a succession of dinners and receptions. Of Sir Robert, Adams was especially fond "not on account of his wit or knowledge, but because he is what a gentleman ought to be." They keenly relished the long-deferred holiday; but Adams did not forget his mission. At a "smart reception at the Foreign Office" he fell into talk with the Foreign Secretary, the unprepossessing Marquis of Salisbury, about the rules of the Record Office which blocked the use of papers after 1802. A letter confirmed their discussion. Adams asked that the ban be lifted to "the year 1810, or, if it is not thought improper, even to the year 1815." Within a week the coveted permission was issued, Adams gracefully protesting in his thanks: "Perhaps it has for me only one disadvantage; if I find anything to rouse my patriotic indignation, I shall hardly feel equal to doing it justice. One can't properly abuse a country which is so good-natured about it." Time blunted that polite scruple. After July 12 he was "pegging away hard" at the bonanza of untouched documents.[4]

"The second act of 'The Innocents Abroad' began," as Marian said, in September when they crossed to France and called on the French Premier, William Waddington, who promised access to the secret papers in the office of Foreign Affairs and the Ministry of Marine. But actual permission was provokingly delayed and all signs pointed to a cabinet crisis. While waiting, Adams decided to try Madrid. He and Marian had been studiously cramming for that journey for several months. There had been Spanish lessons three times a week. "O'nights," said Marian, "we have a blazing fire and read Spanish out loud; a thrilling romance with twenty-five murders in the first four chapters." Adams, sleepy with wading "through cords of plays and novels," begged Lowell: "Teach me to adore Spanish literature, for the more I read of it, the meaner my intelligence seems." [5]

The Spanish archives in Madrid proved even balkier than the French and Lowell, preoccupied with the desperate illness of his wife, could do little for him. The Duke of Tetuan, the Foreign Secretary, protested that there were papers "too delicate to be shown . . . too reserved a character." It was a painful check. The onset of the rainy season made Madrid even more of "a hole." There was only one compensation, the Titians in the gallery which knocked "all his expectations flat." They fled southward. "Andalusia received us with open arms. The sun came out. Cordova was fascinating. The great mosque was glorious." [6]

But while Henry revelled in the scenery, Marian fortunately did not relax her practical vigilance. Aboard the train to Granada she "fell to prattling," as was her habit, with the women members of a family party sharing their compartment. "I muttered to Henry that perhaps the Senor might know the chief of Archives in Seville, and why didn't he make a shot in the dark and see what he could bring down. Henry, true to the characteristics of his first ancestor, wished me to 'bite first.' So, with an assumed air of casual curiosity, I bit deep into the core." Thus they became acquainted with the very charming Don Leopoldo Equilaz, a rich lawyer, antiquarian and professor of Arabic, who did happen to have connections with the national archivist. A devout Carlist, their "Granada Maecenas" painted a gloomy picture of the future of Spain; but Adams as a loyal American hoped that the Republic of 1873 would one day be "firmly planted," for the current regime was just another illustration of the anachronisms of European politics, semifeudal, generations behind America, enveloped in the swirling intrigues and plots of priests, nobles, royalists, and republicans. Their new friend conducted them through the Alhambra and took Adams to explore the old Iberian city. Seeing his interest in ethnology, Don Equilaz urged a visit to Tetuan and supplied them with introductions to the "best Moorish circles." Touched by such overwhelming kindness, Marian philosophized, "A Britisher will do anything for you if he knows you are all right; a Frenchman 'passes by on the other side'; but the Spaniard binds up your wounds." To Tetuan they must go.[7] "One suffers much in Spain," began Adams's extended narrative of the expedition, "but in Africa one is flayed alive." "We escaped the next morning on two donkeys, my wife seated in an arm-chair as a throne supported by a donkey, while I modestly rode in a saddle. We were nine hours on the backs of these animals, and reached Tetuan, 27 miles, in a condition resembling martyrdom; but the ride was almost the most beautiful thing I ever saw, along the Mediterranean all day, with a view that justified self-destruction. We were accompanied by a delightful scoundrel, Juanito, for our *arriero;* a marvelous postman or Rachash, with a turban and long legs, who in youth was a Kabyle robber, and now, having adopted honesty as a profession, was warranted to kill anyone who interfered with us; a white-bearded Jewish rabbi, who sat perched on a donkey with the comical air of a Rafaelitic saint or martyr; and various screaming Arabs. At Tetuan we were deposited at the house of your Consular Agent, Isaac Nahon, an Ebrew Jew, and we occupied his Moorish mansion in company with Sir George Ballas who had come over here from Tangiers. Tetuan is the filthiest hole I ever saw, and the most eastern. . . . I have now seen enough of Jews and Moors to entertain more liberal views in regard to the Inquisition, and to feel that, though the ignorant may murmur, the Spaniards saw and pursued a noble aim." [8]

A four-day public holiday in Seville honoring the wed-

ding of King Alphonso XII to the Austrian Hapsburg Maria
Christina nullified the magic of Don Leopoldo's letter. Adams
was again vanquished, but not so his resourceful wife. "Was
it by chance possible," she asked, "to give a present to
some sub-official who might let us in for the sake of a
new gown for his senora?" It was possible. For three hours
Adams hunted fruitlessly among "the millions of bundles,"
but at least he had the consolation that "no other fellow can
come here and trip him up by later information and spoil
his work." Back in Madrid, Adams found an ally at last in
the Marqués de Casa Yrujo, grandson of the Spanish Minister
to the United States during Jefferson's administration. The key
turned in the lock. He was at last assured of John Quincy
Adams's dispatches.[9]

When, after two months in Spain, they dropped back to
Paris, the smoldering cabinet crisis erupted as if Adams
carried infection in his baggage, a pleasing fantasy that was
to grow with the passing of the years. The political situation in France flattered the *amour-propre* of Americans even
more than that of Spain. The Third Republic harbored a
discordant array of clamorous rivals and bitter hatreds, the
legacy of 1870. Squabbling monarchists had voted a republic only out of mutual spite. The rise and fall of minis-
tries in the ensuing struggle for control gave an impression
of turmoil that the cynical gaiety of Paris did not lessen.
The Catholic party seeking by a coup d'état to restore the
temporal power of the Pope had succeeded only in arousing
a fresh wave of anti-clericalism, touched off by Gambetta's
rallying cry, "Le cléricalisme, voilà l'ennemi!" [10]

For light on the state of France, Adams again looked up
August Laugel, the historian, whom he had met in 1873.
Laugel, a frequent contributor to the *Nation*, represented a
point of view which Adams and his brother Brooks were
later to adopt as they grew more critical of the failings of

democracy. At the moment the Adamses were drawn to the staunch republican Gambetta, Mrs. Adams impulsively affirming, "My sympathies always go with the radicals." In his *France Politique et Sociale*, Laugel decried the passing away of the gracious old order with its familiar loyalties, its respect for authority and for the virtues of the military character. In the current social crisis only the army could be trusted "to preserve the purity of the national character . . . from the insidious passions of a populace at once refined and depraved, and from the levity of [the] prosperous and sceptical bourgeoisie." What was needed was a new Age of Chivalry to revive the medieval military ideal and arrest the racial degeneration of the French which had been exposed by Bismarck's blonde warriors at Sedan. One encouraging effect of the debacle of 1870, said the *Nation*, was the increased interest taken by cultured Frenchmen in the early and medieval history of their country and its literature. As an expert medievalist himself, Adams could refresh his taste for the subject, not only with Laugel but also with the eminent medievalist Professor Marcel Thévenin of the École des Chartes.[11]

Premier Waddington's resignation, forced by the republicans, left Adams up in the air. By coincidence the disobliging Duke of Tetuan had also been deposed in Spain. "See how fate overtakes some ministers who go back on us," Mrs. Adams remarked. Her husband was providentially rescued by Professor Gabriel Monod, youthful editor of the *Revue Historique* and one of his former contributors to the *North American Review*. Other intermediaries also helped untie "the knots in French red tape." A "celebrated French astronomer" supplied an entree to the Ministère de la Marine. The American chargé, Robert Hitt, interposed for access to the archives for 1800–1804, especially those relating to Santo Domingo and Louisiana, describing Adams as belonging

to "une famille illustre," a person of "grand mérite" whose
recent work on Albert Gallatin had had "un légitime succès."
The Second Secretary of the Legation, Henry Vignaud, a
former Confederate captain, agreed to supervise the work of
transcription after Adams left Paris. Suffering setbacks with
some archives, he had phenomenal success with others, so
that there came times when he was "up to his eyes all day
in fascinating work and very happy." By the end of February
1880 he could report, "I never have had a better-employed
six weeks." He was "off at ten every morning, home to
breakfast at twelve, and then off again from one until dark,"
after which he "read hard all the evening." Ahead of him
lay a "mountain of papers and books to digest" and not
"an hour to lose." Once the permissions came for the reserved
archives, he drove himself at top speed, finally calling a halt
on the twenty-fifth when he decamped to London, although
"he could have occupied himself for many more months at
his blessed archives." [12]

In the early fall Paris had been an agreeable place. Henry
still bent on improving his wife had persuaded her, despite
the satire of *Democracy*, to make the pilgrimage to the
great Worth where she commissioned a gown whose colors
suggested "a serious peacock." Her ultra-fastidious husband
insisted on a complete wardrobe, an idea to which she demurred, but he twitted her, "People who study Greek must
take pains with their dress." In any case their Calumet copper
had just touched 200¼ and some extravagance was warranted.
Henry James had come over and they were much together.
For some reason the three friends avoided the French literary
set, although James knew the literary lions as an intimate
of Renan and Daudet. Instead they whiled away their evenings dining about Paris and visiting the theatre, sometimes
joined by the Jack Gardners of Boston. Chill weather blocked
a trip to Mont-Saint-Michel, but Adams managed to see a

few Norman Gothic churches, which delighted him more
than "watering places and casino life" and at his first sight
of Amiens exclaimed it was "a whacker" with features that
"beat anything I knew." [13]

By mid-winter Paris had rapidly lost its charm. Their
English and American acquaintances had flown and James
had gone back to haunt his fireside in London. Except for
a few friends at the American Embassy and infrequent visits
with scholarly associates like Laugel, Monod, and Thévenin,
they were rather much alone, for Parisians were not cordial
to Americans, "in spite of their purchasing power," as the
Nation observed. Adams's letter to the Premier opened no
social doors and he and his wife were left to match each
other's detestation of the great inhabited desert. For her it
was nothing but "a huge shop and restaurant." Henry fretted
even more violently. "At the best of times Paris is to me a
fraud and a snare; I dislike it, protest against it, despise its
stage, condemn its literature, and have only a temperate
regard for its cooking; but in December and January Paris
is frankly impossible." It was all the harder to bear because of
his nostalgia for the Paris of the Second Empire which he had
known as a young man of twenty-two. Then, "the women on
the stage were the freshest young girls in life, and now
they are coarse and big." That was how the Paris stage of
1868 had impressed him. Ten more years had only deepened
his disenchantment.[14]

Dissatisfaction had much to thrive on. The unusually extreme cold of that winter was made even less bearable than
usual for American tourists by the shortage of firewood in
Paris, though the "fearful cold" mercifully abated early
in January. The vagaries of the weather were more than
matched by the howling political tempest. Gambetta, who
struggled to rescue the Third Republic from the royalists,
Bonapartists, and Catholic clericals had their sympathies,

but the turbulence of the debate in the press and the disorderly reflection of the social and intellectual struggle on the stage and in the books of the Naturalist school poisoned the atmosphere. The French seemed intolerably slow in solving the problems that had vanished in America. The recent debates in the Chamber over the bill designed to destroy the Jesuit domination of public education brought the divisive hatreds of the opposing factions into lurid focus. A republican leader defied the anti-democratic coalition: "You . . . have put the word Counter-Revolution in your banner; we on our side, mean to defend the Revolution." Once again at stake were the principles of 1789 and the renewed civil war heightened the bitterness of the controversies over the emancipation of women, the teaching of evolution and materialistic positivism, the increasing advocacy of socialism and pacifism. Religious reaction, long nourished by Pius IX's campaign against modernism, reawakened old hatreds.[15]

With the press still denied full freedom and a general amnesty of the Communards of 1870 still withheld, the protest against the established order found liveliest expression in the theatre where the freedom to give outrage was quixotically respected. The incessant preoccupation of dramatists and writers with illicit love made the Adamses acutely uneasy and resentful. As outsiders they did not perceive that the satirical gibing and the cynicism, the rebellion against virtue and chastity, were all part of the long running warfare with the hypocritical mores of the bourgeoisie and the antiquated marriage laws that flattered the clergy. They had tried a new play at the Gymnase with Henry James, and had found it "very indecent and charmingly acted." If the police had "come in and borne actors and audience to the nearest station house," said Mrs. Adams, "I should have conceded that they had a strong case." The immorality and irresponsibility of the stage — and of all Paris, for that matter — seemed incarnated in the reigning favorite, Sarah Bernhardt. Of course she had to be seen at the Comédie Française in *Ruy Blas* (a timely parable for a divided France) for she was "chic and the rage," but her tantrums and peccadilloes could not be forgiven, especially as these seemed only to endear her the more to her admirers. They joined with Henry James in taking the part of his friend the great Coquelin in his long-standing quarrel with her over the management of the Comédie. They detested her "voice, posing, looks, and all," and adopted Coquelin's angry judgment, "Elle n'est pas sérieuse, ni comme femme ni comme artiste." Their minds made up, they had nothing but scorn for her on her subsequent American tour. Adams shared as well James's rather prudish view of decency in literature. Zola would be his special antipathy. What the *Nation* said of James's *French Poets and Novelists* fitted Adams as well. "He cannot, however, help showing at times the puritanic instincts of a well-bred inhabitant of New England" in his dislike of "Andalusian passions, of ladies tumbling about on disordered couches, and . . . lovers who take refuge from an exhausted vocabulary in *biting* each other." [16]

Cosmopolitan as their tastes were neither Adams nor his wife had the slightest expatriate longings. He was, as his friend Henry Watterson once said, a provincial at heart. "The more we travel," said Marian, "the more profoundly impressed we are with the surpassingly-solid comfort of the average American household and its freedom from sham. They beat us on churches and pictures in the Old World, but in food, clothing, manners and morals, it seems to us we have the 'inside track.' " On Christmas day they looked westward with deep longing. "Pleasant as our seven months abroad have been," went the note to Godkin, "we want to be at home which suits our tastes and tempers better than your effete old monarchies — the unfeeling taunts in your letter about roving habits and nomadic tastes are cruel to homesick Americans." Her husband regularly struck the same chord. America was "a better place than any on this side." [17]

2 Belshazzar's Feast

Everything since their arrival in England the preceding June confirmed their first impression of loss and decay, of the sense of a dying order. What the resident Englishman experienced as the gradual alteration of age and use, the inevitable albeit reluctant accommodation of one generation to the claims of the next one, Adams, after a six-year interval, felt as a sudden disorientation of familiar landmarks. The social parallax drew a livid line across the face of England. Everywhere he and Marian perceived signs of a "great change," a palpable diminution. More of a sentimentalist than he cared to acknowledge, he was easily unsettled by the flight of years and continents and seemed to feel himself a ghost in a strangely different England.[18]

Having talked much to his "liberal friends from John Bright downwards," he considered English politics to be bankrupt and deprecated the political ambitions of his friend Robert Cunliffe. The Liberals had nothing in common "except personal hatred of Dizzy and Salisbury." To build up a party, a liberal leader "must have the nerve to lay his hands on the pillars of the state, and to risk his neck for a distant future." Nor was he encouraged by the shop talk at the home of his old friend William Forster. On the lookout for large principles, he heard only petty chatter about the last debate. There was no "wit, humor, nor taste in it," but it "amused" him because it showed "how a political life vulgarises and narrows intelligent people." His discontent had its origin in a very personal problem, one with which he had so often wrestled inwardly and in debate with his brother Charles, and had not yet wholly settled in his own mind. Should men of talent strike for literature or politics? A number of his brilliant English friends were passing through the throes of such a decision. James Bryce seemed decided on politics and the abandonment of history. George Otto Trevelyan, the biographer of Macaulay, a man exactly his own age, turned to Adams for advice. "It is a terrible business," he said, "to make such a serious decision as that which I have had to make." He justified his acceptance of Gladstone's offer of the post of Parliamentary Secretary to the Navy with an explanation to which Adams could hardly dissent. "I do not feel as if one were living in a literary age of a literary country." [19]

Since Adams's last visit in 1873 England had made great progress toward a new imperium. By threats and masterly bluff Disraeli had thwarted Russian designs on Constantinople and the Dardenelles, cheating her of the fruits of victory in the war with Turkey, and he gave the Turkish empire enough medication to restore it to chronic illness. By another shrewd stroke, without waiting for authority from Parliament, he had bought up the bankrupt Khedive's shares in the Suez Canal and occupied Egypt. By still another stroke he liquidated the East India Company and made Queen Victoria Empress of India. In 1879 a species of peace had descended upon Europe, but he had no time for idleness. To counteract Russian intrigue in Afghanistan, British troops again defiled through the passes to open the Second Afghan war. Meditating on the new turn, Adams speculated that "Afghanistan and India would swamp any ministry." Yet Disraeli hung on. In far off Zululand the last great colonial adventure had already begun. Annexation of the Transvaal led to full scale war with the neighboring Zulus early in 1879. The hordes of ill-armed natives melted away in the fire of the British square, and the land passed to Queen Victoria.[20]

Even as Adams grumbled that his Liberal friends were squandering their talents on politics, the signs had begun to point toward Disraeli's overthrow. Public discontent with the pro-Turkish foreign policy grew daily more intense. Misled by his long-standing distrust of Gladstone, the Liberal party leader, Adams underrated his political energy and sagacity. Months later, in 1880, when Adams relieved the gloom of Good Friday in London by "visiting the monkeys and lions at the zoo," the voters went to the polls to sweep the Liberal party into office by an overwhelming majority. Adams's friends Gaskell and James Bryce were carried in; Forster became chief secretary for Ireland in Gladstone's new ministry. But now that his prognostications had collapsed Adams discounted the development. "We are more startled by George Eliot's marriage to John Cross," he wrote, "than by the elections themselves." Nevertheless, the pair of travelers were impressed, as Marian said, by the "springtide of Liberalism which has risen over the land this week." Especially pleasant was the fact that Disraeli, "that Jew bagman with his quack medicines," had been ordered off the premises." [21]

Looking back from the distant perspective of American progress, English politics and imperial adventures in Turkey, Egypt, India, Afghanistan, and Zululand seemed less important to the Adamses than the state of English society which confronted them. "At this Belshazzar's feast, not only do we see the handwriting on the wall, but the givers of the feast do too, and they are scared, and say it's giving way. On all sides are wails of unlet farms, discontented tenants, no money, good servants who won't wear livery. The 39,000,000 who get no cakes and ale, think it's about time for the

1,000,000 who do, to treat." To Lodge Henry Adams echoed his wife's sentiments. "I am you know a little of a communard myself. . . . In my uniformly untrustworthy opinion, this old shebang will come to grief. Europe has got to do some more heavy revoluting in the next twenty years, and America has a long start." [22]

The marks of the long depression that had begun in 1873 and to which they had grown accustomed in America seemed arrestingly different in England. Parliamentary committees were conscientiously exploring the noisome industrial slums and assembling data for a horrified public. In Lord Morley's words, England was a "paradise for the well-to-do, a purgatory for the able, and a hell for the poor." The Reform Bill of 1867 extended the suffrage to the dim subterranean levels of society, the industrial workers, and the secret ballot law of 1872 made the revolution final. Trade-unions were now legal and strikers could no longer be jailed as criminal conspirators. A new Factory Inspection Act challenged the authority of mill owners by imposing minimum standards for safety. The great older generation of Victorian thinkers and writers — Macaulay, Carlyle, Dickens, Ruskin — saw in all this the advance of social chaos. Not so the Liberals. The path indicated by Mill and John Bright was followed by Gladstone and Morley. The most significant fact of the era, said Morley, was "The rise of the workman to a decisive share in the control of his destinies." That Adams did not more clearly perceive the drift of events at this period and welcome them with greater ardor was a sign of preoccupations in other directions.[23]

3 Old Friends and New

Life in England had an even more magical and charmed quality for him than it had had on his wedding journey, in spite of the vague air of menace that floated like an equivocal second thought about the drawing rooms and country houses which they visited. He wore his "cloak of historian" with graceful authority and Marian had all the serene assurance of a successful Washington hostess. On their return from the Continent they were again deluged with hospitality, resuming the ritual of three and four dinners a week with redoubled zest. London, as James was wont to say, was indeed the "heart of the world," although the vastness of the social world a little daunted their ambitions. Since the Tory "swells" were notoriously inhospitable, they had "no affiliations with that crowd." The one opportunity that Adams had to meet Disraeli was spoiled by two matrons who so harassed him at the Palgrave dinner table that he "came home foaming at the mouth." They drifted into a "respectable, mildly literary and political set," seasoned by the ecclesiastical society of the church historian, Dean Stanley of Westminster, another one of the large circle of acquaintances dating from Adams's earlier visits. The Liberal victory at Eastertime naturally threw a very pleasant social coloring over the remainder of their stay.[24]

They made their headquarters in a house overlooking Bird Cage walk, the great trees beside their parlor window and the quiet surroundings putting them in mind of their beloved Beverly Farms. They reverted to their Washington custom of breakfast at 11:30, having found English luncheons destructive of "time and gastric juices." Afterwards they would often go together to the British Museum to work until closing. They rediscovered the ghostly terrors of a London fog, one as thick as "cream cheese" through which they groped their way at the heels of a pair of link boys with flaming torches. As once before in London Adams was induced to make one of his very rare afterdinner speeches, this time at a Shakespeare Club dinner. With the aid of a couple of American anecdotes he successfully did his patriotic duty. Not all their dining ventures were a success but if they dared to suggest that an English dinner might be a trifle dull, Henry James was always at hand ready to take them to task.[25]

James was their most frequent companion. He would come in almost every day at dusk and sit chatting by the blazing fire or stand "on the hearthrug with his hands under his coat-tails" talking "exactly as though we were in Marlborough Street" in Boston. Sometimes the talk went on till midnight, and Mrs. Adams would threaten to stipulate that she would abandon them at 10:30. One of the chief conversational gambits was James's decision to settle in England, a decision palpably reflected in James's English mannerisms, which must at times have seemed a satire on Adams's own anglicized traits. On this point the Adamses had violent convictions and the debates regularly overflowed into Mrs. Adams's "diary." "What it is that Henry James finds so entrancing year after year we cannot understand — for once it is very nice — but for life it seems to me a weary round — and a man without a country one to be pitied — in ten years I fancy he will understand better what we mean." He seemed almost perversely stubborn. "It is high time Harry James was ordered home by his family. He is too good a fellow to be spoiled by injudicious old ladies in London — and in the long run they would like him all the better for knowing and loving his own country. He had better go to Cheyenne and run a hog ranch. The savage notices of his

Hawthorne in American papers, all of which he brings me to read, are silly and overshoot the mark in their bitterness, but for all that he had better not hang around Europe much longer if he wants to make a lasting literary reputation." [26]

James made the mistake of patronizing his countrymen. "History, as yet, has left in the United States but so thin and impalpable a deposit that we very soon touch the hard substratum of nature, and nature herself, in the Western World, has the peculiarity of seeming rather crude and immature." Adams himself readily conceded the problem faced by the American writer, certainly by the American historian, in the lack of social contrasts; but to him the challenge was one to be met and not evaded. Whatever the limitations of America might be, it alone held the key to the future. When word reached Adams and his wife that they had been missed in Washington, they glowed with pleasure reassured that "it was a wise move to go there to live." They had never flattered themselves "that the Hub missed us." As the end of their stay in England drew near, they eagerly looked forward to escaping the "discipline" of another shivering winter in Europe. "Winter in a first class American coffin" was preferable to "any home on this side." Adams was quite of his wife's "way of thinking and having passed more than eleven years of the twenty two since leaving college on this side of the water he doesn't want to pass any more." [27]

Adams's entree to the spirited art world of the capital was assured by his friendship with Francis Turner Palgrave, art critic and poet, and Thomas Woolner, the sculptor and Pre-Raphaelite poet, both of whom helped him collect drawings and water colors. The sensitive Palgrave was especially voluble with advice, his talk "like Niagara, rushing over one." At the new Grosvenor gallery, "a refuge for the Pre-Raphalites," Adams met all sorts of "queer and pleasant folk" at the exciting series of "tea fights" that launched the exhibitions. Gustave Doré received homage and William Holman Hunt and about them eddied "poets, good, bad, and indifferent; fat duchesses, American beauties with diaphanous reputations; a social ollapodrida." The expatriate American Whistler was a chief curiosity of the show, having been well advertised by his libel suit against Ruskin for describing one of his nocturnes as "flinging a paint pot in the face of the public." The Adamses naturally took Ruskin's part for, on meeting Whistler, they found him "even more mad away from his paint pots than near them." Their own tastes ran to Turner and Bonington, Constable and Corot, though as collectors they were obliged to fight "on the water color line." A little defensive about his thrift, Adams once playfully complained at a diplomatic reception that they hadn't bought a certain painting because "we've spent too much. We're quite ruined." A Cuban diplomat, unfamiliar with Adams's facetiousness, bowed gravely, "It will give great pleasure to lend you any money." Mrs. Adams bemused the diplomat with the remark that it was her "husband's way of talking in December — that on January 1st we should feel quite able to be extravagant." [28]

Wherever they went, Mrs. Adams's reputation for pungent American slang preceded her like an agreeable shock wave. Her inspired figures of speech convulsed her husband as much as they did any other auditor and he would often joyfully appropriate them. Dean Stanley guffawed to hear that General Sherman had "the inside track" to the Presidency or that a dull neighbor did not "enthuse one cent." Her vivid tropes must have had their share in gradually emancipating Adams from the judicial style of his youth. In her letters one catches the ginger hot on the tongue as the characterizations race across the scrawled pages. "A nice, sweet, good woman," she remarked of one aspirant, "but not too deep for wading"; of another, she "has taken to frescoing her face"; and of still another, "fat, rosy, placid, torpid like a feather bed." An actress "looked like a lymphatic tigress draped in yellow Japanese embroidered silk" and "waved up and down the room like a serpent." At a reception the British women were "fat fugues in pea-green; lean symphonies in chewing gum color; all in a rusty minor key." A Boston adventuress "would have euchred Becky Sharp." At a dinner party a baronet made sneering remarks about America. "I laid him out stiff," Mrs. Adams bragged patriotically.[29]

They found many occasions to feel their American superiority. Even at Sir Francis Palgrave's "the social *savoir faire* and ease [was] what one would expect in Pawtucket centre." As devotees of the great Worth, Mrs. Adams and her compatriot, Mrs. Jack Gardner, had to "smile pityingly on the Britons for their awful gowns." Their ultra-fastidious glances searched out the dirty linen that was occasionally more than a mere figure of speech. And yet British society had its puzzling contradictions. "For all that, the men are poets and painters, and the women are intelligent and have fine handles to their names." The most agreeable Englishmen, they became convinced, were those "in the 'upper middle class,' as they call it, whose brains and opinions are not entailed." Their instinctive taste made their house an especially congenial refuge for Henry James as the dowdiness of Englishwomen, their lack of "intellectual grace" and "moral spontaneity" somewhat clouded the felicities of London. They were peculiarly American qualities. Though Mrs. Adams was not a pretty woman, she was, as James liked to recall, "small and graceful and well dressed," and he had admired her above all other young women of his acquaintance because of her "intellectual grace." [30]

Browning they met again as he made his sententious way around the circle of established houses, but resuming the acquaintance did not improve their opinion of the ageing seer. He had "the intellectual apathy in his face of a chronic diner out and talked incessantly in a voice like steel." Matthew Arnold, whom Adams met for the first time, made quite a different impression, at least at first. Adams had long admired the author of *Culture and Anarchy*, seeing in him the image of his own well-bred moral idealism. For a time they encountered him weekly, sometimes at the Forsters' or Smalley's or at their own fireside in Birdcage Walk. The Adamses encouraged him to plan an American tour and Mrs. Adams asked her father to sound out the trustees of the Lowell Institute. "I assured him that he had many readers on our side and would so long as he pounded his own countrymen, that if he took to abusing us he might not find it quite the same." Arnold did not wear well; after a while he seemed a little too facile with a tendency to "slop over." [31]

Of all Adams's new English friendships, the one he most cherished was that with John Richard Green, the brilliant author of the *Short History of the English People*. Almost the same age as Adams, he was one of the most attractive personalities of his time, erudite and yet incapable of being dull, and, what must have specially pleased Adams, sufficiently independent as to take issue with the great E. A. Freeman, whose disciple he had once been. His ideal of history, as a coherent development flashing with picturesque and dramatic incidents, captivated Adams, who was still committed, intellectually at least, to the stringent ideal of Ranke and the pursuit of documents. That drama and narrative color did find their way into his *History* may well have been owing to Green, "that brightest and pleasantest of the men in London." He "bids fair to become my most intimate guardian and teacher," Adams confessed. Green regarded Adams as "one of the three . . . people in the world to whom early history has any meaning." He chaffed his American friend upon the Teutonic erudition of his "Essay on Anglo-Saxon Law," but tendered a crumb of consolation: Adams's fellow contributors were "clean mad." [32]

The only other acquaintance that added "greatly to [his] score" was William Lecky, a vigorous forty-one like Adams, who had recently published the first two volumes of his *History of England during the Eighteenth Century*. Lecky, a pioneer scientific historian, had already demonstrated the validity of the positivist approach to history in two notable books, *The History of Rationalism* and *The History of European Morals*. The first meeting with Lecky in March of 1880 initiated an exchange of several visits at which Adams pursued his double role of student and schoolmaster, putting down his Nilometer into the turbid currents of English positivism. Lecky's home was a chief intellectual center of London. There he met another famous historian whom he had briefly encountered at the Legation many years before, James Anthony Froude, who in his very successful *History of England* rejected any pretense of scientific theory, content to exploit the sheer drama of events. There too at a notable dinner he met the reigning French intellect, Ernest Renan, then in London to give a course of lectures in French. Not until much later did Adams give really close study to Renan's naturalistic and yet reverent treatment of Christianity, but the extraordinary affinity of his ideas and attitudes with those of the sceptical French humanist must have instantly drawn him to the jovial pessimist. Renan shared with the somewhat younger Taine the direction of literary and philosophical positivism in France, though Taine's scientific materialism was of a more rigorous and stoical variety. Even as the apostle of disenchantment Renan clung to an inextinguishable residue of moral idealism. Then at work on the final volumes of his *Origins of Christianity*, he furnished an object lesson of the emancipated intellect which had made its peace with both worlds. Agnostic and seeming materialist, he could yet bend his spirit in eloquent religious homage as in his moving "Prayer on the Acropolis." On Adams, restlessly in quest of an education, the example of such an aesthetically satisfying resolution was not to be lost. Renan showed himself "most sympathetic and chatty" and "very moderate in his politics." [33]

On that memorable occasion Adams also met the great physicist John Tyndall, a pioneer in the field of thermodynamics, and once again he listened to Herbert Spencer, the supreme pontiff of English positivist thought, then at the very height of his enormous vogue. Adams no doubt concurred in the judicial estimate of his wife that Spencer "looks like a complacent crimson owl in spectacles with an assumption of omniscience in manner which is reassuring in this age of unbelief." If Spencer was at all in normal good form, the occasion would have called for him to set the company straight once again on his supposed debt to Auguste Comte, and to point out the inappropriateness of Fiske's appellation, "Cosmic Philosophy" to his "Synthetic Philosophy." Adams had met Herbert Spencer the preceding summer one evening at John Fiske's rooms over "pipes and grog" at the same time that he took the measure of Thomas Henry Huxley. In the intellectual movement of the time, he had long considered Spencer as second only to Darwin. What he thought of Spencer after these meetings he did not say, but his impressions of Huxley and Tyndall he long afterward summed up in the one word, "triflers." [34]

That initial meeting had offered Adams one of those many opportunities which he was so adept at seizing to "learn more out of books than in them" and must have further helped to crystallize his opinions about science, religion, and history. Fiske, the most famous of Spencer's American disciples, was the notorious "positivist" whom Adams had supplanted at Harvard in 1870 but with whom Adams had kept on friendly terms as a fellow member of The Club in Boston. In his London lectures he was now scoring an immense personal triumph, but he still yearned for the post at Harvard which Adams had vacated. Fiske's too-energetic proselytizing for Spencer was not calculated to draw the fastidious and sceptical Adams very close to either master or disciple, whatever his debt to their principles. Nevertheless a certain American quality about Spencer compelled admiration. Adams's Washington friend, Samuel Langley, used to tell them at the Cosmos Club that Spencer defied the graybeards at the London Athenaeum by playing billiards in the basement.[35]

They were all Darwinists who greeted Adams over the pipes and grog, whatever their doctrinal differences. Fiske, the most wholehearted devotee of the group, had once told Darwin that since he first read with "exultation" the *Origin of Species*, " 'Darwinism' has formed one of the pivots about which my thought has turned," freeing him from Agassiz's "pseudo-Platonic attempt to make metaphysical abstractions do the work of physical forces." Henry Holt, another ardent Spencerian and Darwinist and an intimate of Fiske's, may well have been one of the company, for he was then in London and presumably in touch with Adams concerning the printing of *Democracy*. He carefully recorded Adams's remark at that time, "A library should be a big dictionary." Darwin had called Spencer "the greatest living philosopher in England" and had taken from him the phrase "survival of the fittest." Spencer reciprocally had extended Darwin's theory to the formulations of Laplace, Joule, and Faraday in physics and to the wide realms of the social sciences.

Yet beneath the logical beauty of the "Synthetic Philosophy," there lurked somber vistas no amount of convivial talk could hide, least of all from Adams. Spencer, as Holt said, "follows the universe, with all it contains of beauty and emotion, into smash and leaves it there." That sort of apocalyptic vision haunted Adams from his earliest introduction to the new science. In *Democracy* Adams had made Mrs. Lee a student of Spencer's works, though a rather sceptical one, and he made her rather sceptical also of the philosophy of progress for which Spencer stood, widening the philosophical breach between him and men like Fiske and Holt.[36]

In Huxley Adams should have found a congenial fellow sceptic. His turning away from him in the sequel suggests that he probably saw in him too disconcerting a mirror image of his own thought. Huxley, like Adams, had approached Darwin's theory of biological evolution through Lyell's geology. He was now coming round to the position that the theory of evolution did not depend upon Darwin's conception of the gradual modification of species. He inclined rather toward the notion of mutation, nature working by "leaps," as the basic principle, thus practically surrendering Darwin's idea of natural selection. He rejected orthodox religion, but his scepticism extended with relentless honesty to science as well. His just published book on Hume, with which Adams was already familiar, foreshadowed the final movement of his scepticism toward a Schopenauerian pessimism. The cosmic process, the will-to-live, was at war with the ethical process and in the struggle for existence the ethical process must ultimately lose. The morally unfit were fittest to survive, a pessimistic hint which had already made its appearance in *Democracy*, anticipating Adams's "conservative Christian anarchist" of the 1890's.

4   Means and Ends

In Adams's letters to Lodge the practical and more intimate side of his personality found expression. Knowing Lodge's scholarly interest, he kept his friend fully posted on his progress in the spring of 1880. Old newspapers occupied him for a month at the British Museum from 11 to 4 daily, work that seemed "pure loss of time, but inevitable." Actual writing could not begin until his return to Washington and there would come moments when he felt himself becoming a desiccated pedant like George Eliot's Casaubon. So in May he reported that he had "finished with the Record Office, completed my search through newspapers, collected the greater part of my pamphlets, and sounded all the wells of private collections. . . . In Paris and Madrid copyists are at work for me. . . . I foresee a good history if I have health and leisure the next five years, and if nothing happens to my collection of materials. My belief is that I can make something permanent of it, but, as time passes, I get into a habit of working only for the work's sake and disliking the idea of completing and publishing. One should have some stronger motive than now exists for authorship. I don't think I care much even to be read, and any writer in this frame of mind must be dull reading. On the other hand I enjoy immensely the investigation, and making little memoranda of passages here and there." [37]

As a specialist in American history, Lodge had a professional interest in Adams's discoveries in the foreign archives. Adams and he had worked closely together on the American archives for the period out of which had come Lodge's *Cabot* and Adams's *New England Federalism*. He now helped fill in one gap by sending over to London transcripts of envoy Charles Pinckney's notes on the 1802 Claims Convention with Spain. They helped Adams to put the pieces of the historical mosaic together. The American diplomatic maneuvers during the Napoleonic period began to emerge as the materials for Olympian comedy. Pinckney and Monroe "made an awful blunder in signing the treaty; they were fairly scared to death. Now that I see the English side, they appear utterly ridiculous, and poor dear old Jefferson too, but our beloved Federalists most of all. Ye Gods, what a rum lot they were." Later reflection did not change this impression.[38]

Two months later he made his final report of progress and a forecast of the immense task ahead of him. "My work is done, at least so far as it ever will be done. I have made a careful study of English politics from 1801 to 1815, and have got my authorities in order. My Spanish papers have mostly arrived. The French documents are, I hope, coming, although I am still nervous about them. My material is enormous, and now I fear that the task of compression will be painful. Burr alone is good for a volume. Canning and Perceval are figures that can't be put in a nutshell, and Napoleon is vast. I have got to contemplate six volumes for the sixteen years as inevitable. If it proves a dull story, I will condense, but it's wildly interesting, at least to me — which is not quite the same as interesting the public." His estimate fell three volumes short.[39]

Adams had found ample work for his copyists in the Public Records Office. These transcripts alone when he made a gift of them to the State Department in 1900 filled nine large volumes. Through Lord Salisbury's intervention the Records Office suspended the strict rules denying access to the secret papers of the period. One interesting file almost

slipped from his grasp, the papers relating to the notorious
Canadian secret agent, John Henry. These, the cautious
director privately invited the Foreign Office to scrutinize
with special care because of their obviously compromising
character. The agent had ingratiated himself with the Essex Junto crowd in 1808. Four years later he coolly demanded a rumored $160,000 from the English government as
the price of his silence. Failing in this blackmail, he contrived
to inveigle President Madison into buying his secret reports
for $50,000. Adams collated these with the originals only to
discover that the spy had doctored the copies of his reports
with fine professional prudence, cleverly bilking the United
States by selling "as little as possible at the highest price he
could exact." The Foreign Office, evidently satisfied that the
transaction was at least as discreditable to the United States as
to England, passed the whole lot, and Adams secured one of
the most interesting segments of a fantastic intrigue.[40]

Never far from the surface of his thought was the memory
of his own ambition to be "a power in the land." He read
with a degree of envy of Lodge's political activity at the
Chicago convention of the Republican party in 1880. Starved
for political gossip, he grumbled at the failure of so many of
his correspondents to reply to his copious letters. With
Lodge's inside accounts before him he resumed, as in 1876,
the role of political strategist. At all costs the Grant influence
must be counteracted, and the present status preserved because "we have not strength to improve it." Their friend
James A. Garfield seemed to Adams "a very strong candidate" whose influence might be very valuable to Lodge.
Adams counselled that "all your money and work must go"
to the crucial state of New York. As Lodge's political career
had now begun in earnest with his election to the Massachusetts legislature, the time had come for practical advice.

"If you can make friends of the most influential members, including the Speaker, if you can occasionally bring one home to a family dinner, or to a talk in your library; if you can, in short, make yourself important or agreeable to the leaders, you will next year be in a position to claim a good committee and be a leader yourself. I believe seniority alone gives effective influence over assemblies so you can afford to move slowly."

Practicality, however, did not mean hunting for "openings" as his brother Brooks urged. "You know my way of thinking," he reminded Lodge. "I got it from my father, and so I suppose it is merely a piece of hereditary imbecility which I ought to distrust; but at any rate I hold that to be happy in life is possible, so far as it depends on oneself, only by being always busily occupied upon objects that seem worth doing. It is the occupation, not the objects, which makes happiness. . . . As for 'openings,' they lead as a rule to Hell. Blaine and Ben Butler are the ideal of men who go for openings." Then, with characteristic candor — or scepticism — he went on, "This, however, is only written to argue the other side. Probably if Brooks took my view, I should be obliged to take his." [41]

The summer of 1880 wore on. After six intense months they were, as Adams quoted his wife, "pretty well dinnered out." Like sated revellers they sometimes toyed a little dully with their pleasures and the prevalence of "octogenarians," however distinguished, dampened the first flush of enthusiasm. Even Lecky, his head nodding gently on the stalk of his neck, seemed a little preposterous to his American guests when he regretted that England and America did not have a common government. They had had a respite from the London ritual in a short stay with the Russell Sturgises at Grove Farm, Leatherhead, the country seat of the senior partner of Baring Brothers, England's leading bankers. Then James Russell Lowell arrived to brighten the remainder of the season for them. Happy with his appointment as ambassador to England which had ended his ordeal in Madrid, he plunged into London society with his old zest, an elegant personage in his silk stockings and knee breeches. His most delightful conquest came one evening when he gave a "delicious" reading of the "Blue Jay Chapter" from Mark Twain's just-published A Tramp Abroad. For the Adamses it was an evening of pure and patriotic delight.[42]

Early in August, the pair set out for a holiday in Scotland at Sir John Clark's estate at Tillypronie, journeying about in leisurely fashion to historic houses and castles. At one quaint inn they again encountered Bret Harte, who had just been rescued from his exile in Germany by an appointment to the consulship at Glasgow. His friend Hay, now Assistant Secretary of State, who idolized him, had worked hard to have him transferred. King had also "pitched into [Secretary] Evarts." Adams spent the afternoon chatting in the garden with him and fell under his spell almost as thoroughly as had Clarence King and John Hay. Harte had given a successful lecture at Oxford and was hopeful of making a literary comeback. To Adams the creator of "the heathen Chinee" epitomized success in literature and he gladly paid his court.[43]

Before they could sail for home, Adams had yet to wind up the Paris chapter. Crossing the channel again early in September, they found that all obstacles in the bureaus had been overcome. Gabriel Monod received them so warmly that they felt that he and a few like him "redeem this race of monkeys." Even the dreaded session with the Napoleonic Worth became an agreeable chore. The expensive new wardrobe was a triumph and Mrs. Adams had the diverting experience of seeing Mrs. Astor and Mrs. Vanderbilt cavalierly set aside while the master devoted himself to her. Her thirty-seventh birthday was indeed a success.[44]

More than wardrobes and archives, however, required attention. Arrangements had to be made to rent a house in Washington, and there remained the question of what to do with the Marlborough Street house. Still unsold it was "a horrid bore." Business conditions had taken a turn for the better in Boston and the time was at last ripe to sell, but there was little chance that they could realize the $50,000 they had put into it in 1873. Negotiations with Corcoran in Washington went smoothly. They took a six-year lease, with option to renew, on his three-story "White House" at 1607 H Street facing the Square. The six bedrooms and two baths on the second floor would give them ample room to entertain their Boston "constituency." For the modest rental of $200 a month Corcoran agreed, in addition, to provide a five-room annex for servants' quarters above the stable. To the two homesick wanderers the future seemed secure. "I look forward placidly," said Adams, "to recurring winters and summers in Washington and Beverly [Farms], until a cheery tomb shall provide us with a permanent abode for all seasons." [45]

They bade a long farewell to England on September 26. Adams, facing his tenth crossing, dreaded "the horrible ocean before me," but as they stood at the rail of the *Gallia* and watched the foreland recede, they had every reason to be content with their richly varied journey. They departed with "no more regret," in Mrs. Adams's words, "than on finishing a pleasant story, which began well and ended happily and had agreeable characters in it." No slightest hint obtruded itself that the European story as they had read it together was ending without the possibility of a sequel. Two years before, when he was writing *Democracy*, they had convulsed themselves over Henry's gibes at Americans. The European journey softened his discontents and he was returning with his conviction of America's destiny powerfully strengthened. It might be necessary, as a philosopher, "to keep our eyes fixed on the horizon-line or a star, if we don't mean to be seasick," as he lectured Lodge, but for the immediate future at least he would have no need to seek refuge in a pyramid in order to gaze at the North Star, like his heroine, Madeleine Lee.[46]

Chapter Five

The Golden Age of Lafayette Square

1 The Pursuit of Art

CORCORAN's agents labored with a will, but for nearly two months the Adamses languished impatiently at Wormley's Hotel, a short way down the street, rubbing elbows with itinerant diplomats and statesmen while a swarm of workmen rejuvenated the house at 1607 H Street. Henry and his wife debarked in New York on October 4, 1880, and hurried down for a week to survey progress, before making a visit of ten days to Boston "to pull our house to pieces and get out the furniture." Determined to receive the Washington place "in perfect order," Adams encouraged the contractor with suitable "spherical oaths." The thick brick walls allowed them to indulge their taste for capacious fireplaces and fine handmade mantelpieces. One misadventure a little marred their progress. A cornice maker, hopeless of pleasing Adams's meticulous tastes, finally put down his trowel, went home, and unaccountably murdered his wife. By the first of December fifteen wagonloads of furniture sent down from Boston had been finally deployed, the horses stabled, and the winter's campaign of writing and society fully launched. Bent on filling his niche in his own way, Adams urbanely managed to exempt himself from James's current dictum in *Washington Square* that America was a country "in which to play a social part, you must either earn your income or make believe

that you earn it." As a practising historian Adams set out
to enjoy his position as a *rentier*.[1]

The period that now opened in his life had the halcyon
ripeness of early autumn with nothing but bountiful harvests
in prospect. A vista of full and productive years curved
beckoningly across the horizon for the two epicureans. Whatever the chaos of the world outside, within there was an
oasis of impeccable taste and select companionship. Days
were religiously devoted to research and writing, but once
the tea table blossomed, the life of the Adams salon began
and often vibrated with off-the-record politics until midnight.
Not primarily a political house, theirs flourished in the broader
arena of public affairs, science, and the arts. The Lord's
remnant of the Liberal Republican leadership continued to
make its social headquarters there so that within the glow
of his study fireplace Adams still exerted his influence in
behalf of mild reform. A typical entry in Mrs. Adams's Sunday letters reads: "Sunday, a pleasant dinner. Carl Schurz,
Aristarchi Bey, and Mr. Belmont, and Mr. Nordhoff after
dinner — all politics and public affairs." To offset Adams's
preoccupation with history, Mrs. Adams was driven to take
up a hobby of her own, or rather adopted one of Henry's
as an extremely apt pupil. "I've gone in for photography and
find it very absorbing," she wrote in 1883. Of course she felt
she had much to learn, for Henry had had the advantage of
Richardson's instruction. She soon became known as a skillful amateur photographer and her portraits of friends like
Hay and Bancroft were widely admired. Sometimes their
parlor looked like a photographic studio as she posed her
subjects.[2]

Adams and his wife had the collector's instinct and their
house on Lafayette Square reflected it in its profusion of
bric-a-brac, *objets d'art*, oriental rugs and vases, and rare
coins. Their neighbor Mrs. Bancroft once casting an apprais-

ing eye over their possessions remarked, "My dear, I dislike auctions, but I mean to go to yours after you die." Their collection of water colors and drawings earned a two-hour inspection by the art critic of the New York *World*, Mrs. Van Rensselaer, a cousin of Secretary of State Frelinghuysen. The chairs and sofas were in the English style, low and comfortable, but to average-sized humanity they had an absurdly Lilliputian air. No one's feet needed to dangle, least of all the hosts'. Their architect friend, the colossal H. H. Richardson, doubtless thought it a characteristic Adams's jape, a comic revenge on some of his Gargantuan friends. Potted palms, then much in fashion, gave a pleasantly green accent to the rooms.[3]

Alert for neglected treasures, they would sometimes go off in hot pursuit on tips from other connoisseurs. On one occasion Mrs. Adams picked up two Joshua Reynolds portraits of the Groves for $300, which were restored for them by one of their learned friends at the Smithsonian, Dr. Bessels. These went up between the library windows, displacing Tilton's "Venice." Knowing her husband's distaste for portraits, Marian decided that "Henry can look the other way." To her surprise, Henry admitted, "They are charmingly modelled and very dignified." They inherited a Teniers as a memento of Uncle Peter Chardon Brooks and hoped it would adorn their "gaunt library walls thirteen feet high." Thomas Woolner, the English sculptor and Pre-Raphaelite poet, continued to send them gifts of Boningtons, then thought to rank with Turner, until they had four of his scenic pieces. They had also brought back with them many water colors from Woolner's collection of the English school.[4]

The major part of Adams's art collection was probably completed by this period, reflecting as much his wife's taste as his own. Years later when the collection was somewhat diminished by gifts to nieces, visitors particularly noted the sketches by Watteau, Tiepolo, Rembrandt, Michelangelo, and Raphael. A Turner water color of the Rhone valley stood by the library chair; on the wall hung an oil by Constable. The inventory of Adams's estate tells much of his artistic interests. The prizes of the collection were two Turner oils in the dining room, where nine lesser oils also graced the walls, and an imposing Cotman landscape in the reception hall. Forty-four water colors were kept in the library and thirty-two framed prints in the study. The visits to Egypt and Morocco had covered their floors with rugs whose names read like a catalogue of the art: Shiraz, Cashmere, Kurdistan, Baluchistan, Bokhara, Yomud, and so on. Everywhere there was a profusion of Japanese and Chinese vases, bronzes, and porcelains.[5]

The collection had a miscellaneous and even restless character; in painting it leaned strongly to the picturesque. On individual acquisitions Adams frequently had the advice of artists and connoisseurs, Palgrave, Woolner, La Farge, and much later, Berenson, but his taste in art tended toward the well established and the conventional. Like most cultivated Brahmins he looked eastward across the Atlantic, admiring a tradition already being supplanted by the vigorous Impressionists. The vital American art of their own period was largely invisible to his coterie. Winslow Homer and George Innes, Thomas Eakins and Albert Ryder, excited no comment in Adams's correspondence. Insulated from their work by a parochial taste he felt a keen sense of the emptiness of American native culture. For him Ruskin's sentence was final. High art, as Ruskin praised it in Constable, blended the naturalistic and the idealistic; Whistler's heresies repelled him.[6]

Deeply sensitive to art within his range, Adams remained nonetheless little more than a dilettante collector, as he was to admit in the *Education*. The disquieting innovations of Monet and Manet, the opulent vulgarities of Renoir, the eerie jungles of Rousseau, the uninhibited zest of Cézanne and Degas seemed not to seize his imagination. The stranger and wilder horrors that lay across the horizon, the works of the abstractionist and non-objective renaissance were to be even more alien. The "American Artist" Exhibition of 1883 in New York had seemed to Mrs. Adams "as a whole, very poor" and the *Nation* confirmed the judgment of their circle by decrying the "dangerous tendencies rapidly gaining ground in what is called our new art movement." An Adams acquaintance, William M. Hunt, was a member of the group of American experimentalists. He had done the portrait of Adams's father when he was Minister to England, but as the *Education* was to say, "Hunt had no time to sweep out the rubbish of Adams's mind." To the end he retained his "rubbishy" tastes. Though he lived in France almost every summer until the outbreak of the war in 1914, he was never to allude to the revolution in art which took place under his eyes except to dismiss it with a wave of the hand.[7]

2 *Political Ebb-tide*

When Adams got back from Europe, the political picture that greeted his critical eye offered only dubious pleasure. On the train to Washington he had encountered, "luckily for their long famished souls," Wayne MacVeagh, a prominent lawyer and diplomat, notable in Republican politics for his opposition to his father-in-law, the Pennsylvania boss, Simon Cameron. He had much to tell them for he had helped block Grant's renomination for a third term. The full story of the intrigue that produced Garfield's nomination did not reassure his one-time lieutenant of the Gold Conspiracy days. The "Half Breed" insurgents had acquiesced in Chester A. Arthur's nomination to the vice-presidency as a sop to the Grant "Stalwarts," but reformers like Adams saw that in order to get Garfield they had to take Blaine who, unable to win himself, had turned the tide for Garfield. In the confused struggle for power all real issues were swamped in political feuds and Adams hunted vainly for a clue. "Although content to see a Republican triumph," he wrote Lodge, "I am not eager to take a hand in it, and I have too much to condone in the acts of that party and its nominee to make me care to proclaim the condonation." The Democrats offered him even less to admire. Tilden had reputedly turned down the nomination, pleading ill health, but Adams felt sure that the party had let him down and thus thrown away "all the brains they had." They had countered the Republican's General Garfield, the hero of Chickamauga, with General Hancock, the hero of Gettysburg, committing, in Adams's view, "the unutterable nonsense of putting a pure, unadulterated, West Point corps commander at the head of the Democratic party." [8]

The change of administration meant the breakup of familiar associations and the loss of political connections. Schurz would leave the Interior, but what was far more disillusioning, Evarts would be replaced in the State Department by Blaine. John Hay, who had served as first Assistant Secretary of State since November 1879, was eager to disburden himself and return to New York and the editorship of the *Tribune*. Hay, to the lasting puzzlement of the Adamses, who could not understand the sentimental fetish of party regularity, had become an ardent admirer of Blaine and persuaded Garfield to make Blaine Secretary of State. The imp of the perverse seized Clarence King as well, who on Blaine's defeat by Cleveland in 1884 thought his countrymen devoid of sense and gratitude. Henry forgave his friends' aberration, but for himself he held out with stubborn courage against the Blaine enthusiasts. For many months the household nursed its frigid disapproval. Adams gave up his convenient desk in the Department, not wishing to be indebted to a man he despised. "To cut the Secretary of State for Foreign Affairs, without doing it offensively or with ill-breeding, requires not only some courage but some skill," he remarked to Gaskell. He rejoiced at the success of the "rat hunt" which their friend Nordhoff had conducted in the New York *Herald* to expose Blaine's unsavory intervention in the Chile-Peruvian war then raging. When at last Blaine was replaced by the socially acceptable Frelinghuysen, Adams sighed with relief. "I no longer dread going out to dinner for fear I should have to take Mrs. Blaine to table." [9]

The political tension never relaxed for a moment. A kind of breathlessness was always in the air. Each day during the Washington season some new disclosure, some overwhelming turn seemed always to lie beyond the corner. When Henry James visited the Adamses in Washington, his fastidious horror elicited Adams's pitying comment, "Poor Henry James thinks it [Washington life] revolting in respect to politics and the intrigues that surround it." Adams declared that "its only objection is its over-excitement. Socially speaking, we are very near most of the powerful people either as enemies or as friends." In public the stimulus encouraged Adams to indulge to the full his inclination to play the part of political Jeremiah. Shortly before Hayes left the White House, he encountered Adams at a dinner at the Bancrofts and afterwards carefully noted in his diary:

Mr. Adams said, "Our system of government has failed utterly in many respects. The House is not what it was intended to be, a deliberative body. The majority can't control its action. Nothing less than two thirds can control it. Our army is, or ought to be, a mere police. It ought to be called a police. Our navy is nothing. In all ages the difficulty has been how to decide who shall be subs. It is the same here. No means has yet been discovered for doing it peacefully. We have not got it. Our reliance is on the people being so as to need no government."

The point was one which he had vigorously made in the *Gallatin* and reiterated in his letters to his English friends. "Our legislative system broke down long ago. It is absurd to think of doing business with a crowd. Imagine our managing our private property in that way. Nevertheless such is politics and they call it a science." Hayes, evidently intrigued by Adams's authoritative doctrine, invited the pair to one of the last state dinners before Garfield's inauguration.[10]

Toward Lodge, however, Adams took a somewhat less pessimistic tone. Two months after Garfield's inauguration, he declared, "Our fight is now pretty well won. Grantism, which drove us to rebellion, is dead. Not a vestige of it is left. . . . The government is now running on a new track, not much better to be sure, but free from organised corruption. There will be rotten places here, as there were with Hayes — more and worse, I fear — but, as with him, on the whole we may rest and be content." One of the rotten places promptly festered. To pay off one of his political debts Garfield appointed to the lucrative Collectorship of the Port of New York the Blaine man who had "betrayed Grant," as Gail Hamilton viewed it, by swinging the New York delegation at the Chicago convention to the Garfield bandwagon. John Hay had tried to forewarn Garfield when he declined his offer of private secretary, "I woefully fear you will try too hard to make everybody happy — an office which is outside of your constitutional powers." Both New York Senators, Conkling and Platt, resigned in protest, bringing the war between the Half-breeds and the Stalwarts out into the open where the Democrats could delightedly look on in anticipation of the next general election.[11]

Adams had barely become reconciled to the prospect of eight years of well-intentioned bumbling under Garfield, when the assassin Guiteau violently upset his shaky calculations. His friend's death left him curiously unmoved; he took it almost as calmly as he had taken Lincoln's assassination. A week after the shooting he consoled the worried Attorney General MacVeagh, "As for the poor President, let us consider it as a fever, like his wife's; or let us suppose that a brick fell on him from a house-top. . . . Practically this is what has happened. He has been hit by one of the disregarded chances of life. What then? Of course your business is to get him well. In that case he will have an eight-year, popular, irresistible administration. If not! Well! we'll face the alternative when it comes. Luckily we are a democracy and a sound one. Nothing can shake society with us, now that slavery is gone." "*My* devil," he insisted to Godkin, "was Mr. Blaine. Garfield's administration . . . was sort of *delirium tremens* vision with Blaine as the big active snake." With Secretary Blaine gone from the Cabinet, it would be "no small relief" to put up with "a variety of small green and parti-colored serpents."

The trial of Guiteau, the disappointed office seeker, became the sensation of 1881, and the Adamses eagerly accepted an invitation to attend one of the sessions. With his trim pointed beard, the scholarly Adams looked quite at home seated among the sanity experts. Their friend Dr. Folsom of the National Board of Health took them down to the jail after the session to meet the accused. The following colloquy took place:

Said Dr. Folsom, "Well, Grant and Conkling seem to be running things now in the Republican party."

"I think," said Guiteau, "there is more harmony than there was on the first of July."

Said Henry, "What do you suppose Mr. Blaine thinks about that?"

Guiteau gave him a keen look, remarked drily, " 'We won't discuss that.' " It was one of Adams's characteristic thrusts; and squarely hit the shabby mark. Nevertheless, he had no illusions about Guiteau's sanity. "To say that any sane man would do this," he argued to MacVeagh, "is a piece of, not insanity, but of idiocy, in the District Attorney." [12]

The alternative to Garfield had to be faced almost immediately. Arthur took office and the Grant Stalwarts trooped hungrily to Washington. Something more than paradox and pessimism was called for. If Adams did not have time to spend, at least he did have money. The *Nation* was a logical instrument to mobilize public opinion and it needed help. As the New York *Evening Post* had bought it in June, 1881, Adams put himself at Godkin's disposal — with reservations. "This is not my usual way of investing money, for I rather affect business-like principles, but in this case it is with me a question of keeping in with my crowd than of investing money, and I want to do precisely whatever suits best the interest of the paper and its managers. . . . Put me down for $20,000 if it suits your interest to do so." Part of the deal was that Schurz would become editor-in-chief of the *Post*. The prospect of three years of President Arthur and his Stalwart crowd made Adams wail, "I am a bad sailor and easily made sea-sick. For God's sake do keep the E. P. steady." [13]

When Godkin happened to suggest a misgiving about Schurz's tendency toward being "sentimental," Adams reproached him with whimsical ferocity: "If you dry one of his tears, I will denounce you at a stockholders' meeting. Every tear he sheds is worth at least an extra dollar on the dividends. . . . I have always told you that your fatal defect was the incapacity to make a *popular* blunder." Two years later Schurz resigned from the *Post*, unable to stomach longer the doctrinaire economics of his associates, who disapproved of his pro-union stand in a telegrapher's strike. As a heretic in economics he inevitably drifted away from the pessimistic Godkin and the rest of the economic fatalists of

Adams's circle. After the late eighties Schurz's name no longer appears in the voluminous correspondence of Henry Adams.[14] The political complexion of the Adams household was well known. Early in 1881 for example the Boston *Herald* commenting on a passage at arms between Mrs. Adams and Senator Conkling at a dinner at General Beale's home, alluded to her as "a hostess of liberal proclivities." When the Pendleton Civil Service Bill was passed in a manner that discomfited Congressman Kasson of Iowa, he stepped up to the Adamses at a reception given by Secretary Frelinghuysen and "remarked with a good deal of temper, 'Well, the House has passed your *Boston* bill.'" A silent partner in the *Evening Post*, Adams avoided direct interference, preferring to work from the sidelines. Interested chiefly in matters of policy, he stayed away from stockholders' meetings; the financial arrangements he willingly took on trust. "If you [Godkin] or Schurz are about to run away with the bank balance, how the devil am I to stop it?"[15]

His admonitions he saved for matters of editorial policy. The independents he declared had no choice but to support Arthur, distasteful as that chore might be, but at the same time they must carry the fight for good government directly to the people and thus put pressure upon the Administration. One of his directives ran thus: "I want one of you to come on in order to see how and when to begin. I think Schurz had better come now, and you later. Please tell Schurz to hide with me and keep out of the newspapers about ten days hence." President Arthur, across the way, understandably waited some time before inviting the Adamses to a White House reception, but even at a distance he was an object of study. "There goes our chuckle-headed sovereign on his way to church," Marian noted one Sunday. "He doesn't look as if he fed only on spiritual food."[16]

The more he tinkered with political reform, the more frustrated Adams grew. Except on the free trade issue, none of the proposals of their group went much beyond improving the efficiency of governmental operations, hardly a program to capture the imagination of the Grangers and nascent Populists. In the face of public apathy, politics seemed to degenerate into mere intrigue. The moments of disenchantment grew more frequent as he solaced one friend after another on losing office. When Lodge lost the election to the Massachusetts senate, he wrote: "This is one of the drawbacks to politics as a pursuit. I suppose every man who has looked on at the game has been struck by the remarkable way in which politics deteriorates the moral tone of everyone who mixes in them. The deterioration is far more marked than in any other occupation I know except the turf, stock-jobbing, and gambling. . . . It is the curse of politics that what one gains, another man loses. . . . I have never known a young man go into politics who was not the worse for it. . . . They all try to be honest and then are tripped up by the dishonest; or they try to be honest (i.e. practical politicians) and degrade their own natures. . . . My conclusion is that no man should be in politics unless he would honestly rather not be there." Attorney General MacVeagh was another casualty. Failing to extract a bold pronouncement on civil service reform from Arthur, he resigned. The condolence letter to him likewise preached the vanity of human wishes. "As for the office, as you know, I always thought political power the most barren of all forms of success; my conviction is that you are lucky in escaping." [17]

Affairs took a disconcerting turn when Arthur astonished everyone by supporting the merit system in his first message to Congress, thus proving Adams and MacVeagh unduly pessimistic and impatient. Once in office Arthur rose to the challenge. Largely freeing himself from the control of the party bosses, he vetoed pork-barrel appropriations and en-

couraged prosecution of the Star Route frauds. The support
of Arthur which Adams had urged upon the *Post* now took
on a new meaning. Schurz helped found the National Civil
Service Reform League in the autumn of 1881 with George
W. Curtis as president. Early in 1883 the Pendleton Act became law and Arthur won universal approval by appointing
Dorman Eaton first chairman of the Civil Service Commission. A year later more than fourteen thousand Federal em-
ployees had been classified into the service.[18]

A far more difficult cause was the Free Trade movement,
the one great effort of the Independents to solve the economic problems of the nation. Senator Lamar, a chief spokesman for the Adams group, made one of his most eloquent
speeches on the subject. Adams plied Schurz once more. "Of
course the *Evening Post* must above all things be conservative, but I know no reason why you or I should be so, and
as I think conservatism in these days a sign of weak intelligence or advancing years, I prefer radicalism. Therefore I
want to know what the Free Trade organization means to
do if the Democratic party goes back on it, as it has done
in Kentucky. If it falls in your way to get into the councils
of the northwestern free-traders, I wish you would find out
whether we have the means of punishing the Democrats for
this kind of conduct. For my own part I would gladly help
to organise a free trade party, and if we had the strength
to contest a single State, make an independent nomination
for the Presidency." Schurz was already of the same mind,
for what was in the air were the first stirrings of the Mugwump movement of 1884. Under the leadership of Schurz,
Curtis, and Roger Wolcott, the Independent Republicans
were to bolt the Chicago convention rather than accept
Blaine.[19]

Adams agreed to go to the Chicago convention with Mac-
Veagh, but at the last moment changed his mind. "The pros-

pect was too black." MacVeagh himself convinced their group
that "Blaine has a sure thing at Chicago; and, if he fails,
Arthur must succeed." Adams did not attend the great Mugwump meeting in New York which denounced Blaine and
called for support of Cleveland, but he did attend a similar
meeting in Boston of the Massachusetts Reform Club which
repudiated the Republican ticket. His friend Edward Atkinson urged his audience of Independents to "demand the
Tariff of '57." Before rallying his own group to this proposal
Adams took counsel of his old friend Congressman Abram
Hewitt, to ask "whether the idea is a practical one." On one
point Hewitt was to go far beyond the mild palliatives of
their circle and, on the floor of Congress, he boldly spoke
for the day when "the workmen will be the owners of all
machinery" and themselves receive the profits. Adams quietly
overlooked the eccentricity of his influential friend. As the
horizon darkened in the late '80's he chortled sardonically
over the fisheries dispute to Gaskell, "We need a war to clear
away this Irish and socialist rubbish; and a war between
England and America would be interesting, especially as our
generation could look on." [20]

Too busy with his literary labors during the summer of
that campaign to follow his political inclinations, Adams ban-
tered Republican friends like Hay by describing himself as
"a good Democrat" and announcing to all who would hear
that he would vote for Cleveland along with his brothers;
he was "in opposition, fairly and squarely on the free trade
issue." At times he felt a certain irrelevance about all the
political stir. "Our own politics," he explained to Gaskell in
February, 1884, "for the first time in a hundred years, are
almost absolutely indifferent to the people. . . . The truth
is our affairs were never in so good a condition." Four months
later a financial crisis struck. Still sanguine, Adams commented, "The country is richer than ever, but the public

distrusts its financiers. . . . Meanwhile we shall probably
work harder and better for cleaning out the decay." Two
weeks before the election it was apparent that "for the first
time in twenty-eight years [actually twenty-three], a Democratic administration is almost inevitable," which of course
would mean "a step towards free trade." Yet in spite of the
row, he conceded, "no one talks about real interests. . . .
We are afraid to discuss them. Instead of this, the press is
engaged in a most amusing dispute whether Mr. Cleveland
had an illegitimate child. . . ." [21]

Cleveland won by a narrow margin, after one of the most
bitter campaigns in American history. The inauguration was
the occasion for a tremendously stirring parade of war veterans. Adams and his wife rode out on their horses to see
the march past of regiments in Rebel gray and Union blue
and listened to the bands alternately playing "Dixie" and
the "Union Forever." At the head of a Virginia regiment rode
his old classmate "Rooney" Lee, proud on a black horse. For
all the fanfare that ushered in the new administration Adams
anticipated little change in his personal affairs. Only the
State Department concerned him personally. The appointment of Thomas F. Bayard assured him that his privileges
would be unmolested. Reassuring in another sense was the
appointment of his close friend Senator Lamar, an avowed
civil service reformer, to Interior.[22]

Loyal Democrats soon taught their leader the political
wisdom of rewarding the famished faithful and Cleveland
was driven to exasperated fits of swearing and removing
tainted incumbents. The well-oiled veterans' lobby bullied
him into signing pension applications at a faster pace than
any of his predecessors. Free trade collapsed under the
enormous pressure of the high-tariff lobby, so that the tariff
bill emerged a monstrosity. Yet so far as the basic civil service was concerned it appeared that "much had been gained

for reform." Cleveland showed himself "in advance of both parties," according to Henry's brother Charles. In the total framework such achievement gave only small comfort to the more exacting Henry. Inevitably he would turn away from Cleveland as from another clay idol.[23]

Adams made one more effort to make his political influence felt through the *Evening Post* when Cleveland announced the appointment of Daniel Manning to the Treasury who, to Adams, represented "the incarnate machine." He was the choice of Tilden who hoped to play the role of Grey Eminence in the new administration. Adams, learning that the *Post* had agreed not to oppose Manning, sent an angry note to Godkin. "Of course I have nothing to do with E. P.'s policy, and nothing to say in regard to it; but it is only fair that I should give notice of parting company on a point which may prove to be vital." The unterrified Godkin stood pat. An uncomfortable rebuff, it was compounded in another quarter by Cleveland's refusal to listen to Schurz's anguished importunities. Difficult as silence always was to Adams, he had no alternative now but to try to hold his tongue.[24]

One episode in the preceding administration taught him something about the paradoxes of politics and produced the axiom that "as a rule one's opponents are more obliging than one's friends." Arthur had appointed Frelinghuysen to succeed Blaine in the State Department. At first the new Secretary had seemed a political cipher, but he and Adams soon became fast friends. He even made a confidant of Mrs. Adams, inviting her to suggest candidates for the Spanish mission. Shortly afterwards, quite unconscious of any satire, he startled his new friends by offering Adams the mission to Central America in Guatemala City. That this out of the way post should have been proposed in good faith as suitable to a man of his qualifications must have struck Adams as a priceless piece of irony. Upon Mrs. Adams fell the job of gently disabusing the Secretary of State. ". . . I told Mr. Frelinghuysen it was an unwise appointment, that Henry would be in a railroad or job of some kind before he knew it." What Henry thought, he kept to himself. A month after the "offer," he remarked tangentially, "I suspect I might perhaps have an office, if I did not show that I wanted it. At least I might be told that I could be minister to Cochin China or the Feejee Islands, provided I did not take the place." [25]

3 Vanity Fair

The world of Henry Adams as he shared it with his wife in that period which the historians of Lafayette Square call its golden age, was a world of society as well as politics, a world which comes very much alive in Mrs. Adams's uninhibited, Boswellian record of their life. Hers is a kaleidoscopic counterpoint to the graver movement of Adams's sententious reports to his English friends. He looked out upon the show with a patronizing eye, enjoying the role of a Walpole in the chaste precincts of Berkeley Square. His prospectus of November of 1882 could serve as model for the opening of any season from 1881 to 1884.

"Here we are [he reported to Robert Cunliffe] back at Washington at this liveliest of earthly seasons, when we ride every afternoon into the country more wild than most parts of Wales, and as charming as anything I know. In November this place is like Bath or Nice, a sort of off-hand sociable lounging-spot for a set of people who make no money and are generally intelligent. We are mostly poor as the world now goes. Three thousand pounds a year is still a handsome income, and the most important people here have no more. . . . It would amuse you to see what a bright little place it is, and you would understand better why I am not specially anxious to leave it for Europe." [26]

Marriage thoroughly suited him. Long ago he had said with facetious understatement, "From the start, [I] have felt as though my wife were my oldest furniture." Occasionally they might differ in an artistic judgment, Marian having a fondness for portraits, Adams preferring landscapes. But in all else their tastes were remarkably alike and Marian habitually would write "we" when voicing opinions of persons and politics. Children were denied them and that deprivation appears to have been their shared secret sorrow. Adams had the intensest sense of family ties and pride of family, and it must have been deeply disquieting to realize that he would have no descendants to honor his memory as he so filially honored that of his ancestors. As a result he lavished affection upon their nieces, brother-in-law Edward Hooper's five daughters. Hooper, a noted Blake collector and treasurer of Harvard, gradually replaced Adams's brother Charles as a trusted counsellor. When he died in 1901, Adams wrote, "For thirty years he has been the most valuably essential friend and connection I have had. . . . He was one of those central supports without which a house or household goes to pieces." [27]

As the years went by, Adams's protective watchfulness over his wife changed to affectionate dependence, the old dread of a nervous seizure such as had frightened them on their wedding journey on the Nile having practically vanished. Nevertheless, in 1881, when her sister-in-law died, the news was not telegraphed to her until the day of the funeral. "Henry flatly refuses to let me go alone" to help look after the five nieces, she told her father, and she hadn't the heart to drag him off from his work. Two years later at Henry's urging she made a short visit alone to New York to be feted by their friends. It was their first separation since their marriage in 1872. She enjoyed the week's freedom, but Adams, lost without her, in spite of "a charming ladies' dinner and a party at the British Legation," announced that it was "*his* last alone." So far as the weekly and sometimes even more frequent letters to her father show, her health had long since ceased to give cause for concern. There were of course the occasional claims of the dentist, sessions with an aurist for a collapsed eardrum, and a recurring "sick headache." "I suppose a machine is bound to get rickety after running for thirty-nine years," she philosophized. "I earnestly pray that its final fate may be that of the 'one horse shay.'" Sometimes the pace of teas and dinners, followed by evening receptions or champagne suppers at the Legations was too much for her, and her indefatigable husband would go on alone.[28]

In Washington Mrs. Adams found a full theatre for her varied talents. Her passion for novelty, for fresh experience was as insatiable as his, but like his it was often frustrated by an even greater passion for propriety. Washington was a whispering gallery, and few prominent people escaped the rumor factories in such a small society. Gossip writers alert for scandal and infidelities did not hesitate to name names, but the Adamses passed through the ordeal relatively unscathed. Nevertheless, Marian's skill in adding a barb and winged words to a piece of gossip made her many enemies in the outer darkness. Envious and malicious gossip contrived to link her romantically with intimates of their circle, like Hay and King, whose extravagantly gallant attentions piqued curiosity behind the starched lace curtains of the Square.[29]

Adams himself did not quite escape the incessant clack of tongues, for like all the male members of his circle, he idolized and idealized the reigning beauties. In this homage he obeyed the current fashion, the reflex of the extreme emphasis on the gentility and purity of women and the sentimental revival of interest in the age of chivalry. Mark Twain, himself a victim, was already busy satirizing the adolescent cult in *Huckleberry Finn*. Dreiser, speaking of it in *The Titan*, says of the '80's, "Since that day, the maiden and the matron has been schooled to believe that she is of finer clay than man, that she was born to uplift him, and that her favors are priceless." Even the vulgar succumbed. Street car conductors complained that if a pretty woman boarded a car, it soon filled up with a crowd of admiring men. The cult reached its height in literary circles. Richardson and Walpole had each flourished among a garden of exquisite ladies in the eighteenth century. In nineteenth century America Irving and Longfellow had also presided over a court of nieces. Adams's Philadelphia acquaintance, the eminent doctor litterateur S. Weir Mitchell, similarly prospered. The secret of the art was to make every one of these spirituelle divinities believe herself to be the chief confidante. Adams gallantly averred to Hay, "All I care for is a lovely woman," and when a new "stunner" shone in the social sky he promptly made his obeisance.[30]

The most dazzling vision of them all was Elizabeth Cameron, the absurdly young second wife of Senator Don Cameron of Pennsylvania and niece of Senator John Sherman of Ohio. Her Titian hair, incredibly fresh complexion, and inexhaustible vitality amazed society reporters, captivated a host of middle-aged "uncles," and agitated puritanical tongues. Shortly after the Adamses returned from Europe, the Camerons became regulars at their tea-table, though the Senator's wit fell considerably below the required standard. From the start it was evident that the "poor little woman" had "drawn a blank in Don." Nevertheless, they all got on famously, and it was not long before Adams, conquering all aversion, could playfully remark to Hay that Don "loves us like a father. . . ." Excised from the published letter is the amusing and — in

the sequel — significant addition: "*We* were asked to a
charming dinner there the other evening, and I am now tame
cat around the house. Don and I stroll around the house with
our arms around each other's necks. I should prefer to accompany Mrs. Don in that attitude, but he insists on loving
me for his own sake." When the Camerons went to England
in 1883, Adams warmly commended them to Lowell, "Both
my wife and I are very fond of her. Don has good qualities,
and some pretty poor ones, and does not shine in society, but
he is a good deal better than he seems. . . . For our sakes
be kind if you have a chance, to all the Camerons, and especially take Mrs. Don to some big entertainment and point
out to her the people she wants to see or know. You will
fall in love with her, as I have." In a similar vein he was
writing to Hay, "I adore her, and respect the way she has
kept out of scandal and mud, and done her duty by the
lump of clay she promised to love and respect." [31]

Mrs. Adams looked indulgently upon her husband's courtly
admiration of their young neighbor. She too was immensely
drawn to the young "Perdita," who had been snatched away
from them for a year in Europe. "We miss, miss you, miss
you," she exclaimed. Her husband supplied a four-page "word"
of Washington affairs, in which he gently threatened, "All of
your admirers, including myself, are still true to you, but
don't put our loyalty to a longer test." In May of 1884 Mrs.
Don "popped in on the Adamses . . . all in white muslin
and blue ribbons, looking very young and pretty, just back
from a year in Europe and enchanted to get back." The gay
little court of love resumed its sentimental ritual.[32]

Though Mrs. Adams might "for social purposes . . . prefer
the vicious and frivolous" to the merely estimable, she resolutely barred the door to unvouched for or dubious visitors
and sounded the alarm along the threads which held their
society together. Oscar Wilde's celebrated visit to America

early in 1882 probably posed the most serious challenge, but the Adamses met it with stern self-denial. News of Wilde's preposterous affectations had preceded him and when he arrived at the customs house with nothing to declare but his genius, sides had already been chosen. Marian forehandedly asked Henry James, then visiting in Washington, *not* to bring his exotic friend. Lord George Montague, Third Secretary of the British Legation, invited them to receive at the "Bachelors' German" in honor of Wilde. They begged off and Marian entertained her father with an imaginary news item of what might have been. "The guests were received by Mrs. Henry Adams of Boston, married to the scion of a once-honored race. Mrs. Adams has a most queenly presence, an aquiline nose rendered less prominent by full cheeks and wealth of chin. . . . Jewels flashed from her raven tresses and she had a winning Beacon-Street welcome for all. By her side stood her husband, a man of superb physical proportions, two well-set eyes surmounted by a brow of great height and lustre; he ably supported his lady by his genial bonhommie — hereditary it may be, but none the less his own." The local press quietly reported that Wilde "was pleasant and affable and created a very favorable impression." Henry James privately reassured his friends that Wilde was "a fatuous fool and a tenth rate cad." [33]

The bars had also gone up when Sarah Bernhardt made her triumphal tour in America, her occasional "caprices" being whispered about in Brahmin circles with gratifying results. "Our English cousins made such asses of themselves," Mrs. Adams warned her father. "See to it that Boston snubs her off the stage." The Washington performance of "Camille" did not persuade them to reconsider their Paris convictions. The moral quarantine provoked a wave of protest from people who saw in it an unpleasant sign of snobbery and intolerance. "It is the superb actress that people go to see," protested Gail Hamilton in the New York *Tribune,* "not the bad woman." Adams's college crony, Nicholas Anderson, now a Washington neighbor of the Adamses, was also distressed by the outcry. He thought her "superb as of old," and urged his son to "get seats near the stage, for her tones are often low and her expression is wonderful." "Washington is a huge Vanity Fair," he philosophized, "and while many of the good traits of human nature are brought out, clearly observable to one who wants to see them, those which greatly predominate are the worst traits. . . . I am almost disgusted at times with people whom I really like, but who show petty meannesses and vices alien to their real nature. I have seen more symptoms of the world's degeneracy develop themselves in the last six months than in all the last six years." [34]

Society was soon again torn by the arrival of Adelina Patti and Dame Emma Albani in a week of opera. Madame Albani bore a letter from Minister Lowell in London, certifying to her social acceptability, but Patti had no credentials but her art. And in certain Washington and Boston circles the distinction was carefully respected. The beauteous Lillie Langtry also had to run the gauntlet, though Adams realized that he was very much in the minority in his disapproval. "I do not dare hint a doubt of Mrs. Langtry's virtue, for fear of getting myself into trouble. I expect to see her dined by the President and embraced by every staid matron in Washington. It is revolting." [35]

Such prudery was perhaps inevitable in a society that by Continental standards was absurdly unsophisticated, but it was often redeemed by a keen sense of social comedy. One of the most memorable passages at arms took place at a dinner which Bancroft gave for the great English historian, Edward Augustus Freeman, then making a tour of American universities. Adams had once written a hostile review of the *Norman Conquest* for which Freeman had never forgiven

him. Freeman, in Adams's laconic version of the encounter,
"made himself as offensive as usual at the dinner. At the end
he attacked me as I knew he would, and told me he had
replied to my charges, as I would see in the Preface to the
first volume of his third edition of the *Norman Conquest*."
As Marian described it, the scene might have come right out
of Thackeray. "We were first upon the battlefield. . . . [Free-
man] was simply and inexpensively attired in a rusty brown
beard of unusual length. . . . At dinner, the great historian
of the Norman Conquest was on my right; Henry *one* removed from my left. . . . When Freeman informed us that
the Falls of Slap Dash — or some such name — were better
worth our seeing than Niagara 'for the reason that many several streams like your States end in one great *fall*,' we let
the vile insinuation pass, and Edmunds with his best sena-
torial courtesy, said very gently and with no passion in his
tones, 'Where is this fall, Mrs. Freeman?' 'On the *H*adriatic,'
she said, as most Englishwomen would. There was a deathly
stillness, unbroken save for the winter rain beating drearily
against the windowpanes. On we went. The canvasbacks entered. *Three* of them — fresh and fair, done to a turn; and
weltering in their gore. Says Mrs. Bancroft, with a growing
hauteur of manner as of a turning worm, 'Do you appreciate
our canvasbacks, Mr. Freeman?' 'I cannot eat raw meat,' he
said angrily, while a convulsive shudder shook his frame.
Then the *picador* which is latent in me when nature is outraged, rose in me, and I said to him all unconscious of his
theories and the scheme of all his writing, 'I wonder that
you do not like rare meat. Your *ancestors,* the Picts and Scots,
ate their meat raw, and tore it with their fingers.' At which
he roared out, 'O-o-o-o! *Whur* did yer git that?' . . . I did
not know until the next day the exquisite point of my historical allusions. As I casually repeated them Henry became

purple in the face and rolled off his chair, and he, the husband of my bosom, who is wont to yawn affectionately at
my yarns, he at intervals of two hours says, 'Tell me again
what you said to Freeman about the Picts and the Scots and
Anglo-Saxons.' " [36]

A more agreeable English visitor was Matthew Arnold,
who finally embarked on an American lecture tour in the fall
of 1883. Not an accomplished lecturer, he heroically faced
his American audiences, buoyed by the hope that he would
at last be able to clear his only son's name from the stain
of a debt of honor at Oxford. The Lowell Institute proposal
did not bear fruit, and Arnold, anxious to make as much
money as possible, put himself under Barnum's management.
Boston expectantly flocked to his lectures but drifted out in
numb bewilderment, his voice being inaudible beyond the
first rows. In Washington people like Evarts and Bancroft
deprecated the "twaddle" of his first lecture "Numbers" when
its anti-democratic bias became known. On the score of his
writings Adams thought his mind "the most honest I have met,"
but for the man himself he had his fastidious reservations.
Meeting him again at the Bancrofts', Adams felt a certain let-
down. "He is, between ourselves," he admitted to Hay, "a
melancholy specimen of what England produces at her best."
Marian set him down as "St. Matthew . . . Apostle of Sweetness and Anarchy." She felt his "vanity and egotism" had
been "terribly developed by his keeper [Barnum]." Fearful
of heavy hotel bills, Arnold allowed himself to be quartered
on the Leiters as a house guest there to enjoy at first hand
the inspired malapropisms of his hostess. The Adamses felt
he cut a poor figure among them all. It was hard to forgive
an outsider's depreciation of Boston society who at the same
time attached himself to rich and "ungrammatical self-made
men." In time the unpleasant effect fortunately wore off, so

that a few years after Arnold's death, Adams graciously wrote, "I am better pleased to have known Matt. Arnold a little, than any one else of the literary cusses . . ." [37]

Henry James visited Washington for a short time in January, 1882, falling into his old pattern of easy informality at their fireside, but his pose of alienation continued to pique his friends. He seemed little likely to re-acclimate himself to his native land. That he should use an alias to escape the newspapers was hardly a good omen. "The real, live, vulgar, quick-paced world in America will fret him," they said, for he preferred "a quiet corner with a pen where he can create men and women who say neat things and have refined tastes and are not nasal and eccentric." Washington seemed to James, at least in his "darker moments . . . too much of a village — a nigger village sprinkled with whites," to be really habitable. He for his part studied his opinionative hosts with a keenly appraising eye and saved a delicately barbed retort for his farewell note. Marian, he said, seemed to him "the incarnation of my native land." She flared out, "Am I then vulgar, dreary, and impossible to live with? . . . Poor America! she must drag on somehow without the sympathy and love of her denationalised children." Later, when he planned his story "Pandora," he hoped it would allow him to "do Washington, so far as I know it, and work in my few notes, and my very lovely memories of last winter. I might even *do* Henry Adams and his wife." The doing, as it turned out, permitted only a light stroke or two. The "Bonnycastles' [Adamses'] parties were 'the pleasantest in Washington,'" but James caught to the life the special brand of snobbery. "Hang it," said Bonnycastle, "there's only a month left; let us be vulgar and have some fun — let us invite the President." Bonnycastle [an apt epithet] "was not in politics, though politics were much in him." "It struck him," the narrator went on, "that for Washington their society was really a little too good." If a fault were to be found with their salon, "it left out on the whole, more people than it took in." Adams willingly took that risk. "Money," he insisted to Cunliffe, "plays no part whatever in Society, but cleverness counts for a good deal, and social capacity for more." [38]

Adams was accustomed to say that he did not read his "friends' books on principle" but he had enjoyed *Daisy Miller.* Isabel Archer in James's first masterpiece betokened something disturbingly different. Adams frankly owned that he "broke down on the *Portrait of a Lady,*" for a reason supplied by Mrs. Adams. "I shall suggest to Mr. James to name his next novel 'Ann Eliza.' It's not that he 'bites off more than he can chaw,' as T. G. Appleton said of Nathan [Appleton], but he chaws more than he bites off." The picture of "alienated Americans" in the opening installment of the novel sounded to them like "a cry from the heart." Their friends quickly recognized the portrait of Adams's wife in James's "Point of View," published in the *Century* several months after his Washington visit, for the sarcastic criticisms of England and the Continent read like verbatim transcripts. Marian protested that the only character "that can hit me is that of Hon. Marcellus Cockerel," the chanticleer American, but that was sufficient.[39]

Shrewdly perceptive, James identified Marian's somewhat strident opinionativeness with a masculine character. There was indeed a certain swaggering note in her speech and an authority in her manner that belied her small stature. Frank to admit that she did not have a pretty face in a society remarkable for its beautiful women, she endeared herself to men like Clarence King and John Hay by the intrepid qualities of her spirit and her camaraderie. She was never happier than as part of a lively group of Henry's men friends talking gaily or seriously before the fire on terms of intellectual equality. On most women's activities she looked with a masculine scepticism. Women's lunches, especially, were for her "a style of killing time which I detest." [40]

The story echoed the incessant sparring matches between the Adamses and their friend on the relative merits of America and Europe. Paris, said Cockerel, was "the home of every humbug. . . . The theatres over there are insupportable; the atmosphere is pestilential." His travels had enabled him to get rid of a superstition "that there is no salvation but through Europe. Our salvation is here, if we have eyes to see it, and the salvation of Europe into the bargain; that is if Europe is to be saved, which I rather doubt. . . . Disagreeables for disagreeables, I prefer our own. . . . The vastness and freshness of this American world, the great scale and great pace of our development, the good sense and good nature of the people, console me for there being no cathedrals and no Titians." [41]

James's ear infallibly caught the protective optimisms of Henry Adams himself, the optimisms which he patriotically paraded before hostile critics as his friend Lowell did who took one tone in Birmingham, England, and another at Steinway Hall in New York. James's character derided Europe for its jealousies and rivalries, its armies, its social hierarchies, in language that is almost pure Adams. "Once one feels, over here, that the great questions of the future are social questions, that a mighty tide of democracy is sweeping the world to democracy, and that this country is the biggest stage on which the drama can be enacted, the fashionable European topics seem petty and parochial. . . . They talk about things that we have settled ages ago." Adams's intimacy with James lasted through all differences of opinion. He kept a safe distance from the later novels, only by chance being inveigled into reading *The Sacred Fount*. "I recognized at once that Harry and I had the same disease, the obsession of the *idée fixe*. Harry illustrates it by the trivial figure of an English

country-house party, which could only drive one mad by
boring one into it, but if he had chosen another background,
his treatment would have been wonderfully keen. All the
same it is insanity, and I think that Harry must soon take
a vacation, with most of the rest of us, in a cheery asylum." [42]

4 Five of Hearts

Nothing so epitomized the exclusiveness of the Adams
salon from 1880 to 1885 as the tiny club of inner circle intimates that called itself the "Five of Hearts" and exchanged
confidences on specially printed note paper. It probably came
into existence during a merry dinner of the "Hearts" early
in 1881 when Adams, just back from Europe, was renewing
his intimacy with Clarence King and John Hay. Hay's service
as Assistant Secretary of State was then drawing to a close.
The three friends, all "little chaps," as Holt called them,
convivially defied the world's opinion in the privacy of the
Adams home. The two wives, Mrs. Adams and Mrs. Hay,
were the other conspirators in the little game that titillated
the curiosity of their neighbors in the Square. One suspects
that Mrs. Hay, a pillar of Cleveland rectitude and piety, compelled her friends to exercise their irony in all sorts of resourceful evasions. If Mrs. Adams's letters are any gauge,
the minutes of the meetings belonged in Pope's "Rape of the
Lock," where "at every word a reputation dies." Here Hay
no doubt shared — with at least two of the "Hearts" — his
immense delight with Mark Twain's secretly printed "1601."
Here Clarence King found a rapt audience for his inexhaustible supply of puns. Mark Twain himself kept a comfortably
safe distance from Mrs. Hay, for as he once wrote with
elaborate understatement of the situation, "She is very strict
about Sunday." Clemens evidently heard enough about Adams

from Hay to want to do him in his own way. The "doing" produced the satirically incongruous "Henry Adams" of the "£1,000,000 Bank-Note," playing the rough-and-ready Yankee in British high society.[43]

Adams greatly prized the drollery of his friends, their verve and freedom from inhibition. The author of "Little Breeches" still held on, in the company of men, to a good deal of Pike County irreverence. Beneath the dignified demeanor and impressive beard lurked a love of horse play. Once after a bibulous evening at the Century Club Hay, Whitelaw Reid, and Bayard Taylor played leapfrog over the ashcans which lined the sidewalk. But humor is ephemeral stuff. By all testimony Hay and King were inspired raconteurs, yet all Holt could recall of King was a vaudeville jape about a shipwrecked German-Jew who reacted to the cry "A sail! A sail!" with "Mein Gott! I haf no gatalog." When Adams once groused that Boston society existed "in a polar condition of isolated icebergs," King capped the idea with the remark that "Boston was 1387453 years under the ice, and then the Adamses came." Of the unpopular banking firm of Morton and Bliss, King quipped: "If ignorance is Bliss, what the devil is Morton?" When one of the skye terriers showed up with a bad eye, King diagnosed it as a "Tom-Cataract." But what most delighted his homekeeping hosts were the tall tales of his adventures. King too was a restless man, but, unlike Adams, he did not resist the craving. "For me the study or the laboratory would have been utterly impossible," he once said. A working geologist, he took a Byronic delight in seeing "Nature in her wildest and most savage moods."[44]

King was a remarkable mixture of Newport culture and frontiersman. Friends gave wide currency to his classic yarn of Old Man Tison, the braggart mountain man bedevilled by Fresno Pete and Faro Harry. Though he delighted to varnish fact with fiction, he had a far more thorough knowledge of the Far West than either Sam Clemens or Bret Harte. His *Mountaineering in the Sierra Nevadas* was his ticket of admission to Howells' literary circle of which Hay was already a member. According to Howells, King was precisely the sort of literary amateur that Adams always wanted to be. And just as Holt wrote of Adams that he seemed indifferent to ordinary literary fame, so Howells wrote of King that "he was above everything indifferent to literary repute." In both cases the judgment spoke a piquant half-truth.[45]

King evidently was the catalyst that changed the acquaintance between Adams and Hay into an almost rapturous friendship, memorialized in letters which in the earlier years are filled with an adolescent spirit of intellectual romping and playfulness. The three men were as "close as middle aged sinners" could get, as Adams said. By 1881 King had had his fill of government service as much as Hay and as Mrs. Adams remarked, they were "as eager to get out as most fools to get in." Adams, never loth to share his own opinion, gave them the benefit of family wisdom on the vanity of public office, as he had to his English friends. Literature was always the loser. "I grudge you to the law," he told young Oliver Wendell Holmes, when congratulating him on his Massachusetts judgeship, and exhorted him to keep literature before him. Hay's admiration for King was even greater than Adams's. "I never imagined," Mrs. Adams exclaimed, "such fanatic adoration could exist in this practical age." King's opportunity to escape from the Geological Survey to greener pastures came only when President Hayes left office. Thereafter he made his headquarters in New York, running down to Washington for meetings of the Academy of Science or to do his share of lobbying. Soon he involved himself in speculative mining promotions and drifted off to England for a few years. There he hobnobbed with Ruskin and abandoned the finances of his mining company to their incredibly tangled fate. A strange, brilliant, and appealing bird of passage, an exotic among tame doves, he was a fitful correspondent and an unpredictable visitant, rarely arriving when expected. In a mountain camp he sometimes startled visitors by appearing in "immaculate linen, silk stockings, low shoes and clothing without a wrinkle," as if about to be presented at court. The aura of impending failure that clung to him gave him an almost tragic quality in the eyes of his friends. Byronic to the end, King saved one secret, a secret of a double life, that would astonish his friends beyond any literary secrets they had kept. Regarded by all as a resolute bachelor and so listed in all biographical notices, King, at the very height of his social triumphs, became the common law husband of a Negro woman and faithfully supported the children of that union.[46]

King's restless quest epitomized for all of them the lure of what William James called the "bitch goddess" success. How they all hungered for it, never quite sure what the blue bird was, all feeling they were contestants in some kind of desperate foot race. Great wealth was an object, if it somehow could be acquired without chicanery, without the tricks of financiering or political corruption. Yet how? The spirit of Beriah Sellers did not pass them by. Friendly tips were always gratefully received from promoters and engineers like Alexander Agassiz. Calumet Copper runs like an agreeable grace note through the story. Adams's flier in King's Sombrerete mining scheme, on the other hand, returned little more than sardonic amusement as it became "more sombrereteer than ever." He was never a plunger nor did he care to play with the "edge tool" of stock speculation like the astute Hay who prospered "as do the wicked" in that art. "A touch of avarice," Hay was to say of King, "would have made him a Vanderbilt. . . . Yet I fear he will die without anything except to be a great scientist and the sweetest na-

tured creature the Lord ever made." Adams tended toward
the banker's caution of his father and relied on "Ned" Hooper,
his financially conservative brother-in-law, for financial advice. When it came to investing money, he would say, "I
rather affect business-like principles," content with getting
"8 and 10 per cent" on his money.[47]

Hay had the ambitious midwesterner's yearning for the
accolade of Eastern culture. Howells had basked in it; Bret
Harte had been irresistibly drawn; Sam Clemens of Hannibal
had come East to be civilized and to be paid handsomely
for submitting to the process. Joaquin Miller descended on
Washington to commune with nature in his cabin in Rock
Creek Park and be lionized like a literary Sioux. John Hay
had come a long way from Warsaw, Indiana, and Springfield,
Illinois. As a young law student he wrote with considerable
clairvoyance, "I am not suited for a reformer. I do not like
to meddle with moral ills. I love comfortable people. I prefer,
for my friends, men who can read." In the highest degree
Henry Adams met John Hay's ideal. How much he esteemed
that ideal is visible in his anonymous novel *Breadwinners,*
the work which interrupted the endless chore of his biography of Lincoln. He put himself squarely on the side of the
employer in that period of industrial turmoil, but at the same
time he patronized the provincial aristocracy of Cleveland
for their dullness and their lack of the *savoir-faire.* The germ
of *Breadwinners* may well have been cultured in the study
of Henry Adams among the Five of Hearts as one of Hay's
biographers has suggested. The success of the novel produced
a curious about-face in the London *Saturday Review.* Four
years earlier the *Saturday Review* had praised Adams's *Democracy,* as a "masterpiece." Now it praised *Breadwinners*
at the expense of *Democracy,* saying that the latter had been
"ludicrously overrated . . . it has what *Democracy* has not
— it has depth." [48]

Hay's experience with anonymity somewhat paralleled Adams's with *Democracy*. It was bitterly attacked as a crude libel on the labor movement and on midwestern society. Hay, not having Adams's fortitude, fought back in a long anonymous letter to the *Century* which had serialized the novel, a letter which contained an oddly revealing paragraph. "I am engaged in business in which my standing would be seriously compromised if it were known that I had written a novel. I am sure that my practical efficiency is not lessened by this act; but I am equally sure that I could never recover from the injury it would occasion me if known among my own colleagues." In private the friends bandied back and forth with much delight every attribution of authorship as they had done with Adams's novel.[49]

The Adamses helped open doors not only to Washington society but to English society as well, and Hay was everlastingly appreciative. Significantly Adams felt the need of explaining his friendship for Hay to his English "Liberal" friend, Robert Cunliffe. "He [Hay] has everything the world can give except strength. He is amiable and clever, and the only fault I have to find with him is that in politics he has always managed to keep in what I think precious bad company. I never could understand why, except that I never knew more than two or three men born west of the Alleghanies who knew the difference between a gentleman and a swindler. This curious obliquity makes him a particularly charming companion to me, as he knows intimately scores of men whom I would not touch with a pole, but who are more amusing than my own crowd." Adams clung to Hay as one more contact with the world of large affairs. The salutations of their letters tell the story of deepening dependence as each tried to outdo the other in affectionately facetious epithets. Adams would play variations like the fol-

lowing: "My Son John," "Sweetheart," "Dear Heart," "Dear
Oasis," or "Dearly Beloved." Hay would riposte with "My
own and Ownliest," "My beloved Mentor," "My Cherished
Livy," and the improvisations flew back and forth with an
almost feminine verve. The great wealth which came to him
on the death of his father-in-law, and his native talent for
increasing it, made him the "capitalist" of their group. Ill at
ease in Cleveland trying to play the role of a ruthless captain
of finance, Hay now felt free to establish a residence in
Washington whose "best society" was "the most delightful in
the country," according to the *Atlantic*. "There has been
almost an epidemic of building," its correspondent reported.
"The senate is becoming a club of moneyed men." For an
ambitious journalist-diplomat it was a place of promise.[50]

Nicholas Anderson had also yielded to the spell. In Washington on a four-day visit, he had been so charmed that he
promptly bought a house on the Square. Within a few months
he engaged their one-time college intimate, Henry Hobson
Richardson, then at the height of his reputation as an architect, to design a romanesque mansion for him. All of the
friends excitedly pored over the house plans and picked up
the contagion for building. Even the peripatetic Alex Agassiz
was wild to build. Looking at the completed "medieval cas-
tle," as one columnist described it, Adams made "some funny
comments, but was speechless on entering, declaring its arrangements quite perfect." On Thanksgiving, 1883, in Anderson's new mansion, the two old friends passed a sentimental evening recalling their hilarious rendezvous twenty-five
years before at Magdeburg, Germany, with Crowninshield
and the rest. Another memorable occasion of that year was
a farewell dinner for the ill-starred Turkish envoy, Aristarchi
Bey, at which the guest of honor, being in top form, "made
twelve speeches." Anderson, pretending to extemporize in

Greek, recited Anacreon, his hoax detected only by Aristarchi Bey and Adams. Jerome Bonaparte reported that Adams also made "a lovely speech." [51]

Often the lamps glowed late in the study when Brooks Adams came down to beat his obstinate theories into shape with the aid of Henry's trenchant criticisms. He was the most frequent family visitor, limping about with a gouty ailment and "much out of sorts and spirits." When he arrived, Mrs. Adams was hard put to it to "leaven the family dough" with suitable feminine guests. Given always to violent contradiction of each other's opinions, the two brothers had nonetheless grown very close. Brooks was turning from magazine articles to history, and had begun work on his *Emancipation of Massachusetts,* in which he attempted to apply the principles of scientific determinism according to Buckle, Darwin, and Spencer to the process by which the Puritan oligarchy had been overthrown. Perhaps more than any other of his intimates Brooks challenged Henry to increasingly serious thought about the science of history, never letting him forget his role as teacher, guide, and Devil's advocate. Through Brooks Henry kept in close touch with the pragmatic movement in the Harvard Law School of which Oliver Wendell Holmes, Jr., was the natural leader.[52]

Holmes, only infrequently in Washington during this period, brought the kind of intellectual stimulus on which Adams thrived. An intimate friend from their professorial days together, Holmes was welcome also as one of Marian's girlhood circle, his father, Dr. Holmes of the "Breakfast Table" being one of Dr. Hooper's closest friends. Of deepest interest to Adams was the fact that Holmes had greatly extended the institutional approach to legal history, paralleling the work he and his scholars had done in Anglo-Saxon law. Holmes's scientific description of the true character of the common law was already being accepted as a classic formulation. "The life of the law has not been logic: it has been experience. The felt necessities of the time, the prevalent moral and political theories, intuitions of public policy, avowed or unconscious, even the prejudices which judges share with their fellow men, have had a good deal more to do than the syllogism in determining the rules by which men should be governed." Principles like these and the psychological corollaries being developed by their friend William James and James's mentor, Peirce, were bound to erode the remaining a priori principles which Henry Adams had once brought to his reading of Constitutional history.[53]

Brooks, more susceptible to Holmes's positivistic analysis, accepted the implications of this analysis with greater alacrity than his brother. In his course of lectures at the Harvard Law School in 1882–1883, he uncompromisingly developed the intimations of Holmes. "Properly speaking the constitutional law of our country is a collection of customs by which the country is regulated." He found himself obliged to abandon the position which he had shared with Henry concerning the Legal Tender Act. In the early stages of that case Henry had charged that the Act "overthrows the whole fabric of our government." Brooks was now ready to move as fast as destiny. "It is of little moment whether the meaning of our great charter is slowly construed away by the ingenuity of lawyers, or whether it is roughly thrust aside by force: its fate is sealed; it must yield where it obstructs. . . . In our country and our age that which the majority of the people want will be the law, and the President and the Congress, who represent the people, will see that the work is done." [54]

Henry Adams yielded reluctantly to the logic of Holmes and Brooks. He could not gainsay the analysis, but he was inwardly uneasy about the direction of this force of the popular will which had been working its way upward to power since the Reformation. All social, political, and ethical values seemed ultimately at its mercy. Preoccupied during these years with his *History* and its offshoots, Henry Adams could not pursue the implications of the new sociology and psychology with the speculative rigor of his brother. Yet the revolutionary ideas coming from Harvard could not be ignored. They forced upon him the duty of reading history in a quite different light from that of his favorite Macaulay. The task of the prophet and statesman had become enormously more difficult.

By 1884 Brooks had already formulated a preliminary theory of the nature of the struggle between vested economic and political minorities and the repressed and exploited majority. Freedom had come to Massachusetts only when the majority had seized control of the legal institutions by which the priestly oligarchy had maintained their despotism. Henry was not yet ready to move down this path. When in 1884 the Supreme Court finally declared that the Constitution allowed Congress to do what it pleased with the currency, he sadly agreed with Bancroft that the "peau de chagrin" of liberty as guaranteed by the Constitution was rapidly shrinking. Behind the ordered amenities of daily existence in Lafayette Square, the thoughtful bystander could already sense the shape of a wholly alien future.[55]

Chapter Six

Portraits in Acid

1 Virginia Don Quixote

ONCE settled in the Square, owner Corcoran's minions
dispersed, and the plaster dry on the walls, Adams
plunged into the long campaign of writing the *History*. His
determination to meet his own deadlines drew strength from
his wife's firmness. If on rare occasions he showed signs of
faltering, she would hold him to the mark by telling him
how many candles Cousin Bancroft burned at his desk *before*
breakfast. As his "stylographic" moved swiftly over the fools-
cap pages, he pushed forward simultaneously heaping up
his research materials to add to the twenty fat volumes of
transcripts supplied by his European copyists.[1]

He seems at first to have been uncertain in his plan for
opening the work, sketching in later portions while waiting
for a clue. Thus, months after he began, he wrote to Justin
Winsor, the Harvard librarian who had once humored his
demands as a professor there, "Some four or five years of
preliminary work have at last brought me to the point of
beginning on the American newspapers of the time." He
asked Winsor to express six or seven volumes to him at Beverly Farms each week. "My wish," he went on, "is to begin
with the files of 1807 and go on to 1809 without stopping."
Nearly four months later, with the flood still pouring in, he
had made up his mind to a fresh approach, and sent a new
directive to Winsor. "I want to learn all I can about the

social and economical condition of the country in 1800. Can
you send me a few books on the subject in the return box
with the newspaper volumes? . . . I want to find out how
much banking capital there was in the U. S. in 1800, and
how it was managed. I want a strictly accurate account of
the state of education and of the practise of medicine. I
want a *good* sermon of that date, if such a thing existed, for
I cannot find one which seems to be tolerable from a literary
or logical point of view. If you in your historical work have
come across any facts or authorities which would aid me,
I should like to beg them of you, especially if they tend to
correct me. Thus far my impression is that America in 1800
was not far from the condition of England under Alfred the
Great; that the conservative spirit was intensely strong in
the respectable classes, and that there was not only indifference but actual aggressive repression towards innovation;
the mental attitude of good society looks to me surprisingly
medieval. I should wish to correct this impression. Did
Harvard or Yale show anything to the contrary *before* 1800?
I can see that Philadelphia was reasonably liberal and active-
minded; was any other part of the country equally so? Was
there a steam-engine in the United States? . . ." Evidently
what had taken shape in his mind was the pattern for the
opening section of the history, the famous first six chapters.[2]

He now clearly saw his work as the study of a dynamic
development from the datum line of 1800, the opening to be
a kind of continental cross section for the year. In meticu-
lously kept ledgers he set up tables of items: "Population of
the United States in 1800," "Log houses," "Roads," "Diet,"
"drink," "cleanliness," "honesty," and the like with a brief précis
of authorities. On one page under "Literature," he tabulated:
"Newspapers, libraries, schools, universities, writers, belles-
lettres, history." The ordering of facts was one thing, and a
fairly simple one; but the artistic problem was more difficult.

Every objection that Cooper and Hawthorne and Henry James had urged concerning the lack of picturesqueness and drama in American life seemed to rise up in his mind as he contemplated the flat panorama of democracy. The point had long ago been made in one of his early "Bibles," de Tocqueville's *Democracy in America,* which attributed the happy mediocrity of American life to its equalitarian character. He also declared that American literature was handicapped because "There are no dramatic subjects in a country which has witnessed no great political catastrophes." Even the philosophy of history was affected because the individual was far less important than in an aristocratic society. "Historians who live in democratic ages," de Tocqueville explained, "not only deny that the few have any power of acting upon the destiny of a people, but they deprive the people themselves of the power of modifying their own condition, and they subject them either to an inflexible Providence, or to some blind necessity." As his mentor indicated Adams's problem involved not only art but the philosophy of history. In the *Gallatin* Adams had already acknowledged that a determinist theory was unavoidable.[3]

What he thought of the artistic dilemma he expressed in a letter commenting on Lodge's *Short History of the English Colonies in America.* "If fault is to be found, I am inclined, in going over the same ground a little later, to put it on the extreme monotony of the subject, and I have pretty much made up my mind not to attempt giving interest to the society of America in itself, but to try for it by way of contrast with the artificial society of Europe, as one might contrast a stripped prizefighter with a life-guardsman in helmet and breastplate, jack-boots and a big black horse. The contrast may be made dramatic, but not the thing. This is to be, however, the acid test of my own composition, and I am afraid that I shall not succeed so well as you."[4]

The road to the *History* was not destined to be a straight
one. The first interruption came only a few months after he
set to work. His friend John T. Morse, editor of the American
Statesmen series, approached him to do a volume on John
Randolph of Roanoke. Morse must have felt a certain pi-
quancy in inviting the descendant of a house which Randolph
had traduced above all others to sit in judgment upon the
assailant, but his instinct was sound if he wanted a provoca-
tive and hence saleable book. Long afterwards, the climate
of opinion toward the South having changed, Morse professed to believe that he had made a mistake in assigning
the life to such an unsympathetic writer. If it was a mistake,
he made it with his eyes open, for he had read the *Gallatin*
and had reviewed it in the main rather favorably. In that
work Adams had not concealed his contempt for Randolph.
On the contrary, he had given full vent to his detestation
of Randolph's "aberrations" and "eccentricities."[5]

Morse's invitation so thoroughly intrigued Adams that he
could not help playing with the idea like a cat with a ball
of yarn, sending in such a facetiously coy acceptance that
Morse, too much taken in by Adams's chaff, later retained the
impression of "much doubt and little ardor."

"I have had your letter lying on my table for some days,"
Adams replied, "while I tried to screw my courage up to
the point of accepting the burden you want to put on me;
but I am just like the camels I used to see in Egypt, each
with about six attenuated sugar-canes to carry, but groaning,
grunting and scolding as though he was carrying Moses
and Aaron and the tables of the law and the burning bush
and the bronze serpent and in short the whole Panorama
fitout all at once. Did you ever hear a camel scold? Well
that's me, as our French friends say. I have found out that
Carlyle was thirteen years over his Frederic[k], I have lengthened the time for my history to fifteen. Blamed if I'll be

beat by Carlisle [sic] on a detail like that! So I have five years to spare, and perhaps I might squeeze out of them a month or two for your book. If you will agree not to expect a line of it before next November, and not to ask for it ever at all, and not to get mad if I don't do it, and not to call me a liar or a politician or a congressman, or any other name of extreme opprobrium, and not to make any allusions or hints to me when you find me lazy in summer as though you had your eye on me, — then perhaps — well! — I'll think about it. . . .

"If I find Randolph easy I don't know but what I will volunteer for Burr. Randolph is the type of a political charlatan who had something in him. Burr is the type of charlatan pure and simple, a very Jim Crow of melodramatic wind-bags. I have something to say of both varieties." The point settled satisfactorily, Morse asked him to nominate other contributors, which he did but not without protesting Morse's assigning Gallatin to "such an indescribable brute and ass as John Austin Stevens. Schurz was *the* man for Gallatin, and failing him, Frank Walker or old S. J. Tilden or David Wells." [6]

The project had all the attractions of window breaking, of creating a much greater sensation than with his article on Captain John Smith and Pocahontas. Here was an opportunity to debunk another favorite son of Virginia, venerated as a descendant of Pocahontas. Randolph had been a chief adversary of John Adams and John Quincy Adams. "For thirty years," as the biography was to say, "he never missed a chance to have his fling at both the Adamses, father and son. 'The cub,' he said, 'is a greater bear than the old one.' " He had also come to be the sacred symbol of States' rights and nullification to the secessionist South, standing second only to Calhoun for whose doctrines he prepared the way. If Randolph was right, the Adamses and

their anti-slavery associates were wrong. Henry Adams might
well have asked himself dare he allow anyone else to seize
this golden opportunity. Fifteen years had passed since
Appomattox, but there was ample evidence even in the
salons of Lafayette Square that defeat had not brought a
genuine conviction of error to Southern writers.[7]

With what zest Adams went at the writing may be deduced from the speed with which he wrote; it may not have
been a labor of love like the *Gallatin,* but it was if anything
the more congenial labor of detraction. Morse had first
sounded him out toward the end of March. Three months
later, just back from the Harvard commencement, he gaily
wrote, "*John Randolph* is finished. Rah, rah, rah. Now for
Aaron Burr. Rah, rah, '81." By July there was even greater
reason to boast. "I have written two whole volumes in exactly two months," he jubilated. It had been hard work. "Ten
hours a day to get myself on the shelf — my books I mean —
before I am fifty and have lost my powers of work." The
Randolph manuscript did not go immediately to the printer
as he decided to revise it, possibly at Morse's suggestion.
By the first of June, 1882, it was finally ready, if Adams met
the deadline he set in a letter to Morse in March, and it
was published the first of October. The speed of composition
was deceptive. The *Randolph* was no hack work, boiled up
for the occasion, but a return to materials which he had already studied with great care, first for his Harvard lectures,
then re-considered in the light of his painstaking work on
the *Gallatin.*[8]

Thanks to Adams's short biography, the life and character of John Randolph has become a *cause célèbre* of
historical writing. The large scale study of Randolph written
nearly forty years later by William C. Bruce, a Virginia
scholar, spends much of its energy defending Randolph and
Virginia from the alleged calumnies of this "family pamphlet,

saturated with the sectional prejudices and antipathies of the year 1882." Prior to Adams's book, there had been only one important biography of Randolph, that of Hugh A. Garland. Garland, a Virginian and a devoted States' rights partisan, had grown up under Randolph's political influence during the crucial struggles over the tariff and the Bank of the United States. He had eulogized Randolph as the chief architect of Southern statesmanship whose "bold and masterly efforts arrested that centripetal tendency which was rapidly destroying the counterbalance of the States" and he called on Virginia to give adequate recognition to "her wisest statesman, truest patriot, and most devoted son."[9]

Adams's book was a violent refutation of this appraisal. A senator during John Quincy Adams's administration, Randolph became the chief spokesman for the Southern cause and converted John C. Calhoun, Adams's Vice President, to the States' rights position and to the dangerous euphemisms of the doctrine of interposition. Randolph organized the opposition to the administration of John Quincy Adams and with his genius for invective, effectively prevented the reelection of Henry Adams's grandfather. This struggle between Randolph and John Quincy Adams underlies the analysis and gives the biography its peculiar animus.

Henry Adams was as ardent a nationalist as any of his forebears and as ardently anti-slavery, but these ardors conflicted with his conservative view of the Constitution, his attachment to the principle of the division of powers, and his belief that liberty depended on a strict construction of that document. Now that Federal powers had increased far beyond anything his grandfather had envisioned, Adams found himself in acutely distasteful company. On abstract principle, he belonged with the States' rights advocates and the strict constructionists whose stronghold was the South. It was a matter of dogma to him that "Political power had, in all experience, tended to grow at the expense of human liberty. Every government tended toward despotism; contained somewhere a supreme, irresponsible, self-defined power called sovereignty, which held human rights, if human rights there were, at its mercy. Americans believed that the liberties of this continent depended on fixing a barrier against this supreme central sovereignty called national government, which if left to grow unresisted, would repeat here all the miserable experiences of Europe, and, falling into the grasp of some group of men, would be the center of a military tyranny." In the reserved powers of the states, then, lay the main safe-guard against tyranny. Guided by this doctrine, the Republican party of Jefferson and Randolph "placed the good of the human race before the glory of mere nationality." This was the distinguishing feature of the early Virginia school of politics, the inspiration of the Virginia and Kentucky resolutions of 1798.[10]

The one admirable thing that Adams conceded to Randolph was his love of liberty and his detestation of despotic power. He reminded his readers of 1882, "For a generation like our own, in whose ears the term of States' rights has become hateful, owing to its perversion in the interests of Negro slavery, and in whose eyes the comfortable doctrines of unlimited national sovereignty shine with the glory of a moral principle sanctified by the blood of innumerable martyrs, these narrow and jealous prejudices of Randolph and his friends sound like systematized treason; but they were the honest convictions of that generation which framed and adopted the Constitution. . . . a great majority of the American people shared the same fears of despotic government." Opposed to "big" government himself, especially to the post-Civil War version of it in Washington, Adams could not free himself from similar fears. They were the burden of his warning to President Hayes. He conceded that "were Randolph alive today he would probably feel that his worst fears were realized." [11]

Gallatin had confronted the breakdown of the Republican theory in the face of intractable circumstances with courage and practical intelligence. Randolph, on the other hand, visionary and irascible, broke with his party and its leaders, Jefferson and Madison, refused to recognize the force of changing circumstances, and forgetting that States' rights were only a part of republican dogma in 1800, finally made it "his hobby, his mania . . . played tricks with it until his best friends were weary and disgusted." His grotesquely single-minded insistence on the doctrine became "the helmet of this Virginia Quixote, — a Helmet of Mambrino." [12]

Adams set himself to account for Randolph's eccentricity, to make clear that it was an aberration that bordered on charlatanism, and to show that the rightness or wrongness of his political ideal was not really material in the estimation of the character of Randolph. Other Virginia men had begun with the same premises. As for the Constitutional question, the Civil War had not really settled it, as he saw it, but merely postponed it. But the political purist in Adams rebelled violently against the kind of idolatry lavished upon Randolph's memory by a biographer like Garland. Could he permit the man whose quixoticism had reduced a whole section of the country into a sympathetic dementia to be regarded as a hero? To Adams the Southern cause was, from its inception, not so much wrong as wrong-headed and Randolph was the purest exemplar of that wrong-headedness.

The doctrine of States' rights was "isolated, degraded, defiled by an unnatural union with the slave power" because Randolph's personality was twisted and diseased. What he touched, he blighted and he infected his followers with his own abnormality, appealing to the latent irrationality of the Virginia and Southern character. Whether this hypoth-

esis of an individual and a collective psychosis correctly explains Randolph's political career — and the political history
of the pre-Civil War South — is, as Adams was fond of saying, another matter. Now that economic determinism as
the chief explanation of the Civil War has been expertly
modified by emphasis on psychological stereotypes, Adams's
study of Randolph may have greater validity than it once
seemed to have.[13]

As a piece of biographical art, the book illuminates Adams's
rapid emergence as a literary artist. It is a markedly different
kind of work from the *Gallatin*. Impressive as that work is
as a masterpiece of scholarship, it is essentially academic,
addressed to fellow scholars. The documents so dominate
the narrative of Gallatin's public life that the man who
inhabits the monument appears as little more than a model
of Roman virtues. For scientific scholarship in the German
tradition it set a high standard, but its artistry was only in-
cidental.

In the novel *Democracy* Adams had experimented with a
completely new form, one which challenged him to manipu-
late his materials with imaginative freedom and to focus his
analysis of character upon a ruling trait. Through the figure
of Ratcliffe he applied the privileges of fiction to the life
of Blaine; the result was a three dimensional villain. *Democracy* taught him the immemorial lesson of Milton's Satan,
the superior artistic attraction of villainy. Not only did it
liberate him from his documents, it also freed his style from
the excessively judicial tone of his previous writing and
opened up to him the resources of literary allusion, of
dramatic contrast, of narrative pace and timing. The *Randolph* marks a striking departure in his writing, an advance
in artistry if perhaps a retreat in antiquarian accuracy.
Which configuration yields the higher truth remains the
great puzzle of the art of biography. Gamaliel Bradford,

whose sketch of Randolph in *Damaged Souls* was attacked by Virginians as following Adams "in a line of savage criticism which is entirely unjustified by the facts," made the unanswerable defense, "And how is one to know? And how is one ever to know?"[14]

The *Gallatin* had not been planned as a popular book; the *Randolph* was; and its unique character derives from that fact. "I have but one prime test for a popular book," Adams remarked to Lodge. "Is it interesting?" Henry James asked no more — and no less — of the novel. For biography to be interesting to a popular audience, its personages must be treated dramatically. "Your Webster," he said of Lodge's contribution to the series, "should have been an actor like Kemble or Cook. He would have been sublime." The more he looked at history in this fresh light, the more Adams felt its attractions. The posturings of the young Randolph's friends, their bombast and rodomontade struck him as something out of Kotzebue. Jefferson was "a case for Beaumarchais," John Adams "good for Sheridan's school." As an ironist, he tended increasingly to see the persons of history diminished in stature and almost invariably was put in mind of comedy, satirical comedy. Only in the rarest instances did a great tragic figure walk the stage of history and arouse pity and terror. Such a one had been his grandfather, John Quincy Adams. Henry never forgot those despairing, anguished lines of Gretry's opera which had so moved his grandfather. "O Richard, o mon roi, l'univers t'abandonne." "The inevitable isolation and disillusionment of a really strong mind," said Adams, "one that combines force with elevation — is to me the romance and tragedy of statesmanship." By this test, Randolph was not a tragic figure. He had undergone disillusionment with his party and suffered isolation, but, as Adams was at pains to point out, he lacked greatness of mind and moral elevation.[15]

Adams was keenly aware that there was a destructive principle in all biography, even the most laudatory. Under the magnifying lens, all life tended to become Brobdingnagian and beauty vanished, as Gulliver found, in pimples and worse. He read biography and autobiography with a passionate interest and always a little fearfully as if he were himself the subject, for in his imagination he could not avoid feeling himself somehow in the public eye. As an Adams he was a marked man. Some day he too would have to take his chances with posterity. Reading Trollope's autobiography about this time, he shuddered at the spectacle. "I mean to do mine," he promised. "After seeing how coolly and neatly a man like Trollope can destroy the last vestige of heroism in his own life, I object to allowing mine to be murdered by any one except myself." In his letters he remarks the damage that biographies do to the reputations of their subject and vowed to protect himself. Little wonder that as an old man, he thought of his *Education* as a "shield of protection in the grave." [16]

To give the interest that art lends to nature, Adams felt that biography must take its cue from the great novelists to seek the depths of character in the flaws and weaknesses of its heroes. The conventional multi-volumed biography of the period, the official laudations, could hardly be termed readable, condemned as they were to praise their subjects and gloss over the troubled depths. Were he wholly honest with himself he would have had to acknowledge that he had sinned a little himself in the *Gallatin*. Mere adulation violated the principles of the art. It was not enough to portray the strengths, the high lights of a man's career. In his gentle demurrer to Dr. Holmes on the life of Emerson he said, "As a mere student I could have wished one chapter more, to be reserved for the dissecting room alone. After studying the scope of any mind, I want as well to study its limitations.

The limitations of Napoleon's and Shakespeare's minds would tell me more than their extensions, so far as relative values are concerned." As the years passed, the destructive element loomed ever larger, until he was ready to state as the law of biography that "the greatest of them commonly destroy their hero, as Carlyle destroyed Frederic[k] the Great and . . . Morley destroyed Gladstone. . . . The trouble is that any truthful biography must always define the hero's limitations."[17]

What Adams grasped in the case of the *Randolph* was the principle that later writers like Gamaliel Bradford, Lytton Strachey, André Maurois and their school were to employ in making biography a rival of the novel. They would impose upon the amorphous and chaotic materials of man's life, its formlessness and basic incoherence, a unifying insight into the psychology of the subject and select the details which vivify this central intuition of character. Bradford called his studies of damaged souls "psychographs." Yet even as he practised it, Adams could not be wholly comfortable with his principle; the psychological principle opened metaphysical chasms in the realms of being. Reflecting afterwards on Morley's *Gladstone,* he said, "Of course in him, as in most people, there were two or three or a dozen men; in these emotional, abnormal natures, there are never less than three."[18]

Randolph's life lent itself perfectly to Adams's theory. He had been a remarkable individual, a politician of undoubted genius, an extraordinarily effective public speaker whose eccentricities of manner became a trademark. Kinsman of Jefferson and a violent libertarian in the group of men who opposed the Federalists, he had wielded almost autocratic power as chairman of the Ways and Means Committee. Yet he flung away his power to become the turbulent leader of the Southern extremists. The folly of his duel with Henry

Clay was a fitting climax to his misguided crusade. About his personal life there hung strange clouds of abnormality, disease, and a "strange and terrible scandal." [19]

The aura of strangeness and inner horror is heightened by the indefiniteness and mystery of its cause, by the hint of unspeakable scandal. "If disappointment and sorrow could soften a human heart, Randolph had enough to make him tender as the gentlest. From the first some private trouble weighed on his mind, and since he chose to make a mystery of its cause a biographer is bound to respect his wish." And again, "He seems to have been suffering under a complication of trials, the mystery of which his biographers had best not attempt to penetrate." After these hints so strongly reinforced by his outrageous public conduct, as Adams presents it, it comes almost as anticlimax to learn from other sources that Randolph was impotent, enduring gibes on that score on the floor of Congress itself, and that he was haunted by the belief that his sister Nancy was a dissolute criminal.[20]

The great moral crime of Randolph's political career, that which drew to itself all the lesser offenses of his life, was in Adams's somber judgment, Randolph's "prostitution to the base uses of the slave power" of the doctrine of States' rights. How and why did Randolph go astray so as to employ his great talents in such a cause? Working backward from that disastrous betrayal of early principles, Adams postulated a character fatally flawed by weaknesses of body and of mind. A line from Gallatin's curt estimate gave a clue: "Eccentricities and temper of J. Randolph soon destroyed his usefulness." Randolph himself candidly supplied the rest. His own bitter self-judgment gave Adams an appropriate epitaph: "Time misspent, and faculties misemployed, and sense jaded by labor or impaired by excess, cannot be recalled." With this dark thread to lead him through the labyrinth, Adams presents the drama of Randolph's fall as an inexorable descent into the pit like a tarnished Lucifer, but a descent without grandeur or sublimity, merely grotesque as in the grim comedy of his death.[21]

The plantation to which Randolph returned for refreshment after each session of Congress is called "Bizarre." Adams refers to it again and again, sounding the name like a grace note, that soon becomes the dominant tone. Randolph was bizarre in appearance, in manner, in all. By a natural affinity all that was bizarre, abnormal, and eccentric in the Virginia environment drew itself to him. "Extreme eccentricity might end in producing a man of a new type, as brutal at heart as the roughest cub that ran loose among the Negro cabins of a tobacco plantation, violent, tyrannical, vicious, cruel, and licentious in language as in morals, while at the same time trained to the habits of good society, and sincerely feeling that exaggerated deference which it was usual to affect toward ladies; he might be well read, fond of intelligent conversation, consumed by ambition, or devoured by self-esteem, with manners grave, deferential, mild, and charming when at their best, and intolerable when the spirit of arrogance seized him. . . . John Randolph, the embodiment of these contrasts and peculiarities, was an eccentric type recognized and understood by Virginians." They not only understood him, they loved him as a champion, forgave him all, and became implicated in his sins. "As the character of Don Quixote was to Cervantes clearly a natural and possible product of Spanish character, so to the people of Virginia John Randolph was a representative man with qualities exaggerated but genuine; and even these exaggerations struck a chord of popular sympathy." Because of these very weaknesses in him and in his fellow Virginians he was able to mobilize the South in implacable defense of its peculiar institution.[22]

To the "cold-blooded New Englander" who found his extravagance and his plantation manners "obnoxious," Randolph's pride in his Indian ancestry was equally detestable. "It was not the Indian whom they [the New Englanders] saw in this lean, forked figure, with its elongated arms and long bony forefinger, pointing at the objects of its aversion as with a stick; it was not an Indian countenance they recognized in this parchment face, prematurely old and seamed with a thousand small wrinkles; in that bright, sharply sparkling eye; in the flattering, caressing tone and manner, which suddenly, with or without provocation, changed into wanton brutality. The Indian owns no such person or such temperament, which, if derived from any ancestry, belongs to an order of animated beings still nearer than the Indian to the jealous and predaceous instincts of dawning intelligence." The artful characterization, with its subtly contrived rhythm and its covert insult in hinting at the ape, challenged comparison with the eloquent invective of Randolph himself whose ability to "pour out a continuous stream of vituperation in well-chosen language and with sparkling illustration" extorted the envy of his enemies. Again and again, in this fashion, Adams richly pays and overpays the man for his half-century old defamation of John Quincy Adams. Randolph in the course of an excoriating attack upon President Adams and Clay had sneered, "I was defeated, horse, foot, and dragoons, — cut up and clean broke down by the coalition of Blifil and Black George, — by the combination, unheard of till then, of the Puritan with the blackleg." Adams knew his Fielding well enough to feel the full sting of the insult.[23]

Through each phase of the truculent Virginian's career, he shrewdly analyzes the motives that led him to betray repeatedly his principles and pretensions. He prided himself on the inflexibility of his republican principles, yet "he had talked and voted as his interests and passions dictated, supporting the questionable constitutionality of the Louisiana Purchase, intriguing for war with Spain, inciting the war with England." He became a hypocrite in spite of himself because of his inveterate tendency, fatal in a statesman, to allow his feelings to usurp his judgment and reason. In Gallatin's case circumstances had subverted his principles; his moral character remained pure. In Randolph, the antistatesman stood revealed. He subverted his own principles. By his advocacy of protection to the slavery interests he helped create the very centralism which he professed to abhor.[24]

For all his brilliant moralizing he behaved like a party hack in harness. For example, when the objectionable Judiciary Act of 1800 was repealed, Randolph and his party had the chance to apply their States' rights principles to the Supreme Court to prevent its becoming an agency for strengthening the central government. After all his attacks on the Adamses as the "American House of Stuart" he now had the chance to end forever the danger of monarchy or a centralized despotism. This was the crucial opportunity for "laying down those broad and permanent principles which the national legislature ought in future to observe in dealing with extensions of the central power." Instead he lost himself in aimless invective against the "monstrous ambition" of the Federalists to evade the Constitution. "That is all!" commented Adams. "Just enough to betray his purpose without justifying it; to show temper without proving courage or forethought! This was not the way in which Gallatin and Madison had led their side of the House." So once again Randolph forfeited his claim to fame. "He had, it may be, fixed his eyes somewhat too keenly on that phantom crown," said Adams, "and in imagination was wearing it himself — King John II." [25]

Time and again the balance kicks the beam beneath the

weight of Randolph's sins. "He was angry and had forgotten
his principles"; "Not patriotism but revenge inspired Randolph's passion"; "He stood in the gap with a courage fairly
to be called heroic, had it not been to so great an extent
the irrational outcome of an undisciplined and tyrannical
temper"; his rule as chairman of the Ways and Means
Committee was a "fusion of terrorism with lust for power";
he "instinctively disliked what other men adored"; he had
a "rebellious temper"; "his temper, more domineering than
ever"; his vanity was so childish that, "knowing no more law
than his own overseer," he recklessly pitted himself against
the invincible Luther Martin in the Chase impeachment
trial and "at last flung himself like a child on the ground
crushed by the consciousness that his mind could not follow
out a fixed train of thought." [26]

This was the hero whom Virginia had enshrined, a man
with a "devil within his breast." Swept along by the sheer
force of his own impassioned rhetoric, Adams added to
Randolph's burden of failings every weakness which troubled
him in his own temperament, veiled as usual in a broad
generalization. Randolph's was a "mind always controlled
by his feelings; its antipathies were stronger than its sympathy; it was restless and uneasy, prone to contradiction and
attached to paradox. In such a character there is nothing
very new, for at least nine men out of ten, whose intelligence
is above average, have felt the same instincts: the impulse
to contradict is as familiar as dyspepsia or nervous excit-
ability . . . but what was to be expected, when such a
temperament, exaggerated and unrestrained, full of self-con-
tradictions and stimulated by acute reasoning powers, remarkable audacity and quickness, violent and vindictive
temper, and a morbid constitution, was planted in a Virginian, a slave-owner, a Randolph, just when the world was
bursting into fire and flame?" [27]

Randolph's career after he went into full opposition to his party in 1808 Adams dismissed with contempt. It would be mere time lost to follow "the meanderings of his opposition." The break marked the dramatic moment of disillusionment when Randolph became finally convinced that his own party was "not less extravagant and dangerous than those Federalists whose doctrines he had begun by so furiously denouncing. To discover that one has made so vast a blunder is fatal to elevation of purpose; under the reaction of such disappointment no man can keep a steady course. The iron entered Randolph's soul. Now for the first time his habits became bad, and at intervals, until his death, he drank to excess." The program of political perversity that ensued, the rallying of the slave states under the States' rights banner, coincided with the accelerated decay of his mind and character. This fall from greatness provided the artistic denouement of the biography. To this moral catastrophe the plot had moved with all the pace and excitement of a stage play and from it emerges, in a triumph of portraiture, the figure of a malignant and ill-starred political genius, overwhelmed by the very defects of his virtues.[28]

The magisterial authority of Adams's sustained diatribe sweeps all doubts aside and the prosecutor seems sure of a hanging verdict. But at the very end a shadow of a doubt insinuates itself. The whole edifice of the analysis of the motives and character of Randolph may rest after all upon psychological quicksand. Was the moral question really settled? Not until the final page did Adams face the problem of Randolph's sanity, upon which his moral responsibility would have to rest. "On several occasions," he conceded, Randolph "was distinctly irresponsible," but whether he was actually insane or merely in a state of "excitement due to over-indulgence of temper and appetite is a question for experts to decide." Yet after such an uncompromising argument, the admission opened troublesome vistas. If experts pronounced it insanity, the moral condemnation might collapse. The hesitation proved only momentary. "Neither sickness nor suffering," Adams concluded, "is an excuse for habitual want of self-restraint." [29]

The qualities of the New England character that Henry Adams most admired were the Roman and stoical virtues of self-control, moderation, decorum, the neo-classic ideal of the eighteenth century gentleman. All his life he struggled to achieve them, to kennel that rebellious other self of his. An inflammable temper had always been the Adams cross. Franklin had had to cope with it in John Adams; Gallatin saved the Ghent negotiations from the irascibility of John Quincy Adams. Henry's own life had already had its share of passionate antipathies, of whimsical, even fantastic impulses. The imps of perversity, contradiction, and paradox colored his own vision, and he knew it and wittily apologized for them. He attacked these traits in Randolph as if by the very violence of his assault he might uproot them in himself. Somewhat ruefully he would jest that the Adamses always tended to form a party of one when they believed in the justice of their solitary and quixotic cause. In Randolph the trait was intolerable. In Randolph's railing obstructiveness toward the end of his life, when he felt himself in a hopeless minority, Adams may have sensed his own anarchic tendencies, seeing prefigured in Randolph's fate the sort of futility that might threaten his own.

With the cold pages of proof before him and the vehement afflatus gone, Adams disdained his production as "a very dull book," deprecating its shortcomings in his usual fashion. "The fault," he told Hay, "is in the enforced obligation to take that lunatic monkey *au sérieux*. I want to print some of his letters and those of his friends and, in order to do so, was obliged to treat him as though he were respectable."

There rose to the surface again the quaint philosophical strain so abhorred by his practical brother Charles. "Do you know," Henry remarked to Hay, "a book to me always seems a part of myself, a kind of intellectual brat or segment, and I never bring one into the world without a sense of shame. They are naked, helpless, and beggarly, yet the poor wretches must live forever and curse their father for their silent tomb. This particular brat is the first I ever detested. He is the only one I never wish to see again; but I know he will live to dance, in the obituaries, over my cold grave." A whimsical fancy it was, but Hay would have known how much it told of Adams's exorbitant pride and the unruly contradictory impulses that tossed him to and fro. Lodge intercepted one of those impulses a few weeks later while waiting for Adams's opinion of his just-published *Hamilton.* "Much as I want to read your *Hamilton,* the subject repels me more than my regard for you attracts. To say that I detest my own books is a mild expression, and I should be very sorry to feel so towards my friends' writing. I cannot read Bancroft's two volumes [*History of the Formation of the Constitution,* 1882] though the Appendices are very entertaining. Sometimes I seriously think my disgust for history will grow on me until it overpowers my perseverance." [30]

After its publication in October, 1882, John T. Morse hastened to thank Adams for the admirable way in which he had performed his assignment. Adams replied: "If you like 'Randolph' I am pleased, for you are the only person I was bound to satisfy. To me it is an unpleasant book, which sins against all my art canons. The acidity is much too decided. The rule of a writer should be that of a salad-maker; let the vinegar be put in by a miser; the oil by a spendthrift. In this case however the tone was really decided by the subject, and the excess of acid is his." Adams doubtless believed his own protestation, but whether he

sinned by rule or against rule he had once more proved the
family "instinct for the jugular" which had made him such
a formidable journalist. The higher imperative, that of read-
ability, he had fully realized. Several printings were called
for within a few years, the volume proving one of the most
popular in the series, and Adams kept a sharp eye on its
sales for the rest of his life. "After all," he once lectured his
brother Charles, in matters of literary style "it is the public
which controls us and in the long run we must obey the
beast." Harsh as his self-estimate was, he must have glowed
a little when Clarence King rhapsodized: "*Randolph* . . .
is a joy to me page by page . . . a model of literary art.
Seriously, I rank it as the best piece of American work. . . .
Your success is perfect." [31]

Editor Morse's subsequent repentance probably stemmed
from reviews like that of William Henry Smith, the writer
who some years later was to bedevil Adams's *History* under
the pseudonym of "Housatonic." Smith protested that Randolph was an unfit subject for the Series and he saw a "grim
humor" in the choice of Adams as biographer. "Having written the biography of the most malignant enemy that ever
crossed the path of John Quincy Adams, Mr. Henry Adams
should now employ his graceful and impartial pen in sketching the genius and labors of Alexander Hamilton, the man
who did more than all others to cut short the political career
of John Adams." He acknowledged, nonetheless, that Adams
had "made a most readable book, and one that will be useful to the student of American political history." A New
York paper contained "two columns of praise," but the Virginians, reported Mrs. Adams, "are very angry with it —
not that they defend Randolph, but the picture of his surroundings is not pleasing, though true." Adams made a
similar note for Lodge's benefit that "the Virginians are red-
hot at my introductory chapter. . . . Luckily for me, the

book is but a feeler for my history and I want the mud it stirs." Lodge, having praised the *Gallatin,* now contributed an anonymous review to the *Atlantic,* warmly recommending the *Randolph* as "one of the most effective books in the whole range of our historical literature." The *Nation* made reasonable amends for his brother Charles's disciplinary review of the *Gallatin.* True, the new book "dissected" Randolph as if he were a cadaver in a medical laboratory, but it was valuable to the "political student" as the most illuminating study of the decade which ended with the War of 1812. An "excellent piece of work," the small volume had more "general, if less special, interest than is contained in the two larger volumes of his predecessor [Garland]." Moses Coit Tyler's initial impression was unfavorable. He confided to his diary that he "got sleepy over it" and that except for the first two chapters it had "no literary merit"; but his review called it "intensely interesting." The Philadelphia *American* thought it "decidedly one of the best of the series of 'American statesmen.'" [32]

Two generations after the publication of the volume, time has added its own ironies to those of Adams. A Southern biographer of Randolph in 1922, while hotly defending Randolph against what he regarded as Adams's minor errors of fact and major abuses of interpretation, admitted, "There was nothing continental, nothing truly national about him. It will not do to apply to him as a statesman our current tests — an open-minded construction of the Federal Constitution; devotion to the ideal of national unity; faith in our expanding population, wealth and power . . . the awakening sense of international community. . . ." Thirty years later an evangelical reactionary saw him as a heroic disciple of Edmund Burke and a defender of conservatism. "And although Randolph's sovereign states have been beaten down at one time and bribed into submission at another; although every eco-

nomic measure he denounced has been made a permanent
policy of our national government; although the plantation
is desolate and the city triumphant — still, Randolph's system of thought has its adherents. He has helped to insure
us against reckless consolidation and arbitrary power. His
love of personal and local liberties, his hatred of privilege,
his perception of realities behind political metaphysics, his
voice lifted against the god Whirl — these things endure."
Perhaps Henry Adams might counter that once more the
doctrine of States' rights has been perverted to serve a dubious cause.[33]

2   The Mephistopheles of Politics

In later life Adams liked to recall with a certain amount
of sardonic self-satisfaction that he had burned many offending manuscripts to save his self-respect. How far this was
literally true and how far a characteristic exaggeration it is
now impossible to say. But Adams's remark seems only too
true so far as it applies to his biography of Aaron Burr. That
it was completed and practically ready for publication is an
unquestionable fact. Morse evidently indicated sufficient interest in Burr for Adams to plunge into the writing immediately after the draft of the *Randolph* was completed.[34]

Once the *Randolph* was on its way through the press,
Adams glanced again at the *Burr*, which he had set aside in
August, 1881. The manuscript had safely passed Mrs. Adams's
scrutiny; in fact she thought the *Burr* "much better" than the
Randolph. When Hay expressed a "sympathetic interest" in
Adams's "ideal scamp," Adams's reply reflected the growing
uncertainty about its publication. Burr "was never a safe
scoundrel to deal with and may well run away and cheat

the world again; but I tote about a hundred-weight of manuscript far more valuable than his, and he must bide his
time. . . . In truth I rather grudge the public my immortal
writings." The thought mounted, he cantered off as usual.
"My ideal of authorship would be to have a famous *double*
with another name, to wear what honors I could win. How
I should enjoy upsetting him at last by publishing a low
shameless essay with smutty woodcuts in his name." "Smutty"
silently vanished from the published version of this letter.
The matter ceased to be the stuff of whimsy when Houghton
Mifflin declined to publish the book in its series "because,"
as Adams fumed, "Aaron wasn't a 'statesman.' Not bad that
for a damned bookseller! He should live a while at Washington and know our *real* statesmen." It was the second time
Houghton had crossed him. Their first dispute, over the political content of an issue of the *North American,* had induced Adams to resign the editorship.[35]

Nettled by the rebuff, and not knowing that the misgivings
were really Morse's, he told him, "I want you to understand
that my offer to write Burr was an offer to *you,* not to
Houghton, to help you out in your editing. I would not choose
Houghton for a publisher, and for many reasons prefer to
publish in New York or Philadelphia." He would therefore
try Harper or Appleton. Apparently neither firm showed enthusiasm. In December, 1882, he had decided to publish the
following spring "on his own hook." Three weeks later that
scheme was off and he was undecided "what to do with
Burr." Harassed by the pressure of work on the major opus,
he soon wrote fretfully to Hay, "Aaron Burr is not to be
printed at present. He is to wait a few years. I hate publishing, and do not want reputation. There are not more than
a score of people in America whose praise I want, and the
number will grow with time. So Aaron will stay in his drawer

and appear only as the outrider for my first two volumes of history, about a year before they appear, which may give Aaron three or four more years of privacy." [36]

During the winter another member of the Houghton firm, Osgood, offered to publish the book outside of the series. Adams testily replied that he had made other arrangements. Morse, his conscience still uneasy, tried again in the following autumn and drew down another lecture upon his head. Adams would have nothing further to do with Houghton. "Many thanks for your kind interest in Burr. Perhaps it was you who put Osgood up to asking for it last winter. . . . The 'Burr' was written to help your series, if you wanted help. On the general principle of always backing one's friends, if one's friends need backing, I was glad to give you something which I knew would make a sensation. . . . If you want the volume for your series, with your name on it, I will not refuse it; but I don't propose to be dictated to by any damned publisher. . . . I will add that, for reasons connected with the appearance of my 'History,' I have decided in any case to withhold the 'Burr' another year from publication. If the 'history' cannot appear before 1886, the 'Burr' will not appear before 1885." [37]

Beyond these indications there is no further trace of the manuscript of Adams's biography of Aaron Burr nor any further allusion to it in Adams's enormous correspondence. Undoubtedly it was destroyed in one of the periodical holocausts by which Adams purged his files in anticipation of his literary executor. A half century after the incident, Morse said, "If I had desired a life of Burr for the Series, my friend Henry Adams's name would have stood like a forlorn, a very forlorn hope at the bottom of the list of possible writers." Whether he had unintentionally encouraged Adams to expect publication in the series or, having encouraged him, got cold feet when he saw what Adams had done to Burr, remains an open question. Adams's manuscript may well have confirmed Morse's opinion that a life of the traitorous Burr did not belong in a series of American statesmen. One thing is clear, at least, that the firm was willing to publish the book, for its own sensational value.[38]

Why Adams should have suppressed a completed, publishable book is hardly to be explained by mere pique. His ordinary habit was to be economical of his literary materials, to file them carefully, to revise and re-use them. The revisions of *Chapters of Erie* and the salvaging of some of the essays for the later *Historical Essays* suggests his customary thrift. There is no suggestion in his references to the book that Adam was dissatisfied with its literary merits. He obviously thought it good enough for the Statesmen Series. The *Burr* would also have stirred up interest as an "outrider" to the *History* to follow. This important value would be lost if publication were deferred until the whole main project was afloat. Finally, it should be noted that the cost of private publication, if he defiantly elected it, posed no obstacle whatever.

It may well be that the mystery of the destroyed manuscript is simply that there is no mystery, that Adams worked the main sections of the book into the relevant chapters of the *History*, finding it easier to do that than to attempt a wholly fresh departure. Having taken the heart out of the manuscript, he would hardly be tempted to do a new biography and the *disjecta membra* would ultimately find their way to the flames of the study fireplace. A comparison of the structure of the published *Randolph* with the corresponding sections of the "History" suggests what may have happened. In that biography he dealt at considerable length with Randolph's career as majority leader in Jefferson's administration; but once Randolph went into opposition Adams lost interest and hurried over the remainder of his life in a rather

summary way except for his struggle with J. Q. Adams and
Henry Clay. The center of his interest was the administration of Jefferson and Madison and the movement of national
rather than sectional politics. Randolph as a sectional leader
of a lost cause did not fit into the main line of development.
In fact, much the same thing was true of the *Gallatin*. Adams's
overriding interest in Gallatin as a national political figure
precluded much attention to his later career. Burr's significant participation in American national history clearly ended
with the collapse of his treasonable conspiracy. His subsequent travels in Europe and his later career as a New York
lawyer could hardly have tempted Adams's sensation-seeking
pen. Moreover, a long anticlimax would have been inartistic.
The proper dramatic climax is depicted in the *History* at the
close of the chapter recounting the political rivalries that led
up to Burr's duel with Hamilton. Hamilton, made reckless
by hatred and disgust, left a note stating that he would
throw away the first fire. If he were martyred, Burr's power
would surely be destroyed. "The death of Hamilton," wrote
Adams, "and the Vice-President's flight, with the accessories
of summer-morning sunlight on rocky and wooded heights,
tranquil river, and distant city, and behind all, their dark
background of moral gloom, double treason, and political
despair, still stand as the most dramatic moment in the early
politics of the Union." From this moment Burr's own fate
was sealed, though the mad comedy of his conspiracy remained to be told.[39]

Substantial parts of the *History* are devoted to Aaron Burr,
so much space in fact that he afterward felt obliged to ra-
tionalize it as a concession to popular curiosity about Burr.
He figures as one of the three "denationalizing forces" in the
United States. Timothy Pickering and the Essex Junto in
New England were one; John Randolph and his intransigeant
Virginians were another; and Aaron Burr and his fellow

adventurers in Louisiana were the third. One block of five chapters, nearly one hundred and fifty pages, is devoted to Burr's Conspiracy and his attempted escape, a concluding chapter of thirty pages to his trial and acquittal. Setting aside the many other short passages devoted to Burr's earlier political activities, passages probably drafted after he wrote the *Burr*, these six chapters alone would amount to more than half a volume the length of the *Randolph*. Significantly, the space which the *History* devoted to the Essex Junto and the Hartford Convention was less than one-third that given exclusively to Burr. Burr also had had his role in the prelude to the Essex Junto when the extreme Federalists, Pickering and Griswold, turned to him as a possible leader for their faction. The moment was pure theatre. "The idea implied a bargain and an intrigue on terms such as in the Middle Ages the Devil was believed to impose upon the ambitious and reckless. Pickering and Griswold could win their game only by bartering their souls; they must invoke the Mephistopheles of politics, Aaron Burr." Burr's escapade was a more sensational thing and lent itself to more dramatic treatment, but it had little of the importance of the New England movement; its political and constitutional significance was minuscule and its chances for success far more slight. Adams himself says "the conspiracy of Burr was a mere episode, which had little direct connection with foreign or domestic politics and no active popular support in any quarter." [40]

Why he devoted such a disproportionate share of space in the *History* to the Burr Conspiracy may most readily be accounted for by the fact that it was ready to hand as the core of the Burr biography and was undeniably interesting in itself. His laborious experience in transforming the Randolph materials for the *History* must have been instructive — and rather sobering. Having published a political biography

of Randolph, he had to refashion the materials completely to
give them a fresh look for the *History*. Consider, for example, "John Randolph's schism" which in the biography he
had called "The Quarrel." The schism grew out of Randolph's
violent dissatisfaction with Jefferson's secret and devious
scheme to maneuver Napoleon into selling West Florida by
tempting him with an American offer to bar British imports.
The revised version of the transaction required a painstaking
reworking of the narrative; not a line dared be duplicated
except in a quotation. The biography reads as follows:

On March 5, 1806, he [Randolph] began his long public career
of opposition. Mr. Gregg of Pennsylvania had offered a resolution
for prohibiting the importation of British goods. . . . Mr. Crowninshield supported the measure in a speech strongly warlike in
tone. . . . Mr. Crowninshield was a New England democrat, a
thorough supporter of Mr. Jefferson, a 'Yazoo man'. . . . On all
these accounts he was an object of hatred to Randolph, who rose
when he sat down. First he gave Mr. Crowninshield a stinging
blow in the face: "I am not surprised to hear men advocate these
wild opinions. . . . It is mere waste of time to reason with such
persons. They do not deserve anything like serious refutation.
The proper arguments for such statesmen are a strait-waistcoat, a
dark room, water gruel, and depletion." Then, after a few
words on the dispute with England . . . he hit one of his striking illustrations: "What shall this great mammoth of the American
forest leave his native element and plunge into the water in a
mad contest with the shark!" [41]

In the *History* Randolph's opposition received a more powerful and surer handling. "Not until March 5, 1806, did Gregg
call up his Resolution." There followed a long quotation from
Gregg's speech and one from Crowninshield's. The *History*
then proceeds,

When Crowninshield sat down, John Randolph took the floor.
In Randolph's long career of oratorical triumphs, no such moment
had offered itself before, or was to occur again. Still in Virginian
eyes the truest and ablest Republican in Congress, the representative of power and principle, the man of the future, Randolph
stood with the halo of youth, courage and genius round his

head, — a sort of Virginian Saint Michael, almost terrible in his contempt for whatever seemed to him base or untrue. He began by saying that he entered on the subject "manacled, handcuffed, and tongue-tied." . . . and with this preamble he fell upon Gregg and Crowninshield: — "It is mere waste of time to reason with such persons. . . ." The proposed confiscation of British property called out a sneer at Crowninshield. . . . Again and again he turned aside to express contempt for the Northern democrats: — "Shall this great mammoth of the American forest leave his native element and plunge into the water in a mad contest with the shark?"

The quotations from the celebrated speech are largely the same, but the descriptive matrix immensely sharpens the dramatic progression. Instead of blunting that progression by announcing the result at the beginning he saved the summary to the end. "At length, April 7, Randolph committed his last and fatal blunder by going formally into opposition." The most striking addition is, of course, the imaginative tableau of Randolph standing in the well of the House as a "Virginian St. Michael." [42]

Adams obviously viewed the published biography as a preliminary draft and, with his passion for revision, greatly improved it. The animus against Randolph which gave unity of tone to the biography was subdued to the larger perspective of the *History* where his very real virtues are allowed in a measure to extenuate his eccentricities. There are also far fewer condemnatory phrases, perhaps the result of the outcries from Virginia. But the significant point is that not only is Randolph somewhat more humanized, there is a more discriminating depiction of his personality as an actor in the political serio-comedy.

The treatment of Burr and his conspiracy in the *History* exhibits an oddly different spirit even though one concedes the justice of Ford's remark that "the historian who discovered Aaron Burr was Henry Adams." Burr in the extended account of the plot and the trial scarcely emerges as an individual;

the felicitous epithets that surround the image of Randolph and lift him from the background are absent. There is hardly any sustained effort to vivify him as the "ideal scamp," to expose the "charlatan," or dramatize the "Mephistopheles." The only truly sensational aspect of the story is the evidence that shows the dishonorable conduct of General Wilkinson, the American general-in-chief, who received a secret retainer of $2,000 a year from the King of Spain, a treasonable relation confirmed by documents Adams had obtained from the Spanish archives. The hundred page section on Burr that followed the material relating to Randolph has little of the literary glow so marked in the treatment of Randolph. There is, of course, the intrinsic excitement of the melodramatic intrigue, of the chase and final capture, a glimpse of Burr in a sleazy disguise, another briefer glimpse of his attempt to elude his captors by leaping off his horse, a succession of "dramatic tableaux" as Ford has called them. But the sense of comedy is asserted rather than shown. "Between Captain MacHeath and Colonel Burr was more than one point of resemblance, and the 'Beggar's Opera' could have been easily paralleled within the prison at Richmond; but no part of Burr's career was more humorous than the gravity with which he took an injured tone." [43]

From an Olympian standpoint Burr's grandiose schemes were hardly the stuff of unquenchable laughter and Adams's feeling of wry humor remains largely private. The final trial scene at the Eagle Tavern, where the reader catches his last view of Burr, is singularly lacking in color, though the legal and political interest was in fact intense. Burr is simply extinguished as a cowardly and vulgar swindler, a kind of cipher at his own trial. The descent from Vice President to swindler may have been more comic than tragic, but Adams let the opportunity slip for a final touch of either John Gay or Beaumarchais. The absence of personal shading, of psychological insight, and artistic emphasis, all the qualities which marked the revised portrait of Randolph, suggest that Adams lost interest in Burr and incorporated large portions of the manuscript without rewriting them in the way he rewrote the Randolph materials. However, in spite of its depreciation of the man, Adams's account of Burr had the very considerable virtue of bringing him out of the shadow of the duel with Hamilton. Long afterward, brooding over the obstructionist tactics of the Senate, he recalled Burr with a certain respect, saying, "I have always been impressed by the parting speech of that otherwise overrated scoundrel Aaron Burr, on going out of office as Vice-President: 'If the Constitution is to perish, its dying agonies will be seen on this floor.'" [44]

In adapting the Burr narrative there would not have been the same necessity for revision since the Burr biography was unpublished when the corresponding section of the *History* was being written. If, as here suggested, a substantial part of the *Burr* was incorporated, without significant change, Adams's plan to publish it as an "outrider" was no longer feasible, the outrider having been impressed into the ranks. He would have had to turn once more from the *History* and rework the biography in order to give it an independent character, a thankless task at that point. Moreover, his annoyance with the publishers for turning down the manuscript was real enough. He was sensitive as well about the sales of the *Gallatin* and the *New England Federalism* and had already convinced himself, with a degree of wry petulance, that "there is a rooted opposition which amounts to conspiracy" against the reading of his books. The idea of being obliged to publish the rejected manuscript on his own could hardly have pleased his second thoughts as a practising historian. The silent assimilation of the book into the *History* would cut all the knots with a single stroke.[45]

3 Work and the Flight of Years

With the two maleficent figures exorcized, as if they were
fetish counterparts of Blaine and Conkling, Adams resolutely
turned again to his *History*, a little ashamed of his preoccupation with the two most fantastic personalities in the Jeffersonian entourage. "I have worked very steadily and have
felt for the first time a sort of nervous fear of losing time,"
he apologized to Lodge to explain his neglect of friends. "I
have but one off-spring, and am nearly forty-four while it is
nothing but an embryo." There was little time to brood about
the fate of the Burr manuscript. "Life is passing too fast for
me to bother much about anything." By the end of January,
1882, he had gotten "to the end of Chase's impeachment and
the close of my first four years, the easiest quarter of my
time. Heaven only knows whether the result is readable. As
yet I have not yet put it together so as to be read, but I
keep hammering ahead, day by day, without looking back-
wards." Reminded of the new biographies of Cobden and
Lyell, men whom he had known well, he felt a shiver of
incredulity. "It is not only the *fugaces annos*, but the *fugaces
continentes* that bewilder me with a sense of leading several
lives." [46]
Nonetheless he felt that he had hit his stride. Life was
full to overflowing: five hours daily at his desk writing, two
in the saddle, and the remainder, society. He hugged his
satisfaction close. "Indeed, if I felt a perfect confidence that
my history would be what I would like to make it, this part
of life — from forty to fifty — would be all I want. There
is a summer-like repose about it; a self-contained, irresponsible, devil-may-care indifference to the future as it looks to
younger eyes; a feeling that one's bed is made, and one can

rest on it till it becomes necessary to go to bed forever." [47]
The summer of 1882 whirled by at Beverly Farms in a
surge of unremitting labor. He had gone north again with a
certain feeling of relief, for as the Washington season closed,
he had felt himself surrounded by "a hospital of broken-down
family and friends," his father "an amiable and contented"
wreck, his mother ill, his brother Brooks, who had languished
with him for three weeks, "in pieces, used up," Hay "barely
able to get home to Cleveland, with palpitations of the heart."
King had nearly died in the wilderness from "the opening of
an old rupture," and his third friend, Richardson, stricken
with Bright's disease, defiantly joined the other two for a
jaunt to Europe. Contemplating the somber outlook in the
Quincy homestead that year, he reported his musings to
Gaskell. "A very few years more will bring me and my generation into the fifties and start us down the home quarter.
I am working very hard to get everything out of my brain
that can be made useful. If my father is a test, I can count
on twenty years more brain, if the physical machine holds
out. Do you know that you and I have corresponded for
about that time? The other day it occurred to me that
Thackeray had written a ballad about an old man alone and
merry at forty, dipping his nose in the gascon wine, and I
laughed as though it were a joke." [48]

The turn of the year found him "grinding out history with
more or less steadiness," occasionally fretful against the tyr-
annies of on-coming middle age, the recurring bouts of
rheumatism, the traitorous behavior of his teeth, and the old
enemy that sometimes interdicted the joys of the table. "I
am very irritable," ran one note to Hay, "and several gentlemen who have been dead these fifty years, are catching
singular fits in Hell on account of my dyspepsia." In this
mood he looked with jaundiced eye upon Jefferson, Madison,
and Monroe. He found himself "incessantly forced to devise

excuses and apologies or to admit that no excuse will avail. I am at times almost sorry that I ever undertook to write their history, for they appear like mere grasshoppers kicking and gesticulating on the middle of the Mississippi River. There is no possibility of reconciling their theories with their acts, or their extraordinary foreign policy with dignity." He was resolved in spite of the handicap that his work should be "readable," at least as readable as Macaulay, whose life he was then enjoying in the English Men of Letters series. His target now was to get out two trade volumes in 1885, covering the first administration of Jefferson.[49]

Another summer came and he secluded himself in the playhouse in the woods which his wife had built for her nieces, working at his typewriter "like a belated beaver," according to his wife, "from nine to five every day, garbling the history of his native land as run by antedeluvian bosses." His version to Hay sounded a plaintive note. "I toil and moil, painfully and wearily, forward and back, over my little den of history, and am too dry-beat to read novels. [An allusion to Hay's *Breadwinners*] I would I were on a mule in the Rockies with you and King, but at forty-five every hour is golden and will not return. I painfully coin it into printer's ink, and shall have a big volume of seven hundred pages to show *you* next winter. As it gets into type I cower before it in hope and fear, for it is all I shall make of this droll toy called life." Sometimes the fear was strong. Perhaps he would not publish. "Keen Savvy? as our slang goes. I would rather let the stuff lie till I'm dead." And in the same mood to Gaskell, "There is a kind of pleasure and triumph in proving to oneself that one does not care a nickel cent for the opinion of one's fellowmen." After all his work amused him and seemed "worth quite as much as the work I see of other people." He saw no use "in fashing oneself about success." [50]

It was hard to make up one's mind wholly about this craving for success that drove his friends, as well as himself, in almost hysterical pursuit of the phantom. His own notion of it had its touch of Romantic disdain. "The world is made up of very few *real* people," he said to Holmes, congratulating him on his appointment to the Massachusetts Supreme Court; "only a few score, I think; and anything which encourages in the hope that we are one of these realities is the highest encouragement." Sardonically, he foresaw the fate of his own work in the "humiliating" reception of Francis Parkman's *Montcalm and Wolfe*. A first edition of only fifteen hundred copies was printed, "when," as he said, "ten thousand ought to be a very moderate supply." It was patent that his chief reward would have to be "the brevet of literary aristocracy." Yet as a historian he would have to run the gauntlet of popular criticism. Under such conditions of national intellectual apathy, the presumption of the average critic seemed more intolerable than ever, all the more so perhaps because his own conscience was not clear on that score. Adverse criticism had always made him suffer. Commiserating with Hay for the attacks on *Breadwinners,* he confessed, "Every now and then in my life, my critics succeeded in making me feel very seasick for a day or two. I am a sensitive cuss and a coward. When I get a real whipping, I feel kind of low about it." Recalling his own career of lethal journalism, he formulated the strategy by which he would abide; "I never fight except with intent to kill, and you can't kill a critic. . . . Reply is like scratching their match for them. I have been one, I know." [51]

Chapter Seven

The Warfare Between Science
and Religion

1 A Literary Conundrum

FOR a temperament as restless as that of Adams the only relaxation which he could allow himself was a complete change of pace, a new project, as if the freedom from the necessity of earning his living imposed a higher imperative of deserving his freedom. The moment that he came to a halting place in the seemingly interminable *History*, he turned to the writing of another novel, *Esther*. Presumably he wrote the novel in an extraordinary burst of creative activity during the latter part of the very quiet summer at the seashore, for early in November, 1883, he was simultaneously correcting proof on it while reading proof on the first volume of his history. And with his left hand, so to speak, he turned out a historical article in French for his friend Gabriel Monod of the *Revue Historique*.

By some miracle of domestic management all these projects raced on without interfering with an extraordinarily active social life. Henry and his wife commonly avoided large receptions as "twaddle business," even begging off once from a diplomatic gathering across the way at the White House to which the Secretary of State had personally invited them. The "nauseating society rabble" was not for them, but private receptions and dinners and theatre parties were another mat-

ter. Once again Mrs. Adams's letters of that season read like
a roll call of the eminent. More than ever Washington permitted "the kind of dinner one can have only here and the
only kind that amuses us." Still there were frequent quiet
evenings reading by the fire and the oft sighed-for pleasure
of an early curfew. Photography became a deepening preoccupation as Marian mastered the new platinum-type process. When the artist F. D. Millett came down to lobby for
removal of the tariff on works of art and spent a few days
with them, there was a great flurry of picture taking, the
artist draping his pretty wife in statuesque poses.[1]

Their friend Gilder of the *Century* pressed Adams to do
a sketch to accompany Mrs. Adams's fine photograph of old
George Bancroft, but she declined for both of them saying,
"Mr. Adams does not fancy the prevailing literary vivisection.
The way in which Howells butters Harry James and Harry
James Daudet and Daudet some one else is not pleasant."
For Hay's understanding eye, Adams remarked, "The mutual
admiration business is not booming now. Between ourselves,
there is in it always an air of fatuous self-satisfaction fatal
to the most grovelling genius." [2]

A fresh and agreeable distraction seized them before the
end of 1883. They decided to build a house. Corcoran had
sold the lot next to their house at 1607 H Street and plans were
ominously afoot for a seven-story apartment house. For more
than a year they had been uneasy "about our future life —
in this world," doubtful of the smoke and darkness that would
be cast upon them and of the chance their absurdly moderate rent would soar. Hay, a millionaire since the recent
death of his father-in-law, leaped into the breach and bought
the entire corner tract, conveying the west 44 feet to Adams
on January 14, 1884. Squarely opposite the White House it
was indeed, as Adams crowed, "a swell piece of land." Even
before the deal was concluded, Adams had "drawn to scale

the whole interior." They knew just what they wanted, "a square brick box with flat roof — pine finish — " and fireplaces, of course, in every room, and not subservient to steam heat as in the Anderson mansion where the fireplaces were "only for show." People born west of the Alleghenies did not "understand cosiness in the New England sense." For $30,000 they counted on getting a "squalid shanty — no stained glass — no carving — no nothing," a thoroughly functional house and small stable. One feature would be decidedly omitted, "a company parlor." They did not wish "a fine house, only an unusual one." Amazed at her own impulsiveness, Mrs. Adams wrote, "I who have always been utterly opposed to building am the one who jumped first. I like to change my mind all of a sudden." [3]

They engaged H. H. Richardson as architect, now much in demand after his triumphant — and expensive — design for the Nicholas Andersons. They planned at first for adjoining entrances with the Hays on H Street, but Richardson, insisting on a symmetrical treatment of the double mass, was inexorable. Hay must face on 16th Street. After a session with the ebullient Richardson, Adams chortled that their house would be simply "unutterably utter . . . a laughing stock of the American people for generations to come." Hay ought to hurry back from Cleveland for another "architectural Belshazzar." Richardson, enormous of girth and height, regal in a bright yellow waist-coat, his rush of speech made turbulent by a slight halt in his utterance, swept his clients away with him. Dilatory as usual he did not get the plans to them for six more months, but they conceded he dealt with their sketches "like a master." There remained much negotiation as Hay wanted more land for a rose garden, and in the middle of things he dashed off to London for two months with King, leaving Adams with a power of attorney and a free hand to get the two houses under way. Being next door to the site, husband and wife could watch "every brick and plank," and make photographs of the progress. Fascinated by the details of allocating costs, Adams sent on to Hay elaborate tables of figures, finally arriving at his share of the price of the land as approximately $28,000.[4]

In the midst of all this delightful stir, the more serious business of Adams's career went on with extraordinary intensity and concentration. The private edition of six copies of the first massive volume of the *History* was at last on his desk in the first days of February of 1884, the wide margins and interleaved blank pages ready for the comments of the little group of private critics to whom he sent copies, George Bancroft, Hay, Abram Hewitt, Carl Schurz, MacVeagh, and his brother Charles. He thought he would be ready to "reprint" the book in two conventional volumes in 1886. He felt sure he had made it readable, though not to Englishmen, for as he explained to Gaskell, "I am writing for a continent of a hundred million people fifty years hence; and I can't stop to think what England will read." [5]

But the *History*, consciously aimed at American posterity, gave little scope for the tumult of his thought as he responded to the fresh currents of ideas that were eroding all familiar mental landmarks in his society. It was that other book, *Esther*, so quietly and circumspectly issued in March, 1884, as to die still-born, that leaped into existence out of the deeper levels of his being. He must reach not posterity but America of the present, tormented moment. He too felt obliged to come to grips with the issues that were agitating social thinkers everywhere, issues that had sprung forth from the Pandora's box of modern science, overshadowing even politics and economics. Science, as Clarence King had said, was "clearing away the endless rubbish of false ideas from the human intellect," but that clearing away had now reached the foundations of the great social institutions, the Church and the Family, and the old and the new order challenged each other in attitudes ranging from despairing hostility to hopeful reconciliation under the rival shibboleths of Religion and Science.[6]

The circumstances of the publication of *Esther* are not the least of its interest. Adams was in a mood to experiment, to play a kind of serious hoax, to prove something to himself like one of Hawthorne's characters in the grip of an obsession. Annoyed by what he thought was the parasitic nature of the book publishing business, he persuaded Henry Holt to publish the novel without the customary advertising, wanting to see whether it could make its way in the world without factitious aids and puffing. Perhaps he was taken with the quixotic idea of reviving the amenities of eighteenth century England, when reputations were made by the word of mouth of discriminating readers and authorship carried social consideration, if a gentleman writer chose to make himself known. Naturally he guaranteed the costs of the experiment. To make sure that the book should be judged solely on its merits, Adams adopted the pseudonym Frances Snow Compton. Reluctantly Holt humored his friend's whimsical scheme, issuing the book as the third in his new dollar series of quality novels. This time he maintained absolute secrecy about the authorship after due warning by Adams. The few, who in time were let into the secret, were equally discreet, and the identity of the author did not become known until 1918. There seems no reason to doubt that Marian Adams, who was constantly with him, was in on the secret and read the novel as his favorite private critic. Her unpublished letters of 1883–1885 to her father show that she kept the secret of the authorship of *Esther* as well as she had kept that of *Democracy*.[7]

The title was left out of the publisher's regular advertising and no review copies seem to have been distributed in the

United States, except to the *Publisher's Weekly*. That publication limited itself to a paragraph which reads very much like the conventional publisher's handout.

Quite unconventional in plot, characters, and denouement. Esther is a New York girl of good social position, who has been educated in an unusual manner. She has been taught no religious belief, and has been allowed perfect independence in choosing her friends and arranging her life. She is a fine artist, and her studio is the lounging place of several notable men. One of them, an Episcopal clergyman, loves her, and is after a struggle accepted by her. The story shows their mutual unfitness for each other — neither being willing to make any concession of opinion — and the final rupture of their engagement.

Adams held out against Holt's suggestion for "whooping up" the book, but by early January of 1885 he was ready to concede, "My experiment has failed." In his own circle the book sank without a trace and he was denied the pleasure of listening to sophisticated comments about the work of his "double" while hugging the secret of its authorship. "So far as I know," he complained to Holt, "not a man, woman or child has ever read or heard of *Esther*. . . . My inference is that America reads nothing — advertised or not — except magazines." [8]

The disappointment was all the more keen because there was no question in his mind that the novel deserved success alongside the flood of mediocre potboilers, an opinion that can still be sustained by a careful reading of the novel. In spite of the deliberate conspiracy of silence, five hundred copies of the edition of one thousand were sold the first year. The circulating libraries acquired copies and many nameless folk who knew nothing of Lafayette Square and its genteel vagaries presumably enjoyed the work. [9]

Possessed by his maggot, Adams was helplessly borne along. He urged Holt to try a further experiment; "I want to test English criticism and see whether it amounts to more

than our own. As you know, I care very little for readers
and dread notoriety more than dyspepsia; but I like the
amusement of a literary conundrum." He proposed that Holt
should bring out *Esther* in England and pair it with one
other novel in the new series. "Both to be advertised in the
same words and places. No clue or hint should be given that
might give one volume an advantage, or offer a stimulus to
the critics." He proposed the use of two books, fearing that
the "single challenge" by *Esther* alone "might suggest a clue
which I meant to hide." Mrs. Ward's shrewd guess about
Democracy suggested dangers. Practical difficulties of book-
keeping and copyright, of secretly underwriting the financing
of the companion volume by another author finally led to the
abandonment of that part of the new test, and *Esther* faced
its English audience alone. The one review in the *Athenaeum*,
a piece of superficial journalism, left the conundrum essentially unsolved. "Like many another American novel," the
reviewer declared, this one was "clever and inconclusive. It
gives the reader the impression that the writer's chief object
is to show that she is up to the mark in art, science, religion,
agnosticism, and society. . . . The study (for it can hardly
be called a story) is wanting in human interest." [10]

Whimsy aside, Adams's reasons for anonymity in this case
were probably much the same as those which applied to
Democracy. Again it was a *roman à clef*, a number of his
intimates serving as models or supplying traits of character.
One of the most prominent, Strong, clearly showed the linea-
ments of Clarence King. Esther, the central figure, drew very
heavily on Marian Adams. Marian's father figured importantly
in it as did La Farge, Elizabeth Cameron, and Phillips Brooks.
Having seen the virulence of the attacks on the labor and social thesis of Hay's *Breadwinners* as well as the storm raised
in the United States by the iconoclasms of his own *Democracy*, he was understandably reluctant to be drawn into con-

troversy over the explosive religious issue. It was enough that
the family was already notorious for political heterodoxy
without adding religious to it. In any case, Adams preferred
to wait until his *History* had made its mark before he challenged critics in his own name. "Remember," he told the impatient Holt, "that authors, if not publishers, have to look
many years ahead and yet sometimes miss their mark. Five
years, at least, is necessary for me to get ready for pushing
things. If I die meanwhile, you have a sure card, and need
not be uneasy about holding it back." Moreover, if the book
were to be reprinted, he planned, as he said, to make a few
minor revisions.[11]

In the light of his practical — and impractical — calculations concerning it at this time, the reader must be wary
of treating *Esther* too exclusively as a symbol of his marriage.
Unquestionably it was a deeply felt exploration of his mind
and feelings, but it was no thinly veiled confessional. Like
many another literary artist, he freely exploited himself and
his immediate environment for the purposes of his novel and
with sufficient detachment to make it a tour de force of ideas.
The only other allusions he made to the book came after Mrs.
Adams's tragic death, when it was inevitable that he should
read back new meanings and should feel a special sacredness
about it for its many private echoes. The ambiguity about
the precise autobiographical bearing of the novel derives
chiefly from a comment he later made about it. Allowed at
last to read it, Hay sent his fulsome praise to Adams then
seeking diversion in Japan and urged him to avow authorship. "Perhaps I made a mistake even to tell King about it,"
Adams replied; "but having told him I could not leave you
out. Now, let it die! To admit the public to it would be
almost unendurable to me. I will not pretend that the book
is not precious to me, but its value has nothing to do with
the public who could never understand that such a book

might be written in one's heart's blood. Do not even imagine
that I scorn the public, as you say. Twenty years ago I
would have been glad to please it. . . ." Five years later
when the *History* was at last a fully accomplished fact, he
wrote to Mrs. Cameron, "I care more for one chapter, or any
dozen pages of *Esther* than for the whole history, including
maps and indexes; so much more indeed, that I would not
let anyone read the story for fear the reader should pro-
fane it." [12]

The *Esther* of these two letters is obviously a quite different thing from the matter-of-fact subject of Adams's negotiations with Holt. In a long facetious letter to Hay, when
the book was going into proof, and Adams was making some
rather shrewd if topsy turvy criticisms of Hay's novel, he
gave not the slightest hint of any soul-shattering creative
experience or ordeal just finished. He believed that the higher
reaches of feminine character had yet to be adequately explored by a novelist. "Howells cannot deal with gentlemen
or ladies; he always slips up. James knows almost nothing of
women but the mere outside; he never had a wife." In *Esther*
Adams attempted a more authentic "portrait of a lady." In
the light of what subsequently happened, it is easy enough
to see the reason for Adams's altered attitude and to understand the extraordinary emotional fetish that he attached to
the book. There was a sufficient vestige of superstition in his
sceptical make-up that the book must have come to seem
a piece of genuine clairvoyance, as if somehow he had pierced
the visible mask of reality. Clarence King afterwards spelled
the matter out to Hay with his usual clarity. Henry "conceived the quaint archaic project of putting forth the novel
without any notices or advertisements to see if a dull world
would do their own criticising and appreciate his work. Later
came to his mind a second reason why he should let the
novel lie where it had fallen in the silent depths of American

stupidity and that was a feeling of regret at having exposed his wife's religious experiences and, as it were, made of her a chemical subject *vis à vis* religion, as in *Democracy* he had shown her in contact with politics. Later when Dr. Hooper died of heart failure, as the old man in *Esther* died, he felt that it was too personal and private a book to have brought into its due prominence, so he has let it die." [13]

2 The Dilemmas of Determinism

The novel undoubtedly germinated in the highly charged intellectual atmosphere of the Adams salon where the Five of Hearts held a kind of communal court. All was grist to the mill of conversation, one may be sure, but once facetiousness and wit had their inning at the dinner table, good talk, like brandy and cigars, would assert its claim to the chief place before the hearth. The skirmishes which Adams had witnessed as a young man at the American legation in London, his head whirled about and intoxicated by the promise of the new science, the great emancipator of the mind, could now be seen as only the prelude to a vast intellectual and social revolution. Comte had taught his age: "Ideas govern the world, or throw it into chaos." On every hand there were growing signs of chaos. In America as in England, Darwin's evolutionism was the catalyst idea, but in America it immensely accelerated the disintegrative effect of the belated industrial revolution that came in the wake of the Civil War. In a world of atomized institutions, no anchor seemed capable of holding against the current which was dislodging so many settled attitudes and values. Society was becoming secularized. Most conspicuously, philosophy was being divorced from theology, just as long ago art and architecture had been fatally divorced from the Church. As Ruskin was still teaching Adams's generation, never had the past seemed so at odds with the future. Deeply implicated in the uprooting process was a cloud of subsidiary issues, the rival claims of intellect and feeling, reason and intuition, head and heart, male and female. And all of these found their due place in the design of the novel.[14]

Darwin, of course, had professed that his theory was consistent with Theism, but that avowal brought no peace and was succeeded by an era of furious debate whose end is not yet in sight. The literature of the reconcilers and quasi-reconcilers of religion and science during this period is immense for every serious writer of the period tackled the subject. The most influential book of the decade had been John W. Draper's *Conflict between Science and Religion,* published in 1874, which particularly attacked the obscurantist trends of the Roman Catholic church and its "war" on modern civilization. Draper identified the scientific habit of mind with freedom of conscience and political freedom. At the popular level Colonel Robert Ingersoll brought the Higher Criticism of the Bible to the grass roots and helped populate the land with village atheists.

Hardly a season passed without a major contribution to some aspect of the question by a friend or acquaintance of Adams. Asa Gray attempted mediation in *Natural Science and Religion* [1880]. In England Sir John Seeley, professor of history at Cambridge, attacked supernaturalism in his book *Natural Religion* [1882]. Leslie Stephen's *Science of Ethics* of 1882 presented the position of the highly cultivated agnostic of the school of Mill and George Henry Lewes. In Washington Frank H. Cushing of the Bureau of Ethnology and a fellow member of the Cosmos Club, brought out his book *The Myths of Creation* in 1882. At the Philosophical Club a presidential address on "Modern Philosophical Conceptions of Life" set off a train of acrimonious rejoinders.

The speaker derided Herbert Spencer's chemico-physical hypothesis of life, "the fashionable faith of the hour," and cited Du Bois-Reymond's famous warning of the limits of scientific thought. To explain mental phenomena "we are logically compelled to invoke the existence of a vital principle." Major Powell opposed vitalism either old or new style; for him mind was "only matter in motion." William Harkness, the mathematician, avowed "belief in force, and hence vital force, and further in a little religion," but his presidential successor, William Taylor, urged doubts to them that fear. "The induction seems natural that outstanding mysteries — the ultimate constitution of matter, the nature and genesis of life and mind itself — must in time yield to the same persistent siege of searching analysis and be reduced to subjection . . . of an all-embracing mechanical philosophy." [15]

One of the most important questions with which the novel wrestles is the grounds for religious belief, involving that perennial of metaphysics, the freedom of the will. Crushed to earth by material science, it managed always to rise again in every discussion of philosophical determinism and natural ethics. His friend William James argued vehemently, "Metaphysics of some sort there must be. The only alternative is between the good metaphysics of clear-headed Philosophy and the trashy metaphysics of vulgar Positivism." In the realm of moral judgment a scientific theory like mechanistic determinism might be rejected precisely because it did not accord with one's subjective preferences, quite apart from any question of absolute freedom of the will, which may or may not be metaphysically true. Faith, like the working hypothesis of the scientist, can be "verified" by what it enables man to do.

James rejected Huxley's accusation that to believe because one desires to believe is the "lowest depth of immorality" as a "ridiculous veto" which would "paralyze two of our most

essential faculties: that of aiming at an object, as a result of
an act of faith . . . and that of courageously undertaking an
action in those cases where we have no advance assurances
of success." Belief was the source of moral energy. The proof
was that men did move mountains.[16]

Shortly before James revisited Europe in the fall of 1882,
he sent the sceptical Adams two of his recent essays, "Rationality, Activity and Faith" and "Great Men, Great
Thoughts, and the Environment." One bore upon the religion *versus* science question; the other called into question
the basic premises of Adams's historical writing. In the first
he suggested that mechanists like Adams were guilty of a
contradiction. They conceded "the necessity of faith as an
ingredient in our mental attitude. . . . But by a singularly
arbitrary caprice they say that it is only legitimate when used
in the interests of one particular proposition, the proposition,
namely, that the course of nature is uniform." This, said
James, was the true "dilemma of determinism," hence it was
a mistake to believe "that the juice has ages ago been pressed
out of the free-will controversy." Committed to philosophical
mechanism, Adams had cut himself off from the inner sources
of moral energy that produced socially useful citizens, opti-
mists. In his sardonic moments, which now came increasingly
often as he played the disenchanted bystander in Washington, "nirvana" and "pessimism" came easily to his lips. As a
very young man he had denounced the futilitarian philosophers "singing that old song, *Vanitas Vanitatum.*" Now James
reproached him for becoming one of them.[17]

What William James thought — and possibly — said of
Adams's fastidious pessimism may be inferred from his review of Renan's *Dialogues*. These he characterized as "simply priggishness rampant, an indescribable unmanliness of
tone compounded of a histrionically sentimental self-conceit,
and a nerveless and boneless fear of what will become of the

universe if 'l'homme vulgaire' is allowed to go on . . . a man
savouring his *dédain* and enjoying the exquisitely voluptuous
sensation of tasting his own spiritual pre-eminence. "As Adams
drew closer to Renan's congenial scepticism, the reproach
would come even nearer home to him, as it did to his fellow
sinner, Henry James.

The article instantly aroused in him the demon of contradiction, even as it left a potent residue that would ultimately undermine his own scientific dogmatism. He pounced
upon the practical religious bearing of James's article.

"As I understand your Faith, your X, your reaction of the
individual on the cosmos, it is the old question of Free Will
over again. You *choose* to assume that the will is free. Good!
Reason proves that the Will cannot be free. Equally good!
Free or not, the mere fact that a doubt can exist, proves that
X must be a very microscopic quantity. If the orthodox are
grateful to you for such gifts, the world has indeed changed,
and we have much to thank God for, if there is a God, that
he should have left us unable to decide whether our thoughts,
if we have thoughts, are our own or his'n.

"Although your gift to the church seems to me a pretty
darned mean one, I admire very much your manner of giving
it, which magnifies the crumb into at least forty loaves and
fishes. My wife is quite converted by it. She enjoyed the
paper extremely. Since she read it she has talked of giving
five dollars to Russell Sturgis's church for napkins. As the
impression fades she talks less of the napkins." He would
obviously agree with John Fiske that "the free-will question
is a great opener of the floodgates of rhetoric." [18]

Adams was violently sceptical also of James's attempt in
the second essay, "Great Men, Great Thoughts and the Environment," to give scientific support to the great man theory
of history. The essays were complementary, for if in practice
latent moral energy freed the will, a man greatly endowed

with such energy could alter society. The great man, the genius, or the hero, said James, arose by a process strikingly analogous to mutation, producing a "sociological variation." "The mutations of societies from generation to generation are in the main due directly or indirectly to the acts or example of individuals whose genius was so adapted to the receptivities of the moment, or whose accidental position of authority was so critical, that they became the ferments, initiators of movements, setters of precedent or fashion, centres of corruption, or destroyers of other persons, whose gifts, had they free play, would have led society in another direction." [19]

To this shining generality Adams interposed his own: "With hero-worship like Carlyle's, I have little patience. In history heroes have neutralized each other, and the result is no more than would have been reached without them. Indeed in military heroes I suspect that the ultimate result has been retardation. Nevertheless you could doubtless at any time stop the entire progress of human thought by killing a few score of men. So far I am with you. A few hundred men represent the entire intellectual activity of the whole thirteen hundred millions. What then? They drag us up the corkscrew stair of thought, but they can no more get their brains to run out of their especial convolutions than a railway train (with the free will of half an inch on three thousand miles) can run free up Mount Shasta. Not one of them has ever got so far as to tell us a single vital fact worth knowing. We can't prove even that we are." What William James made of this *soufflé* of free-hand paradoxes he seems to have kept to himself.[20]

Adams's parting shot that accumulated genius had not yet delivered a single vital fact worth knowing and that existence itself was unproven characteristically leaped upward into the blue of metaphysics, into those proscribed reaches of thought which irresistibly drew him away from the too sober realms of physical science. James would have to finish his *Psychology* to answer those posers of epistemology and ontology. Yet it was a shrewdly calculated shot. Perhaps his position was vulnerable, but so too was James's. Beneath Adams's surface assurance about historical determinism, doubts were already accumulating. James's premises carried a real threat, for almost alone among qualified scientists he contested the idea of a closed system and reassured the ministry that scientific psychology was on the side of the angels. He offered a kind of scientific Arminianism to combat the scientific Calvinism of his friend; salvation of sorts was open to all. The optimistic idealism of the American dream was entitled to respectable standing in modern philosophy.[21]

Though he contradicted James, Adams clearly had ambivalent feelings about his own pessimism. In a very real sense James spoke to his buried self, the shy idealist whose winning charm occasionally flashed upon his intimates. A residue of practical optimism lingered on in spite of his carefully cultivated cynicism. Sometimes he was forced to admit that the plain evidence of his senses contested his logic. "There are some difficulties," he wrote Gaskell, "in the path of all pessimistic reasoning which makes its conclusions doubtful, and for some centuries yet may seem to confute its truth. Man is still going fast upward." Henry George's lamentation in *Progress and Poverty* seemed to him without foundation. "My own belief is that the average man here is really twice as well off now as in 1800 in spite of Mr. George. I do not believe that the great millionaires in the country affect the distribution more than five per cent." He sent on to his English friends an article which he had persuaded his friend Henry Gannett of the Census Bureau to contribute to Morse's *International Review* which showed by tables of statistics that the standard of living had steadily risen; people no longer brought up families on salt pork having learned to prefer fresh meat. He hoped that the English statistics might show that "this ratio is to be constant, for if it is, the world has settled its material problem and will soon turn to its intellectual one." He looked out upon the new America and the prospect seemed good to him. "So far as I can see, we are all right here. The country is at last filled out; railways all round and through it, and everyone satisfied." The building boom in Washington was ocular evidence. "There is a tremendous amount of activity in every direction; and another generation will see the result. I consider ours to have already done its work, and on the whole it is the biggest on record." [22]

The question of intellectual progress was, however, deeply implicated with the religious question and that question turned loose upon man all the ambiguities of the Socratic command, Know thyself. The thread of Ariadne led inward to the mystery of the self. What was man and what was consciousness? "We can't prove even that we are," Adams had gibed. Perhaps not, but all around him in that era of excited controversy writers challenged the point, often with a certain pious desperation; for the destructive criticism of supernatural and transcendental religion had produced a crisis in popular philosophy. If not in Revelation, then the proof of the existence of God would have to be found within the individual consciousness. In the very same issue of the *Princeton Review* in which Adams read James's article on "Rationality, Activity, and Faith," the noted Yale theologian, George P. Fisher in the "Personality of God and Man," attempted precisely that proof.[23]

The striking likenesses of thought between Professor Fisher's argument and the sermon of Adams's hero, the Reverend Stephen Hazard, in the opening scene of *Esther* suggest that it was probably that article that provoked Adams to attempt his own contribution to the great debate. "Belief in the personality of man and belief in the personality of God," said Fisher, "stand or fall together. Recent philosophical theories which substitute matter, or an 'Unknowable,' for the self-conscious Deity . . . cast away the personality of man as ordinarily conceived." Pantheism was equally destructive of the self. "On this fact of our own personality the validity of the arguments for theism depend." This is what Descartes meant by his intuition, *"Cogito ergo sum,"* I think, therefore, I am. "Only that Personal Power which is exalted above Nature, the creative principle to which every new beginning is due, can account for self-consciousness in man." [24]

The implications of such a view were too serious to ignore. Could a mechanistic science of mind be harmonized with a religion of consciousness? On every hand the issue leaped to Adams's attention. In the *North American Review,* for example, the Hegelian William Torrey Harris declared that "the intellectual problem of the age is how to bring into harmony the scientific view with religious faith." In the midst of the writing of *Esther* Adams's good friend Charles Nordhoff dropped in to leave a copy of his textbook on natural religion called *God and the Future Life,* he having been induced to write it because he believed that the "recent and very important discoveries and new theories in science" had needlessly aroused concern over a supposed conflict between science and religion. More than twenty years had passed since Adams's father had sent to him in Berlin an anxious letter on the subject, worried that he may not have impressed his sons "so much as I ought to have done with my idea of the importance of an earnest religious faith." He hoped that Henry's residence "in a country too much tainted with the sophistry of the modern speculative infidelity" would not prevent him "from a regular attendance upon religious worship of some kind and a frequent meditation upon serious subjects." The churchgoing had long since ended, and *Esther* was in a sense Henry's long-meditated private justification.[25]

3 *As Sight of God*

The novel opens appropriately in a church where the
struggle of ideas comes to a natural dramatic focus. "The
new church of St. John's, on Fifth Avenue, was thronged
the morning of the last Sunday of October, in the year 1880."
The time, in effect, was the present.

The sermon dealt with the relations of religion to society. It
began by claiming that all being and all thought rose by slow
gradations to God, — ended in Him, for Him — existed only
through Him and because of being His.

The form of act or thought mattered nothing. The hymns of
David, the plays of Shakespeare, the metaphysics of Descartes,
the crimes of Borgia, the virtues of Antonine, the atheism of
yesterday and the materialism of today, were all emanations of
divine thought, doing their appointed work. . . . The preacher
then went on to criticise the attitude of religion towards science.
'If there is still a feeling of hostility between them', he said, 'it is
no longer the fault of religion. There have been times when the
church seemed afraid, but she is no longer. Analyze, dissect, use
your microscope or your spectrum till the last atom of matter is
reached . . . you will find enthroned behind all thought and
matter only one central idea, — the idea which the church has
never ceased to embody, — I AM! Science like religion kneels
before this mystery; it can carry itself back only to this simple
consciousness of existence. I AM is the starting point and goal of
metaphysics and logic, but the church alone has pointed out
from the beginning that this starting-point is not human but
divine. The philosopher says — I am, and the church scouts his
philosophy. She answers: No! you are NOT, you have no existence
of your own. You were and are and ever will be only a part of
the supreme I AM, of which the church is the emblem.

Adams acknowledged that in this disquisition "perhaps the
preacher rose a little above the heads of his audience. Most
of his flock were busied with a kind of speculation so foreign
to that of metaphysics that they would have been puzzled to
explain what was meant by Descartes' famous COGITO ERGO

sum, on which the preacher laid so much stress." With this challenging résumé of the position of a conservative theologian like Professor Fisher, Adams opened the first phase of his novelized argument, the relation between theology and art in the world of modern science.[26]

Somewhat justly the critic William Roscoe Thayer has remarked that in *Esther* the "persons talk like the embodied doctrines which we used to read in dialogues." Inevitably a novel of ideas and social purpose runs such a risk, but there is a great deal more than a Platonic symposium in the pages of the novel. Adams achieved an astonishing tour de force in the way in which he made the intellectual questions central to the action of the story. The tension between religion and science, the past and the future, arises in a rich psychological context and with a strong sense of the social and cultural implications of the question. There had been articles and treatises in plenty on the place of religion in society, yet no novelist in America had attempted to deal seriously with what was the most controversial subject of the time and show its full bearing upon the life and thought of the American intellectual.[27]

An ideological novel, its realism is wholly internal, uncompromisingly probing into the beliefs and motives of a group of highly sensitive and cultivated persons, in effect the members of his own circle. There is only the sketchiest indication of the social setting. Evolution, heredity, education, and wealth have already done their work. Adams brings the struggle between religion and science to its sharpest form in the practical question of intermarriage, for marriage was the most formidable of all social relations. He often wondered privately "how any man or woman dares to take the plunge." Intermarriage between persons of different religious faiths was a commonplace; but in this novel the question is one of intermarriage between a believer and an agnostic. To give it its most uncompromising form the novel presents the believer as an Episcopal Church rector with evangelical tendencies who is determined to honor the religious claims of the past. In such a conflict ideas must have consequences. But more than the struggle between belief and unbelief is at issue; there is also involved the struggle of wills, the timeless struggle of the man and the woman for mastery. Law, tradition, and the marriage service required that a woman submit her will as well as her person to her master. In the conflict of two such opposed minds, the role of love or passion becomes peculiarly interesting. All for love is a romantic — and compelling motive, but in finely constituted and scrupulous minds that "all" involves intellectual and moral integrity. Granted that the heart has its reasons, might it not equally be true that the mind has its reasons which the heart was bound to respect? [28]

As in *Democracy*, the central figure is once again a woman, the model obviously Marian Adams. Esther, a distinguished amateur painter in New York City, lives with her long-widowed father, William Dudley, a one-time colonel of New York volunteers in the Civil War. A substantial inheritance long ago relieved him from the need for seriously practising law. Esther, his only child, has for fifteen years been absolute mistress of her father's house. Her semi-invalid father, knowing that he has not long to live, is worried about her. "Poor Esther has been brought up among men and is not used to harness. If things go wrong she will rebel, and a woman who rebels is lost." The parallel with Marian's situation is close. Her mother had died when she was five and for several years after the marriage of her elder brother and her sister, she had all the privileges of an only child. As a result, as Adams had written during his engagement, "she has grown up to look after herself and has a certain vein of personality which approaches eccentricity." Her father, Dr. Hooper, was a professional man, an oculist, and he like Mr. Dudley had inherited enough money to be indifferent to his practice. Marian's Puritan ancestry went back to earliest days of the Bay Colony as did Esther's. Significantly, Esther, like Mrs. Adams just before her marriage, is no longer a debutante but a mature young woman of nearly twenty-six. The Reverend Stephen Hazard, her suitor, is about thirty-five. At the time of Adams's marriage, he was thirty-four and Marian was twenty-eight. In retrospect he always regarded their experience as striking close to the ideal. "In my opinion," he once remarked apropos of an imminent marriage, "twenty-seven is better. A woman does not get her courage till then, or her head." [29]

Esther is the center of a group of five characters. One of them is her cousin George Strong, an adventurous professor of geology, also about thirty-five, a thoroughgoing sceptic and as incurably facetious and high-spirited as Adams's friend Clarence King, who obviously supplies the main features. When asked what kind of artist is Wharton [La Farge] he replies with King's characteristic chaff, "A sort of superior housepainter. . . . He sometimes does glazing." Strong, like King, is an authority as a practical geologist, though in his obsession with giant fossils he resembles another member of the Washington circle, Othniel Marsh. Strong, too, is given to unpredictable absences on scientific expeditions and all in all is too erratic to be a good match for Esther although they hover vaguely on the edge of romance. As a kind of elder brother of Esther he plays the role of intellectual mentor. Strong calls Esther the "sternest little pagan I know," an epithet equally appropriate to the agnostic Marian with her extreme moral and social scruples. In fact it is the company of talented and well informed men which spoils Esther for ordinary society for she has no serious interest in the conventional dancing partner. Like Marian she had given up waltzing, at which she had been very good, for a more intellectual social life. Strong is invested also with some of Adams's own physical characteristics, notably a high bald forehead and a dark beard which produce a look of strong character. Like Adams he had inherited enough money to be a professor for the fun of it.[30]

Paired with the hard-headed, rationalistic Strong is the most vividly drawn character of the whole group, the artist Wharton, Strong's friend, who has been engaged to do the murals for the new church. As Strong lives for science, so Wharton lives for art. The most complex figure of the group, he reflects the challenge of John La Farge's personality. La Farge had been a lecturer on art at Harvard when Adams was there and Adams came to know him as part of his brother-in-law's artistic circle of friends. In the fall of 1876 La Farge had been brought in by Richardson to do the remarkable murals in nearby Trinity Church, where he later fashioned the lancet windows. Reared as a Roman Catholic La Farge had a strong feeling for religious art. He approached things intuitively, as Adams was wont to say, rather than intellectually like himself. Wharton similarly "felt rather than talked." Moody, idealistic and intensely opinionated, it is he who best intuits Esther's character. He terms her "one of the most marked American types I ever saw," echoing Henry James's comment about Marian Adams. She epitomized the intellectual riddle of America, "whether American types are going to supplant the old ones, or whether they are to come to nothing for want of ideas," extinguished by middle class materialism. Wharton views Esther with the same cool detachment with which Adams had studied Marian. "Her features are imperfect," says Wharton. "Except her ears, her voice, and her eyes which have a sort of brown depth like a trout brook, she has no very good points." But Esther's potentialities fascinate Wharton, as Marian's fascinated Henry

Adams. "I want to know what she can make of life. She gives
one the idea of a lightly-sparred yacht in mid-ocean; unexpected. . . . She sails gayly along, though there is no land
in sight and plenty of rough weather coming." And then
Adams added his teasing private joke almost as if he had his
letters to Gaskell lying before him, "She never read a book,
I believe, in her life. . . . She picks up all she knows without an effort and knows nothing well." Thus Adams affectionately patronizes his heroine — and his wife, for Marian
though an omnivorous reader had little taste for abstruse
science and the learned talk of her husband's friends in the
Geological Survey bored her. Perhaps that is why Adams
puts into the mouth of Esther's father a sweeping condemnation of the tortures of indiscriminate reading.[31]

Esther meets the third of the trio of serious-minded men,
the Reverend Stephen Hazard, an intimate of her cousin,
when Strong takes her to the first service at St. John's Episcopal Church. For the character of Hazard, Adams drew
liberally upon his second cousin, Phillips Brooks, rector of
Trinity Church in Boston. Hazard had been brought from
Cincinnati to New York as Brooks was brought from Philadelphia to Boston. His popularity with transient audiences
and his slightly latitudinarian views have earned for him, as
they did for his prototype, a certain amount of criticism
from the ultraconservative members of the congregation. The
real and the fictional rectors are both men of the world,
widely read, and keenly interested in art and science. Hazard
works closely with the architect as Brooks had worked with
Richardson. The endless discussions between Strong and Hazard on the relation of science and religion reflect one of the
main staples of the conversations of their circle at the Cosmos
Club and the Century. Phillips Brooks once remarked, "You
will get more live talk about first principles in either our
Boston or your New York club in an hour than from any

gathering of London clergy in a year." The opposition of
ideas between Hazard and Strong vividly appears in the
repartee of an encounter between them in which Strong
fancifully suggests that the Reverend Mr. Hazard should
ride the dragons of geological science. Hazard demurs, "There
are dragons enough at St. John's." To which Strong retorts,
"You are throwing away your last chance to reconcile science
and religion." [32]

When Adams became intimate with Richardson late in 1881
during the planning of Nicholas Anderson's house, Richardson was full of great projects for the further improvement of
Trinity — the addition of a front porch, a chapter house, and
a daring scheme of mosaics to cover the great piers. After a
lively summer with Phillips Brooks touring France and Italy
in quest of architectural ideas, he returned in the fall of
1882 to become an even more frequent dinner guest at the
Adamses. Much as Adams relished Richardson's convivial
gaiety, Adams drew out his serious side with the professional
skill of the one-time professor of medieval history. It was the
heyday of Gothic restoration and imitation and the world of
architecture resounded with the debate. Richardson, full of
his theory of Romanesque architecture, opened Adams's eyes
to the simple grandeur of the twelfth century church. Adams
later said, "I caught the disease from dear old Richardson."
Hazard, full of "thirteenth century ideas," is similarly made
a victim of the same infection. Brooks, Richardson, and La
Farge had all studied the work of restorers like Viollet-le-
Duc, the reigning authority, and his associates, if only to
rebel against the new Gothicism. Endlessly they debated the
question of how to solve the relation between the church
building and the doctrines which echoed down its aisles. The
debates between Wharton and the minister Hazard undoubtedly recall the frequent conferences of Richardson, La
Farge and Phillips Brooks over the decoration of Trinity

Church. Richardson with his pronounced ideas on ornament must often have clashed with the purist La Farge. From such stimulus it is understandable why nearly the first half of the novel has for its principal setting the scaffolding and vaults of the new church where the murals are being belatedly completed just as they had been at Trinity, and why the question of church decoration should play such a leading role.[33]

The quiet tenor of Esther's life, which heretofore has moved gracefully between her studio and a children's hospital where she serves as the benign story lady (perhaps a reminiscence of Marian's visits to the Worcester asylum with her father) is interrupted by the arrival of Catherine Brooke from Denver. She is an exquisitely beautiful "child of nature" and the idealized prototype of the admiring company of nieces in fact and "in wish" who come to Lafayette Square. Adams lavishes on her his most sentimental figures of speech — "fresh as a summer's morning," a complexion "like the petals of a sweet brier rose," "natural and sweet as a flower." "No one could resist her hazel eyes or the curve of her neck, or her pure complexion which had the transparency of a Colorado sunrise." Adams's opinion of his own connoisseurship may be educed from his remark in the novel about Esther's uncle, Mr. Murray, that he "had a sound though uncultivated taste for pretty girls."[34]

Catherine, not yet 21, is brought on the New York scene, an orphan left to the charge of Esther's aunt, Mrs. Murray. She is to be ushered in to the great world of New York culture and refinement and to undergo an education which shall give her "a soul," for as Wharton says of her, she "stood nearer nature than any woman he knew." Brought up a strict Presbyterian, she is now introduced to "a new world of imagination," the world of novels which she had been brought up to regard as wicked. Strong gives her Dickens's *Old Curiosity Shop,* and Stephen Hazard chooses novels to give her a sense of the past. She gains confidence and a sophisticated self-consciousness, posing for her portrait in a way vaguely reminiscent of Donatello's in the *Marble Faun*. Catherine's impact upon the sophisticated group becomes the mainspring of what little overt action takes place. It is she rather than Esther who dominates the first half of the novel.[35]

Her fresh, dewy-eyed charm recalls at once Elizabeth Cameron, whose extreme youth and beauty had captivated Adams and his wife. They had in a sense taken her under their protection and helped advance her career as a Washington hostess and stimulated her interest in books and art. Coming from an Ohio family, there was enough suggestion of the West about her to warrant Adams's fiction of residence in Denver. Esther paints her portrait as the "Sage Hen," Catherine's name as an "adopted" Sioux, with appropriate Western props supplied by Strong. Her education in art gets under way and opens the debate on art. Esther had adopted Hazard's suggestion that "beauty of the subject is the right ideal" in art. Wharton however objects that "the merit of a painting was not so much in what it explained as in what it suggested," and with characteristic candor and earnestness proposes that Esther give up her amateur dabbling and turn professional by painting one of the mural figures high on the transept wall at St. John's. This she does.[36]

Once again Catherine sits as model, but now not for her surface beauty but to be spiritualized as St. Cecilia. Wharton imposes rigorous discipline demanding that the artist must transfer his soul to the painting itself. Catherine objects that Wharton is trying to make Esther paint like a man. Wharton sternly replies, "An artist must be man, woman and demi-god." He must be above his subject. "Put heaven in Miss Brooke's eyes!" he exhorts Esther. "Heaven is not there now; only earth. She is a flower, if you like. You are the real saint. It is your own paradise that St. Cecilia is singing about." In

the vaulted transept of St. John's Esther undergoes the discipline of "space and silence . . . color and form." Here the
rector visits his two charming protégés and the work becomes
"an ecclesiastical idyll," with Hazard engaged in a friendly
rivalry with Wharton for control of Esther's taste. Hazard
would prefer that the traditional figures be represented with
the simple direct symbolism of the medieval painters. Esther
is unsure of her powers for as Wharton had warned Hazard,
she has "nothing medieval about her," but belonged to the
spiritualized paganism of the future.[37]

Wharton, obsessed with a sense of the modern alienation
of religion and art, cries out, "I am sick at heart about our
church work. It is a failure. . . . The thing does not belong to our time or feelings." His religion is of tougher fibre
than the high-church theology of the rector, with its in-
tellectualized ceremonies and pantheistic overtones. "To me
religion is a passion. To reach Heaven, you must go through
Hell and carry its marks on your face and figure." Wanting
to express "beauty of form," Wharton collided with the
wishes of Hazard and the church committee who preferred
the severities of early Christian art, with its stiff, conven-
tionalized and Byzantine representation. It was this tradition,
he felt, and Esther agreed, that gave a theatrical aspect to
the church. He wanted to "go back to the age of beauty, and
put a Madonna in the heart of their church. The place has
no heart." When he corrects Esther's drawing by giving it
"an expression of passion subsided and heaven attained,"
Esther recognizes it as "Nirvana," the final blessedness of
Buddhism, the reunion with Brahma. Wharton explains, "Nirvana is what I mean by paradise. It is eternal life, which,
my poet says, consists in seeing God." This poet, we soon
learn, is Petrarch, whose ideal of Christian renunciation is
thus identified with the ideal of self-escape.[38]

Thus Adams incorporated another significant strain in contemporary religious and artistic thought. The spread of pessimism from the dark fountains of German thought had brought with it a side of oriental speculation largely ignored by Emerson and the Concord school. Schopenhauer found in the Nirvana of Buddhism an appropriate symbol of the rejection of the will and he and his disciple Hartmann helped make the term one of the clichés of educated circles. Sir Edwin Arnold's florid epic poem, *The Light of Asia*, celebrating the life of Gautama Buddha, "The Teacher of Nirvana and the Law," was now at the height of its immense vogue, for the scientific study of mythology, as it diminished the authority of Christianity, turned many minds to the exotic religions of the Far East. Raphael Pumpelly, whose far ranging orbit often brought him back to the Adams drawing room, had been a pioneer orientalist and La Farge, who contributed a chapter on Japanese art to Pumpelly's *Travels Through America and Asia*, had actively proselytized the cause in the early seventies.[39]

Wharton's troubled career owed some of its features to still another remarkable visitor at the Adams home, William Sturgis Bigelow, a favorite cousin of Mrs. Adams. After a bohemian existence in Vienna and Paris as a medical student, he had returned to lead a rootless existence, unable to settle down in his profession. In Washington he had become infatuated with the vivid Emily Beale, much to the Adamses' displeasure. Suddenly, as Marian Adams surmised, "the sawdust came out of [the] California doll." Disenchanted with life and love, Bigelow took refuge in Japan in 1882, going there to collect art and study philosophy and soon became a convert to Buddhism. Something of his cosmopolitanism and Baudelairean anguish finds expression in Wharton. He too has explored the charnel house for artistic materials in a kind of Gothic quest. After an unhappy marriage to a

French actress, a romantic temptress who had abandoned him, a woman who might have posed for "Semiramis, Medea, Clytemnestra" — a figure highly suggestive of Sarah Bernhardt — Wharton for a time took refuge in Vaucluse where he romantically identified himself with the most celebrated of all jilted lovers, Petrarch, and there, with Hazard's help, translated the sonnets.[40]

Out of the youthful past of the two men, Petrarch's poetry enters the story to illuminate from a fresh angle the relation of religion to love and marriage. Petrarch's melancholy destiny never to win the shadowy Laura symbolizes the lot of the two men. In Wharton's case the Petrarchian renunciation has already taken place, but for Hazard it lies hidden in the future. He too is doomed to be a Petrarchian victim. Once more Adams touched the life of one of his models. The Reverend Phillips Brooks, now a confirmed bachelor at forty-six, had himself once been engaged to marry. The romance had been broken off to his lasting regret. Petrarch's renunciation of Laura seemed to Wharton the tragic victory of the soul over the senses, the attainment of the sight of God through denial of the sight of the world. As Adams once said of Emerson, "In obtaining extreme sublimation or tenuity of intelligence, I infer that sensuousness must be omitted." Wharton falls in love with the uncorrupted Catherine Brooke, but his wife melodramatically appears at St. John's and shatters the idyl of poetry and painting. She is conveniently bought off and Wharton is assured of a divorce; but the spell is broken. His fate had already been foreshadowed on the church wall where Hazard sketched him, ironically at Catherine's urging, as Petrarch in the guise of St. Luke. There on the wall he is fated to look toward his second Laura, Catherine, painted as St. Cecilia, in an allegory of earthly passion overcome.[41]

The leitmotif of love and religion is expressed again and again like a reprise in a few pregnant lines from Petrarch:

> As sight of God is the eternal life,
> Nor more we ask, nor more to wish we dare,
> So, lady, sight of thee, ...

Uttered first by Hazard, in Adams's translation, they afterwards haunt Esther's lips in the Italian with the talismanic force that they were in later years to assume for Adams himself. Hazard warns her that in the end Petrarch repented the time he had thrown away on Laura. Approving the moral of Petrarch's sonnet, he implies the theological terms on which he himself might love. Could Esther, as a woman and an agnostic, accept this stoical valuation of earthly love? Could she treat love and marriage as a mere means to salvation, the traditional Christian view, and regard it, so far as it was sensual, as an impediment to grace? Could she be more than Laura to this priestly Petrarch? The Nietzchean Strong cannot help her at this juncture for he no longer hovers between two worlds but has become a stoical and solitary wayfarer in the cold wastes of a scientific future, a future which must create its own values and illusions.[42]

The problem becomes urgent for her when she loses her two main props. First, the virtual finishing of the murals leaves her without a sense of purpose, for her venture into professionalism has spoiled her taste for amateur painting. When Wharton reminds her that "much of the best work in the world has been done with no motive of gain," she philosophizes that women cannot work alone; they must have companionship. Her second loss, the death of her father, is infinitely greater, as it leaves her utterly "alone to meet the buffets of life." Her father, a stoical and gallant freethinking sceptic to the end, tries hard to infuse her with his courage. Deeply, even obsessively, attached to her father,

Esther had now to face her final emancipation. She could
not confront her fate, truly, until she confronted it alone.[43]
One is immediately struck by the dramatic parallel with
Mrs. Adams's own situation. In so closely transferring
Marian's problem to fiction Adams seemed to be trying to
work out by artistic insight the question that they would
inevitably have to face when Marian's ailing father should
die. That there would be great peril could easily be foreseen; yet, unconsciously at least, he must have awaited his
wife's release with restless anticipation. His marriage could
not really be complete so long as he had to share so large a
portion of Marian's love with her father. Much as he respected his father-in-law, he was far too sensitive and romantic not to have felt the unspoken rivalry. When at the
end of the novel, Esther finally rejects her clerical suitor,
saying that if she married him she would have to share him
with his church, she breaks out passionately, "Of all things
on earth, to be half-married must be the worst torture." [44]
Perhaps Adams guessed the tragic truth of his half marriage,
but it was an inadmissible thought.

In the novel Adams carries Esther safely across the abyss
of "moral strain" and "physical fatigue." Her dying father
places his hand in hers "but she imagined that he had meant
not so much to ask for the strength of her hand as to give
her the will and courage of his own, and she felt only the
wish that he might not doubt her answer to the call." Long
accustomed to the ritual of funerals and mourning, Adams
depicts his heroine in the usual succession of psychological
states: the "inevitable depression," "days of vacancy," seeking "refuge in trifles" but finding that "the needle and scissors
are terrible weapons for cutting out and trimming not so
much women's dresses as their thoughts." She turned for a
short period to talking mysticism with Stephen Hazard for,
as Adams comments, "Most women are more or less mystical

by nature, and Esther had a vein of mysticism running through a practical mind." [45]

Hazard discusses with her "the purity of the soul, the victory of spirit over matter, and the peace of infinite love" and self-confidently sweeps aside her fear that having no heart in his work she will ruin his life. She luxuriates briefly in the surrender of her will to his, but when she attends the church service her old scepticisms return and her discontent is aggravated by the thought that she would have to share her husband with the congregation. Desperately, she immersed herself in books of theology hoping to reason her way to share Hazard's faith. "A terrible fascination impelled her to read on about the nature of the Trinity and the authority of tradition and to explore the apostolic succession with Newman." She exhausted herself to tears and was in danger of making herself ill over trying to fathom the doctrine of the atonement, and the Athanasian creed, the archsymbol of dogma. Hazard, as a latitudinarian, avoided strict inquiry or dogmatic interpretation, anxious to soften difficult doctrine by symbolic interpretations very much as Phillips Brooks did in the pulpit of Trinity Church, an evasion that stirred up controversy in and out of his congregation. Strong, the cynical intellectual, plays devil's advocate for his friend Hazard. It was indifferent whether Esther converted Hazard or Hazard Esther. "It's a case of survival of the fittest." Whatever happened in a world of scientific determinism was unavoidable.[46]

To Mrs. Murray, the convenient aunt and duenna of the story, churchgoing is a matter of social discipline rather than theology. Disturbed by the growing church gossip, as well as the practical incompatability of the lovers, she determines to break up the romance. A thorough pragmatist, she is impatient with Strong's Olympian detachment. *He* should have married Esther. His defense is simple: marriage

was not a matter of logic but of love. Mrs. Murray's tart
retort to this plea indicates the keennness of Adams's self-
scrutiny. "You and he," she says, referring to Hazard, "and
all your friends are a sort of clever children. We are always
expecting you to do something worth doing, and it never
comes. You are a sort of watercolor, worsted work, bric-a-
brac, washed out geniuses, just big enough and strong enough
to want to do something and never carry it through." [47]

"Is religion true?" Esther demands of Strong. "Ask me
something easier!" he replies. "Ask me whether science is
true!" He had leagued himself with science "because I want
to help in making it truer." The fact of the matter was that
"There is no science which does not begin by requiring you
to believe the incredible. . . . The doctrine of the Trinity
is not so difficult to accept for a working proposition as any
one of the axioms of physics." Thus Adams epitomized the
position to which he himself was being driven, the stand
taken by his English statesman-friend, Arthur Balfour. The
whole of science, Balfour had recently written, "is incapable
of any rational defence. The premises of science are not yet
properly determined." Even Huxley had said, "I am too much
a sceptic to deny anything." Strong repeatedly sounds the
note: "Mystery for mystery science beats religion all hollow.
I can't open my mouth in my lecture room without repeating
ten times as many unintelligible formulas as ever Hazard
is forced to do in church." For himself, he had put the
formulas of the past behind him and had committed himself and his free-thinking scepticisms to the future.[48]

What Esther must have, said Strong, was faith: "You can
never reason yourself into it," he warned. "If you have faith
enough in Hazard to believe in him, you have faith enough
to accept his church. Faith means submission. Submit!"
Piteously, Esther cries out, "I want to submit. Why can't
some of you make me?" This was the crux of the matter.

How was the will to be forced to deny itself? For Strong
the agency for denial was science. To Esther he proffered
from the studio mantel an ivory crucifix, the all-powerful
symbol with which the Roman Church had dealt with rebellious wills. Like a medieval penitent, she presses the cross
with desperate force against her heart. But no authoritarian
rite of self-humiliation can help her; she was born without
the capacity for faith and Strong realizes that his "little
bluff" of free will has failed.[49]

Henry Adams deliberately adopted the name of his heroine
from the central figure in Hawthorne's "Old Esther Dudley."
Her father had taken "a fancy to the name when he met it
in Hawthorne's story." Perhaps there lurked in Adams's
mind the recollection that in the distant past one of Marian's
ancestral cousins, the Tory "King" Hooper, had turned his
back upon the future, like Old Esther Dudley, to remain
faithful to the old order. Perhaps Hawthorne's tale gave
Adams a key symbol of a loyalty that like Maule's curse had
descended upon the Esther of his novel and from which she
would have to free herself whatever the cost. Adams's debt
to Hawthorne plainly goes farther than the borrowing of
the name and the theme of opposed loyalties in that story.
Hawthorne's dramatic explorations of moral questions strongly
attracted him, as passing references in his letters indicate.
His temperament found an answering echo in the somber
twilight of Hawthorne's universe, in which freedom of the
will had little scope and in Hawthorne's obsessive sense of
ancestral influences and tradition as in *The House of Seven
Gables*. Salem oppressed him and he sought escape as Adams
had from Boston and with equal unsuccess. "The spell sur-
vives," said Hawthorne, "and just as powerfully as if the
natal spot were an earthly paradise." [50]

The work of Hawthorne's whose spirit is most strongly
reflected in *Esther* is *The Marble Faun*, the study of the

moral and intellectual education of the faun-like Donatello. Donatello had a pagan quality, a kind of primitive purity and capacity for enjoyment, lost to Christian civilization. Esther too had something of that nature. When the artist Wharton praises the extraordinary originality and individuality of Esther, Stephen Hazard asks with a touch of facetiousness, "What sort of a world does this new deity of yours belong to?" Wharton replied, "Not to yours. There is nothing medieval about her. If she belongs to any besides the present, it is to the next world which artists want to see, when paganism will come again and we can give a divinity to every waterfall." [51]

In *The Marble Faun*, painting, architecture, sculpture, and religion form a complex symphony of themes. In both novels some of the characters appear in a double guise, as persons and as idealized portraits, and there is a special symbolism in the portrayals. In *The Marble Faun*, for example, Miriam paints a self-portrait. The pure Hilda paints a copy of Guido's Beatrice, the "fallen angel," and reveals strange spiritual insights. Kenyon, the sculptor, does a symbol-haunted bust of the enigmatic Donatello. Adams presents a similar pattern of mirror images. Esther Dudley first paints Catherine as the "Sage Hen" (Cf. Hawthorne's Hilda as "The Dove") and then, with fresh insight, as St. Cecilia. Hazard himself draws a cartoon of Wharton as Petrarch, though ostensibly representing St. Luke. The symbolical Petrarch thus confronts a symbolical Laura concealed in the representation of St. Cecilia.

Hawthorne's Hilda is greatly tempted by the Catholic Church and seems almost on the point of conversion, but as "a daughter of the Puritans" she cannot repudiate her deep loyalties. She is tempted by the comfort of the church, the strength it offered for one's weakness, the subtle appeals of art and ritual to the senses, but hers is a secular non-theological faith. Confronted by unyielding dogma she at last turns away. Hazard tries to convert Esther, whose "paganism" has a distinctly Puritan and spiritual cast, to the Episcopal Church, the gulf essentially no wider than between Hilda's mild New England unitarianism and the Romish communion, and in Esther's case dogma also bars the way.

In Hilda's feeling toward the church Hawthorne also epitomized the spiritual struggle to be experienced with increasing frequency by so many esthetic New Englanders as they made their cultural pilgrimage to Rome or to the Episcopal Church. Hazard's enthusiasm for medieval church art reflected one side of the religious reconstruction — or reaction — of the time. Hawthorne suggests as well a rationale for the turning of so many New England Brahmins to the figure of the Virgin Mary. Hilda defends her unorthodox worship by saying, "A Christian girl — even a daughter of the Puritans — may surely pay honor to the idea of divine Womanhood without giving up the faith of her forefathers." And Hawthorne adds the benignant comment, "If she knelt, if she prayed, if her oppressed heart besought the sympathy of divine womanhood afar in bliss, but not remote, because forever humanized by the memory of mortal griefs, was Hilda to be blamed? It was not a Catholic kneeling at an idolatrous shrine, but a child lifting its tear-stained face to seek comfort from a mother." [52]

4   The Lesson of the Falls

The closing scene of the novel strongly recalls the confrontation scene in *Democracy* in which Ratcliffe tries to overcome Madeleine's political scruples. Hazard has followed Esther to Niagara Falls in the dead of winter and he is

constrained to argue his case for supernatural religion, not
from the strategic elevation of the pulpit but in competition
with the thundering cataract. Obliged at last to abandon the
philosophical rationale of Descartes' *Cogito* as the basis for
the proof of God, Hazard adopts the practical one of Pascal.
He confesses that he too has been tormented by doubts,
but his study of atheism and materialism brought him "at
last a result more inconceivable than that reached by the
church, and infinitely more hopeless besides. The atheists
offer no sort of bargain for one's soul." Pascal had long ago
made the point in his figure of the wager. "Their scheme is
all loss and no gain. At last both they and I come back to
a confession of ignorance; the only difference between us
is that my ignorance is joined with a faith and hope." It
was precisely the ground that William James took in his
defense of religion. "If you win, you have infinity; if you
lose, — if atheism is right, — you lose nothing." [53]

But Esther balked at violating the integrity of her mind
by giving lip service. To trust Hazard and surrender her
judgment to him would not free her from the tyranny of
the will and the self but more deeply enslave her. The
doctrines of his church seemed to her even more pagan than
the ceremonies. The truth was that the church was not
really spiritual. "It is all personal and selfish." Personal immortality and the resurrection of the body seemed to her
"a shocking idea. I despise and loathe myself, and yet you
thrust self at me from every corner of the church." Hazard,
his cause already lost, angrily reproaches her, "Can you . . .
think of a future existence where you will not meet once
more father or mother, husband or children? Surely the natural
instincts of your sex must save you from such a creed!" To
the scrupulously rational Esther such an argument was base.
"Why must the church always appeal to my weakness and
never to my strength! I ask for spiritual life and you send

me back to my flesh and blood as though I were a tigress you were sending back to her cubs." The struggle was over. Esther was free at last.

But if like her Puritan forebears Esther had clung unshaken to her principles her victory, like all triumphs of the spirit over the flesh, came high. Strong learned this when he congratulated her on having fought her "battle like a heroine." Stirred out of his usual cynicism he proposed that she marry him. Her reply is the final line — and paradox — of the book: "But George, I don't love you, I love him." When Adams allowed King to read the novel, King objected to the palpable evasion. Adams should have made Esther "jump into Niagara as that was what she would have done." Adams acknowledged, "Certainly she would, but I could not suggest it." [54]

Esther's tragedy, if tragedy it is, is that of her whole sex. Perhaps nature has fatally divided woman's soul. Her aunt had suggested as much when she stoically remarked, "Marriage makes no real difference in their lot. All the contented women are fools, and all the discontented ones want to be men." Into her mouth Adams put a favorite epigram of Clarence King. "Women are a blunder in the creation, and must take the consequences."

What positive religion would meet Esther's lofty criteria is only dimly suggested. At the beginning Hazard had propounded what seemed to her a medieval theology predicated on self-consciousness in man and his God. At Niagara Falls their roles are reversed. For here Esther seems to stand in her own church, a harbinger of a new paganism, as Wharton had once prophesied, with the Falls as a primal altar from which a male divinity spoke in a great parable of nature. [55]

Adams had once visited Niagara late in January and had been roused to extraordinary enthusiasm by the sight. That deep impression wells up in these striking pages of the

novel. A Sunday morning has come again like the memorable
Sunday morning of the preceding autumn at the opening of
the action, when she first heard Hazard speak on Descartes'
great text. "A ludicrous contrast flashed on her mind between
the decorations of St. John's, with its parterre of nineteenth
century bonnets, and the huge church which was thundering
its gospel under her eyes." She wondered how "after listening
here, any preacher could have the confidence to preach again."
Here before her "eternity, infinity and omnipotence" were
"laughing and dancing" in her face.[56]

To steel herself for her final interview with Hazard, Esther
had taxed her cousin Strong to state his religious views.
His reply fairly represented Adams's own guardedly agnostic
position. He did not believe in a personal God. Future re-
wards and punishments were simply "old women's nursery
tales!" He could only affirm that there was a "strong probability of the existence of two things . . . mind and matter."
It was not a pleasant doctrine and as for converting anyone
to his view, "Great Buddha, no!" He could not deny the
possibility of a future life, if the idea were purged of all
temporal associations. Developing the idea which Adams had
flung after William James, the failure of man to acquire
"a single vital fact worth knowing," Strong went on to say,
"If our minds could get hold of one abstract truth, they
would be immortal so far as that truth is concerned. . . .
Hazard and I and everyone else agree that thought is eternal.
. . . The only difficulty is that every fellow thinks his thought
the true one. . . . We may some day catch an abstract truth
by the tail, and then we shall have our religion and immortality. We have got far more than half way. Infinity is
infinitely more intelligible to you than to a sponge. If the
soul of a sponge can grow to be the soul of a Darwin, why may
we not all grow up to abstract truth?" Esther queried, "Does
your idea mean that the next world is a sort of great reser-

voir of truth, and that what is true in us just pours into it like raindrops?" Tempering the masculine abstraction for her feminine mind, Strong admitted that "the idea is a little of that kind." Esther linked it at once with the symbol before her eyes: "After all I wonder whether that may not be what Niagara has been telling me!" In this speculative union between Platonism and Darwinian evolution, with its residue of incorrigible idealism, all except the hardiest scientific materialists were steadily being driven to ground. It marked out for Adams the highway of thought which he would henceforth follow.[57]

Chapter Eight

The Forsaken Garden

1 Point of No Return

B^Y May 1884 the new house, which was still in the planning stage, had become Adams's chief interest. After that
he listed the politics of the Mugwump compaign. Construction was to begin within a month. The twin houses began to
rise almost simultaneously, their highly conspicuous situation opposite the White House immediately inspiring widespread curiosity and a share of Washington legend. Wise-
acres promptly built a communicating door in the party wall,
a door whose existence was entirely imaginary. A much
more curious and malicious legend, published many years
ago, is a variant of the first one. Adams is supposed to have
"refused his wife's request to cut a door through a partition
for the convenience of spirit visitors." In view of Mrs. Adams's
scorn for such credulities, one surmises that the story is a
solemn echo of some hoax played by the Five of Hearts to
discourage vulgar curiosity.[1]

The social aloofness of the two friends was effectively
translated into the handsome dark red brick Romanesque fa-
çades that rose majestically to the steeply gabled roofs. The
Adamses did not get their flat roof, but the treatment was
far simpler than the array of intersecting gables and pointed
turrets on Hay's structure. Rows of deep windows lanced
the thick walls, those of the fourth floor rounded at the top
as in a medieval abbey. The crypt-like recesses of the two

arched bays on the ground level accentuated the Romanesque aspect. Their friend Anderson, whose struggles with the architect had so often amused them, now had his goodnatured innings. "The two houses exteriorly do not meet public expectations," he wrote to his son, "and are ranked after ours, but their interiors will be of unusual magnificence and beauty and corresponding costs." An art historian, Larkin, has called them characteristic of Richardson's genius, the bold outlines and heavy geometric accents symbolical of American strength and self-reliance. However, Richardson's good friend and first biographer, Mrs. Schuyler Van Rensselaer, art critic of the New York *World* who had once called to see the Adams art collection, thought them not representative of the architect's best work because of the limitations imposed. One architect even called them "relative failures," the great hall of Hay's house being the only redeeming feature. The red brick represented a compromise, for the original elevation called for stone which would have produced an even more dignified façade and a better scale. But $30,000, the first estimate of the Adamses and curiously out of proportion to the cost of the site, would never have realized Richardson's dream, nor in the end did it cover the compromise by a long way any more successfully than in Anderson's case.[2]

Mrs. Van Rensselaer thought that in spite of "the singular plan" which Adams insisted on, there was "no decrease in excellence." She has left a careful description of the unusual interior. "The chief rooms were to be upstairs, and the ground floor was to be divided longitudinally by a wall — the hall and staircase lying to the right, the kitchen apartments to the left of it and communication effected only at the back of the house. . . . [The architect] clearly marked this division on the exterior by designing his ground-story with two low, somewhat depressed arches with a pier between them. Within one arch is the beautifully treated main doorway, and behind the other, masked by a rich iron grille, are the windows of the servants' quarters, while the door that leads to these lies beyond the arch to the left. Inside, the hall with its great fireplace and its stairway forming broad platforms is as charming as it is individual. . . . The fireplaces are their chief features — wide and low with jambs and mantels of rich-toned marbles."

Progress was slow, the construction taking almost a year and a half as architect and clients debated costs and esthetics with friendly vehemence. The work going on practically under his study windows made for considerably more distraction than Adams had bargained for. "Ten times a day I drop my work," he reported to Hay in the following autumn, "and I rush out to see the men laying bricks or stone in your house. Mine is still where it was when you were here. . . . The brick-work is beautiful." Mrs. Adams practiced her photography on the clutter of scaffoldings. No amount of resolution could withstand their imperial and mountainous friend. "Richardson put back into my contract every extravagance I had struck out, and then made me sign it. . . . He is an ogre. He devours men crude, and shows the effect of inevitable indigestion in his size." Richardson's methods tended toward the bizarre, as La Farge once noted. He did not allow blue-prints to stifle his conception, but working from the drawings of his assistants he commonly kept his "building in hand, as so much plastic material." Adams lectured him; even the opulent Hay sometimes demurred, but Richardson disarmed them both with his "ravishing designs." [3]

The ground note of his correspondence during this hectic period was always the house. He hunted stone for the main fireplace like the most fastidious of sculptors, going through the whole Smithsonian collection for a suitable sample of porphyry. Temptingly he described his find to his wife, "a

small slab of Mexican onyx of a sea-green translucency so
exquisite as to make my soul yearn." In spite of cost, the
Mexican onyx went in. During the final months of the
project in the summer of 1885 while the Adamses kept to
the seclusion of Beverly Farms, their friend Dwight, librarian
at the State Department, was left in charge of their Washington establishment as a kind of general factotum, the prelude to his becoming Adams's private secretary. Adams kept
firing off admonitory bulletins. "If you see the workmen
carving a Christian emblem, remonstrate with them like a
father. . . . I wanted a peacock. The architect wanted a
lion. Perhaps you could suggest a compromise, — say a figure
of Mr. Blaine, Conkling, or Bayard." Usually, protest was
useless. "Your account of the cross and carving fills my heart
with sadness, and steeps my lips in cocaine. I can neither
revolt nor complain, though the whole thing seems to me bad
art and bad taste. . . . Don't quote me, or repeat my grum-
blings. Our dear Washingtonians chatter so much that one is
forced to deny them food for gossip." When at last the façade
stood fully revealed, Adams conceded that Richardson had
"toned down the worst carvings," but the newspapers preserved an "ominous silence." [4]

Between architecture and politics, he yet managed to wind
up work on the second administration of Jefferson, finishing
the draft in the summer of 1884. Shortly before the end of
the year, he could tell Parkman, "My own labor is just half
done. Two heavy volumes have been put into type, partly
for safety, partly to secure the advantages of a first edition."
At least his scholarly priority would be established. He was
impelled to take stock of his achievement, especially because
of the political upheaval they had just witnessed in the election of Cleveland which had ended twenty-three years of
Republican rule, swept out of the way, so it seemed to him,
by forces as inexorable as those which had carried Jefferson

and Madison helplessly down the stream of history. The immense political machine built up under Lincoln, Grant, Hayes, and Arthur seemed to have dissolved as inevitably as a salt in a chemical solution. The matter required an appropriate generalization: "The more I write, the more confident I feel that before long a new school of history will rise which will leave us antiquated. Democracy is the only subject for history." [5]

The six copies of the second volume went out to the same loyal band of readers who had received the first. One of them, George Bancroft, reciprocated by sending over his monumental revision of his own history for Adams's eye. Enviously — or at least with gracious flattery — Adams remarked, "In you I detect no sign of the weariness and languor which mark the close of other men's histories, and which, I regret to say, have descended on the middle of mine." That a sense of languor should have overtaken him after five years of extraordinary application was hardly surprising. Not only had he brought his own huge project to the halfway point and the end of an era, he had produced two biographies and two novels in the same period. It had been the most intensely cerebral five years of his life, with his first novel marking the first break-through of his imaginative perceptions from the bonds of polemics and scholarship. *Esther* signalized another stage in the growth of the artist, the development of poetic insight. Clearly the inner war had deepened over his true role as a writer. He had succeeded too well as a historian, too rapidly, having in fact become a leading authority before the appearance of his major work. Already he seemed aware of a kind of anticlimax in his effort. The political revolution that he thought he witnessed confirmed the sense of break and transition. Chester A. Arthur's almost silent disappearance from the scene, the epitome of political frustration, must have seemed an artistic parallel of Jefferson's

inglorious departure at the end of his second term, swept
out on a political ebb-tide.[6]

In that slack-water his personal situation, however, was
secure. "My history will go on, I hope, as quietly under Mr.
Cleveland as under Mr. Arthur." But the work was not destined to go on quietly in 1885. The distractions of building
were about to be multiplied by far more alarming difficulties.
Moreover, the very materials of Madison's first administration
defied enlivening. The whole intricate tangle of diplomatic
cross purposes and political bumbling that only the outbreak of the War of 1812 would untie, resisted every effort
of dramatic contrast. "Executive Weakness," "Legislative Im-
potence" were the characteristic labels for this sterile period.
Some of the gray coloration of his domestic life that summer
seems also to have diminished the luckless Madison. After
the greater Jefferson left the stage, "a well-graced actor,"
the colorless Madison was pure anticlimax.[7]

The personal crisis which Adams had foreseen in *Esther*
broke upon him in March, 1885. Mrs. Adams's seventy-four
year old father, Dr. Hooper, had been ill for some months
suffering the agonies of angina pectoris. He now suddenly
took a turn for the worse. His devoted "Clover" and Henry
reached his bedside in Cambridge almost as rapidly as her
Sunday letter, which bubbled with news of the "Mugwumpish
tendencies" of Cleveland's appointments. Her Thursday "Special" had regaled her father with the picturesque highlights
of the inaugural parade. She had felt something of the
same girlish excitement of twenty years before when she
had cajoled her way down to Washington to see the Grand
Review of Grant's and Sherman's victorious armies. "Clover"
stayed on with the anxious family in Fayerweather Street
to help nurse the old man whom she idolized, the person
who since her early childhood had been both father and
mother to her. For a month she endured the round-the-clock

ordeal, gallantly facing the grim event like Esther. Next door her five young nieces demanded attention. One of them remembered how Aunt Clover summoned an Adams nephew from Harvard one evening to help with a dancing lesson for the older girls.[8]

Adams's letters to his wife during this month were the first he was ever under the necessity of writing to her. He felt a sensation of strangeness with the first letter, he who had written thousands to others. "As it is now thirteen years since my last letter to you," he rallied her, "you may have forgotten my name. If so try to recall it. For a time we were somewhat intimate." He had inspected the new house once again. He could assure her that it would be even more handsome than the Hays'. In any case the twin result was bound to "make a sensation." He could send "only a little crumb of love . . . the dogs need so much." Poetically addressed, "Dear Mistress" and "Dear Angel" they are, at the same time, astonishingly devoid of tenderness, filled with the surface concerns of household and society, visits to the dentist, dinners with Hay and other friends, queries about library fixtures and bells for the new house — all the small talk of a busy household. Solitude, the isolation that he always dreaded, had one compensation; he had escaped the terrors of his habitual insomnia, sleeping "for once, without waking from twelve till nine o'clock." [9]

The mercurial Hay was in the dumps again about his house, then Nick Anderson burst in like a gale to cry out that Hay's house is "the finest thing in existence" and up went the "dear Hay's spirits." Clarence King sent them a white porcelain tea set. Lowndes had "beat his head off at chess." Some antic of La Farge's showed he was "insane, — literally," which in Adams's lexicon meant *figuratively*. Alex Agassiz had popped in again "brown and burned" from the study of the Hawaiian coral reefs. Russell Sturgis, Eugene

Schuyler and he had browsed in a Japanese art dealer's shop, hunting bronzes. Richardson and he had called on President Cleveland. "We must admit," he said of their new neighbor, "that, like Abraham Lincoln, the Lord made a mighty common-looking man in him. I expected it and was satisfied. He was very quiet and said little." However, the President's serious-minded sister talked deferentially with him about George Eliot's biography.

There were recurring alarms, so that Adams bolted "forward and back like a brown monkey" between Washington and Cambridge, feeling thoroughly useless and unwanted. On a return journey he bumped into King on the train. King, on his way to Mexico and the dubious Sombrerete mine, was just home from Europe and full of his experiences with Ruskin, from whom he had bought a Turner from the same series as their own "Martigny." Adams busied himself with everything but history though he was pleased to allow Mrs. Bancroft to read the new volume because she was "by all odds the most intelligent woman in Washington." [10]

For the first time Adams watched the delicious overture of spring along the bridle paths without his wife's companionship, but he reported Nature's progress to her with the loving detail of a Thoreau in Walden woods. "April 10, 9 a.m. . . . The day was fine though cool (Therm. 44°), and I took my first three-hour spring excursion round by the dog-tooth violets and Rigg's farm. A few maples showed a faint flush here and there, but not a sign of leaf is to be seen, and even the blood-root and hepatica hid themselves from my eyes. A few frogs sang in the sun, and birds sang in the trees; but no sign of a peach-blossom yet, and not even the magnolias and *Pyrus Japonica* [flowering quince] have started." Like a true Thoreauvian he carefully checked Nature's performance against his journal record of other springs. "In 1878 the magnolias were in full flower and killed by frost on March 25, and in 1882 the frost killed them on April 10. I have not even seen the yellow forsythia in flower, though it should have been out as early as March 15. Last year the *Pyrus Japonica* was reddening on April 2." What Mrs. Adams's response was to her husband's diverting barrage of news and gossip does not appear, for her letters to him have vanished. The strain of the vigil was evidently very great. One cryptic telegram summoning him to Cambridge "at first," as he told her, "frightened me out of my wits." But Richardson reassured him, "declaring he would give anything in the world if his wife would send such a telegram to him." [11]

At last on April 13, 1885, the ordeal came to an end. "Poor Dr. Hooper," as Adams tersely reported to Hay, was dead "of heart disease." In his will he named Adams one of the three trustees of the half-million dollar estate, of which one-third of the income was to go to Mrs. Adams. Outwardly composed, Mrs. Adams thanked the Hays for their sympathy, sadly recalling how they had "gone over the same road," after the suicide of Mrs. Hay's father, "without the comfort or even gayety with which my father walked to his grave. His humour and courage lasted till unconsciousness came on the 9th and on the 13th he went to sleep like a tired traveller." She too could be gay. "I send you something which will amuse you," she added, "Henry James, Jr. again!" The full impact of the shock was yet to be felt. For Clover it would mean the end of the strongest attachment of her life, the arrest of the years' long ritual of letter writing to which father and daughter simultaneously consecrated a portion of every Sunday of their lives. Adams might well have hoped that out of this season of aimless drift would in time come a deeper communion between his wife and him, a strengthening of that dependence upon each other which, as he once observed, the absence of children made necessary. Anxiously Adams waited the outcome, hoping that the real-

life Esther would safely re-cross the abyss. Here was another
prophetic likeness between Carlyle and him. Mrs. Adams had
not long since jested about that "painfully droll couple" and
she had teased him as *her* "man of genius" when they read
Mrs. Carlyle's letters. Carlyle too had prepared him; for the
death of his wife's father "in a sense almost broke her heart,"
as Adams read in the *Reminiscences*. "To the end of her
life his title even to me was 'he' and 'him.'" [12]

In June the Adamses quietly sojourned at Old Sweet
Springs, West Virginia, enjoying long saddle rides on the
mountain trails. Here they were joined by a Washington
intimate, Rebecca Dodge, whose blue-stocking interests Adams
gently rallied with verses from a Milton sonnet:

> Lady that in the prime of earliest youth,
> Wisely hast shunned the broad way and the green,
> And with those few are eminently seen,
> That labor up the hill of heavenly truth.

He had cast about at once for diversion, asking Pumpelly
to arrange a tour of western Canada for them. Then thinking that too strenuous, he got his friend Arnold Hague to
plan a six-week pack trip for them in the Yellowstone country.
This trip too was abandoned in favor of Old Sweet Springs.
A change became apparent in Mrs. Adams and, as a result,
instead of renting out the Beverly Farms place as they had
planned they took refuge there. [13]

During the summer Adams, supplied with boxes of materials for his desk, thought to end the hiatus of two months in
his writing, but he found it "almost impossible to resume
historical work. The muscles seem to refuse to respond to
the will." Doggedly he pushed on. "History is always with
me, — and be hanged to it." "We vegetate," he wrote their
old family friend, John W. Field; "I do what I still call
history, which is now a mere mechanical fitting together of

quotations." He also diverted himself constructing elaborate genealogical tables of the Adamses and the Hoopers, "but I lose my temper when I cannot find a missing grandmother, and the temptation to swear becomes irresistible." The months passed in a kind of nightmare as his wife's iron composure gradually gave way to nameless fears. Not since their wedding journey on the Nile, thirteen years before, had she experienced such a seizure of depression, but that had been short-lived. She rallied sufficiently by the end of the summer for him to put in an appearance at the second annual meeting of the American Historical Association at Saratoga Springs in September. He and his Washington friend Eugene Schuyler, the diplomat, had no academic connections but were received as "eminent specialists." His old colleagues, Ephraim Gurney and Justin Winsor, were also there and his former students, Ephraim Emerton and Edward Channing. He had not attended the founding meeting, the previous year, being weighed down then with printer's proofs, but had joined as a life member shortly afterwards. His brother Charles immediately followed suit, as did Brooks the next year.[14]

The outgoing head of the association, President Andrew D. White of Cornell, had thoughtfully distributed his address, waiving the reading of it out of deference to Goldwin Smith of Toronto, but not foregoing an oral commentary. Before the end of the meeting he also read an extremely long paper on "A History of the Doctrine of Comets," reviewing the superstitions attaching to them. Charles Kendall Adams pontificated more informally. It was too much for Henry. "The prevalence of Andrew D. White and C. K. Adams," he remarked with acerbity, "was rather disastrous to History." He fled without waiting for Schuyler's paper, even though he had something of a vested interest in it, "Materials for American History in Foreign Archives." That a woman historian, Lucy Salmon, was also on the program, did not raise his opinion of the proceedings. "Unless we get more history into our management," he angrily commented, "we shall not get far towards omniscience except in cemetery theory and female story-telling." [15]

Once more in a hopeful mood the Adamses busied themselves getting ready to reopen their Washington establishment. They reached town in mid-October. Suddenly Mrs. Adams was overwhelmed by a profound depression of spirits. "We lead a quiet and very retired life at present," Adams explained, "as my wife goes nowhere." Their friend Anderson gloomed, "I am afraid I am bitterly revenged on the Adamses for the fun they had with my architect troubles, for their house is not nearly finished and Mrs. Adams is suffering from nervous prostration." With rigid self-control the unhappy Adams drove ahead with his research at the State Department library, hampered by Dwight's temporary absence because he had come to rely upon him as an assistant. At this moment in mid-November, Henry Holt, unaware of the critical strain, proposed actively pushing *Democracy* again. Adams wrote a nervous veto. "By-gones are pretty well by-gone, and I am not so particular as I was; but, all the same, I am peculiarly anxious not to wake up the critics just now. Luckily they have not seen my little red flag. [*Esther?*] for the fellowship of the Holy Saints, do not wave it at them! I never had so many reasons for wishing to be left in peace, as now." [16]

Disturbed as he was by his wife's mental state, he did not yet suspect its full gravity and he did not think to call in their Baltimore friend Dr. S. Weir Mitchell, one of the most eminent neurologists of the day. Masking his disquiet, he sent off one of his periodical eight-page letters to Cunliffe, allowing himself to say only that his wife had "been, as it were a good deal off her feed this summer and shows no such fancy for mending as I could wish." For the rest he delivered a shrewd disquisition on English politics, Cunliffe having lost his seat in Parliament at the recent election. Gladstone's Tories had undercut the liberals by appropriating their program. Adams reflected, "A very curious law seems to rule elections. I have had occasion to notice here, where no real principle divides us, that some queer mechanical balance holds the two parties even, so that changes of great numbers of voters leave no trace in the sum total. I suspect the law will some day be formulated that in democratic societies, parties tend to an equilibrium." In the face of this political entropy, he proposed new alignments, as the middle ground was disappearing. "The Whigs, from Edmund Burke to Carlo Gaskell and even yourself," he pointedly remarked, "were always conservatives at heart." They would have to frankly join the Tories or make their peace with Joseph Chamberlain's Radical wing of the Liberals. "As an American I want to see all traces of medievalism preserved in Europe; — otherwise Americans will be left without a single place to study history and bric-a-brac; but, American as I am . . . I admit that neither the Church nor the Peerage strikes me as likely to satisfy any radical like myself who happens to be in their shadow. Therefore, if I were one of your party, I should be obliged to follow the potent Chamberlain. . . . We radicals mean to reform the whole concern; and if we are to fail, we might as well fail under conservative rule as under any other." [17]

But if Adams could find surcease in the accustomed round of thought, his wife could see no light in the darkness of her despair though, mercifully, she continued to be lucid. With gathering swiftness the depressive phase of her illness ran its course, accompanied by the usual sense of profound unworthiness. She rallied briefly in accord with the inexorable pattern of manic-depressive psychosis. On Sunday morning, December 6, a week after the letter to Cunliffe, she sat at

her writing desk again. It was useless now to think of the
accustomed letter to her father. Once she had thoughtlessly
jested about such things to him, having heard that a noted
friend of theirs had voluntarily gone to Somerville for treatment. "The insane asylum seems to be the goal of every good
and conscientious Bostonian, babies and insanity the two
leading topics. So and so has a baby. She becomes insane
and goes to Somerville, baby grows up and promptly retires
to Somerville." Dr. Hooper himself active in the affairs of
the Worcester Asylum had reproached her for her "taste for
horrors" when she asked him to brief her on the season's toll
in Boston. Marian defended her curiosity with grim wit. She
only wanted to prepare herself for her annual return, "otherwise in June I must visit Somerville and ask to see the patients' book, and then explore Mt. Auburn for new-laid
graves." She had cause now to repent her satire. Lost in an
anguishing sense of guilt, she wrote to her sister, Ellen: "If
I had one single point of character or goodness I would
stand on that and grow back to life. Henry is more patient
and loving than words can express. God might envy him —
he bears and hopes and despairs hour after hour. . . . Henry
is beyond all words tenderer and better than all of you even."
The note remained on the desk, unsent.[18]

The next day the evening issue of the Washington *Critic*
carried the following item:

— Death from Heart Paralysis —

Mr. Henry Adams of 1607 H Street, while leaving the house
yesterday morning for a walk, was met at the door by a lady
who called to see his wife. Mr. Adams went upstairs to learn if
his wife could see the visitor, and was horrified to see her lying
on a rug before the fire, where she had fallen from a chair. He
hastened for assistance, after placing her on a sofa, and meeting
Dr. Charles E. Hagner they returned, when the physician stated
that she was dead and had probably died instantly from paralysis
of the heart . . .

The *Post* report of the same date added a few details.

Mrs. Adams had been an invalid for several months but had been quite rapidly recovering. Indeed yesterday morning she told her husband, in reply to questions concerning her health, that she was better than she had been for a long time. Her appearance certainly indicated as much, and Mr. Adams noted a marked improvement in his wife's condition. The unexpected suddenness of her death made the blow all the more severe. . . . Mr. Adams has been erecting a very handsome residence at the corner of Sixteenth and H Streets, which he had contemplated occupying next month.

In the *Evening Star* on the following day President Cleveland's first message to Congress promising "reform and retrenchment" and condemning silver coinage and polygamy among the Mormons crowded out all mention of the tragedy except for the briefest death notice.[19]

The true story could not long be suppressed. On Wednesday, the ninth, the Washington *Critic* asked — and answered — the shocked surmises behind all the fashionable doors of the capital.

Was it a case of Suicide?

The certificate of Coroner Patterson and Dr. Hagner in the case of Mrs. Henry Adams, who died suddenly in this city on Sunday last, is to the effect that she came to her death through an overdose of potassium [cyanide], administered by herself. A New York *Sun* correspondent states further that there is no doubt Mrs. Adams intended to take her own life. She was just recovering from a long illness, and had been suffering from mental depression. Mrs. Adams was formerly Miss Marian Hooper of Boston. She was well known and highly esteemed in society in that city and in Washington, which had more recently been her home. She left no children.

There was a crushing finality in the last sentence that only those who knew them well fully appreciated. One of Mrs. Adams's oldest friends, Mrs. Whiteside, from whom she had grown apart in recent years, now remarked with severe piety:

"How often we have spoken of Clover as having all she wanted, all this world could give, except children — and not having any was a greater grief to Mr. Adams than to her. And now at forty years old [42], down comes a black curtain, and all is over. Yet in my unorthodox mind I can't help hoping that hers was invincible ignorance, and that somehow and somewhere she is learning better things." Even to the unorthodox, Marian's frank agnosticism could not go unchided. The correspondent for the New York *Sun* added a macabre touch for its more jaded readers: "Although she was still warm they could not revive her. The fumes of the poison and the empty phial that contained it, told plainly enough the cause of death." [20]

In this sensational fashion the tragedy was trumpeted to the social and political world of Washington, New York, and Boston, where they and their families were widely known. All their lives they had lived in terror of clacking tongues. Throughout the years of their marriage they had successfully defended their privacy from the society columnists. Adams himself had always loved to make a "sensation," but on his own terms. Unfavorable publicity had made him acutely miserable. He never forgot or forgave the drubbing the London *Times* gave him when the editor stumbled upon his authorship of the letters in the Boston *Courier*. He had also had a succession of *mauvais quart d'heur's* in the days when Senator Howe sneeringly advertised him as a "begonia." The front-page newspaper headlines would have made a far less sensitive man cringe. One can imagine his humiliation and panic, especially when he saw that there were those in the press who were not above petty revenges.

Less than a week after the tragedy the Washington *Critic* earned its name with a story whose blunders at least must have offered sardonic amusement to the bereaved husband.

In effect it repeated the retaliatory gossip of Senator Blaine's friends.

The late Mrs. Henry Adams is generally supposed to have been the author of 'Democracy,' a novel in which the society of Washington was almost savagely criticized. She had a reputation of saying bitter things of men and measures, and of her fellow women too, and although an entertaining talker, was generally distrusted and failed to become socially popular. Her husband, Mr. Adams, is also an author of some note, having contributed a life of Calhoun [sic] to the Statesman series, and also [sic] one of Albert Gallatin.

The New York *World* followed the *Critic*'s lead, observing in its gossip column, "Prominent People," that Mrs. Adams "was the possessor of that most dangerous woman's weapon, a sharp tongue, and was not at all popular in society. She was believed to be the author of the anonymous novel 'Democracy,' which created such a sensation in Washington and was regarded in England as the great American novel of the year." Even a year later an echo of the event sounded in the gossip column of an Iowa newspaper. The reporter, writing of the new twin houses on Lafayette Square, said: "Mr. Adams, next door, has a splendid home, but his wife in a temporary fit of insanity committed suicide a year ago, so that the shadow of such a great sorrow prevents ostentatious living." [21]

Against the harsh detractions could be placed, however, the sympathetic and respectful obituary in the Boston *Transcript*, an estimate which was to set the tone of all future published references.

In the death of Mrs. Henry Adams, Washington loses one of its most brilliant and accomplished women. Her house was the pleasantest resort of the cleverest men and women who live in and who visit the capital. She came nearer being the head of an intellectual coterie than any woman there, and to be asked to her home was a privilege which comparatively few obtained, and to which many aspired. Mr. Adams who is the son of Charles Francis Adams and was once professor of history at Harvard University and his wife cared less for public rank than any people in a society where rank is naturally greatly regarded. They took Presidents, and Cabinet officers and senators at their worth, and high rank of itself gave no one a passport to their house.

Mrs. Adams was a sincere as well as an accomplished and witty woman. Those who knew her will always cherish her acquaintance as an honor, and her sudden death will bring great grief to them all. She was the daughter of the late Dr. Hooper who died some months ago and a sister of Mr. Edward Hooper who was the treasurer of the corporation of Harvard University. Her husband has the sincere sympathy of many friends in Massachusetts and throughout the country.[22]

In a first report of the tragedy the Washington correspondent of the New York *World*, after glossing over Mrs. Adams's death as "caused by heart trouble," had added appreciatively, "She was a very skilful amateur photographer and was a member of the Amateur Photographers' Club here. She has made a number of very artistic negatives of distinguished people among her friends and acquaintances." It was among the chemicals used in her photographic darkroom that Mrs. Adams found the means of her self-destruction.[23]

2   Between Oneself and Eternity

The terror that had motivated Mrs. Adams's act had had its fictional counterpart in Adams's novel. Esther's father, incurably ill, feared going "off by bits, as though I were ashamed to be seen running away . . . instead of going off suddenly and without notice as a colonel of New York volunteers should." Dr. Hooper's lingering death of angina pectoris confirmed the worth of the principle. Marian's own phrase to her father, as she once joked about a passing illness, was that she hoped her final fate would be that of the

One-Hoss Shay. The horror of prolonged illness and enfeeble-
ment of the mind haunted both Adams and his wife. In his
father's humiliating mental decline in Quincy, Adams imagined
he saw the shadow of his own fate, and the calendar of lucid
years still left to him seemed written on his study walls.
The thought made him anxious to hurry on with his writing.
In the preceding year, when an aunt of hers was languishing
in extremis, Marian Adams wrote to her father, "My silent
prayer is for heart disease or lightning when my time comes."
Years before when their painter friend William Hunt "put
an end to his wild, restless, unhappy life," she philosophized,
"Perhaps it has saved him years of insanity, which his temperament pointed to." She wrote in a similarly stoical vein
of another acquaintance, "What the use is of prolonging existence with a stone in one's heart I can't see." Was not her
favorite Jane Carlyle to be envied that her fervent wished
for "death from the Gods" had been graciously granted? [24]
    The hypothesis first advanced by Katherine Simonds that
Henry Adams unconsciously caused his wife's death by in-
fecting her with his scepticism and pessimism and thus un-
dermining her will to live seems far-fetched and even sentimental. Married at twenty-eight, her character fully developed
and already given to eccentricity, as Adams's own early characterization of her made clear, inured to the society of brilliant and heterodox people, Marian was hardly an impres-
sionable young girl to be robbed of her faith in the church
of her fathers. Maturity came early in Boston and New York
society, as her friend Henry James noted of one of his heroines: "At the age of twenty-two [she] was, after all, a rather
mature blossom, such as could be plucked from the stem only
by a vigorous jerk." [25]
    What the faith of her father was is portrayed in the char-
acter of Mr. Dudley in *Esther* whose lack of religion was a

discouraging example in the eyes of Esther's aunt. Mr. Dudley "never sat in his pew, and never expected to do so; he had no taste for church-going." In this respect Mr. Dudley reflected her father's practice. As a proprietor of King's Chapel in Boston, Mrs. Adams's father had kept a pew there for decades, but rarely occupied it. In a brief memoir of their father, Marian's brother Edward wrote with a certain euphemism that Dr. Hooper's "religious feeling was strong and constant but rarely expressed except in his personal character." When the Adamses first came to Washington, Marian already had a violent distaste for churchgoing and the sanctimonies attached to Lent. The death of Pope Pius IX aroused the militant rationalist in her. "How depressing to Pius the IX to wake up in another world and find himself 'sold' the remains of an exploded fallacy beginning life as a street sweeper in the New Jerusalem." Irreverence was her most natural state. Bored by the Comédie Française, she ejaculated, "It's duller than King's Chapel." She shared her scorn for Nordhoff's *God and Future Life* with her understanding father, "To me it is incomprehensible stuff — but life passed between Mrs. Nordhoff and the New York *Herald* office may account for a good deal." In her hundreds of letters to her father there is no hint that he ever reproached her for her irreligion, though he took her to task occasionally on other matters. Amused once by the advertisement of her cousin Russell Sturgis in a Boston paper, "Wanted a Christian cook — none other need apply," Mrs. Adams "went him one better and tried for a free thinker, but had to compromise on a 'hardshell baptist.' " [26]

The entries in her letters to her father expressing annoyance with occasional indispositions are hardly to be taken as signs that her religious beliefs were being undermined by her husband. Though not a robust person, she was an expert horsewoman and keenly enjoyed their long daily rides in the open air, summer and winter. She easily laughed off being accidentally flung into a swamp. Moreover, the tone of her latest letters is as buoyant and animated as the earliest. The onset of middle age seemed to disturb her far less than it did Henry Adams who was hagridden by the sense of the flying years. "When one is forty and on the home stretch," she wrote with witty stoicism, "it's consoling to find it suits one better to look ahead than behind. If Lot's wife hadn't been a morbid conservative she would have had a sweeter old age and been a pillar of strength to her reprehensible husband." [27]

It may be that the perfectionist Adams set such very high standards for social and intellectual intercourse as to put his wife too continuously on her mettle to be a witty and accomplished hostess; yet she played her role with enormous relish, often greater than her husband's. He had indeed good-naturedly patronized her before their marriage as someone considerably younger and less sophisticated than he, but his jocular critique was not much more than the defensive apologies of the somewhat embarrassed bachelor who has finally capitulated. Actually, his wife had lived in an intensely social and intellectual atmosphere long before she met him, her father's house on Beacon Street being a symbol of their aristocratic position. For years before her marriage she had been hostess for her widowed father and intimately acquainted with distinguished older friends of his like Dr. Oliver Wendell Holmes. Cambridge academic, literary and artistic circles were opened to her through her eminent brother and her brother-in-law, Professor Gurney. It was a world that set very high standards for an avidly intellectual and imaginative young girl, so that from the beginning she could hardly have avoided feelings of inadequacy and a pressure to excel. Her experience at the temple of Karnak on her wedding trip was only a fresh reminder of limitations which her ambitious nature was always striving to overcome. "How true it is," she had confided to her father, "that the mind sees what it has the means of seeing. I get so little, while the others about me are so intelligent and cultivated that everything appeals to them." [28]

Yet if disapproving blame cannot properly be placed at the door of Adams's intellectual pride, he himself behaved as if tormented by some obscure sense of guilt. What followed in the wake of that calamitous Sunday suggests an over-mastering impulse toward expiation and self-mortification. He had, it was true, unwittingly helped forge a link in the fatal chain by initiating his wife into photography, which called for the use of one of the deadliest of all poisons, potassium cyanide. He had indeed been careless to allow such a deadly agent to be accessible to his wife in her terribly depressed state. So much blame he could hardly have avoided imputing to himself. A simple precaution and she might have still been alive. Beyond that there was something that may have been far more subtly disturbing to so fine a conscience as his. Could he be sure that he had not wished the death of Marian's father? In his novel he showed a vivid awareness of the latent hostility of a father-in-law. When the talk turned to Esther's possible marrying, her father is made to say with sardonic humor, "It is not she, but her husband who is on my mind. I have hated the fellow all his life. About twice a year I have treacherously stabbed him in the back as he was going out of my own front door. I knew that he would interfere with my comfort if I let him get a footing. After all he was always a poor creature, and did not deserve to live. My conscience does not reproach me." Even more shattering must be the doubt that Marian's grief for her father was stronger than her love for her husband. How painful also to realize that it was her act that made him a marked man, obscurely suspect.[29]

Adams's first impulse was to hide from his friends. He sent "a pitiful cry from the heart" to their neighbor Miss Dodge, "to keep everyone away." It was an unlucky impulse. Nick Anderson wrote in bafflement to his son, "I called as soon as I heard it, and offered to do all I could, but Henry refused to see anyone. I appreciate his state of mind, but I am sorry he would not let me show my sympathy by my acts. Until his family arrived he saw, as far as I can learn, no one whatever, and I can imagine nothing more ghastly than that lonely vigil in the house with his dead wife. Poor fellow! I do not know what he can do." Other residents of the Square wondered also as they saw him stare fixedly out of the window.[30]

Many years later he thought he remembered the "awful horror of solitude for the hours before friends could reach one, in the first instants of prostration." But memory was deceiving him again. Similarly, when someone inadvertently mentioned the name of his wife in his presence, he said sadly, "I have not heard my wife's name spoken for over twenty years. That was a great mistake." One of his auditors could not forbear adding that the blame for the mistake rested on Adams himself for he had made it only too obvious that he did not wish his friends to mention her name.[31]

Henry had instantly telegraphed his brother Charles, who reached Washington the following afternoon, soon after the arrival of Edward Hooper, sister Ellen, and her husband Ephraim Gurney. At dinner, moved by a sudden impulse, he startled the family by coming down wearing a bright red tie and tore off the mourning crepe from his arm and threw it under the table. His wife would have understood the gesture, for as a Sturgis she scorned such tokens of mourning. Charles laconically recorded in his diary that the next day he "drove with Henry out of town and took a walk with him." One matter that would have to be attended to was

Marian's estate. Her trust interests would of course expire, but of the rest of her small fortune of $40,000 and the house at Beverly Farms, which had been owned by her, Henry was the sole legatee, and very soon afterwards he followed the Brahmin custom of putting the entire estate in trust, naming himself as beneficiary, but he treated the income and, at his death, the principal as belonging to his wife's five nieces. Their future, as he explained to one of the trustees, "is much more on my mind than is my own." [32]

John Hay had wired at once from New York and followed the telegram with a letter. "I hoped all day yesterday and this morning to hear from you, and thought it possible that you might summon King and me to be with you at the last. . . . I can neither talk to you nor remain silent. The darkness in which you walk has its shadow for me also. You and your wife were more to me than any other two. I came to Washington because you were there . . . Is it any consolation to remember her as she was? That bright, intrepid spirit, that keen fine intellect, that lofty scorn of all that was mean, that social charm which made your house such a one as Washington never knew before, and made hundreds of people love her, as much as they admired her."

The most wayward of the "Hearts," Clarence King groped with a curiously strained awkwardness for "those few words of heart-felt condolence which seem every moment on my lips." Misunderstanding the announcements, he waited in New York expecting to see Adams as he passed "en route to lay the form of your wife near Boston." Hay's telegram, the first shocked reflex of his sympathy, did not go unanswered. Adams's unfalteringly precise script crossed Hay's touching tribute in the mail. "Never fear for me," he reassured his anxious friend. "I shall come out all right from this — what shall I call it? — Hell!" As witness to his self-command, he declared that he would go ahead with a trip to Japan "just as we planned it together." [33]

By the eleventh Gurney was able to assure Godkin that Adams "has in a measure recovered his tone, and is setting his face steadily towards the future. He is anxious to go into the new house, — or rather to go out of the old, as soon as possible, and settle down to his routine life and work. . . . [Theodore] Dwight, librarian at the State Department, who occupied their house during the summer will take our place when we go, and will remain with Henry for an indefinite time." To the ever-solicitous Hay, Adams sent assurance that he "was getting through the days somehow."

"You will understand as I do that my only chance of saving whatever is left of my life can consist only in going straight ahead without looking behind. I feel like a volunteer in his first battle. If I don't run ahead at full speed, I shall run away. If I could but keep in violent action all the time, I could manage to master myself, but this wretched bundle of nerves which we call mind, gives me no let up, and I am only grateful beyond words that it allows me to sleep." He therefore urged the Hays to come on to Washington and occupy their house. He meant to sleep in his before New Year's. "We can hardly make matters worse." [34]

On December 30 Marian's sister sent a further report to Godkin: "I hear from Henry constantly — far better news than he or C[lover] could have dared hope [re the house]. I trust he will be in his new house tonight. The associations of the old were too intense to be safely borne. Dwight is balm. He says if I'm not peaceful he will send him on. Henry rides — moves his books — looks out of window — is like a small child — reads Shakespeare aloud evenings — has several familiar friends of theirs — mostly Mrs. Field and women just now." His favorite, Mrs. Cameron, was one of the loyal company who ministered to him. A recent news story about her in the Washington *Critic* offered passing amusement. "Although the stepmother of six children she still presents a brow unlined by care, and a voice and manner as gay and youthful as possible. Constant late hours and the wear and tear attendant upon the onerous task of continued entertaining which her husband's position exacts has not told upon her at all." [35]

Cossetted and mothered in this fashion, Adams now set out on the long career which was to be lived increasingly among an entourage of women, of nieces real and imaginary, in fact and in wish. The turning was almost a reflex action. A worshipper and idealizer of Woman from his earliest days — for example, he treasured to the end of his life the little note that his grandmother sent with her gift of the *Vicar of Wakefield* — Adams came to prefer "women's society," as his brother Brooks recalled, "in which he could be amused and tranquillized." There was in truth a feminine quality in his fastidious withdrawal, a withdrawal that would become the "ostentatious retirement" whose ceremonials charmed his intimates.[36]

Not only did the mother-image draw him on and with such strength that in his letters he would sometimes play with the fancy of being a small boy at a mother's knee, but also the old family trait of "self-mortification" which all of the Adamses had, as he said, "inherited from Calvinism" asserted itself. In such an access of self-mortification he declared that he had "also died to the world." "I have had happiness enough to carry me over some years of misery: and even in my worst prostration I have found myself strengthened by two thoughts. One was that life could have no other experience so crushing. The other was that at least I had got out of life all the pleasure it had to give. I admit that fate at last has smashed the life out of me; but for twelve years I had everything I most wanted on earth." He was never to relinquish this tragically sentimental role. What remained to him could only be a kind of posthumous existence. He had no more interest in life, he said, "except as a bystander." The role came easily to him, for he had always prized his vantage point on his stool high above the crowd. Now there was a special sanction for his habitual disclaimer of responsibility. "When one cares for nothing in particular, life becomes almost entertaining. I feel as though I were at a theatre — not a first class, but a New York theatre." His life with Marian was "closed forever, locked up, and put away," as he would write, "to be kept as a sort of open secret, between oneself and eternity." The private drama of his mourning sometimes startled an acquaintance. When the president of the American Academy of Arts and Letters once invited him to prepare an address for a public meeting, Adams turned to him "with a quizzical look, as if [he] were the most ignorant person in the world, and said: 'Do you know, Mr. Johnson, that I have been dead for fifteen years.'" Like Conrad Aiken's Mr. Arcularis, he found that the role permitted him "a mild, cynical tolerance for everything and everyone," a perpetual license for a wry and world-weary amusement.[37]

The experience was the first of a long series of portentous "notices to quit" that the death of persons close to him announced. He grew to feel himself the grim recording secretary of his circle, as if they were all playing some sort of obstacle race to the grave. In his copy of the 1898 *Report of the Class of 1858* he painstakingly added asterisks as the black-bordered cards arrived until the original necrology of thirty-eight grew to sixty-seven, while his posthumous life went merrily on.

The manner in which he wore his grief may have been strange and excessive, but it was a period in which mourning often took exaggerated forms and found expression in curious self-imposed taboos. It was the fashion to be "half in love with easeful Death," to seek new ways to cultivate sorrow. The morbid mood found expression in books of poems like that of his friend Dr. S. Weir Mitchell, *Psalms of Death*. Had not Tennyson sung of "seas of Death and sunless gulfs of doubt"? When Lowell's wife died, he too like Adams declared it had broken his life in two. His favorite, Carlyle, every detail of whose life interested him, had set a kind of model. Carlyle had written that the death of his wife had "smitten my whole world into universal wreck." Among Adams's intimates, the restless Agassiz, a widower for many years, sometimes gave frightening hint of his suffering, acting, as he said, "a constant lie." At a reference to the death of his wife, he held up his hands and said, "I cannot bear it!" with such a look of agony that the subject was never again mentioned. He too had "died" with her. Sometimes the ritual of grief went to grotesque extremes. Queen Victoria had her husband's evening clothes laid out every night as a memorial. Rossetti buried all his unpublished manuscripts with his wife's body. The conspicuous silence of *The Education* concerning his wife was to be one of Adams's contributions to this tradition. Mrs. Adams had once told of a prominent couple whom they knew never again appearing in society or even dining out after the death of their daughter four years before. In Adams's case his dark humor seemed to justify itself like the minister's black veil in Hawthorne's story for a grim succession of deaths soon began among friends and relatives.[38]

Faithfully nurturing his own grief, he became a master of the condolence letter, each one falling gently upon its recipient like a sad accolade of initiation into "the Hearts that Ache," as he termed their fraternity. In 1892 when Nick Anderson died, he stoically reviewed his own plight. "He is almost the last of my college companions, and sad as I am to bid him goodbye, I have long ago looked on my own life as quite finished, and have accustomed myself to the idea of waiting only a little while more or less, before joining him and the rest. Three of us have gone in little more than a year, comparatively young all of them, and the two or three of them who remain must make ready." He little dreamed that he would have to hold himself in readiness for twenty-six years more.[39]

The new house into which he moved on the very last days of 1885 became a kind of symbolic tomb for him and he inhabited it with a macabre gaiety, renouncing the world like a Buddhist monk in pursuit of Nirvana. On Christmas day he sent to Mrs. Cameron, on the other side of the Square, "a little trinket . . . a favorite of my wife's," asking that she "sometimes wear it, to remind you of her." To the Corcoran Gallery of Art he gave as a memorial the two Joshua Reynolds portraits whose discovery had so delighted Mrs. Adams.[40]

The mood of almost Gothic sensibility in which he now luxuriated had its literary and poetic preparation in the prescient pages of *Esther*. The sonnets which he had translated out of Petrarch were now suddenly clothed with tragic personal meanings. How often he had sounded the note, unaware of waiting fate, of the lover faithful unto death who finally turns through his spiritualized love to a contempt for the world. Indeed the sombre fantasy of having died with the death of the loved one was a favorite theme of Petrarch.

> In her I lived, with hers my life is sped
> The hour she died I felt in my heart death . . .

and again

> And she is dead! and dead my soul in me . . .
> Ah, sick and sightless stares the human will!

and despairing still

> Why leave me here, so blind and so bereft,
> Since she, in whom mine eyes found light and grace,
> Departs, and only the throbbing night is left.[41]

His mood fed also on the romantic despair of Swinburne whose poems he read with undiminished excitement as each volume appeared. They still belonged, he felt, among "the best English work" of the time. In reading the *Poems and Ballads* of 1882 he had mused pencil in hand over such ecstasies of disenchantment as "Ave Atque Vale" and "A Forsaken Garden" with its funerary line: "O dust and ashes, once thought sweet to smell." To Adams the lovely house and the acres of woodland by the sea at Beverly Farms became for him his own "forsaken garden by the sea," the dead lovers gone. He resolved never to return to it and kept the resolve until almost the last year of his life. His library held his wife's precious copy of Swinburne which she had bought in London in 1866, the volume containing the haunting "Itylus," a poem filled with the same lyrical pain as one of the sonnets translated in *Esther*, "Wherein a grieving bird reminds him of his own heavier anguish."

> Oh, little bird! singing upon your way,
> Or mourning for your pleasant summer-tide . . .
> But now the gloom of winter and of night
> With thoughts of bitter years for leaven,
> Lends to my talk with you a sad delight.

More than thirty years afterward, the news of Henry James's death touched a long-hidden spring and the words of "Itylus" came again to his pen. "I have been living all day in the seventies," went his meditation to Elizabeth Cameron, "Swallow, sister! sweet sister swallow! indeed and indeed and indeed, we were really happy then." On every anniversary of

Clover's death one of their young friends, the faithful Rebecca Dodge Rae, placed a bunch of white violets, one of her favorite flowers, upon the grave. "I think that now," Adams wrote to her in 1896, "you and I are the only ones who remember." [42]

Chapter Nine

The Season of Nirvana

1 Floating down Niagara

A DAMS's original plan to make a tour of Japan had been
motivated by intellectual curiosity and love of the picturesque. The illness of his wife added a fresh motive. After
so much talk of the Orient in their circle and so much interest
in Chinese exploration and Japanese art and religion, Adams
had succumbed to the courteous proselytizing of his friend
Yoshida, the Japanese ambassador who had returned to Japan
in 1881. There is the revealing allusion in *Esther*, when Hazard
confesses to the heroine that she tempts him to run away
from his ecclesiastical labors. "How pleasant it would be
to go off to Japan together and fill our sketch-books with
drawings." To which Esther, seized with delight, cries, "Oh,
are you in earnest? . . . I could crawl and swim there if you
would go with me." [1]

With the first half of his history safely in print and in the
hands of his little corps of critics for their comments, Adams
felt the need for a long holiday which might restore his wife's
health. The few weeks at Old Sweet Springs in West Virginia
had unaccountably worked no magic. Perhaps a long ocean
voyage to the Orient would divert her mind from her stubborn
grief. Cousin William Sturgis Bigelow, now happily studying
in Japan, was sending them fascinating reports. He would
make an agreeable ally. But the new house in Lafayette Square
would not finish, as Richardson continued to dab at his

architectural palette with inspired improvisations. "No Mikado for me yet," Adams groused to Hay on October 1, 1885, "If I run away and hide in Japan, can I furnish from there?" Now, with his wife dead, the making of the trip seemed a kind of moral duty. But he could not and would not travel alone, having a horror of loneliness. He set about to find a companion for his journey. Who was free to go with him to the ends of the earth? King was mired again in England; Hay had his wife and "babes" and his *Lincoln* on his hands. Pumpelly, the far wanderer whose Mexican journey had recently thrilled all of them, had his professional interests; Alexander Agassiz, back from India on one of his many quests for health, was preoccupied with Calumet and Hecla in the Michigan peninsula.[2]

Chance played into Adams's hands. La Farge had reached an impasse in his design for the famous "Ascension" painting in the Tenth Street Church of New York, baffled how to achieve the mystical effect of levitation for his angels. Adams approached him at precisely the right moment. La Farge had also been auditor, as a house guest, when his one-time collaborator, Pumpelly, dazzled them with talk of far-off places. Vaguely, La Farge thought he might capture the right atmospheric effect in the mountains of Japan. As for the wherewithal, Adams, his purse always open to his friend, temptingly offered himself as host, for La Farge led a somewhat hand-to-mouth existence, maintaining his large family in Newport while he kept bachelor's hall in New York. His devoutly Catholic family, already long accustomed to his Bohemian independence of life, would as usual find sustenance in prayer. What made him an especially desirable companion to the fastidious Adams was his unusual decorum, for an artist. La Farge's clerical son used to puzzle himself over his absent father's susceptibility to the "white magic" of beautiful women, but Adams, willing to shut his eyes perhaps, tolerantly recalled that "unlike most men of genius he had no vices I could detect." [3]

Tall, impressive in his black beard, a charming conversationalist, an original genius, he had his depths. "My temper is frightful," he once told Adams, "and the world is stuffed with sawdust." He could hardly have supplied a more congenial view at that moment. The Faustian side of La Farge was already familiar to Adams for he had put it into the character of Wharton in *Esther*. Fifty-one to Adams's forty-eight, La Farge was the ideal complement to him. He could match Adams's chronic dyspepsia and insomnia with an impressive array of what his wife called "diplomatic illnesses." Highly intuitive, even mystical in his approach to art and life, a poetical philosopher and an enraptured colorist in painting and stained glass, his was an outlook that would now give a fresh vitality to Adams's perceptions. Insatiably intellectual, Adams was ready to explore deeply areas which he had only glimpsed before. La Farge was wont to say, "Adams, you reason too much." For five months he was now to go to school to La Farge to try to absorb something of La Farge's intuitive receptivity to experience, to try to loaf and invite his soul. The two friends had resolved to seek a creative rest, to find, as La Farge said, "a bath for the brain in some water absolutely alien." They had agreed to "bring no books, read no books, but come as innocently as we could." The innocence was a bit of poetic license. La Farge was already something of an expert on Japanese art. He had contributed an authoritative chapter on the subject to Pumpelly's *Across America and Asia* in 1869 in which he had praised "the marvellous decoration" and the "intellectual refinement" of the handling of color, acknowledging at the same time that the "subtlest, deepest, and most complicated feelings of the mind" present in the Christian art of Leonardo and Michelangelo were as lacking in Japanese art as in that of pagan antiquity. [4]

Early and late, Japanese and Chinese art and life had attracted the Adamses; their collecting was well under way even before they came to Washington. In Paris they patronized Sturgis Bigelow's art dealer friends. They made allies of oriental art dealers in Washington and New York as they had in Boston and hunted eagerly for kakemonos. Adams's collector's judgment was already a byword among their friends. To check the provenience of a Chinese vase he turned with practiced eye to the authoritative works in his library. Not only had he cultivated the Japanese and Chinese envoys in Washington, but long before when a Japanese visitor came along they would "pump" him unmercifully for light on what Adams fell to calling "the Asian mystery." [5]

Adams had begun looking toward the Far East as long ago as 1869, three years before his marriage. Bored by the stagnation of Quincy and restless for change, he vowed "to go to the Pacific" in 1871.[6] His Harvard professorship had cancelled that jaunt. Afterwards in Washington the Orient grew even more attractive in the company of Baron Yoshida and Chen Lau-Piu, the Chinese envoy. He enjoyed the tea ceremony and tried to get the men to dine in their national dress. Not only their curios but their archaic law interested him. Adams, then fresh from his study of Lewis Henry Morgan's *Ancient Society*, had found a congenial fellow student of archaic society in Yoshida. Japan offered a remarkable field of study of the phases of progress with its enclaves of aboriginal tribes and its feudal system in process of sudden dissolution. Morse's *International Review* of 1881 reported the progress of the social and industrial revolution and the movement toward representative government. The flower of the samurai chivalry had risen in revolt in 1877 and had been destroyed. A scientific historian might be an eyewitness to historical evolution speeded up as in a vast laboratory, the dynamic Westernizing movement, with its exaggerated individualism pitted against the quietism of an otherworldly religion, whose ideal was Nirvana and the annihilation of self.

The interest in Japan had engrossed many of their Boston friends, largely as a result of the Lowell Institute Lectures of 1881. Professor Edward Sylvester Morse of Salem, recently returned from the Imperial University of Tokyo, talked with such enthusiasm of Japanese folkways and the "beauty and dignity" of daimyo and samurai art and life that a whole movement started up in Boston's intellectual life. Because of him Percival Lowell and William Sturgis Bigelow made the hegira. And the adventurous friend of the Adamses, Mrs. Jack Gardner, responded to the stimulus by visiting Japan on her round-the-world trip in 1883. Ernest Fenellosa had already gone out to Japan to teach political economy and philosophy in 1878, shortly after his graduation from Harvard. The very first edition of John Murray's *Handbook for Travellers in Japan* came out in 1884, with its spartan challenges, to initiate the tourist flood. It was high time therefore that Adams should survey the field.[7]

The journey had finally arranged itself after six rather desultory months in Washington. As was natural for the period of mourning, social life came to an end. Through an exaggerated sense of delicacy friends like Secretary Lamar stopped their regular visits and Adams was suddenly withdrawn from all except a few of his closest intimates, like the Hays, the Camerons, and the Bancrofts. Dwight had become a kind of personal secretary though he still lingered on at the State Department. The great echoing new house could be safely left in his charge with a staff of three servants. Furnishing the new house provided a useful anodyne during the months of condolence calls when "all society . . . seemed to drop its mask for a moment and initiate me into the mystery." A certain determined gayety returned as he jested with Hay about his success in looting the shops of New York and

Washington for objects of art. He was going to Japan, he said, "for no other object than to buy kakemonos for my gaunt walls." He urged Hay to move in quickly, offering the hospitality of his house while the Hays settled, willing to risk the mute reproaches of Mrs. Hay for his refusing the solaces of religion.[8]

Though he went through the motions of research, his history languished in dead-water. Paul Leicester Ford copied some Harrison letters for him. Ford's mother sent him the manuscript of her biography of Noah Webster for criticism. Feelingly he commented, "a great mass of material is almost as troublesome to a biography as a short allowance." He knew the hypnotic fascination of family trees. Genealogy "has a curious, personal interest, which history wants." Her work forcibly recalled him to his own tormenting editorial creed: "My criticisms are always simple; they are limited to one word: — Omit! Every syllable that can be struck out is pure profit, and every page that can be economized is a five-percent dividend. Nature rebels against this rule; the flesh is weak, and shrinks from the scissors; I groan in retrospect over the weak words and useless pages I have written; but the law is sound, and every book written without a superfluous page or word is a masterpiece. All the same, no one cares to apply so stern a law to another person. One has a right to be severe only with oneself." [9]

Late in April the American Historical Association held its annual meeting in Washington as a tribute to the president, the aged George Bancroft. On terms of agreeable familiarity with leading American historians who flocked to Washington for the homage to Bancroft and who between meetings congregated at the Cosmos Club in Lafayette Square, Adams obviously enjoyed his role as one of the hosts. At one of the sessions he fell back easily into his old role of classroom cross examiner when a young Harvard Law School student, John

M. Merriam, attacked Jefferson's "Use of the Executive Patronage" as a repudiation of principle, incautiously alluding to a
Jefferson letter "published curiously enough" in Adams's
edition of the Gallatin Papers. Adams having gone over the
whole ground in his yet unpublished first volume, could point
out that "on both sides the game was selfish." Jefferson was in
fact the victim of his own conciliatory tactics and had to face a
revolt in his own party for not ousting Federalists rapidly
enough. His remarks must have had an arresting quality. In
the only such entry in the minutes of the entire Proceedings,
Secretary Herbert Adams wrote that it was "a suggestive
paper, provoking some comment by Mr. Henry Adams of
Washington." [10]

He sent his regular summing up of the season to Gaskell.
"With its usual exasperating coolness the world has gone on,
carrying me with it, as though I were a stray monkey floating
down Niagara on a handorgan. . . . I have decided to get
myself quite out of the way. Fortunately Washington is a
cheery place where people take life gaily and I have been by
no means solitary or deserted. All winter I have never left my
house except to ride, or for a short walk; nor seen society except for the old friends who came to see me. Luckily for me
John Hay and his family came in January . . . but the winter
has been dark with deaths among my oldest and closest
friends." Having decided to go to Japan he had characteristic
second thoughts about the abhorrent sea voyages and the
Japanese "whom I do not in the least pine to see." Yet he was
not ready for Europe. "It is full of ghosts." [11]

But he did feel that he had recovered himself. Once more
he had a practical interest in "the world's affairs." It seemed
to him that "the world really has suddenly made a great
change; and that it is not merely I who have had a mental
shock. Both here and in Europe a vast revolution seems to
have occurred within a year past. Our politics are already old-

fashioned — quite thrown aside by new social movements."
The English Liberal movement had been diverted and
hampered by the Irish troubles. To him there was only one
solution, a free Irish parliament. "Absolute independence
might be not the worst result." England seemed to him a
stranger country than ever. "I have become an old man in a
twelvemonth. The future no longer belongs to us." The new
society coming into being would be so different from theirs
that it would bore them. But for him who liked to look on,
he accepted it. "I always did like the theatre, though my only
ambition was to write the play." [12]

One more blow fell before he would get away. The in-
domitable Richardson died of Bright's disease at 47, light-
heartedly defying his doctor's orders to the very end. In a
long editorial the New York *Times* eulogized him "as one of
the chief forces in modern architecture," one whose genius
flourished in a way that would not have been possible in
France where architecture had developed an official style as
the special preserve of the government and the Beaux Arts.
Adams and Anderson were the only ones of the Washington
circle to go to Boston for the funeral, which was held in his
masterpiece, Trinity Church, Boston. Thus came to an end
one of the most promising careers of his generation, one which
had begun in the '60's when he and "Fez" Richardson roamed
Paris together. Henry's brother Charles eulogized him at the
Harvard Commencement, "large in everything — large in conception, large in soul. . . . His presence filled the mind as it
did the eye." [13]

Richardson's overwhelming style had left its mark. Having
designed houses for Henry Adams, Hay, Anderson, and Mac-
Veagh, he had in effect conducted a school of architecture for
his friends and clients. It was he who had employed La Farge
on Trinity, and Saint-Gaudens and Stanford White had been
his chief draftsmen. His ideas on church architecture swept all

before him. Before Richardson Adams had been a rather un-critical student of the great Viollet-le-Duc. Richardson eman-cipated him. Adams's letters with their sprinkling of allusions to Richardson show the depth of his tender regard. In the *Education* he valued no college mate higher. He had a "sort of overflow of life" that made him "irresistible." Twenty-seven years after the death of this Titan, Adams, speaking of the Worth dresses he was providing for Ruth Draper's appearance before Queen Mary, was reminded of one of his sayings, "As poor old Richardson used to say, they will *feel* it." [14]

Adams had summoned neither Hay nor King on that black day in December; but before his departure to Japan he made amends with a peculiarly meaningful gesture of friendship. To King, transiently back from England, he disclosed the secret of *Esther,* for King more than any other person perhaps, except Adams himself, had shared the freedom of Marian Adams's thoughts and feelings. Then having let King into the sacred place, he felt compelled to admit Hay as well. The day he left New York, he gave King leave to tell Hay but "under injunction of a secrecy far more careful than that required for *Democracy*." [15]

2   Antechambers to Mystery

Luck was with him when he set out from Boston on June 3, 1886. The directors' private car of the Union Pacific was being deadheaded West. Thanks to his brother Charles, president of the railroad since 1884, he and La Farge had the palatial car to themselves. There had been a farewell gathering in New York with King and Saint-Gaudens at which he may have first broached the plan for the Rock Creek memorial. Full of high spirits, the two travelers dashed for the train, La Farge having spent the day, as King gaily put it, "dodging creditors and

sheriffs . . . and trying to borrow a few thou' right and left
wherewith to paint Japan red." Safely under way, Adams
entertained Madame Modjeska and her husband at a twelve
o'clock breakfast aboard the train, clear proof, as he said, that
he was "a breakfasting animal." In spite of a promise to
preserve his innocence of mind, Adams whiled away the long
hours by studying Buddhism, with its Four Noble Truths and
the Noble Eightfold Path by which Nirvana was to be attained.
La Farge surrendered to the intoxication of the Western
scenery and sketched. An alert newshawk at Omaha, spotting
the private car, clamored for a story. He lost the story but
won the encounter; "for when in reply to his inquiry as to our
purpose in visiting Japan, La Farge beamed through his
spectacles the answer that we were in search of Nirvana, the
youth looked up like a meteor and rejoined: 'It's out of
season.' " [16]

That day the press was filled with news of Cleveland's
honeymoon in the White Mountains and the indictment by a
blue ribbon grand jury of the anarchists in Chicago for the
Haymarket tragedy. Neither event roused interest or even
satire in Adams's high spirited farewell from San Francisco:
"My ship is in the bay, all ready at the quay, but before I
wend my way, good-bye to thee John Hay. . . . If you and
King were with us, we would capture the ship, turn pirate,
and run off to a cocoa-nut island. As it is we shall be sea-sick
without crime." [17]

It had been fifteen years since he had ridden West to follow
the trail of the Fortieth Parallel Survey. He had been single
then; once more he was alone. The two journeys enclosed a
whole vanished world of experience and the ironies of his
situation haunted him. To his seneschal Dwight he forlornly
commented, "I can only hope I am better company to others
than to myself," but to Hay he was determinedly gay. As the
train rushed westward toward the sunset and he read of

Buddha and Nirvana and the annihilation of self, the ideal
of the East began to have an absorbingly personal meaning.
The orthodoxies of Christianity repelled him. As he said of the
"four female missionaries" aboard ship, "They sing and talk
theology, two practises I abhor." Buddhism attracted him by
its freedom and imaginativeness.[18]

The voyage which began on June 12 belied everything that
Clarence King and Arnold Hague had told him about the
repose of the Pacific. "We have been more miserable by the
linear inch than ever two woe-begone Pagans, searching
Nirvana, were before." Yet La Farge's charm was so irresistible
that they managed to stay as "gay as petrels" and unrepentant
in their seasick misery. They arrived on July 2, 1886, to find
Japan in the grip of a frightful cholera epidemic and broiling
under a summer sun. The guidebook's elaborate cautions
about Japanese cuisine and hotel accommodations away from
the treaty ports turned out to be judicious understatements.
Even the hotel food had "a pervasive sense of oily nastiness"
and every journey was a full-fledged expedition requiring
"food, sheets, flea-powder, and if possible drink." The overpowering stench of the streets and paddyfields had one compensation; it proved to him he had not wholly lost his sense of
smell. Somehow they managed to escape with only the briefest
attack of cholera.[19]

Sturgis Bigelow took charge of them, acting as "courier and
master of ceremonies" and interpreter. The learned Ernest
Fenollosa lectured and bullied them on what to admire,
rousing the picador in Adams. "He is a kind of St. Dominic,
and holds himself responsible for the dissemination of useless knowledge by others. My historical indifference to everything but facts, and my delight at studying what is hopefully
debased and degraded, shock his moral sense. . . . He has
joined a Buddhist sect; I was myself a Buddhist when I left

America, but he has converted me to Calvinism with leanings towards the Methodists." [20]

In spite of the homilies of their expatriate friend, the extraordinary discomforts of travel, the baffling barrier of language, and the utterly alien quality of their surroundings, Adams acknowledged that Nikko at least was "worth coming to see." But getting there while weak from a bout of cholera, jounced about for twenty miles beyond the railhead over execrable and muddy roads, staggering up the steep rises afoot in 90° heat were factors that gave a certain bite to his admiration. "Japan is not the last word of humanity, and Japanese art has a well-developed genius for annoying my prejudices; but Nikko is, after all, one of the sights of the world. I am not sure where it stands in order of rank, but after the pyramids, Rome, Mme. Tussaud's wax-works, and 800 16th Street [Hay's residence], I am sure Nikko deserves a place." The economics of this manifestation of religion staggered him. "When you reflect that the old Shoguns spent twelve or fourteen millions of dollars on this remote mountain valley, you can understand that Louis Quatorze and Versailles are not much of a show compared with Nikko." He busied himself making scores of photographs of the exquisite temples and mausoleums, but as he said these could give no idea of the extraordinary unity as of a single ingenious composition of twenty acres of temples on the mountain flank. When they passed through the long anteroom of the vast shrine of Yeyasu with its carved and inlaid ceilings, its gilded pillars and flowers and mystic birds, Adams echoed the rhapsodies of La Farge: "The impression is that of a princess's exquisite apartment, as if the Tartar tent had grown into greater fixity, and had been touched by a fairy's wand." He was not to feel the same impression again until he saw the "private apartments" of the Virgin at Chartres.[21]

Fascinating as are Adams's letters from Japan with their intense alertness to the picturesque sights and smells and sounds of the places they visited, they did not pierce beneath the surface. He contented himself with humorous remarks on the strange customs, on the universal habit of meaningless laughter, on the mechanical doll-like movements of the women, on the startling nudity of the sexes at the public baths, on the disconcerting absence of privacy, and on the triumphs and failures in pursuit of curios. Japan was quaint to him. "The only moral of Japan is that the children's storybooks were good history. . . . The whole show is of the nursery. Nothing is serious; nothing is taken seriously." So too Pierre Loti was to write, aware of his European superficiality. When Adams visited a back country village and saw the whole town bathing "naked as the mother that bore them . . . as their ancestors had done a thousand years ago" he "broke out into carols of joy." Here was his archaic society. The prudery that had once led him to argue the superiority of draped Venuses to undraped ones began to slip away. When he saw at one of the temples the many signs of phallic worship, he conceded "one cannot quite ignore the foundations of society." At the same time he could not "conquer the feeling that Japs are monkeys, and the women very badly made monkeys." There were exceptions, however, and he could not avoid admiring "one pretty girl of sixteen, with quite a round figure." It was on that occasion — or possibly another — that La Farge recorded for *Century* magazine that his companion "cannot yet quite get over the impression made upon him by the pretty young lady near whom he stood under the eaves of the bath-house where he had taken refuge from the rain, and whose charming manners were as charming as her youthfulness, and had no more covering." [22]

What he saw at the public baths of Yumoto left him with

a somewhat troubled conscience. He could imagine the scoffing laugh of the uninhibited Hay and the mocking scepticism of King the sensualist. "In spite of King," Adams protested to Hay, "I affirm that sex does not exist in Japan, except as a scientific classification. I would not affirm that there are no exceptions to my law; but the law itself I affirm as the foundation of archaic society. Sex begins with the Aryan race." The succinct "law" was still another characteristic and dubious generalization, this one reflecting his study of *Ancient Society*. In the archaic society of the Indians, Morgan wrote, "the passion of love, which required a higher development than they had attained, was unknown among them." It was Morgan's thesis that the Aryan peoples had taken the lead in the progress from barbarism to civilization. The "passion of love" was one of their beneficent inventions. The imagined absence of sexuality explained for Adams why the beautiful wife of a Japanese marquis was simply a "successful bit of bric-a-brac" rather than a woman.[23]

In the light of these reflections there is a curious aptness in La Farge's comment on their life in the little house by the waterfall in Nikko that he was Huckleberry Finn and Adams was Tom Sawyer. Like Sam Clemens of Hannibal they cherished their peculiarly American naiveté about sex. Nor could they escape what has been called the universal "fetish of racial attraction and repulsion." There was also an uncomfortable paradox in what Adams saw. He found himself in a society that outwardly at least seemed to conform successfully to the chaste ideal of Christian asceticism, the ideal which had always tormented and baffled the average sensual man of the West. Men and women displayed no public interest in sex. It was inconceivable that Japanese decorum surpassed that of Beacon Hill or Lafayette Square. Such an idea contradicted the moral superiority of the visitors. Wherever he turned, the challenge seemed to trouble him.

It was a constant irritation that the women seemed not women. They were "badly made and repulsive." The contrast with the feminine visions of Washington society struck him at every turn, though at the Nō theatre La Farge did perceive "much refinement and sweetness in the faces of the women." The superb Geisha ball on the eve of their departure seemed to him "an exhibition of mechanical childishness" in which "the women's joints clacked audibly, and their voices were metal." His very interest in archaic society and its presumed "laws" led him astray, for he was yet bound by the stereotypes that passed for science at the meetings of the Anthropological Society of Washington. The sexual freedoms and taboos of the Orient were yet to be understood. It would take still another venture in education before Adams should discover sex as a universal energy.[24]

Contemporary Japan was too chaotic and strange for understanding. Japanese politics were as opaque as all other aspects of contemporary Japanese life. Adams gave no sign of responding to the new social movement or the political revolution going on under his eyes. The politics and history of the Orient still hid from his vision. However, he was on other ground when he contemplated Japanese art and architecture. Here he felt in his element, continually urging La Farge to attempt serious work. Adams's impromptu lectures supplied a steadying corrective to the Pre-Raphaelite dreaminess of La Farge's aesthetic. La Farge set to work at last. As he explained it, his resolutions were started by Adams's "analysis of the theme of their architecture, and my feeling a sort of desire to rival him on a ground for fair competition. But I do not think that I could grasp a subject in such a clear dispassionate and masterly way, with such natural references to the past and its implied comparisons, for A[dams]'s historical sense amounts to poetry, and his deductions and remarks always set my mind sailing into new channels."[25]

Adams collected curios, porcelains, kakemonos, Hokusai drawings, and silken gowns for his friends' wives, spending at least a thousand dollars on his own account. The gowns were virtually to set a fashion at Newport. But this tourist bustling about did not go to the essence of his experience. What deeply moved him was the past, the great symbols of a once stable tradition, the monumental past of incalculably costly temples and shrines. They made Japan seem to him a kind of gilded Egypt. He saw them as symbols of a vanished order and dignity, of ideals that were passing. In the great temple at Nikko he talked with La Farge of the character of the great feudal overlord Iyeyasu and "of the deadening influence of the Tokugawa rule, of its belittling the classes whose energies were the true life of the country." But democratic doctrines were hard to hold on to before the great tombs and impressively wrought relics. When silence fell on their talk, these asserted their deep authority and Adams strove with the aid of all of La Farge's intuitions to grasp the solacing inwardness of Buddhism.[26]

Unlike Adams, La Farge liked to give himself up to lazy contemplation and drifting, heedless of time and schedules. Sketching in the bathroom of their pretty doll-like house overlooking a waterfall and the temple beyond, La Farge imposed moments of serenity upon Adams, when he grew weary of climbing about with a bulky camera. They studied the great tomb, built as La Farge said not to defy time but to accept "eternal peace." Slowly returning through the incredibly beautiful corridors, they felt the contrast between an art indifferent to time's waste and the "permanence and the forces of nature." What Adams had seen symbolized in Niagara Falls seemed oddly echoed here. Here the two friends shared the "feeling of humility and of the nothingness of man." In that place of tombs, with the figure of the goddess Kwannon looking down compassionately from the wall, art spoke with serene authority, "We are the end of the limits of human endeavor. Beyond us begins the other world, and we, indeed, shall surely pass away, but thou remainest, O Eternal Beauty!" Adams's quixotic search for Nirvana did not succeed, could not except indirectly as Galahad and Faust demonstrated of such romantic quests. "If only we had found Nirvana — " La Farge lamented; "but he was right who warned us that we were late in this season of the world." Still Adams did find in Japan a symbol for his grief to which his poetic and emotional nature could cling.[27]

At Mount Vernon the tomb of Washington had seemed to the heroine of *Democracy* "the only restless spot about the quiet landscape." At Nikko, however, the problem of art and nature had been solved. Inevitably Adams thought of his own problem, what sort of monument should he erect to his wife's memory — and his buried life? La Farge complained that in America it was almost impossible to find an artist capable of making a monument, "a tomb, or a commemorative ideal building — a cathedral, or a little memorial" because there was "no *necessity* for such forms of art" in a society devoted to "usefulness, getting on," to all the ways which destroy integrity. Only in such things could art be expressed "pure, by itself," anonymously, belonging only to those who come to it "for love, for the deep desire of enjoyment," such as might be felt before fragments of Greek or Gothic ornament. Thus La Farge lectured Adams on the antidote for what "Stanford White once called our 'native Hottentot style.'"[28]

What even a superficial acquaintance with Buddhism taught was that the greatest art would seek beauty as the soul sought Nirvana in self-absorption into the universal and the infinite, in anonymity, in the extinction of the restlessness of the will. Art and philosophy thus merged in the greatest of the ideal sculptures of Northern Buddhism in Japan, the great statue of the contemplative Buddha at Kamakura. Rising beyond self, the ideal transcended the flesh and fused the male and female halves of the world's body into the image of the world soul. This lesson of how the spirit might free itself from the body's clamor took deep root.[29]

Equally compelling were the representations of the Goddess of Compassion Kwannon, sitting beside the "descending stream of life," shrouded in flowing drapery. This figure drew them back again and again, touched them most, "partly, perhaps, because of the Eternal Feminine," as La Farge mused. La Farge, like Pumpelly, perceived the similarities between Buddhism and Catholicism. The "Queen of Heaven," the Compassionate One, had its counterpart in the Virgin of the Christian world; but Kwannon was more than compassionate; she gave to those who invoked her fearlessness and serenity in the face of earthly troubles.[30]

The brooding spirit of Nikko took possession of Adams. "One feels no impulse to exert oneself; and the Buddhist contemplation of the infinite seems the only natural mode of life. Energy is a dream of raw youth." Slowly the weeks went by, the Fenollosas and Sturgis Bigelow summering in nearby homes. They all made pilgrimages to the shrines and sacred waterfalls. Bales of merchandise arrived from Tokyo, in which they hopefully rummaged for the always elusive examples of high art. The broad and infinite variety of their meditative talk together, the echoes of the esoteric disquisitions of Fenollosa and Bigelow, provided a running gloss for the mysterious objects of their daily view. History and myth, old custom and legend, fell evocatively upon their ears. The soft and misty outlines of those conversations took shape in La Farge's philosophical "vagaries," but in Adams the inner struggle still prevented his full release.[31]

While at Nikko, Adams received a letter from John Hay praising his "melancholy little Esther" and urging him to republish it under his own name. He recoiled with a kind of horror. The suppressed anguish that began when his wife was called to her dying father's bedside rose up with a rush. "Today, and for more than a year past, I have been and am living with not a thought but from minute to minute." He was pleased that his book had found "one friend," but the desire to suppress it as an act of mourning, to celebrate a kind of spiritual suttee, had swallowed up all lesser vanities. He was now carefully tending his grief with a touching ceremonial of poetic meditations.[32]

In one of his little pocket notebooks, he copied out the octave of De Musset's romantic idealizing of Beatrix Donato of the white bosom and divine figure,

> Beatrix Donato fut le doux nom de celle
> Dont la forme terrestre eut les divine contours
> Dans sa blanche poitrine un esprit sans détours
> Le fils du Titien pour la rendre immortelle
> En fit ce portrait, témoin d'un mutuel amour
> Puis cessa de peindre, à compter de ce jour
> Ne voulant de sa main illustrer d'autre qu'elle.

Thus the poem sang the legend which told that the son of Titian had painted her portrait, regarding it as the immortal witness of their love. From that day he did not paint again, not wishing, as the poem said, ever to celebrate any one else. De Musset too had known the crushing loss of love. The uncopied sestet said more perhaps than Adams could bring himself to set down; beautiful as the painting was, it was not worth as much as the kiss of its model.

> Vois donc, combien c'est peu que la gloire
> Puisque, tout beau qu'il est, ce portrait ne vaut pas
> (Crois-moi sur ma parole) un baiser du modèle.

Beneath the poem, like a talisman, appeared the date 1838, the year of Adams's own birth. On the opposite page stood a companion sonnet, "The Son of Titian," eloquent with the Petrarchian mood of *Esther* which now suffused Adams.

J'ai le coeur de Pétrarque et n'ai point son génie;
Je ne puis ici-bas que donner en chemin
Ma main à qui m'appelle, à qui m'aime ma vie.

Shyly, he too wished to hold out his hand to one who called him, to whom his soul might be drawn.[33]

Swept by crowding impressions, welling up from within, as he sat on the veranda of their little house near the burial place of the Shoguns, Adams would often look up from the pages of Dante's *Paradiso* to contemplate the great temple of the Buddhist Mangwanjii beyond the waterfall. He jotted down little notes as if in an effort to bring into some kind of harmony the ideas of East and West, of the Nirvana of Buddhism with the heavenly paradise of Christianity, of nature with truth. The upward ascent, guided by Beatrice, her account of the scheme of man's redemption, the exhortations of St. Thomas Aquinas and the wisdom of the learned doctors of the church, all had a strange relevance to what he found about him. The Eternal Feminine of Kwannon had its echo in the spiritualized beauty of Beatrice. How to reconcile these two images of the eternal woman? In the difficult Canto XIII in which St. Thomas Aquinas illuminates the superiority of God to nature, Adams carefully fixed the epigram in mind. "Nature is always imperfect like the artist." In another Canto Dante doubtful of himself wonders how much he dare publish for his ancestor, Cacciaguida, charges him to speak the truth. Adams paused to render the homely phrase, "Let there be scratching where the itching is." So in the pages of his notebook the pendulum of his thought swung back and forth.[34]

They had arrived at Nikko, some ninety miles north of Tokyo, on July 12. After six weeks of leisurely exploration of the shrines in the environs of that summer resort country,

whose scenery and temperature were much like Virginia
Springs, they were ready to concede the truth of the Japanese
proverb, "Do not use the word magnificent till you have seen
Nikko." When they got back to Yokohama on the 29th of
August, the sun was still broiling, but the pursuit of curios
went on with redoubled zeal. Extremely fine things were
scarce and costly, but the stuffs were "cheap and beautiful"
and Adams yielded to temptation. His notebooks testify to
the incredible cheapness of the acquisitions, so that his statement is not wholly fanciful that he had bought curios enough
to fill a house, some two thousand dollars' worth, half of it on
Hay's account. To avoid the reputed severity of the San
Francisco custom house, he planned to send most of his things
by tramp steamer via Suez to New York.[35]

The time of their stay drew to a close. On September third
they made their expedition to the great Buddha of Daibutsu
at Kamakura, and Adams duly photographed it, borrowing
a priest's camera. On the way back to Yokohama they tried
unsuccessfully for a view of Fuji. Adams, overwhelmed by
the heat, carried his clothes in his hand and waded through
the surf. Finally he resigned himself to the rickshaw and
hurried through the darkness past the open walled houses, his
eyes awhirl "with the wild succession of men's legs and of
women's breasts, in every stage of development and decomposi-
tion, which danced through the obscurity." They reached
Kobe on the ninth after a short and seasick run in a steamer,
and installed themselves royally at nearby Kioto. Their letters
of introduction performed the usual magic and they went
about "followed by a train." [36]

Kioto seemed to Adams as charming as Granada, scenically
at least. Playing host in Japanese dress, he found his legs
would not fold beneath him gracefully nor comfortably. He
watched his guests get thoroughly drunk on saki while the
Geisha troupe he had hired solemnly executed the formal

dances for which he had no taste. After much search he arranged for the Butterfly Dance at a nearby temple. His notebook entry for the day also mentions a sword dance of their guardsman and the curious sight of two court nobles playing hide and seek. There followed another' picturesque journey, thirty miles by rickshaw to Nara, the ancient capital, and other excursions about Yokohama, sometimes in the bone-breaking comfort of a kago or litter. Finally they caught a satisfying view of the great mountain, Fuji, near Kambara on the gulf of Suruga Bay. Adams made a tiny sketch of the peak and clouds to remind himself of the astonishingly sudden slope of the sacred mountain. La Farge put the scene into words: "At the end of the great curve of the gulf stretched the lines of green and purple mountains, which run far off into Idzu, and above them stood Fuji in the sky, very pale and clear, with one enormous band of cloud half-way up its long slope, and melting into infinite distance toward the ocean. . . . Below its violet edge the golden slope spread in the sun, the color of autumn leaf. . . . As A[dams] remarked, it was worth coming to far Japan for this single day." [37]

Adams took his last look at the pale, watery light of the coast from the deck of the *City of Peking* on October 2. Running a genius had been a fascinating experience for him. Heat and discomfort had occasionally driven him to contradiction and perverse satire, but he had been enormously diverted. He could readily agree with the celebrated Mrs. Bishop, who had preceded him, in her temperate judgment, "I found the country a study rather than a rapture, [but] its interest exceeded my largest expectations." [38]

The eighteen day return voyage across the Pacific astonished him; for once he did not suffer badly from seasickness, though he did take the precaution of religiously dosing himself with acid phosphate. He had the uncommon pleasure of being able to smoke his cigar occasionally, the severest test of sea legs,

Except for one short violent bout, the cholera epidemic had passed them by. With the learned Fenollosa as a fellow passenger, he could thrash out at leisure the meaning of his three months' education in Japan, his first experience with a completely exotic culture. He could hardly wait to send his newest generalization to Hay, a "nugget of golden learning." As soon as he got ashore on October 20, he wrote, "Japan and its art are only a sort of antechamber to China and . . . China is the only mystery left to penetrate. I have henceforward a future. As soon as I can get rid of history, and the present, I mean to start for China, and stay there. In China I will find bronzes or break all the crockery; . . . Five years hence, I expect to enter the celestial kingdom by that road, if not sooner by a shorter one as seems most likely to judge from the ways of most of my acquaintances at home." [39]

The news that greeted him was gloomy enough to test his most sardonic resolutions. His old Harvard colleague, Professor Ephraim Gurney, had just died of pernicious anemia, a "savage blow" indeed for his childless widow, Ellen, who had lost her father, Dr. Hooper, and her sister Marian in little more than a year. Moreover, his own father's decline was now so rapid that Washington would have to wait while he hastened to Quincy to perform the familiar ritual of the "death beds one has to watch." [40]

His brother Charles was waiting for him at the quayside to take him home by way of southern California over the Atlantic and Pacific Railroad. The route took him along the great Sierra Nevada range so often described by Clarence King, then through the Mojave Desert and across the vast wastelands of mesquite, yucca, and cactus to Albuquerque, rejoining Charles's railroad, the Union Pacific, at St. Joseph, Missouri. It was one of the increasingly rare moments for the two former allies to be so long in each other's company. Charles had reached the pinnacle of the active life as head of

THE SEASON OF NIRVANA

the Union Pacific. What Charles could tell him of that impressive achievement was hardly the stuff to fire the ambition of middle age, but rather make the pursuit of Nirvana doubly attractive. In *Chapters of Erie* the two brothers had studied and damned the brilliant depredations of Jay Gould. The rape of the Erie had been followed by that of the Union Pacific, which Gould then abandoned to build up his own Southwest railway empire to the Pacific with the loot. Henry and Charles rode eastward from California through that enormous rival domain with ample time for sardonic reflection. At least they were keeping the memory of Gould's sins green, for they had that year republished *Chapters of Erie*. Charles's opening remarks even more aptly expressed their joint thoughts in 1886 than when first published in 1871. "Call things by their right names, and it would be no difficult task to make the cunning civilization of the nineteenth century appear but as a hypocritical mask spread over the more honest brutality of the twelfth." 41

Charles had confidently accepted the plundered legacy of Gould two years earlier and had sacrificed to the work of rehabilitation "private business, literary work, leisure and comfort" hoping to put the line "on a firm financial footing" through "measures of development and improvement which alone have any attraction for me." He soon discovered that he had underrated his adversaries in Wall Street and the railroad lobby in Washington. The results? "Literally nothing!" Thus in the pages of his journal he reviewed his work a few years later. "So I pass my life, contending with debts and disappointment, — in contact with men like Plumb and Ingalls in Washington, or men like Villard and Smith in Wall St; and my life all the while ebbing — ebbing away. What folly!" 42

At Quincy the darkness was slowly deepening upon the deposed head of the House, the centers of memory quite gone. Quietly on November 16 Charles Francis Adams drifted into the deeper forgetfulness of death. To the four sons gathered about his bedside it was a moment for the most sobering reflection. The old man's motto had been "Work and Pray." Prayer had long been lost to them, but all of its intensity had been transformed into an infinite capacity for work. They had inherited the old man's fierce probity and ambition, but an ambition fatally compromised as it became in him by a sense of the vanity of things. At seventy he had written to young Henry Cabot Lodge, "When I was entering into life I was disposed to mount a high horse and challenge the world to disputation for prizes which now I would not cross the room to secure." Lodge had shrugged off such disenchanted wisdom. In the sons it was bred in the bone.[43]

For three generations politics had been the natural habitat of the family, but as Charles somberly wrote in his diary, "The experience of my family for a hundred years ought to be a warning to me there. They had all that political preferment could give. Were they made happy or contented by it? . . . I am tired; and the prizes I am after, well, if I gained them all, are not worth having. Political preferment I do not want, — power and patronage have no charms for me, — social distinction and excitement I am not adapted to getting, nor in the past, has it afforded me anything I now look back upon with satisfaction; — curiously enough I am an artist! — I love literary work for its own sake. I like to sit among my books in the sun-light of my library, and investigate and write of the past." For all his reproaches he had come round to Henry's attitude. The moment must have given Henry a certain hollow satisfaction. How curiously the hereditary bent asserted itself. Their father and his father before him had also found solace in their sunlit studies, in the tranquillizing work of the pen, even in writing epic poetry as John Quincy Adams had done. Henry made the application personal. "To me," he admonished an office-seeking friend in England, "politics

have been the single uncompensated disappointment of life —
pure waste of energy and moral. I hate to see other men hope
where I think myself wiser. It reflects on my character and
veracity." [44]

But if Henry and Charles were disillusioned, their younger
brother Brooks still had a certain leeway, according to Henry's
maxim, "Men of fifty ought not, and generally are not able, to
be revolutionists." Brooks, moody, irascible and lonely, "a kind
of exaggerated *me*" to Henry, had just finished his *Emancipation of Massachusetts,* an attempt at a scientific case study of
historical progress. The lesson for him of that moment in family
history could only be that there must be a revolution in their
political thinking. Only Brooks was left to undertake the revolution. Their eldest brother John Quincy stood somewhat
apart from the others, somehow spared his portion of the irritable genius of the family. As Henry said, "John was the
only one of the family who can make one laugh when one's
ship is sinking." [45]

On July 4, 1887, Henry's cousin, William Everett, delivered
the eulogy in Quincy as Henry listened approvingly. The
choice of their cousin Everett had historical fitness. Nearly
forty years before, William's father, the great Edward Everett,
had in the same place delivered his eulogy of John Quincy
Adams whose unyielding austerity had kept his generation
at bay. Outwardly Henry's father had been cold and reserved,
but within the family circle he had tried in his fashion to
drop the mask which protected him against public hostility
and suspicion. For Henry he had had a special fondness.
When Henry had gone to Europe as a youth of twenty, his
mother wrote him, "Papa is a baby about you all" and quoted
his plaint, "I miss that boy terribly. I have been really unhappy all morning." His lifelong anxiety about his ambitious
children inspired countless homilies on the one great theme:
"Above all . . . the study of ethics is of the greatest value

in active life." How often his father had lectured him on "the modern speculative infidelity" and urged him to attend church regularly. Advice long unheeded now. On Henry's side, what great things he had once expected for his father — and for himself! How he had urged his mother to be glad that duty and ambition came together. He had written proudly, "You know I'm ambitious; I needn't remind you of it: not on my account; but as a family joint-stock affair." But even then he had sensed his father's fatal weakness. He was too fastidious. "He doesn't like the bother and fuss of entertaining and managing people who can't be reasoned with." For himself he had discovered after painful trial that he was his father's son. Besides there had been practical impediments. "My father and brothers block my path fatally, for all three stand before me in order of promotion." [46]

Everett acknowledged that Charles Francis Adams was cold, but the truth was that his countrymen deserved no greater show of warmth. "They carefully inform the descendants of heroes exactly what his ancestor's virtues were. . . . And while thus sedulously explaining to him what a load of ancestral duties is entailed of him, they remind him carefully that an American has no ancestral rights; that while his blood or name may set him on a compulsory pinnacle of notoriety, he need not suppose that it entitles him to any confidence." At the outset of his political career Charles Francis Adams had made a painful discovery, recorded in his diary, "Strange as it may seem, the distinction of my name and family has been the thing most in my way." Every one of the sons listening could feel the force of their father's chagrin.

Charles Francis Adams had never practiced law, said Everett, partly because of the prejudice which keeps law business out of the hands of wealthy men's sons and then blames them for living on their father's income. When his estate was probated it was apparent that he had managed his patrimony with frugality and shrewd judgment, the total inventory amounting to slightly over a million dollars. In language that now seems quaintly formal, he aimed at scrupulous justice among his four sons and daughter, his wife having been "so amply provided for" under her father's will. "I have thus far had abundant reason to thank God, that I have had no occasion to make any distinction of affection between my children." He exhorted them against "unworthy jealousies or contentions." His valuable "cabinet of coins and medals founded by my father, but greatly enlarged by five and twenty years of collecting myself," he gave to Henry to keep as a memorial of his family.[47]

How much Henry Adams's income was enlarged by his inheritance it is hard to estimate. Already the beneficiary of a number of trusts and himself active also as a trustee, he was extremely knowledgeable in financial matters. Seven years before he had talked of being used to getting 10 per cent on his money. Currently he thought himself lucky if he could "net four per cent for those whom I protect, soon it will be three. . . . When I was a boy and until fifteen years ago, six per cent was the rule." Of course this left out of account the often spectacular yield of common stocks in his own portfolio like Calumet and Hecla. As a young man in England during the Civil War he had frequently reviewed the American investment situation for his brother Charles and given detailed instructions, embroidered with frequent objurgations about the "damned banks," for the investment of his modest funds. Ward Thoron appears to have begun acting as his Washington financial agent about this time while Edward Hooper looked after his interests in Boston. His income may now have reached as much as $50,000 a year, of which he habitually reinvested half.[48]

His brother Charles had, of course, prospered far more than he, adopting a scale of living that was to make the

thrifty Henry increasingly uneasy. Two and a half years after
their father died, Charles, reviewing his twenty years of sala-
ried railroad work, felt his bitterness offset somewhat by the
fact that he had grown rich by his own efforts, his inheritance
having played a negligible role. In twenty years his annual
income had grown from $5,000 to $120,000; he could pride
himself, "I have thus picked up a fortune by the way — and
kept it."

In spite of himself Charles had been drawn into the intrigue and stockjobbery of Wall Street to protect the Union
Pacific and he knew he had failed for he had neither the stomach nor the talent for Wall Street intrigue. "A man stands
about the same chance there that a woman would stand in a
brothel." Such was the lesson he could read for his two philosopher brothers, Henry, and Brooks, and leave for them to
draw a moral for the rest of their lives. "The men of whom one
hears so much there, — the Goulds, the Vanderbilts, the Vil-
lards, the Sages, the Drews and the Fisks, — are neither great
nor interesting nor amusing. They are simply material." [49]

What Henry Adams felt about his father's passing, he kept
out of his letters, trusting perhaps that his friends would
know how to construe his reticence; a just estimate would
take time and a careful inward scrutiny. He had learned the
lesson of silence and repose in Japan; grief needed to be as
anonymous as the tombs of Nikko. Ironically, the task of
preparing the epitaph for the grave at Mount Wollaston fell
to him as the most literary of the four sons. Posterity, at least,
could learn its obligations.

> Trained from his youth in politics and letters
> His manhood strengthened by the convictions
>   Which had inspired his fathers . . .
> He failed in no task which his government imposed
>   Yet won the respect and confidence of two generations. . . .

Would every beholder sense the anguish and the scruple of that single word "imposed" or the deep frustrations it hinted at?

In the melancholy winter that followed Henry faced stoically ahead and preached the need of stoicism in the world. The pessimistic clamor of Tennyson's *Locksley Hall, Sixty Years After* seemed to him to violate all decorum, "an unmelodious shriek . . . undignified even if the universe were shrivelling." Tennyson besought his reader: "Patience! let the dying actor mouth his last upon the stage." But his exacting reader said that "old men should know how to make their exit with grace and humor." Mankind may be on the highroad to perdition, "but I do not think that art or manners require us to fling the fact constantly in our neighbors' faces." On this score also Adams would change his mind, remembering in his own way Tennyson's line: "Chaos, Cosmos! Cosmos, Chaos! Who can tell how all will end?" [50]

More to his taste was John Hay's poem "Israel" in the *Century,* elaborately illustrated with mythological figures of the Fates and Jacob and the angel. Hay also queried the riddle of the universe, the name and nature of God. Thus Jacob taxed the angel, "Tell me, I pray Thy name," but the angel answered not. All questions were answerless and science as helpless as the rest. Adams passed on to him King's quip that they all ought "publish our joint works under the title of 'The Impasse Series' because they all ask questions which have no answers." He added his own endorsement, "but nothing has any real answer, and when one walks deliberately into these blind alleys where Impasse is struck up at every step, one cannot, without a certain ridicule, knock one's head violently against the brick wall at the end. Victor Hugo did this, to the delight of Frenchmen; but for our timider natures, let us go on, as before, and, when we see a brick wall, take off our hats to it with the good manners we most affect, and say in our choicest English: 'Monseigneur, j'attendrai.' You have done it charmingly." Another friend, James Russell Lowell, posed his own version of the "impasse" in his current satire "Credidimus Jovem Regnare," which also asked, "Whence? Whither? Wherefore? How? Which? Why?" It too suggested that science was no more successful than religion in unveiling the eternal verities.[51]

The winding up of family affairs in Quincy depressed him almost beyond endurance. His mother, to whom he was deeply attached, got about painfully in her wheel chair. Brooks was impatient to begin his studies in Vienna, especially of the military leaders who seemed to him the last line of defense against the vulgar materialism of the "gold bug" speculators and bankers. He was ready to take up de Tocqueville's challenge, uttered a half century before: "A new science of politics is needed for a new world." Having shown how the Puritan oligarchy had been overthrown, Brooks determined to get at the nature — and weakness — of the new Leviathan which threatened liberty. Henry knew that his summers must henceforward belong to his mother. But Quincy now spoke of death and decay. As he walked through the orchard and the well-kept paths of the rose garden, he realized with a pang that his dulled senses no longer caught the rush of springtime fragrances. "The worst of a childhood's haunts like this place," he said, "is that it forces on one's mind the passage of time." [52]

3   Through History to Buddha

Back in Washington with his cargo of Japanese art objects in place, Henry Adams sat down at his desk once more chastened and a little dubious of success, but determined to boil up his old interest and bring his history to a close. Through his letters there now began to run a trickle of bantering reports of progress. He began to be obsessed with the idea of getting off to China. "Every day I pass at my desk is passed in the idea that it is so much out of my way." He saw himself setting out "after the manner of Ulysses, in search of that new world which is the old." He began to learn Chinese, spending two hours a day on it after a stint of six hours making the history "dance." He entertained Hay with his dictionary version of the First Beatitude: " 'Pure heart of man is possess blessing of, for has God, kingdom approach are of kingdom.' What it means I can't say." 53

The draft of Madison's first administration now went swiftly on. When the winter's work was over and "China so much nearer," a new impulse struck him, perhaps the result of Alex Agassiz's enthusiasm. He would do Hawaii the following year and then Peking. On his way north he paused briefly in New York to visit with La Farge and Schurz. A new reader whom he had pressed into service, Samuel Gray Ward, the New York representative of Baring Brothers, returned the first two draft volumes and these Adams left with Schurz. Hay's opinion of the draft was lyrical. "It is, in my impartial opinion the best piece of writing this generation will see from the hand of a Yankee," he wrote their friend Sir John Clark at Tillypronie and added admiringly, "He is up to his eyes in Chinese art, history, and geography, and proposes to leave Marco Polo out of sight in his travels and explorations." 54

Boston and family affairs had depressed him sadly on his spring visit. Summer in Quincy fulfilled his gloomiest expectations. His ailing mother injured her foot in the elevator and the House was overhung with anxiety. The urge to be quit of all burdens harried him. There could be no thought now of issuing his work in leisurely installments. He would finish and decamp. Anyway, long-drawn-out publication blunted the impact of a work. He would take his own advice to Parkman, "Swing the whole at the head of the public as a single work. Nothing but mass tells." Already Hay's *Lincoln* was finished. Hay had dashed off to England for a holiday, leaving Adams chained to his documents and the intricate narrative of the War of 1812. When Hay returned to prepare the ten volumes for publication, Adams in friendly rivalry, now projected a ten-volume set of his own, planning to eke it out with a volume of historical essays. A decade had passed since the project had begun to take shape in 1878 and the work had become an incubus. Word of its progress had got around among historians and his wide circle of friends so that much was expected. In self-defense, he forbade his "eternal history" to be mentioned in his hearing, "the bore of my friends and myself for ten years," making it a point of his social relations not to discuss his books at all, even with close intimates, except when he sought criticism. Friends, like Mrs. Cameron, prided themselves on respecting the taboo. "I have never talked to you of your books, have I?" [55]

Settled down in the churchly quiet of the Stone Library, adjoining the Mansion House, he fell into his usual Spartan routine. Writing "history as though it were serious, . . . and when my hand and head get tired, I step out into the rosebeds and watch my favorite roses," for he had "taken to learning roses" as a diversion. Seized with fits of impatience he took a savage pleasure in lengthening his stint like a conscience-stricken monk. "I work near ten hours a day, and shall soon finish the cosmos at this rate." Confronted by masses of "old international law," he wished for Dwight's expert help. But Dwight had not yet cut his ties at the State Department. The pressure to finish grew more intense. "I must explode into space somewhere, after this summer of galley slave toil," he fumed. "My comfort is to think that the public shall suffer for it, and any number of defunct statesmen will howl, in the midst of their flames, at the skinning they are getting this season, owing to my feeling cross." [56]

By the end of August, 1887, he saw no alternative to employing a stenographer, as Hay had been driven to do — not without protest, however. "With this vile modern innovation I shall spoil my work," he wrote his "dear Prodigal" Hay, "but I shall either be in my pleasant grave on this day two years, or my history will be done and out. I have notified the Japanese government to begin operations in China at that date." He drove his blonde "calligraphess" through nearly a chapter a day, a pace that kept him "on the intellectual jump." In three weeks the revision of Madison's first administration was ready for private printing. "The beautiful typewriter," he reported, "is dismissed." It had been "a month of dry rot" to him but the reward was before him, the steady flow of proof sheets from Wilson the printer. But he insisted on his jest to Hay: "I am seasick every time I see a proof. The sense of its being a baby becomes overpowering." He was ready to "start at any time, with anybody, for anywhere." He took aim with King at Mexico, but news of floods and fever balked them. He fretted in his new greenhouse, "forcing roses" and complaining of the expense. Deeply dejected he studied his reflection in the mirror, more conscious than ever of his gray hair and bald head, and "the crows-feet that are deep as wells under my eyes." [57]

When his wife was alive, she had always succeeded in teasing him out of his recurring mood of dust and ashes, a mood which from the earliest years of his marriage he felt was honestly his through "race and temperament." Marian used to subdue his violent tirades against the inadequacies of the human race to mere "grumbling." Now no one stood between him and his determined melancholy. He summed up his plight for Gaskell: "I am well, as far as I know, with everything in the world except what I want; and with nothing

to complain of, except the universe." Where Marian would
have gaily derided his self-pity and pessimistic vaporings, his
court of ladies listened with romantic sympathy.[58]

His eldest niece, Mary Adams, a vivacious girl of twenty,
had come down to what King liked to call "Adams's expur-
gated tea house" in Washington for her second season as "niece-
in-residence," the first of a succession of blithe and faithful
spirits who helped brighten Adams's celebrated "breakfasts."
He watched their flitting about in Washington society with a
benevolent and paternal eye. There were moments when the
froufrou of silk about the table grew cloying. There was much
affectionate fussing over Mrs. Cameron, who was soon to
present her impassive husband with a daughter, a little to
the embarrassment of the grown step-children. Sometimes
Adams longed for Hay's salty wit. "My breakfast table is
crowded to suffocation and famine; Mrs. Don [Cameron]
is tender and is going to Beverly, and has taken me to call
on Mrs. Cleveland; Miss Lucy [Frelinghuysen] comes at one
o'clock; Rebecca Dodge is affectionate; Sally Loring, bright;
Miss Thoron, Catholic; and they are all as one family; but oh,
my blessed Virgin! they feed my soul with but thin nectar." [59]

The engaging young British diplomat, Cecil Spring Rice,
joined the privileged circle at 1603 H Street, to begin a thirty-
year friendship. He was one of the first of the young "nephews
in wish" in whom Adams sought the authentic marks of the
new men of the future. Twenty-eight to Adams's forty-nine,
the personable young secretary of the legation was an instant
success. Adams thought him "an intelligent and agreeable
fellow" with "creditable wits." "Mad, of course, but not more
mad then Englishmen should be." He paid for his meals "with
a certain dry humor, not without suggestions of Monckton
Milnes's breakfasts of five and twenty years ago." His wit had
a congenially acid bite. "Nobody can deny," he wrote to a

friend, "that [the United States] is the dullest country in the world to be rich in and the bitterest to be poor in." [60]

Spring Rice found his host a fascinating enigma and already a legendary figure in Washington. "The Adams family are as odd as can be," he wrote home. "They are all clever, but they all make a sort of profession of eccentricity. . . . Two of them were arguing. One said, 'It seems to me I am the only one of the family who inherits anything of our grandfather's manners.' 'But you dissipated your inheritance young,' answered the other. . . . I like the one here, who since his wife died has no friends and no absorbing interest and takes an amused view of life, tempered by an attachment to Japanese art." Spring Rice was very soon on the most cordial terms with Adams, but continually amazed by his personality, he kept returning to the puzzle. After a little more study he wrote, "He is queer to the last degree; cynical, vindictive, but with a constant interest in people, faithful to his friends and passionately fond of his mother and of all little children ever born; even puppies. He lives in a Japanese house full of strange trophies from Japan and a precious idol given him by the Japanese Minister. He has no cards and never goes out. A friend of Aubrey de Vere's lives with him [Theodore Dwight]: an ideal librarian: small and dark: always arranging books and living all day in the library of the State Department like a spider in a web watching all the books that fly through the world and digesting them slowly. Next door is the house of John Hay, the poet, who drops in to talk and chat and argue and compare notes: the best storyteller I have ever heard and such a good sort, too." In 1890, five years after Mrs. Adams's death, Spring Rice, again stationed in Washington and a constant dinner guest of Henry Adams, was still able to write that he "never goes out." [61]

It was not long before Spring Rice was as hopelessly en-

amored of Mrs. Cameron as Adams and Hay. He is "chanting
your hymns," Adams told her. "He is certainly better worth
having in your train than most of us others who are there.
He has more of the charm of the most agreeable English
society than any Englishman we have had. He has also another quality which is worth considering, for he is a gentleman,
and the species has become rare in his profession." Spring
Rice's sonnets to her beauty challenged Hay and Adams to
chivalrous rivalry. It was an exquisite game of adoration such
as true Pre-Raphaelites might delight in, imagining themselves
as Petrarchs and Dantes. The Senator had little appetite for
such frivolities, being busy with the guerrilla warfare of Pennsylvania politics but, a little flattered perhaps by the distinguished persons in his wife's train, looked on indulgently. As
senior courtier, Adams's dependence on their young charmer
grew and he haunted the Cameron drawing room, a "tame
cat" like Stephen Hazard in *Esther*. For a while he had a
gay companion again for his horseback rides and a confidant
to whom he could send a casual note across the Square for a
diverting cup of tea or ride under the winter sun. "The roses
are sweet," ran one missive. "I feel very belle. How about our
ride? Is it off?" The congenial group broke up early in 1887.
Mrs. Cameron took the Adams house at Beverly Farms to
spend the summer there with her infant daughter, Martha.[62]

The child was born in Washington in June of the preceding year. Adams, famished for a child's affection, worshipped her as if spiritually to make her his own. His
attachment to the infant drew him even closer to her mother,
so that he found himself helplessly whirled along in her
train, his thoughts leaping ahead in anticipation of their
meetings or sinking despondently when they missed them.
Involved with his mother's troubles at Quincy, Adams yearned
to visit Mrs. Cameron but an indefinable dread held him
back. "I can't quite make up my mind to go to Beverly; not
because it would give me pain so much as because I am

no longer able to feel it. . . . Pain is not so bad as some
other things, and just now I have my hands full." One rainy
Monday she, "the nearest reasonable approach to an angel,"
visited Quincy bringing more joy than he had felt "in these
many moons." When he thought he could get off to Mexico
with King, his only regret was that she could so easily spare
him. "I am sorry," he said, "for time does not seem to clear
away the wreckage of life, or to show how to climb over it." [63]

Fate was by no means done with his sensitive nerves. Another blow fell. His widowed sister-in-law, Ellen Gurney,
ill in mind as Marian had been, wandered off from her sick
room and was fatally injured by a Cambridge freight train.
The shock-brought on a nervous breakdown in her brother,
Edward Hooper, and prostrated him for six weeks. Adams
hurried north in the hope of being useful and meanwhile he
visited his mother, "very infirm and complaining." The cumulative tragedies were enough to try the most sardonic of stoics.
This kind of *joie de vivre* only a Zola could celebrate.[64]

Adams's state of mind for the ensuing year and a half can
be followed in a remarkable twenty-five page fragment of
his Diary which somehow escaped the periodic winnowing of
his papers. The Diary significantly fills out the story told by
his published and unpublished letters. The entries were usually
made on Sunday, apparently summarizing the notes of a
pocket journal. Most of the entries prosaically narrate his com-
ings and goings or the progress of the *History,* but these are
occasionally interspersed with passages of troubled introspection:

February 12, 1888 — The winter drags along about as miserably
as it began. I am still quite off my balance, and have been
peculiarly depressed by an attack of what seems malaria, perhaps
the growth of my greenhouse. . . . My little knot of friends are
steady in their allegiance, and Mrs. Cameron more winning than
ever, but Clarence King telegraphs that he will be ready to
start next Thursday. [For a trip to Cuba]. . . . I am weary of

myself and my own morbid imagination, but still more weary of
the world's, and the dreary recurrence of small talk. History is in
Chapter VI of Book II. No proofs of [Draft] Vol. III this week.

King, suffering from chronic illness, was forbidden to go to
Cuba. Hay, ill with a chronic throat, dropped out after two
weeks in Florida. Adams resolutely pushed on with the third
valetudinarian, Dwight.[65]

His travel letters provide an interesting contrast of attitudes
as he adapted his tone to each reader in turn. To Gaskell he
somewhat deprecated the whole trip, mentioning only in passing his seeing a bull fight. To Mrs. Cameron, however, he
confessed his great excitement at witnessing his first *corrida*
and sent a vivid and, in spots, macabre account of it, some
dozen pages long. "The show was just thrilling but what
turned my poor old addlebrain on end was the dozen or two
ladies in more or less soul-moving costumes." One ravishing
creature made him wish he was "a picadero or a peccadillo,
or anything to her." The picturesque opening ceremony recalled the Roman arena and Heliogabalus: "I felt that life
was still left in the worn-out world. My true archaic blood
beat strongly in my heart." Then with sick fascination he
watched the goring of the horses. When the bull was finally
brought to his bloody finish and the men howled, Adams,
unimpressed by the moment of truth, quietly observed, "On
the whole I was too unwell to watch long; and the moment
the bull was dragged out of the arena, I told Dwight I would
keep company with the bull." He swaggered about in a big
straw hat, feeling that Havana was more Spanish than Spain,
and even the omnipresent dirt recalled the pleasures of his
Spanish journey with Marian nearly ten years before. The
architecture struck him as agreeably genuine. "They knew and
still know how to make arches." Like the Spaniards they were
also capable of bad rococo as in the cathedral front. Recalling
the month-long trip for his Diary he acknowledged, "If it

was not happiness, it was at least variety." At Vedado, "I looked out seawards and asked myself whether honestly I wanted or not to return. As near as I could tell my real feeling, I had not one wish ever to see Washington or home again. . . . If it were not for Mrs. Cameron and John Hay, I should turn and run." [66]

For a week he was poised at his desk doing "one small chapter of history," then he was off again for a jaunt to Norfolk with King and Hay. Refreshed by travel, he felt ready for the final push. "I have not suffered much from depression, and not at all of late, from excessive and alarming turns of temper." A week later he probed inwardly: "At work again on History. . . . Spirits much better, and almost no acute depression; only indifference and tedium." One sure distraction for his tedium lay across the Square at the Ogle Tayloe house, now the Washington residence of the Camerons', for there the baby Martha took full possession of his heart. "I have made love to Martha Cameron," he confided to his Diary on May 6, 1888, "and by dint of incessant bribery and attentions have quite won her attachment so that she will come to me from anyone. She adores Del Hay's pigeons, and takes a fearful joy in visiting Daisy in my stable. Her drawer of chocolate drops and ginger-snaps; her dolls and picture books, turn my study into a nursery." Soon he was to keep an elaborate doll's house behind a sliding panel in his library.

The sense of living on the edge of life, shadowed by death and extinction, rose often to the surface of consciousness. In one such mood he made a "noble present" of his books on early German law to Oliver Wendell Holmes, Jr. "Put them all to the best use in your power, and I shall then feel as though I were still teaching." But when he despaired most he would seize upon the vague hope of a brave new life that might lie beyond the Pacific horizon when he should be "set free forever from my duties in life, as men call occupations they are ashamed to quit, but are sorry to follow." [67]

As the Washington season drew to an end once more, he saw no escape. The record took on an even darker tone. What he once wrote near the close of his life was never more appropriate than during these months when his spirits reached bottom. "Thank God, I never was cheerful. I come from the happy stock of the Mathers, who, as you remember, passed sweet mornings reflecting on the goodness of God and the damnation of infants." Doggedly he marked his progress through the War of 1812 like a staff officer with a map before him. "May 13 [1888]. Finishing the Northern campaign. . . . May 20 . . . the Washington campaign. . . . I see the day near when I shall at last cut this only tie that still connects me with my time. . . . I am almost alone except for an occasional visit from Martha and her mother, and I have been sad, sad, sad. Three years! . . . . June 3. A gloomy week, not quite so desperate and wild as in my worst days, but, so far as I can remember, equally hopeless and weary." The Lodges dragged him from his desk for a visit to Mount Vernon but to no avail. "The dissipation cost me three days of despondency. . . ." The black mood suited a new project, the final ordering of the vast store of family papers at Quincy. "Dwight has left the State Department and come into our family service." [68]

The return of summer obliged him to "repeat the old desperate Quincy effort," for it was his turn to look after his mother. He found her "sensibly declined in body and mind. . . . A quick and easy end would be a great blessing for her. . . . I might say the same for myself. I would certainly be quite willing to go with her. . . ." The writing resumed. "June 24 . . . am at Ghent. Dwight has arranged with Burlingame of Scribner & Co for publication." July 22. "Deep in Ghent negotiations. . . . Interesting to me more than most. . . ." August 12. "I have taken up my Chinese again and

find I recover it fairly quick. I mean to make a new attempt
to learn a thousand characters fortnightly. . . ." September
9. "Contract made with Stanford White for stone work of
Buddha monument at Rock Creek. Have written to Saint-Gaudens to send his contract for signature." Again he surveyed
his manuscript. He was nearing "the end of Chap. IV, Book
V, which closes my narrative, March 4, 1817. Tomorrow I shall
reach that point. Four economical and literary chapters remain
to be written, and I hope to have these in shape before I return to Washington. I think I never before wrote eight chapters in less than two months; but I have now nothing else to
do. Life is at least simple. If I have no satisfaction, I have
little interest. I am nearly Buddha. . . ."

In the next entry he tasted to the full the bitter fruit of his
scholar's triumph. "Sunday, September 16. The narrative was
finished last Monday. In imitation of Gibbon I walked in the
garden among the yellow and red autumn flowers, blazing in
sunshine, and meditated. My meditations were too painful to
last. The contrast between my beginning and end is something
Gibbon never conceived. Spurred by it into long meditated
action, I have brought from Boston the old volumes of this
Diary, and have begun their systematic destruction. I mean
to leave no record that can be obliterated." He seemed to
write with a certain terrible relish, as if he might thus destroy
the "double" that haunted him. Again to the *History.* "Of the
four concluding chapters, I have already written one third,
and all are in my mind, outlined and partially filled in. . . .
Nothing yet from St. Gaudens whose contract is the one
serious undertaking now left." Another week of despair. "Sunday, September 23. No sunshine since last Sunday, and floods
of rain. In the midst of gloom and depression I have come to
the last page of my history. I wish I cared, but I do not care a
straw except to feel the thing accomplished. At the same time
I am reading my old Diaries, and have already finished and

destroyed six years, to the end of my college course. It is fascinating, like living it all over again; but I am horrified to have left such a record so long in existence. My brain reels with the vividness of emotions more than thirty years old." Looking out at the dripping garden he again felt the mocking contrast with Gibbon. "I am sodden with cold and damp, and hunger for a change," ran his fretful counterpoint to Hay. "All because I was filial and gave up Fiji to nurse my mother whose health is as good as my own." The macabre ritual before his study fire went on and on. "Sunday, September 30. Steadily working ahead towards my demise. . . . I have read and destroyed my Diary to the autumn of 1861. Nothing in it could be of value to anyone, but even to me the most interesting part was my two closing college years. Much is unpleasant and painful to recall. Sunday, 6 October. . . . Continue reading old Diary, but I hesitate to destroy much of the record since 1862, not that I think it valuable, but that I may want to read it again. Portions are excessively interesting to me; nothing to anyone else." On that tantalizing note the immaculate script comes to an end.[69]

With the publication of the *History* begun, Adams got off on October 12, 1888, to join his friend the baronet, Sir Robert Cunliffe, on a western tour. They were indefatigible sightseers, making the grand circle from the falls of the Shoshone in Idaho, to Portland, down through the length of California, across the Southwest by way of El Paso, with a stopover at New Orleans to visit the famous battlefield. Having no entrée to New Orleans society there was no cause to linger and they hastened back to Washington having "travelled in all about nine thousand miles with perfect success." The Diary account served as a prosaic *aid memoire*. The color, the dust, the picturesque adventures, the sublime landscapes, the adventures and misadventures, he worked up with appropriate ironic gaieties and exaggerations in his letters to Gaskell and Mrs. Cameron. But the heartiness of manner and his best travel letter style did not wholly cover the malaise that lay beneath. "I took my baronet out to the Cliff House, where the Pacific was rolling in its long surf in the light of a green and yellow sunset; and there I pointed to the Golden Gate and challenged the baronet to go on with me. Ignominiously he turned his back on all that glory, and set his face eastward for his dear fogs; and I, too, for the time, submitted; but the longing was as strong as ever. [If I had not wanted to see Martha once more, I am not quite sure that I would not, then and there, have run for it."] [70]

His letters to the infant Martha played a poignant and affectionate counterpoint which only her mother could understand as she read the palimpsest messages. Beneath the playful chatter of gumdrops and of dogs ran a vein of pathos that must have touched her mother to tears as she read the romantic fancies to her prattling babe: "I love you very much and think of you a great deal, and want you all the time. I should have run away from here, and looked for you all over the world, long ago, only I've grown too stout for the beautiful clothes I used to wear when I was a young prince, and I've lost the feathers out of my hat, and the hat too, and I find that some naughty man has stolen my gold sword and silk stockings and silver knee buckles. So I can't come after you, and feel very sad about it. If you would only come and see me, as Princess Beauty came to see Prince Beast, we would go down to the beach, and dig holes in the sand; and would walk in the pastures, and find mushrooms which are the tables where the very little fairies take dinner. . . ." To Mrs. Cameron herself Adams sent a steady flow of gossip and persiflage, paying homage with graceful bagatelles or turning a Shakespearean compliment. "I will not question in my jealous thought where you and Martha may be, or your affairs suppose, but like a sad slave stay . . ." [71]

His "haunting anniversary," December 6, turned his thoughts again to the Saint-Gaudens projected statue. The idea for the memorial had taken shape in Adams's conversations with La Farge in Japan. Not long after they returned, the two of them sought out the young Japanese scholar Okakura, whom they had first met in Japan, to discuss with him the symbolisms of Buddhist art, especially of the figure of Kwannon. The idea of timeless contemplation seemed the perfect note, and they hurried to Saint-Gaudens at his studio in west Thirty-Sixth Street. On the spur of the moment Saint-Gaudens posed an Italian boy mixing clay in the studio, no female model being handy, and flung a blanket about him. Adams vetoed the first pose: "No, the way you're doing that is a 'Penseroso.' " Not at all sure just what the figure should be, Adams was positive on one point: it should fuse the art and thought of East and West.[72]

After the initial spurt of interest, progress was excruciatingly slow, as always with the temperamental Saint-Gaudens. Adams became increasingly anxious about the work. The Diary and the extensive correspondence record the years' long struggle with Saint-Gaudens and Stanford White to finish. The reason for the delays is suggested in the following entry: "1888 April 22. I saw La Farge and St. Gaudens, and made another step in advance towards my Buddha grave. Nothing now remains but to begin work, and St. Gaudens hopes to play with it as a pleasure while he labors over the coats and trowsers of statesmen and warriors." The friendship of the men made bargaining peculiarly difficult, but Adams was insistent that a business-like contract be drawn so that there might be some probability of early completion. Saint-Gaudens, at a loss to know "what to ask" for his share of the work, tried to take refuge in Edward Hooper's remark that Adams would spend $10,000. White's share for the foundation, however, would probably run to $7,000. The mere casting of the bronze figure would come to another $3,000. Perplexed, he asked Adams to "state a limit," adding, "I have not the 'cheek' to ask any sum of a friend for a work that may not set the world afire." Stanford White, more practical, sent on his contract for the foundation and headstone "against which Saint-Gaudens' masterpiece is to rest," and urged Adams to get Saint-Gaudens to commit himself in writing. "Even with a contract and a time and a price set, it is hard enough to get anything out of him." Meanwhile, Adams made his preparations, recording on September 30, "Have sold at a sacrifice two thirds of all the railroad stock I still own, and am beginning to provide twenty thousand dollars for Saint-Gaudens and Stanford White . . ." [73]

In November, 1888, Saint-Gaudens began the work, the contract calling for completion in May, 1890, though Saint-Gaudens hopefully expected to finish by the preceding autumn. He asked for the return of the photographs of the boy who had posed in the studio. Adams dropped off again at the studio on his way back from Boston. "We discussed the scale, and I came away telling him that I did not think it wise for me to see it again, in which he acquiesced." Another month went by; the sculptor asked for photographs of Chinese Buddhas which Adams had set aside for him in Washington "and any book *not long* that you think might assist me in grasping the situation." One further preliminary needlessly troubled him, as he soon discovered. "I have had my conversation with La Farge apropos of our work and in an hour I got all I wished from him as you predicted." To bring the chaotic suggestions to a focus he jotted down: "Adams. Buddha. Mental repose. Calm reflection in contrast with violence of nature." Two of the early sketches foreshadowed the final hooded figure, but a third, a sketch of a seated Socrates, reflected the initial uncertainties. Still he kept after Adams to drop in and see "the result of Michelangelo, Buddha, and

Saint-Gaudens." As the work went on he sometimes used a man for a model, sometimes a woman, the idea of the sexlessness of the figure already taken for granted.[74]

As Saint-Gaudens slowly and painfully worked free from the oppressive philosophic abstractions of Adams and La Farge, he moved with surer instinct back to a figure he had designed a dozen years before, the "Silence," in which, avoiding the suggestion of any particular mode, Greek, Roman, or Egyptian, he created his own "Style Libre." He had wanted "a heavy kind of veil that covers the head, drooping over the face so that it throws the face in shadow and gives a strong impression of mystery," but his client overruled him, insisting on fine drapery. He would also have liked the left hand to cross the body and be concealed in the drapery, for he found hands troublesome. In the new figure he was able to satisfy both desires. All that he ever wished to change, afterward, was the long fold falling between the knees, which he thought "somewhat amateurish." With the finished plaster figure before him, Saint-Gaudens proposed to Adams that, instead of casting the work in parts, as had become common, he cast it in bronze "virtually in one piece." Ashamed of the further delay this would entail, he volunteered to set the cast up in position for Adams's approval, especially of the face. "The face is an instrument on which different strains can be played," he wrote anxiously. "With a word from you I could strike another tone with as much interest and fervor as I have with the present one." Adams managed to avoid seeing the models of the final design, getting reports at second hand from La Farge, who acted as a kind of referee and agent. Stanford White's sketches for the architectural setting impressed Adams as a "stunning scheme" but he passed on to La Farge the final voice with the proviso that the architecture "have nothing to say," and above all that "it should not be classic," but Stanford White resisted

and Saint-Gaudens succeeded in winning agreement to a
"small classical cornice." [75]

6 *Preparing for the Press*

As the end of his dedicated labor hove into view he redoubled his efforts. "To admit the truth, the frenzy of finishing
the big book has seized me." He hurried off the chapters as if
they were letters. From his beleaguered study he fired off a
stream of bulletins on the many problems connected with
publication, for as he said, "On that depends my departure
for China." At first he hoped for a symmetrical eight volumes,
four for each administration, and queried Hay on how long it
would take to print them, each to be five hundred pages. To
Dwight had fallen the responsibility of initiating the negotiations for publication with Charles Scribner, but the arrangement seems to have complicated matters more than they
simplified them. Adams's presence was more strongly felt
through an intermediary than directly. As matters followed a
more and more tortuous path, he had increasingly to be
consulted. Adams took much the same patronizing tone toward
Scribner as he took toward the indulgent Holt; but Scribner
was less ready to humor his whims. [76]

A month after Dwight had sounded Scribner and got a
tentative acceptance in advance of seeing the work, Dwight
forwarded Adams's memorandum of terms:

Eight volumes, five hundred pages each
Every pair of volumes to make a separate work with title page
and index. . . .
The whole work to be printed and ready before any portion
is published. . . .
After the expenses of publication are repaid . . . the author ought
to share equally with the publisher. H.A.

What Adams balked at were the advertising and promotion expenses. Scribner counteroffered with a fifteen per cent royalty arrangement, to which Adams replied at great argumentative length.

. . . If I were offering this book for sale, I should, on publisher's estimates, capitalize twelve years of unbroken labor, at (say) $5000 a year, and $20,000 in money spent travelling, collecting materials, copying, printing, etc., in all $80,000, without charging that additional insurance, or securing percentage which every businessman has to exact. . . .
    As I am not a publisher but an author, and the most unpractical kind of an author, a historian, this business view is mere imagination. In truth the historian gives his work to the public and publisher; he means to give it. History has always been for this reason, the most aristocratic of all literary pursuits, because it obliges the historian to be rich as well as educated. I should be sorry to think that you could give me eight thousand a year for my investment, because I should feel sure that whenever such a rate of profit could be realized on history, history would soon become as popular as magazine-writing, and the luxury of its social distinction would vanish.[77]

Unduly pessimistic about the sales of the work, Adams submitted his detailed calculations countering those of Scribner and renewed his offer to share equally after all costs were met, but excluding "advertising, rent, salaries, putting on the market, etc."

Appalled at the accounting aspects of such a partnership Scribner riposted with a "firm" offer of 20% royalty after 2000 copies. Adams capitulated. To his Diary he grumbled, "I expect no 'afterwards,' but if my book has the large sale of five thousand copies, I shall receive twelve thousand dollars for twelve years' work, or one thousand dollars a year. I have spent more than that on it." It was difficult to resign himself to the truth of his own proposition that a historian's work was necessarily a gift to the public. He took sardonic refuge in the hope that his work would be pirated, a fact alluded to by Richard Watson Gilder when he tried to persuade Adams to join the copyright law campaign. "As to lobbying we will give you five cents a day for the rest of the winter, if you will say five words a day to your boon companions in the lower house in favor of international copyright; but I am afraid your influence will be the other way in your great and avowed desire to have your book stolen." If Adams's irony needed any buttressing his royalty checks were to furnish it. After ten years these amounted to $5000. The contrast between his experience and that of Gibbon and Macaulay could only confirm his impression of the swift decline of American culture. Macaulay's *History* had sold 140,000 copies.[78]

Scribner was willing to forgive much as he soon perceived that he had achieved a publishing coup. "It is a great book," he told Adams, "and will create a profound impression among students of history and thinking men generally." What followed was something of an ordeal for author and publisher. Adams's own frequent letters exchanged with Scribner were paralleled by a far greater number between Dwight and the publisher. There were countless details about typography, maps, setup, paper, and binding. On every point Adams had very definite opinions, and no detail was too small for his careful consideration. He was concerned especially about the aesthetic appearance and the symmetry of the chapters, organizing the pages so as to get effective division into volumes. He insisted on personally supervising the indexing.[79]

The printing was to be done from the three printed draft volumes with their corrections and insertions and directly from the manuscript of the fourth large volume, the draft of which was finished by September 23, 1888. Convinced of the value of a clean, simple page, Adams strove to avoid any cluttering of the text. The text was all important and he wanted it to read as a continuous narrative without marginal notes. "They were never of use to me in any book, except Coleridge's 'Ancient Mariner.'" Page headings, too, seemed a

waste of effort. The typography of the first volume he felt to
be crucial. The proofreading should be "exceptionally careful."
"Everyone criticises first volumes. No one cares much afterwards." At his own expense he ordered a *de luxe* edition of
twelve copies of the initial two volumes on thin paper for a
"Ladies Edition," for himself "or family and a few special
friends," repeating the flattering largess with the second two
Jefferson volumes.[80]

One matter that perplexed him was how the introductory
chapters should be handled. He felt that precedent was against
introductions: "Gibbon ran his introductory chapters into his
narrative, and Macaulay actually broke off his narrative to
insert his introductory chapter. On the other hand I admit that
my first seven or eight chapters are wholly introductory not
only to my sixteen years but also the century. They ought to
stand by themselves." Scribner immediately replied; "As to
the question of setting apart the first eight chapters and
heading them *Introduction,* we are decidedly opposed to that
idea and think they should formally constitute a portion of
the work to which really they integrally appertain. It is *your
work* and not the epoch that is designated by the title, it
seems to us, and your work begins at its beginning, of course."
His view prevailed. Indeed it may have been his idea that
led to dropping the too pat division of the original draft into
four sections of five books each, a device which would have led
to the awkward splitting of the larger sections, as happened,
for instance, with Bancroft's history.[81]

With the long-standing examples of his friends, Green,
Bancroft, Parkman, and Palfrey before him, it had been
natural that he should have decided at first to adopt the
scheme of breaking the long narrative up into volumes or
parts, books, and chapters. Macaulay had settled on book-
length chapters of a hundred pages each, a heavy tax on the
reader's sustained attention. He also had eschewed chapter

titles, but as Scribner could point out, had allowed running heads. On this point Scribner also had his way. Bancroft's title pages showed a busy array of titles and sub-titles of Parts and Epochs that spilled over from one printed volume to the next. Palfrey had been unable to make his books and volumes gibe, the six books occupying five printed volumes. By the time Adams was ready for publication fashions had changed. The revised posthumous edition of Green's *History* had already abandoned book divisions in favor of chapters and sections.

Adams's methodical scheme, settled on fairly early, had been to devote one large draft volume to each administration, each one to make two published volumes. Too hopefully, he had expected to issue the first pair about 1885. In spite of the delay in publication or "reprinting" as he called it, he adhered to his scheme so that each administration appeared in two volumes with independent index. The first two volumes ran light, thirty-five chapters, including the introductory six chapters; the second and third pair had thirty-nine chapters each. The fourth manuscript volume covering Madison's second administration evidently ran to forty chapters, including the "Epilogue" of four chapters. This fourth manuscript volume did not go through a private printing, but was published as three volumes, to make a total of nine. The first six volumes ran 450 to 500 pages each, but try as he would he could not conveniently bring the last four years "within the compass of two volumes," particularly as he planned to add "four chapters in the nature of an Epilogue." Moreover, space would be needed for the cumulative index, 127 pages as it turned out.[82]

The neat plan of five "books" for each administration, each book running seven or eight chapters, imposed a coherence on events that was frequently arbitrary. A certain rhythm of alternation was of course possible between domestic and foreign affairs. Moreover, the Louisiana negotiation formed a natural center for one group of chapters; the Burr conspiracy for another; the military campaigns for still others; but the web of interaction was far too subtle and complex for maintaining what became increasingly arbitrary divisions and Adams and his publisher wisely dropped the scheme which would have needlessly complicated the already complicated numbering system of the published volumes. As a complete set these were numbered from 1 to 9. In addition the "pairs" were numbered 1, 2; 1, 2; 1, 2; 1, 2, 3.

The following excerpts from the Diary open the door to Adams's study during the final months of rewriting. "September 30. [1888] My third volume [draft] is at last printed though I have still a second revise of the last chapter to correct." "Sunday 6 October. Preparing to print. Saw Wilson last Tuesday and Wednesday about a specimen page." "Sunday 16 December. Cunliffe sailed last Wednesday. I have since worked desperately to prepare my first chapters for the press. Gradually I am beginning to rewrite the whole first volume." "Sunday 23 December. Very hard work preparing copy for press. . . . At last I am launched and must take my final course. I am pleased with the new page, which is that of Froude's cabinet edition; but I am troubled about the form of my introductory chapters, as I am in effect rewriting them, and can no longer meditate over choice of changes." "Sunday 6 January [1889] Another year nearer the end, thank time. Copy, copy, copy! Disgusting labor. I can write faster than I can prepare for the press." "Sunday 13 January. Shocking labor over first volume of history which has to be rewritten. I have only sent about one-fourth of it to the printer. . . ." The next sentence suggests other distractions as well. "My brother Brooks is here." Invariably that meant the hardest kind of debate about historical theory.

Brooks had been disappointed by the reception of his *Emancipation of Massachusetts,* a work which he had thoroughly discussed with Henry. In fact he had begged Henry's aid in promoting the book: "I want some public statement of my book: that it is not an onslaught on the Puritans but an attempt to apply general laws to a particular phase of development. You, my dear fellow, are, permit me to say, almost the only man who has understood the point — and you could by about ten lines to the *Nation* put me in the position which I want to hold. At present I am read for the story and I shall miss my whole aim unless I am careful. I may have been wrong not to put on a full preface, but I thought people would be brighter than they are." Henry, burdened with his own work, put him off and urged him to plead his case in the newspapers.[83]

The Diary entries marched steadily on. "Sunday 20 January [1889]. Work on the history is easier now that I have got into diplomatic affairs . . ." "Sunday, January 27. Always hard at work . . . have done about 350 pages of the old volume, which contains 580; another week or two ought to complete it, and then I can begin rewriting my last volume. The work is trying; when I quit it, at three o'clock in the afternoon, my nerves are raw, as though I had scraped them." He had to have a respite. The moment the copy for the first two volumes went to Wilson, Adams's Cambridge printer whom Scribner had consented to employ, Adams dashed off for a three months' holiday this time "knocking about an unknown region called the North Carolina sounds" and "as far south as Savannah." He joined two lively young men, Tom Lee and Billy Phillips. Adams thrived on the rough discomforts, vainly hunted duck, fished for shad, lost at euchre and poker, and happily trudged about Raleigh's Lost Colony. He sent off for his dress suit and plunged into Savannah society for a few days' agreeable dissipation, Phillips having the all-important entrée. He had to be persuaded to return to Washington in time for the inauguration of Benjamin Harrison, but the advent of his new presidential neighbor bored him and he shut himself up in his study.[84]

"Sunday 17 March [1889]. I am rewriting the concluding chapters of my last volume. Very quiet season. Brooks has been here. He goes to Europe again. My society is wholly Martha Cameron and her mother. . . ." "Sunday 31 March. I have prepared all the copy for the second volume, and am rewriting the eighth. . . . President Harrison is amusing me by developing all the characteristics peculiar to Indiana politicians. Hay's private account, derived from Blaine of Harrison's behavior, is convulsing." "Sunday 7 April. I have set a type-writer to work at the beginning, while I write back from the end. The world is still tedious and flat." "Sunday 21 April. I have rewritten the Battle of New Orleans. . . ."

The entry has a special significance for he dwelled on the New Orleans victory with a certain patriotic fervor, as demonstrating American superiority. The proportions of this episode and of the Burr narrative troubled him and he felt called on to defend them to Roger Burlingame, editor of Scribner's. He gave so much space to the Battle of New Orleans, he said, because it has held "an undue place in popular interest." "I regard any concession to popular illusions as a blemish; but just as I abandoned so large a space to Burr — a mere Jeremy Diddler — because the public felt an undue interest in him, so I think it best to give the public a full dose of General Jackson." [85]

As the proofsheets passed back and forth over his desk, his mind turned with growing anticipation to the China voyage. Pumpelly, the Asian expert, came to dine again, Hay and Mrs. Cameron sharing the enlightenment. The Diary entry for Sunday, May 5, was not easy to make. "Mrs. Cameron left here last Tuesday and sailed for Europe. I went to Baltimore with them." His little world was breaking up for the year. As offset, Clarence King dropped in and there was much "Central Asian talk." In spite of departures Washington became livelier for him. He was seeing "rather more society than usual," dining at Mrs. Cabot Lodge's, whose charm did much to palliate her husband's aggressiveness, doing "Sinfony concerts," and riding the nearby trails. He called on the Russian chargé "to give information of our intent to visit Central Asia." Rosen offered "no objection to our Asiatic mystery, and I expect to make a sort of Marco Polo caravan." [86]

The final event needed to round out his practical Calvinism now broke with the rush that the long-expected catastrophe sometimes takes. His eighty-one-year-old mother, to whom life had become increasingly painful and burdensome, was to be spared no horror. In May her mind gave way. Henry's eldest brother, John Quincy, wrote worriedly about the burden thrown on her companion Miss Baxter. She fell into a drugged lethargy and when he arrived in Quincy after his customary spring visit in New York with King and La Farge, she was already unconscious. His Diary recorded the event with stoical restraint: "She died at half past ten o'clock, Thursday evening, June 6. I was present. We buried her yesterday [Saturday] afternoon by my father's side at Mt. Wollaston. I shall remain here this summer with Miss Baxter and Dwight." Attached as he had been to her as a favorite son, he could not but welcome her enfranchisement, as well as his own, for the outrages of time had done their worst. Another valve of feeling went shut. Her nature was so much a part of his, even to the complaints and forebodings, as he always said, that grief was irrelevant and he never betrayed their timeworn bond by futile tributes. She would join Marian in the limbo of his silent mourning. A gray atmosphere hung over the family house, that retreat to which his presidential ancestors had come back "to eat out their hearts in disappointment and disgust." None of the sons wanted the house; they had no love for it. Adams thought he would be the last to occupy it, but he was forgetting Brooks and the tenacity of even the most irksome tradition.[87]

Toward the end of the summer he was wound up, as he would say, in a perfect coil of activity. The draft volumes circulating among his little staff of readers had to be called in and gone over. Scribner kept pressing him for copy, eager to publish promptly. Certain of publication, Adams now luxuriated in fits of cynicism. Delay was indifferent to him, "the longer, the better for my objects — but I would much prefer to be free of the whole job as soon after January, 1890, as possible, so that I can go abroad in that year." Then he added a comment which was all too firmly based on fact: "I have only two wishes: one is to be free, and the other to escape the annoyance, which to an author is considerable, of infuriated grandsons and patriotic women-critics crying for redress." He had already had a specimen of that indignation from Paul Hamilton, grandson of the South Carolinian Paul Hamilton, Madison's Secretary of the Navy. Unsuited for his Cabinet office, he had been obliged to resign. Adams, hoping to unearth the private reasons for his failure, had sent an inquiry to the grandson, accompanied by a patronizing little lecture. "The whole country south of Virginia is removed from the region of intellectual phenomenon, capable of study," especially because the absence of private records made it impossible for historians to "describe or understand what kind of men they were." Hamilton proudly retorted that "the private life of our great men, though above reproach, has ever been considered sacred." As for the absence of records, he coldly added, "all relics of that kind, in Carolina, were destroyed by the vandal hordes of Sherman and Potter." [88]

This had been but a foretaste. Before the first Madison volume appeared, General Joseph Wheeler, a Georgia Congressman, approached him on behalf of General Willian Hull's grandchildren who feared that Adams would accept the court martial version of their ancestor's surrender at Detroit. Adams agreed to let them see the page proofs. Confirmed in their suspicions, they then submitted a legal document of protest and requested that the imputation of cowardice be withdrawn. Adams toned down a few sentences and included the concession that considering the constitution of the court martial, its judgment "could not command respect." A protest of another sort was to follow him to the South Seas in the shape of a two-part letter to the editor of the New York *Tribune*, signed "Housatonic." Even as late as 1910 irate grandsons pursued him. A Southerner protesting a slur in *Randolph*, published nearly thirty years before, wrote to him with some bitterness that others had similarly protested "without a reply from you." [89]

The initial pair of two volumes, the first administration of Jefferson, was published October 2, 1889, in an edition of 1500 copies. The second set appeared February 8, 1890, the printing of 1500 increased to 2000 in the course of the year. Pleased at the progress, Adams wrote to Cunliffe, "Four volumes are now out, about equal to four volumes of Froude. Five volumes are to come." Alluding to his neighbor busy with Nicolay on the ten-volume *Lincoln*, he cast up accounts in American historiography, "Hay and I are racing and carry about the same weight. Between us we have pretty well disposed of the History of the United States. Another generation will have other methods and objects, but I hear of no one among our contemporaries who proposes to jostle us from our seats." By July he was impatiently poised for escape to Samoa, his itinerary having been changed again, held back only by the Index and La Farge's tantalizing hesitation. The world, he mused, would "go along just as straight, whether I drop out or not." He felt a wave of self-pity. "The flop of a winged bird always did jar my nerves." He left the last proof sheets for

Dwight and headed westward again from New York with La Farge on August 16, 1890. Thereafter the third set (Volumes V and VI), the first administration of Madison, appeared on September 26 in an edition of 2000. The final set (Volumes VII–IX) came out January 10, 1891, 2300 copies being printed the first year.[90]

Chapter Ten

Decline and Fall of the Hero

1   The Social Dynamics of Democracy

THE four thousand pages of the *History* do not lend themselves to easy summary or neat analysis for they are the
culminating expression of many motives and of many con-
verging themes. They have something of the complexity and
the philosophic drift of Tolstoy's immense historical "novel"
of the Napoleonic epoch in Russia. Adams's pages are as
defiantly American as Tolstoy's are Russian, yet they have a
common preoccupation in the laws of universal history as
scientifically determinable. Both turned to the same period of
revolutionary change to illustrate them. Standing on the
periphery of Napoleon's turbulent empire, both Russia and
America were profoundly affected by the forces which he
symbolized. Both nations experienced a powerful impetus in
new directions of national development, a development which
inspired de Tocqueville's remarkable prophecy that the two
countries would share the mastery of the world.[1]

The similarity of ideas between the two works arrestingly
illustrates the time spirit, for Adams did not acquire a copy of
War and Peace until he bought the French edition of 1884
and that edition did not contain the extraordinary epilogue
on the laws of universal history expanding the briefer philosophical asides which dot the novel itself. Yet both works
sounded the same all-encompassing themes: the unimportance
of the hero in history, the mechanical determinism which

governs the interplay of social forces, the absence of freedom
of the will in the historic process. The similarity goes even
farther, for Russia's role in Pan-Slavism is as inevitable a part
of the historic process as the Manifest Destiny of American
democracy.[2]

To Adams as to Tolstoy, history was a vast irony, a web
of paradoxes in which man was enmeshed. Habitually unable
to foresee the necessity of circumstances man became the
victim of them. The element of individuality, as he once
objected to Tilden, was "the free-will dogma" of current
historical writing, a dogma which drove historians into contradiction and statesmen into hypocrisy. Jefferson's policy
toward the Indian was a striking case in point; avowedly
humanitarian, he was obliged by the logic of national expansion to encourage ruthless measures by his willing instrument Governor William Henry Harrison. The Governor's
report "of Indian affairs," said Adams, "offered an illustration
of the law accepted by all historians in theory, but adopted by
none in practice; which former ages called 'fate,' and meta-
physicians called necessity, but which modern science has
refined into the 'survival of the fittest.' No acid ever worked
more mechanically on a vegetable fibre than the white man
acted on the Indian." In like manner, Tolstoy wrote that "the
actions of Napoleon and Alexander, on whose words the event
seemed to hang were as little voluntary as the actions of any
soldier who was drawn into the campaign by lot or by con-
scription." He declared that "we are forced to fall back on
fatalism as an explanation of irrational events," but the fatalism
was that of the laws of physics. Just as the course of a battle
could be "represented by the diagonal of a parallelogram of
forces," so on a vaster scale "the only conception that can
explain the movement of peoples is that of some force com-
mensurate with the movement observed."[3]

The disproportion between men's belief in their power to

control events and their inability to do so gave to history its chief literary motifs or emotions, its tragedy and its comedy. Adams imagined a traveller in the Washington of 1800 musing "among the unraised columns of the Capitol," unable to find rational grounds for believing the grandiose aspiration to be realizable. One senses a veiled hint of the moment when Gibbon, among the fallen columns of the Forum, grasped the historical clue. From his study windows Adams gazed upon a modern enigma. The rise of this new Rome challenged explanation as much as the fall of the old. What really was to be the character and destiny of this new empire; what fate awaited *it* in the struggle for existence among the nations?[4]

Europe and England had poured their contempt upon America at the first indication that she was taking a different path. So effective had been the propaganda that, as Adams said, many Americans were prepared to agree that they were "degenerate Englishmen." Even science had supported the chorus of depreciation as when Buffon asserted that the animals of the New World were smaller and inferior to their counterparts in the Old. August Comte declared in 1842 that there was no hope that the United States would achieve the positivist felicities of the "ulterior state," in spite of material advantages because intellectually it was handicapped by the negative ideas of the Protestant Reformation — freedom of thought, equality, sectarianism, and doctrinaire legalism. Matthew Arnold's pious homilies were but the latest of these aspersions and they were echoed by the expatriate James. No refutation had yet been made in terms of the new science of dynamic sociology. Henry Adams undertook the task.[5]

He did so with a large degree of confidence, for he believed that with relation to England and Europe, America stood far ahead in the march of progress. In his letters to his English friends, he never tired of pointing out that America had solved the social and political problems with which England and the

Continent were still clumsily fumbling. There were indeed weaknesses which he felt as keenly as Lowell and Whitman, as *Democracy* testified, but material progress was indisputable throughout the century. The census figures proved it. By 1815 "the increase both in population and wealth was established and permanent, unless indeed it should become even more rapid." Adams prudently left his theory of progress open-ended: "If at any time American character should change, it might as probably become sluggish and revert to the violence and extravagances of Old-World development. The inertia of several hundred million people, all formed in a similar mould, was as likely to stifle energy as to stimulate evolution." The scientific prophet could do no more than point out that all avenues of destiny were still open to national endeavor and place appropriate warning signs beside each one.[6]

The famous questions at the end of the "Epilogue" are, therefore, more rhetorical than real. They neatly parallel the equally rhetorical and ambivalent questions at the end of the introductory six chapters. Could American society, Adams asked his readers, "physically develop the convolutions of the human brain?" It was the same challenge he had thrown down to William James. Returning to the charge in his summing up, he queried, "They were peaceful, but by what machinery were their corruptions to be purged? What interests were to vivify a society so vast and uniform? What ideals were to ennoble it? What object, besides physical content, must a democratic continent aspire to attain? For the treatment of such questions, history required another century of experience." Three quarters of the century of experience had already run by and progress had followed the lines traced out between 1800 and 1815. "Only in the distant future could serious change occur, and even then no return to European characteristics seemed likely." Every man of Adams's contemporaries could see about him the accumulated evidence of American progress and feel the force of the ironic perspective which projected the past into the present as prophecy fulfilled. The good and evil of the present were the product of inexorable evolution and defined the bounds of variation between which the America of the future must develop. What Comte had taught his generation he had put into practice: the philosophical historian must as in all other sciences learn "to predict the past, so to speak, before we can predict the future." [7]

Bancroft in his history had assured Americans that their destiny was the special charge of the Deity; in the long run of our history "the selfishness of evil defeats itself, and God rules in the affairs of men." Such a naïve theory was no longer tenable. Nothing quite so vividly shows the difference in approach between the two friends than an analogous passage from Adams: "The laws of human progress were not matter for dogmatic faith, but for study." America was not exempt from "the common burdens of humanity." She must "fight with the weapons of other races in the same bloody arena; . . . she could not much longer delude herself with hopes of evading laws of Nature and instincts of life." [8]

If the laws of progress obeyed the laws of nature, their discovery, said Adams, must be the work of scientific history. History stood, therefore, at the crossroads. "No historian cared to hasten the coming of an epoch when man should study his own history in the same spirit and by the same methods with which he studied the formation of a crystal. Yet history had its scientific as well as its human side, and . . . in American history the scientific interest was greater than the human. Elsewhere the student could study under better conditions the evolution of the individual, but nowhere could he study so well the evolution of a race. The interest of such a subject exceeded that of any other branch of science, for it brought mankind within sight of its own end." [9]

Buckle, who had attempted to do for English history what

Adams was now attempting for American history, had given ample warning of the difficulties which Adams faced.

The unfortunate peculiarity of the history of man is, that although its separate parts have been examined with considerable ability, hardly any one has attempted to combine them into a whole and ascertain the way in which they are connected with each other. . . . Every generation demonstrates some events to be regular and predictable, which the preceding generation had declared to be irregular and unpredictable: so that the marked tendency of advancing civilization is to strengthen our belief in the universality of order, of method, of law. This expectation of discovering regularity in the midst of confusion is so familiar to scientific men, that among the most eminent of them it becomes an article of faith: and if the same expectation is not generally found among historians, it must be ascribed partly to their being of inferior ability to the investigators of nature, and partly to the greater complexity of those social phenomena with which their studies are concerned.

What history needed were historians on a par with "Kepler and Newton." Buckle anticipated the historical determinism of the *History*. Human actions result from motives; these follow from "antecedents; . . . if we were acquainted with the whole of the antecedents, we could with unerring certainty predict the whole of their immediate results," but he had also shown the impasse that faced historians. Among Adams's colleagues, John Fiske agreed that "the law of progress, when discovered will be a law of history," but more cautious than Adams he saw the enormous difficulty of any dynamic theory of history: "A formula which is to include in one expression phenomena so different as the rise of Christianity and the invention of the steam engine must needs be eminently abstract," just the sort of correlation that Adams would one day attempt to make between the Virgin and the dynamo.[10]

Whatever the difficulties, Adams believed, as he once privately remarked to Parkman, that "should history ever become a true science, it must expect to establish its laws, not from the complicated story of rival nationalities, but from the

economical evolution of a great democracy." Only in America
existed the necessary preconditions of scientific study, a society
"large, uniform, and isolated as to answer the purposes of
science." Comte had first enunciated the axiom: "The laws
of social dynamics are most recognizable when they relate to
the largest societies, in which secondary disturbances have the
smallest effect." De Tocqueville almost simultaneously had
made the first tentative application, postulating that "America
is the only country in which it has been possible to witness
the natural and tranquil growth of society." [11]

Europe defied scientific study because as a result of the
fierce military rivalries its societies were too often disintegrated
to allow the study of evolutionary sequences. But it was
precisely this military struggle that made European history
more attractive for it gave prominence and dramatic interest
to the exploits of the individual and made history the personal
arena of the hero. Denied the hero, scientific history must be
dull and incapable of competing against such rivalry, for in
America "historians and readers maintained Old-World standards." [12]

The problem of the true importance of the hero in history
could not wholly be dismissed and it lurked troublesomely
in the background. Going over the American record a third
time when he turned to the *History,* Adams propounded to
Tilden that Jefferson, Madison, and Monroe were in no sense
heroes. "They were carried along on a stream which floated
them, after a fashion, without much regard for themselves."
Yet as he wrote on, he could not help but feel the tug of contradiction and in the final reassessment he left the point
ambiguous. "Whether the figures of history were treated as
heroes or as types, they must be taken to represent the
people. . . . Readers might judge for themselves what share
the individual possessed in creating or shaping the nation;
but whether it was small or great, the nation could be under-

stood only by studying the individual." The admission seems almost a surrender of the "science" of the history.[13]

The ambiguity mirrored the violent debate that raged all about him. Comte had set it off perhaps by deprecating the importance attributed to genius. They were "essentially only the proper organs of a predetermined movement. . . . In politics, as in science, *opportuneness* is always the main condition of all great and durable influence, whatever may be the personal value of the superior man to whom the multitude attribute social action." Powerful individuals left no trace if they moved in "a contrary direction to modern civilization." Gallatin's great merit, in Adams's eyes, had been that he learned to move with his generation. Spencer, too, had declared that heroes were merely the "product of the age," provoking William James to make a slashing attack in defense of individual initiative. Fiske countered that Spencer did not really mean to disparage the importance of the individual. On the other hand, another Spencer disciple, Grant Allen, went all the way, "No individual initiative has any effect in determining the course of human destiny," or as Tolstoy had put the matter, "In historic events, the so-called great men are labels giving names to events." Yet in spite of determinism which, as Lester Ward wrote, made man "the product of an infinite series of infinitesimal impacts in one general direction . . . no more remarkable than the evolution of a metal or a crystal," Adams could not abandon his belief in the directive value of an élite class. After all, what gave the world value to him was its "very few *real* people." Galton in his "scientific" study of hereditary genius acknowledged that there were "very few first-class men, prodigies — one in a million, or one in ten millions" who competed for the same prizes, but even so the number of family reservoirs of genius was impressive and the Adams family headed the list.[14]

Deeply affected by this current of ideas, Adams found

himself in an increasingly serious dilemma. Macaulay's triumph
was already a legend and the envy of every other historian.
His most recent biographer had singled out for highest praise
his ability to evoke the dramatic *mise en scène* of historical
events. But Macaulay had succeeded by deliberately refusing
to bow to the ukase of the sciences and in defiance of the
spirit of the age had aimed at making his history a "true
novel." Adams professed to be "willing enough to write history
for a new school"; but, as he said, "new men will doubtless
do it better, or at least make it more to the public taste." If
his own form was avowedly transitional and hybrid, he could
say in its defense that in America the time was not yet ripe for
treating American history purely as "a mechanical evolution"
because of the psychological need for Americans to believe in
heroes. Though it was too late to attempt to rival Macaulay,
he was confident, he assured one of his friends, that he had
made his history readable. Unable to transfer his entire
allegiance to the new school, he felt he had managed to divide
it with more or less success between science and art.[15]

It is apparent from all the scientific allusions that pervade
the *History* that he believed that there was one scientific
hypothesis by which the data of history could be successfully
organized, the evolutionary hypothesis of Herbert Spencer.
John Fiske's popularization had made it one of the leading
commonplaces of educated circles. Fiske asserted "that the
evolution of society, no less than the evolution of life, conforms
to the universal law of evolution discovered by Mr. Spencer."
That law reduced the cosmic process to a universal energy
system in which the components moved according to the
familiar figure of the parallelogram of forces, the resultant of
each correlation of forces becoming in turn the component
of a new and more complex figure and so on *ad infinitum*. In
his exegesis Fiske went on to explain that "social progress
consists primarily in the integration of small and simple com-

munities into larger communities; and in the more and more complete subordination of the psychical forces which tend to maintain isolation, to the psychical forces which tend to maintain aggregation." Here science appeared to supply to Adams the rationale for the centralizing and nationalizing movement in American history. It was all a matter of dynamics. In fact Comte had titled one of his own chapters "Social Dynamics; or a theory of the Natural Progress of Human Society," and Fiske could say in 1874 that the great difference between the past and the present was "this habit of looking at things dynamically." Adams had therefore ample precedent for declaring conventional history already outmoded in a dynamical age.[16]

Spencer's influence could not help but be pervasive, given Adams's long-standing commitment to the New Science, especially in geology and physics, but the influence can be more particularly detected in certain key analogies. Perhaps the most famous dynamical figure of the conclusion of the *History* is the following: "Travellers in Switzerland who stepped across the Rhine where it flowed from its glacier could follow its course among medieval towns and feudal ruins, until it became a highway for modern industry, and at last arrived at a permanent equilibrium in the ocean. American history followed the same course. With prehistoric glaciers and medieval feudalism the story had little to do; but from the moment it came within sight of the ocean it acquired interest almost painful . . . science alone could sound the depths of the ocean, measure its currents, foretell its storms, or fix its relations to the system of Nature. In a democratic ocean science could see something ultimate. Man could go no further. The atom might move, but the general equilibrium could not change." The figure elaborated the suggestive observation he had once made to Tilden: "History is simply social development along the lines of weakest resistance, and that in most cases the line of weakest resistance is found as unconsciously by society as by water." [17]

Obviously he had taken a more than cursory glance at his copy of Spencer's *First Principles* if not also at Fiske's commentary in the *Outlines of Cosmic Philosophy*. Water, said Spencer, in its various forms exhibited the universal law, the tendency of energy to move "in the direction of least resistance." Fiske echoed, "It is sufficiently accurate to say that motion follows the line of least resistance." No matter how complex the social mechanism became, "The direction of motion must be the resultant between the lines of greatest traction and least resistance." The very raindrops, said Spencer, showed the immutable pattern of nature. "In every rill, in every larger stream, and in every river, we see them descending as straight as the antagonism of surrounding objects permit." Elsewhere, returning to the water image, for it was a favorite with him as later with Adams, Spencer proposed the following model for the evolutionary progress of society. "Evolution has an impassable limit. The re-distributions of matter that go on around us, are ever being brought to conclusions by the dissipation of the motions which effect them. . . . Descending from clouds and trickling over the earth's surface till it gathers into brooks and rivers, water, still running toward a lower level, is at last arrested by the resistance of other water that has reached the lowest levels. In the lake or sea thus formed every agitation . . . propagates itself in waves that diminish as they widen and gradually become lost to observation . . . [until] quiescence is eventually reached. . . . In all cases then, there is a progress toward equilibrium . . . the ultimate establishment of a balance." [18]

This equilibrium did not imply the death of society or the "degradation" of its societal energies; on the contrary society would have reached its highest state, a state of "moving equilibrium" and not one of complete stasis. There would be a "disappearance of some movement which the aggregate had in relation to external things," but only the "centre of gravity" would lose its motion: "the constituents always retain some motion with respect to each other — the motion of the molecules if none else." In the ultimate phase of democracy, ran Adams's version, "Man could go no further. The atom might move, but the general equilibrium could not change." Spencer thus postulated "a gradual advance towards harmony between man's mental nature and the conditions of his existence" which would bring "mankind in sight of his goal," or, as Adams put the idea, "within sight of its own end." [19]

Assuming that this was a satisfactory description of the process by which mankind would reach its "end" the question arose what that goal might be and how inevitable was the process. On these points there was no clear agreement. Given sufficiently remote time for the working out, one could predict an optimistic issue, and the popular imagination seized upon the scientific second coming, but among the leaders of thought there was no such easy optimism as a later generation has glibly supposed. Comte looked toward a planned society, but he restricted to very narrow limits the Lamarckian theory of the inheritance of acquired characteristics and dismissed as chimerical the possibility of "unlimited perfectibility." Fiske cautioned that "far from being necessary and universal, progress has been to an eminent degree contingent and practical. Its career has been frequently interrupted by periods of stagnation." Lester Ward uttered a similar warning in 1883, "We must divest our minds of the current notion that evolution necessarily implies higher and higher organization." The crux of the matter was, as Adams had jeered at William James, that the mind even of genius could not get free from the material convolutions of the brain; intellectual progress had its mechanical limits. Yet every dream of perfection demanded that somehow man escape from the trammels of necessity. The leap from a mechanically determined past to a future controlled by mind could not be made without assuming a scientific miracle.[20]

The inherent contradictions already had begun to puzzle Adams and the bafflement left its mark on the *History*. In spite of cautious reservations, the dynamic theory of the Social Darwinists had distinctly eschatological overtones, promising a scientific millennium in which man's history would somehow escape the tyranny of time and change. So Fiske wrote of mankind's goal: "As surely as the astronomer can predict the future state of the heavens, the sociologist can foresee that the process of adaptation must go on until in a remote future it comes to an end in proximate equilibrium. The uncanny interdependence of human interests must eventually go far to realize the dream of the philosophic poet, of a Parliament of Man, a Federation of the World . . . when the desires of each individual shall be in proximate equilibrium with the means of satisfying them and with the simultaneous desires of all surrounding individuals." [21]

The utopian dream would be subject to the working out of remote sidereal equilibriums which in the far reaches of time would put an end to earth's measureless felicity when the heavens themselves moved toward their ultimate equilibrium. This cosmic eventuality did not sadden Spencer, for the overwhelming grandeur of the process was too sublime for mortal regret. After all, as Lowell was reminding pessimists, science had immensely lengthened man's stay on earth beyond the meagre chronology of Bishop Usher and in its calculations of the life of the sun had added millions of years to his expectations. Fiske even suggested that the question of the death of the sun was by no means closed, that there existed the possibility of the indefinite continuation of the human race.

But the spectre of that inevitable cosmic catastrophe haunted Adams's imagination and insensibly darkened every vision of the interval of possible felicity and placed an overwhelming question beside every scientific conjecture.

2 A New Order of Man

Having formed the habit of looking at things dynamically, the age also followed Comte in trying to determine the "direction" and the "rate" of human progress. One of Adams's early mentors, Charles Lyell, had written in 1863: "The rate of progress in the arts and sciences proceeds in a geometrical ratio as knowledge increases, and so, when we carry our retrospect into the past, we must be prepared to find the signs of retardation augmenting in a like geometrical ratio." Lewis Henry Morgan fused the evolutionary ideas of his predecessors with the dialectic conception of Comte's historical phases, laying down the following principle: "Inventions and discoveries stand in serial relations along the lines of human progress, and register its successive stages." "Social and civil institutions exhibited a similar register of progress." Hence "by reascending along the several lines of human progress toward the primitive ages of man's existence . . . the advance made in each period will be realized." [22]

Adams adopted the hypothesis that the period 1800 to 1815 was a phase of American civilization as distinct as any described by Comte or Morgan, and employed for his external organization the sort of scheme once proposed by Spencer in his famous book on education. "We want all the facts which help us to understand how a nation has grown and organized itself. . . . And then the corresponding delineations of succeeding ages should be so managed as to show us, as clearly as may be, how each belief, institution, custom, and arrangement was modified; and how the *consensus* of preceding structures and functions was developed into the *consensus* of succeeding ones." In effect this was the method of "historical comparison" advocated by Comte, to "show the growth of each disposition, physical, intellectual, moral, or political, combined with the decline of the opposite disposition, whence we may obtain a scientific prevision of the final ascendancy of the one and the extinction of the other." [23]

The opening and closing sections of the *History* provide the required frame of social dynamics. In the first six chapters Adams analyzed the forces and the inertias at work in the United States of 1800. What made this energy system unique in the world was that it was called upon to sustain "the experiment of embracing half a continent in one republican system," the one step the United States had thus far made "in advance of the Old World." What pattern of order would the chaotic forces take? Would the resultant of these social forces take the direction aimed at by political leaders? Whose plan represented the keenest prevision of events, that of Washington or of Jefferson, that of the Federalists or the Republicans? The equilibrium of forces in colonial America had been disturbed by the introduction of the new force of independence. Whether the new force was a Comtian "idea" or a Spencerian "feeling" or both, a whole new series of equilibriums had ensued, but now on a national scale. The new aggregate, the nation, had now to maintain itself in the dynamic "struggle for existence" among nations, while the whole international machine was being whirled into new combinations by the influx of supranational forces like the revolutionary movement spreading out from France. Internally, the unifying forces had had to overcome the disintegrating and denationalizing ones, all without substantially altering the unique direction of American progress.[24]

The datum line from which man's progress in America —

his civilization as Adams conceived it, might properly be measured was that drawn by his mastery over nature. That line revealed an amazing paradox which Adams exploited at every turn. The retrograde forces and inertias seemed on the surface greater than the progressive ones. "No civilized country had yet been required to deal with physical difficulties so serious, nor did experience warrant conviction that such difficulties could be overcome." The unfinished Capitol symbolized "the immensity of the task and the paucity of means." The first hard fact of the race for world power was the discrepancy in numbers. The United States had only one-third the population of England and one-fifth that of France. The geographical obstacles to political, economic, and social unification were enormous; barriers to travel were "almost insuperable"; besides, the European experience gave no clue to a solution, for in communications Europe was still in the "age of the Antonines." In short, "Nature was rather man's master than his servant." [25]

The inertias were more than material. "The greatest obstacle of all was in the human mind." At the national level the American mind "except in politics, seemed . . . in a condition of unnatural sluggishness." The antiquated educational system was inadequate to overcome "popular inertia in a democratic society." Though "every American knew that if steam could be successfully applied to navigation, it must produce an immediate increase of wealth, besides an ultimate settlement of the most serious material and political difficulties of the Union," the prevailing "old-fashioned conservatism" of mind delayed the adoption of this means. From the very nature of American problems the United States would have to become "a speculating and scientific nation," yet "Science, the tool most needed, generally languished," hardly keeping "pace with wealth and population" and the people were hostile to a national banking system, though it was indispensable for business enterprise and expansion.[26]

For his evidence Adams ranged exhaustively through newspapers, economic reports, books of travels, census statistics, memoirs, and belles lettres, anatomizing in successive chapters the "intellect" of New England, of the Middle States, and of the Southern States. Since thought was, as all social philosophers agreed, the ultimate form of human energy, Adams gave it the position of highest importance in his survey. But here he confronted the acknowledged dilemma of the social scientist. "The growth of character, social and national — the formation of men's minds, — more interesting than any territorial or industrial growth, defied the tests of censuses and surveys. No people could be expected, least of all when in infancy, to understand the intricacies of its own character." Newspapers, travelers' accounts, could give little more than impressions. "From materials so poor no precision could be expected. A few customs more or less local; a few prejudices, more or less popular; a few traits of thought suggesting habits of mind — must form the entire material for a study more important than that of politics or economics." Thus Adams put his reader on notice that the emphasis of the subsequent narrative would be unavoidably misleading because of the disproportionate richness of documents in politics and foreign affairs.[27]

Having painted in darkest colors the inertias and obstacles to success, Adams turned to the agencies which were to accelerate the national movement. The chapter is appropriately called "American Ideals," the opposite extreme of the "physical" considerations with which the analysis opened. The transformation of language is equally notable. The opening had been as low-keyed and matter of fact as the statistics employed; now the tone rose to impassioned eloquence. "The mass of Americans were sanguine and self-confident. . . . If they were right in thinking that the next necessity of human progress was to lift the average American upon an intellectual and social level with the most favored, they stood at least three generations nearer than Europe to their common goal. The destinies of the United States were certainly staked, without reserve or escape, on the soundness of this doubtful and even improbable principle, ignoring or overthrowing the institutions of church, aristocracy, family, army, and political intervention, which long experience had shown to be needed for the safety of society. . . . There was a chance, if no greater than one in a thousand, that America might, at least for a time, succeed. If this stake of temporal and eternal welfare stood on the winning card; if man actually should become more virtuous and enlightened . . . ; if the average human being could accustom himself to reason with the logical processes of Descartes and Newton! — what then? Then, no one could deny that the United States would win such a stake as defied mathematics." [28]

For that sublime gamble America held a better hand than Europe or, changing the figure to one that better typified the contrast, that of the prize ring, he glorified the American in these words. "Stripped for the hardest work, every muscle firm and elastic, every ounce of brain ready for use, and not a trace of superfluous flesh on his nervous and supple body, the American stood in the world a new order of man." American society even then was organized so "as to use its human forces with more economy than could be approached by any society of the world elsewhere." "Compared with this lithe young figure, Europe was actually in decrepitude. Mere class distinctions . . . raised from birth barriers which paralyzed half the population . . . endless wars . . . huge debts . . . aristocracies, sucking their nourishment from industry . . . social anomalies . . . better fitted for the theatre or for a museum of historical costumes than for an active workshop preparing to compete with such machinery as America would soon command . . . as incongruous as would have been the appearance of a mediaeval knight in helmet and armor, with battle axe and shield, to run the machinery of Arkwright's cotton-mill." [29]

From the standpoint of the 1880's America had indeed outstripped England and Europe. Her free institutions had enabled her to economize her forces, her means, her money. Europe might well have foreseen, as far back as the opening of the century, that "when the day of competition should arrive" as it had by the time of Adams's writing, "Europe might choose between American and Chinese institutions, but there would be no middle path; she might become a confederated democracy, or a wreck." Relative to Europe then even in 1800 "the American social system was proving itself to be rich in results. The average American was more intelligent than the average European, and was becoming every year still more active-minded." Europe had not had the wit to foresee the inevitable, and even the romantic Wordsworth fell victim to the blind clichés of the critics of America and joined in the stupid libels of America. In this fashion Adams drove home his evangelical creed.[30]

When he came to revise the introductory section for publication, the graphic scenes of the War of 1812 glowed fresh in his mind and he heightened the coloring with patriotic vehemence. "To their astonishment and anger, a day came when the Americans, in defiance of self-interest and in contradiction of all the qualities ascribed to them, insisted on declaring war; and readers of this narrative will be surprised at the cry of incredulity, not unmixed with terror, with which Englishmen started to their feet when they woke from their delusion on seeing what they had been taught to call the

meteor flag of England, which had burned terrific at Copenhagen and Trafalgar, suddenly waver and fall on the bloody
deck of the 'Guerrière.' " [31]

The sectional types characterized in the introduction become key terms in the subsequent narrative and are made to
represent dominant ideas or energies contributed to the
republican experiment. These "local influences which shaped
America" were the unique evolutionary product of each
section, the result themselves of the interplay of physical,
economic, and intellectual forces. At the two extremes, representing centripetal and denationalizing forces, were the New
England, and more specifically the "Massachusetts school" of
thought and the "Virginia school." Mediating between the two,
tempering their excesses, deflecting and opposing their direction were the centers of the Middle states, New York, and
Pennsylvania. A little later, as the century got under way, there
would be thrust into the vortex of national power a fresh aggregation of forces: the "Western school" of Henry Clay.[32]

Most important was the Pennsylvania school which had
adopted the national point of view the most rapidly of all the
states. It was the "ideal American state, easy, tolerant, and
contented." If their leaders were commonly mediocre and
"gravitated like inert weights to an equilibrium, they were sure
in the end to get" what they wanted. The Virginians, on the
other hand, professing the most elevated political ideals, were
the most provincial and lacking in balance; their disasters re-
sulted more from their own impatience and temper than the
skill or acumen of their enemies in Congress. Paradoxically, the
two great Virginia leaders, Washington and Jefferson, did not
run true to type. They were like and yet unlike their school
and hence were among those few capable of dragging society
forward, in a sense mutation figures in the evolutionary
dialectic. The energies most vitally useful for national development were those of the New York school whose leaders

were unhampered by the metaphysical absolutes of Massachusetts or Virginia political ideas or by the moral scruples of New England.[33]

Step by step Adams assembled the infinitely complex parts of the social mechanism and then set the figure in motion. But the movement could not be made as clear as the scheme promised. Everywhere he was faced with the lack of reliable evidence. Even more baffling were imponderables like Napoleon. The "mysterious processes" of his "strange mind" could not be fathomed. He was "incalculable . . . and not a man like other men." American society bristled with riddles and contradictions. No single term recurs more often than "chaos." Society blindly searching for order and unity seemed always on the verge of degenerating into chaos. At the beginning the Constitution "restored order in the American chaos," but the return to chaos was incessant. The narrative as it records the collapse of Jefferson's expedients and the immoderate struggles for power among the antagonists, explodes into such phrases as "chaos in American society," "confusion became chaos," "chaos prevailing in the White House was order compared with the condition of Congress." With the declaration of war against England "chaos seemed beyond control." The rise of the war spirit showed that "illogical and perverse, society persisted in extending itself in lines which ran into chaos." [34]

In only two areas was Adams reasonably sure of his ground: finance and military affairs. The figures of foreign trade permitted an almost graphical representation of the relative movement of economic forces. The turning of the exchanges against England, reflecting the shift of the balance of trade in favor of the United States, could be tabulated and measured. But even more significant to Adams were the data supplied by the military and naval engagements. Here he could indulge his passion for statistical calculation. A decade later when he was carrying on his enormous colloquy with his brother Brooks about the relative energies of the power combines open to American diplomacy, he remarked, "More than ten years ago I labored to get at a numerical value of the energies, in the last three volumes of the History [chiefly discussing the military and naval campaign of the war of 1812], and I figured it then as about two to one against England, and four to one against Europe." [35]

The opposition of forces in the military actions was treated almost as a problem in physics. In almost every engagement Adams listed from the most authoritative reports from both sides, the number of men engaged, the reserves, the exact number of killed and wounded, the number and character of artillery. The naval battles permitted even closer calculations than those on land. For example, in the engagement between the American *Wasp* and the British *Frolic,* "The two vessels were equal in force, for the 'Frolic's' broadside threw a weight of two hundred and seventy-four pounds, while that of the 'Wasp' threw some few pounds less." Their other dimensions were roughly equivalent. As the action was fought with "the two sloops running parallel, about sixty yards apart, in a very heavy sea, which caused both to pitch and roll . . . marksmanship had the most decisive share in the victory." In the forty-three minutes of battle, the British losses in dead and wounded were nine times the American loss.[36]

From such comparisons, certain vital deductions could be made about the relative mental and moral energies involved. The famous victory of the *Constitution* over the *Guerrière* showed that the power to inflict damage was far greater than the disproportion of physical power. This was the objective evidence. The reasons for the disproportion were that the Americans were "better and more intelligent seamen" and their "passionate wish to repay old scores gave them extraordinary energy." Hence, though the "physical" superiority was as ten to seven, the "moral superiority" counted as ten to two. The "best test" of "relative skill" in the use of artillery came in the battle at New Orleans. There fifteen guns of various calibres were pitted against twenty-four British guns; "the weight of metal was at least three hundred and fifty pounds on the British side against two hundred and twenty-four pounds on the American side, besides two howitzers against one." After about two and a half hours the British batteries were silenced and the guns abandoned. The British losses were more than two to one, proof again of the superior moral energy of the Americans.[37]

Financial and military energies were not the only ones susceptible of scientific analysis. Jefferson's embargo had provided almost a laboratory experiment. Like his fellow visionaries of the "Virginia" school, Jefferson thought that America could use this "engine of coercion" without the expense of war, an error based on ignorance of the dynamics of political action. "The law of physics," said Adams, "could easily be applied to politics; force could be converted only into its equivalent force. If the embargo — an exertion of force less violent than war — was to do the work of war, it must extend over a longer time the development of an equivalent energy." He had to admit that Jefferson's fear of war reflected the popular attitude. "War, which every other nation in history had looked upon as the first duty of a state, was in America a subject of dread, not so much because of possible defeat as of probable success." Americans feared the rise of a military oligarchy.[38]

To Adams this fear seemed utterly groundless. No Nietzschean, he nevertheless had some of his brother Brooks's admiration for the glories of war. It was "the cradle" of arts and liberty. "If war made men brutal, at least it made them strong. It called out the qualities best fitted to survive in the struggle for existence. To risk life for one's country was no mean act even when done for selfish motives; and to die that others might more happily live was the highest act of self-sacrifice to be reached by man. War, with all its horrors, could purify as well as debase; it dealt with high motives and vast interests; taught courage, discipline, and stern sense of duty." [39]

So far as he was able within the sequences of events Adams isolated the major movements as competing constellations of power. In the historical narrative these movements form the episodes. The juxtaposition of didactic "science" and historical narrative therefore runs throughout all nine volumes. One may disregard the science and enjoy the brilliantly written bravura sections in which the artist triumphs over the social scientist, but only at the risk of misreading the total work. The science of it is obviously the indispensable "myth" of the whole literary structure. Questionable as it may be, it makes the vast array of materials cohere; the alternate gathering of forces, their collision and recombination, determine the interweaving of the episodes. So far as his habit of self-depreciation would allow, Adams believed he had successfully fused science and history. Only much later, after the *Mont-Saint-Michel* and *The Education*, did he conclude that "narrative and didactic purpose and style" could not be successfully mixed.[40]

3   *Toward a Theory of Progress*

Although the *Gallatin* — and to a lesser degree the *Randolph* — had anticipated the themes of the *History*, Adams contrived to give his narrative an extraordinary air of novelty. Freed from the restrictions of the biographical format, especially the need of keeping his subject constantly in the foreground, he was able to greatly increase the scale. Gallatin was now subdued almost to the role of a monitory Greek chorus. The hapless Jefferson bustled about the center of the stage, but only as a nominal hero for whom fate provided the wrong lines, a victim of political ventriloquism. Trapped in the swirling currents of "necessity" and "the struggle for existence," Jefferson found himself at the center of a system which dangerously "continued to lose energy" while incessantly threatened by the "impending collision of forces." At the same time the inertias of his thought and that of his party were involved in the dynamics of much larger periodic movements. By 1811, said Adams, the reaction against the spurious "Jeffersonian revolution" of 1800 brought a third twelve year cycle to an end "in a sweep toward still greater energy; and already a child could calculate the result of a few more such returns." [41]

One of the greatest irruptions of new forces began on the second of May, 1808, when Madrid "rose in an insurrection" against Napoleon. It was a small, if bloody affair, but "it had results which made the day an epoch in modern history." It touched off revolutionary movements from Europe to South America in which "the Bourbon rubbish was swept away from Madrid." Yet because American affairs were already inextricably involved in European power politics "the stronghold of free government drew back and threw her weight on the opposite side," against the democratic movement. The succession of realignments that followed grandly illustrated for Adams the mechanical sequences of history. "The workings of human development were never more strikingly shown than in the helplessness with which the strongest political and social forces in the world followed or resisted at haphazard the necessities of a movement which they could not control, or comprehend. Spain, France, Germany, England, were swept into a vast and bloody torrent which dragged America, from Montreal to Valparaiso, slowly into its movement; while the familiar figures of famous men, — Napoleon, Alexander, Canning, Godoy, Jefferson, Madison, Talleyrand; emperors, generals, presidents, conspirators, patriots, tyrants, and martyrs by the thousand, — were borne away by the stream, struggling, gesticulating, praying, murdering, robbing; each blind to everything but a selfish interest, and all helping more or less unconsciously to reach the new level which society was obliged to seek." [42]

Far away in America another small and violent event similarly initiated its vast chain of consequences in a sequence of historical energy that would add its resistless current to the same stream. "As in the year 1754 a petty fight between two French and English scouting parties on the banks of the Youghiogheny River, far in the American wilderness, began a war that changed the balance of the world, so in 1811 an encounter in the Indian country, on the banks of the Wabash, began a fresh convulsion which ended only with the fall of Napoleon. The battle of Tippecanoe was a premature outbreak of the great wars of 1812." Once again the interconnection of American affairs with Europe demonstrated the reign of scientific law amid apparent chaos with the certainty of Newton's physics.[43]

Adams was not explicit about the nature of the great undercurrent forces in American life, nor did he attempt to evaluate their components. Reviewing his work during the revision, he keenly felt the limitation. "Readers," he remarked, "will be troubled, at almost every chapter of the coming narrative, by the want of some formula to explain what share the popular imagination bore in the system pursued by government . . . but nothing was more elusive than the spirit of American democracy." The very difficulty of scientific measurement continually threw him back upon a *mystique* of force, a hypostatized something that mysteriously united all phenomena, physical and psychic, into a cosmic machine. Such was the American trend toward nationalism, "the silent undercurrent which tended to grow in strength precisely as it encountered most resistance from events." The paradox suggested the familiar principle of physics, Newton's third law, that every action is accompanied by an equal and opposite reaction. No historic irony was greater than the struggle between conscious and unconscious thought: "The wit of man often lagged behind the active movement of the world." Parliament and the British navy may have tried to interdict American commerce with the West Indies, but "geography and Nature were stronger." [44]

Within such a framework of analysis the moment of the conjunction of forces was of peculiar interest for it indicated a moment either of sudden acceleration or of change of direction, the entering upon a new phase. Dates and single events had a crucial significance. Scientific history sought to detect these turning points and these in turn provided the dramatic climaxes of the literary narrative. The famous Second of May which "swept the vast Spanish empire into the vortex of dissolution" had its predecessor dates which marked the "breaking up of the old European system of politics": for the English, July 4, 1776, opened a "new era"; for the French, the fall of the Bastille. Similarly decisive were such events as the Congressional debate over the Louisiana purchase act. "This moment was big with the fate of theories." The act gave a fatal wound to the strict constructionist theories of Jefferson's party; "old political theories had been thrown aside." [45]

The cold-blooded aggression of the British frigate *Leopard* upon the *Chesapeake* similarly had momentous consequences. "For the first time in their history the people of the United States learned, in June, 1807, the feeling of a true national emotion." Democrat and aristocrat were made to "writhe alike" in common misery. The circumstances which led to the issuance of the notorious Orders in Council required elaborate exposition because they "gave an impulse so energetic to the history of the United States; they worked so effectively to drive America into a new path, and to break the power and blot out the memory of Virginia and Massachusetts principles."

The victory of the *Constitution* over the *Guerrière* though small "on the general scale of the world's battles, . . . raised the United States in one half hour to the rank of a first-class power." The American invention of the lightly sparred privateer schooner whose speed and maneuverability made possible the virtual blockade of the British Isles marked another phase of energy. Now for "the first time when in competition with the world, on an element open to all, they proved their capacity to excel, and produced a creation as beautiful as it was practical." [46]

There were many other decisive moments as the parallelograms of force succeeded each other: the adoption of the Twelfth Amendment, the unsuccessful impeachment trial of Chase, the passage of the Embargo Act and its repeal, the declaration of war, and the like. Amidst all these events in politics and foreign affairs, the most important for the future was one whose force was to be felt only after the close of the fifteen year period. "Another event, under the eyes of the American people, made up a thousand-fold, had they but known it, for all the losses and risks incurred through Burr, Bonaparte or Canning. [The date] which separated the colonial from the independent stage of growth [was] the 17th of August, 1807 . . . for on that day, at one o'clock in the afternoon, the steamboat "Clermont," with Robert Fulton in command, started on her first voyage. . . . The problem of steam navigation, so far as it applied to rivers and harbors was settled, and for the first time America could consider herself mistress of her vast resources. Compared with such a step in her progress, the medieval barbarisms of Napoleon and Spencer Perceval signified little more to her than the doings of Achilles and Agamemnon." [47]

Perhaps nothing pleased Adams's historical imagination so much as the beautiful irony of the event. "Few moments in her history [America's] were more dramatic than the weeks of

1807 which saw the shattered *Chesapeake* creep back to her anchorage at Hampton Roads, and the *Clermont* push laboriously up the waters of the Hudson; but the intellectual effort of bringing these two events together, and of settling the political and economical problems of America at once, passed the genius of the people." In one of the most poignant of the many might-have-beens of his *History*, Adams declared that Fulton's steamer armed with a single gun would have been more effective than Jefferson's whole gunboat navy, "but President Jefferson, lover of science and paradox as he was, suggested no such experiment." The case was a capital illustration of the mental inertias to be overcome.[48]

For all the science of his analysis, Adams could not escape the contradictions and dilemmas of the effort to harmonize mechanistic evolution, necessary and inevitable as the formation of a crystal or the growth of a tree, with the imperatives of abstract morality. His hypothesis left him with an unslaked thirst for something higher and better in man.[49] What moral qualities were being fostered adequate to survive "violent tests"? If Adams showed a lack of sympathy for the "people," it was not wholly because he was an aristocrat. He demanded moral striving for them as he did for himself. So he wrote in a famous passage: "The American people went to their daily tasks without much competition or mental effort. . . . Every day a million men went to their work, every evening they came home with some work accomplished; but the result was matter for a census rather than for history. The acres brought into cultivation, the cattle bred, the houses built, proved no doubt that human beings, like ants and bees, could indefinitely multiply their numbers, and could lay up stores of food; but these statistics offered no evidence that the human being, any more than the ant and bee, was conscious of a higher destiny, or was even mechanically developing into a more efficient animal." He could not have been

truer to his Puritan heritage than by demanding a consciousness "of a higher destiny." Life must be moral or it was not
worth the history that recorded it. The effort to resolve the
complex movement of society into simple, component energies,
as in the succinct view of labor as economic man, threw him
back upon morality by its patent inadequacy and the revulsion indicated his own idealistic impatience with the theory
of history to which he was committed. The American people
were more pure in morals than Europeans but he shrank from
relating — or degrading — morality to an economic nexus like
the utilitarian philosophers.[50]

If the signs of consciousness of a higher destiny were not
present in the mass of men or at any rate not necessarily reflected by their industry, sobriety, and prudence, they were
lacking in higher circles as well. One of the conspicuous
themes of the *History* is the moral shortcomings of those
higher circles, especially the Federalists. Adams's scorn falls
heavily on the so-called "wise and virtuous," "the best people
of Boston," on those who formed "the whole of fashionable
society," on those who were the recruits of the Essex Junto
and ready to join England in subverting the Union. John
Quincy Adams, who had suffered so much at the hands of the
Junto, could rest content in his grave that his grandson had
evened every score before posterity. "In truth," said Henry
Adams, "Burr's conspiracy, like that of Pickering and Griswold had no deep roots in society, but was mostly confined
to a circle of well-born, well-bred, and well-educated individuals, whose want of moral sense was more proof that the
moral instinct had little to do with social distinctions." In
fact he suggests that in 1808 the terms "gentlemen" and "conspirators" were synonymous. "The most aristocratic American
of the twentieth century will probably agree with the most extreme socialist that Congress, in 1808, might with advantage
have doubled its proportions of tailors and swindlers if by do-

ing so it could have lessened the number of its gentlemen." His brother Charles liked the characterization but persuaded him to change "gentlemen" to "conspirators." The scepticism parallels Jefferson's despondent reflections, as Adams quotes them. "I fear from the experience of the last twenty-five years that morals do not of necessity advance hand in hand with the sciences." [51]

If the rhetorical questions at the conclusion of the opening chapters are translated into the propositions which they imply, the utopian character of Adams's theory of progress clearly emerges. "Complete success" of the new American society required that "it transmute its social power into higher forms of thought"; that "it provide for the moral and intellectual needs of mankind"; that "it take permanent political shape"; that "it give new life to religion and art"; that "it create and maintain in the mass of mankind those habits of mind which had hitherto belonged to men of science alone"; that it produce or be compatible with "the differentiation of a higher variety of the human race." Plato's *Republic* hardly asked more of its guardian-philosophers. [52]

4 Resolution of Forces

As the *History* approached the close of the War of 1812, the military, diplomatic, and political lines of force moving toward the long moment of equilibrium which would be symbolized by the Treaty of Ghent, Adams began to take his pointer readings along each line. A "new epoch began" with the signing of the treaty, though, as befitted the ironies of history, the treaty left "every claim on either side open for future settlement." But if on paper the Americans seemed "the chief loser . . . they gained their greatest triumph in referring all their disputes to be settled by time, the final negotiator, whose decision they could safely trust." To Gallatin he gave chief credit for saving the treaty against the fractiousness of John Quincy Adams and Henry Clay, the over-zealous spokesman for the new West. Obliged to sit in judgment upon his forebears, Henry Adams added a touch of dynastic history — and extenuation. "In 1814 as in 1783 John Adams clung to his trophies, and his son would have waged indefinite war rather than break his father's heart by sacrificing what he had won [i.e., the fisheries rights off Canada]; but at Ghent the son stood in isolation which the father in the worst times had never known." Clay obstinately refused to concede the *quid pro quo*, free navigation of the Mississippi, and thus balked the diplomacy of the Adamses.[53]

The end of the war allowed the people to "turn their energies to undertakings of a wholly different character" and they made the turn with such speed, "almost in a single instant," as to rival "the transformation scene of a pantomime." The spectacle of England brought incontinently to the peace table baffled "the most intelligent and best educated" circles in America and England. It was as if "a village rustic, with one hand tied behind his back, challenged the champion of the prize-ring, and in three or four rounds obliged him to draw the stakes." That village rustic represented the new economies of forces of democracy whose lithe strength Adams had celebrated in the lyrical passages of the introduction. As might be expected in a more mobile and adaptable society, "the long, exciting, and splendid panorama of revolution and war, which for twenty-five years absorbed the world's attention . . . vanished more quickly in America than in Europe, and left fewer elements of disturbance." [54]

The remaining two years of Madison's administration required but three cursory chapters. So far as Adams's thesis was concerned the critical movements had been brought to equilibrium in 1815. The "chief historical interest" of Madison's Annual Message of December, 1815, "lay in the lines of future party politics that Madison more or less unconsciously sketched." It embraced the idea of a strong central government — national roads and canals, national defense, protective tariffs; and took its stand "beyond further possibility of change, on the system of President Washington." The new Congress "in contrast with the imbecility of many previous Congresses" showed remarkable "vigor" and a new scale of government was established. A National Bank came into being and supplied the *sina qua non* of Adams's political theory, the resumption of specie payments. Granting that "population and wealth had increased," what was more significant was that in political experience "the people had advanced more rapidly than their numbers or capital." The elections of 1816 demonstrated, in spite of appearance and dogma, that "in truth parties had outgrown their principles." From the standpoint of 1815 "great changes in the American people struck the most superficial observer." Successfully disengaged from the orbit of European politics, Americans now concerned themselves with the price of cotton rather than with the Rights of Man of fifteen years before. Yet they would have resented any imputation of sordidness in themselves or their representatives. For example, they howled down a proposed salary increase for Congressmen, for as Adams sardonically remarked, they desired, in imagination at least, "to be represented by something nobler, wiser, and purer than their own average honor, wisdom, and purity." [55]

With the retirement of Madison, the moment arrives for the second "consensus," the cross section drawn athwart all the lines of national energy. The closing analysis parallels the opening scheme as closely as good art would allow. The movement in economics fufilled the demands of the theory postulated to account for it. The graph of population growth promised a doubling in twenty-three years, though the drift of population already showed significant losses to New England and Virginia, foreshadowing the shift in the centers of power. To estimate the increase in wealth Adams employed several formulas to interpret the available statistics. All showed, again in accord with the theoretical requirement, that both North and South, wealth increased faster than population. The geographic barriers to transportation and communication were decisively conquered. Thanks to the new economic instrumentality, the steamboat, "the continent lay before them like an uncovered ore-bed. They could see, and they could even calculate with reasonable accuracy, the wealth it could be made to yield. With almost the certainty of a mathematical formula, knowing the rate of increase of population and of wealth, they could read in advance their economical history for at least a hundred years." [56]

Adams concluded that "the movement of thought, more interesting than the movement of population, or of wealth, was equally well defined." Unfortunately this movement was difficult to represent, as he had warned in the beginning, and his summary treatment of it recalls John Richard Green's somewhat similar résumés which eke out the political narrative. The political, diplomatic, and military history had been recited in the greatest detail of fact and document, and the threads of development kept distinct with the utmost nicety, but a similar analysis in literature and art proved impossible. [57]

Material progress showed a steep ascent, but the same rise could not be descried in religious and political thought. No great philosophical or theological movement unified the mind of America. The new religious sects reflected only a change of direction in the national character, "emotional rather than intellectual." The Unitarian revolt against "Calvinistic severity in New England" showed "the same humanitarian tendency" and "warmth of emotion" of the more popular dissident sects. All agreed "in relaxing the strictness of theological reasoning." The unity of the New England church fell victim to the peace, for the conservative clergy, outraged by Jefferson's democracy, with its deism and utilitarianism, had supported the Hartford Convention. In spite of the innovating movement, "the old churches were not capable of destruction" and the new and old dogmas continued to exist side by side with no tendency toward union.[58]

In political *theory* Adams could detect no progress. The sixteen years were "singularly barren of new political ideas." The excessive political speculation in the twenty-five years before 1800 had "exhausted the energy of society" leaving in Americans only an interest in "the practical working of their experiments." But the weakness of the pragmatic resolution was that it rested on the tacit "agreement not to press principles to a conclusion." In the Chase impeachment, for example, "no point was decided." And on the question of States' rights "no one could say with confidence what theory of the Constitution prevailed." Practical politics had made its day to day solutions; but constitutional interpretation had "stood nearly still." [59]

The theoretical nature of the new sovereignty generated by the stress of war remained "a matter for future history to settle"; but there could be no doubt that the practical advantages of political centralization had not been cheaply purchased. The institution of the "previous question" in 1811 clearly "marked deterioration," for in permitting debate to be stifled, the House was responding to "the blind instinct for power" with the methods of those "great usurpers of history, Cromwell and Napoleon." The action paved the way for such evils as the Legal Tender Act. Thus when the Supreme Court confirmed the constitutionality of that act in 1886, a decision concurred in by Adams's one-time law tutor, Justice Horace

Gray, Adams wrote to Bancroft, "Although we are quite aware that the path of 'sovereignty' — which our grandfathers called tyranny — cannot be longer blocked or impeded, we are bound to record, as the government moves, the distance it has gone, and the shorter stage that remains before it." [60]

All the lines converge upon the last chapter, "American Character," lines which began with the mere counting of heads on the first page of the history. In 1815 "American character was formed, if not fixed," and "the American, in his political character, was a new variety of man," although his antipathy to war and military organization revealed a serious flaw in administrative capacity. In one of his Orphic allusions, reflecting perhaps a certain fatigue or confusion in his analysis, he added that politically sagacious societies like those of Massachusetts and Virginia "admitted failure" in dealing with issues so simple that the newest societies, like Tennessee and Ohio, "understood . . . by instinct," but he avoided specifying the issues. Pushed by his scheme to pass final judgment, Adams equivocated. "Opinions might differ whether the political movement was progressive or retrograde." Forced to chew on the politics of 1885, that were "meaner than ever," he evidently could not bring himself to say more, at least for home consumption.[61]

In the social sphere the situation was clearer. Here he recapitulated the superiorities in seamanship, in naval warfare, in marksmanship, in military engineering, in the steamboat. The fast sailing schooner with its pivot gun, as it grew "out of the common stock of nautical intelligence — best illustrated the character of the people." Average intelligence like average morality surpassed old world standards and corresponded with the "wants of a growing democratic society," but it remained an open question whether "the result was a high or a low national ideal." If the ultimate achievement of a moral utopia seemed doubtful, Adams could at least confidently assert that in contrast to England there was a more rapid movement of thought in America, a greater readiness to adopt new ideas in politics, religion, and art, a disposition to surrender tradition more rapidly, and an optimistic mildness in religion reflecting the easing of the "struggle for existence." [62]

With these conclusions established Adams announced the *Q.E.D.* of his long-sustained analysis: "The traits of American character were fixed [a third reprise]; the rate of physical and economical growth was established." Henceforward the chief task of history must be the appraisal of moral and spiritual progress. For such a consensus, Adams suggested the satisfyingly round figure of a hundred years' experience, roughly 1917. As he wrote later, the work "was intended only to serve the future historian with a fixed and documented starting-point." The long demonstration that began nearly a decade and a half before in 1876 with the noble patriotism of his review of von Holst's *Constitutional and Political History of the United States* had at last come to its close. The positions taken in that review now rested upon the most massive documentation. The law of centralization in American political development was the practical consequence of the political experiment initiated by the Constitution. Theory and practice had achieved a working equilibrium during the critical period of 1800–1815. What he said in "*my* Centennial oration" in the *North American Review* in 1876 he held to in 1889. Beneath the chaos of energies, the complexities of "personal motives and idiosyncrasies," the historian "cannot but become conscious of a silent pulsation that commands his respect, a steady movement that resembles in its mode of operation the mechanical action of Nature herself." In the *History* that great "silent pulsation" became the irresistible "silent undercurrent" of the democratic experiment. The *History* reflected much of the patriotic optimism of 1876. In fact the heroic exploits of the War of 1812 inspired so many eloquent passages that his brother Charles took him to task in the margin of the draft copy: "In writing history suppress the patriotic glow." Henry had not glossed over inexcusable faults, but he had made his monumental answer to "foreign criticism" like that of von Holst.[63]

Chapter Eleven

Art and Scholarship

1 In the Dissecting Room

THE *History* is commonly regarded as an anti-Federalist document and there is truth in the characterization; yet it is equally true that it unmercifully exposes the failings of the Jeffersonians. The exceptions in each party define Adams's ideal of American democracy. Gallatin, though a Jeffersonian, was saved from the excesses of the Virginia school by two circumstances. He was of foreign birth and grew up a Pennsylvanian. The perfect balance of his virtues, of the practical and the theoretical, won him election to the United States Senate as the candidate of both parties. John Quincy Adams was the other exception. Though a professed Federalist, he ultimately broke with his party over the Embargo and was driven from office by his arch-rival, Senator Pickering, who put the interests of New England above the Union. "Alone among the prominent Federalists," Henry loyally recorded, John Quincy Adams attended a public meeting in Boston to protest the attack on the *Chesapeake*. In the margin, George Bancroft with his shaky pen queried, "Federalist? *sic et non.*" On this point Adams would not yield. "Federalist" it stood.[1] If the party was subverted, it was by State Street and not by Quincy.

The quarrel with State Street marked impassable limits on one side; that with Jefferson's political heirs bounded the other. As old men, John Adams and Jefferson had made their peace, the bitterness of the Campaign of 1800 gracefully erased in the noble philosophical discussions of two Immortals. Their quiet deaths on the same day, July 4, 1826, should have been an omen of unity, but the character assassination of the Campaign of 1828 reopened old wounds for the son, John Quincy Adams. The motley coalition under Jackson re-invoked the spirit of the earlier Jefferson and drew again on the libels of 1800. Reflectively weighing the whole course of affairs, Henry Adams saw no reason for discarding his inherited feelings "toward Jefferson, Pickering, Jackson" and the rest of his ancestor's enemies. For Alexander Hamilton and Timothy Pickering the aversion had all the venom of personal hatred; but toward "poor dear old Jefferson" Henry Adams had ambivalent feelings.[2]

The contradictions in Jefferson's character fascinated him. Unlike his fellow statesmen, Jefferson "could be painted only touch by touch, with a fine pencil, and the perfection of the likeness depended upon the shifting and uncertain flicker of its semi-transparent shadows." Hereditary feelings or no, Adams could not help but identify himself with Jefferson. In spite of the stern morality and sober common sense in which he had been bred, there was in his character a love of wit and elegant refinement that drew him to the man whom tradition required him to patronize. He seemed to hold the mirror up to himself as he dwelt on Jefferson's complex sensibility. "The rawness of political life was an incessant torture to him, and personal attacks made him keenly unhappy. His true delight was in an intellectual life of science and art . . . his writings often betrayed subtle feeling for artistic form, — a sure mark of intellectual sensuousness. He shrank from whatever was rough or coarse, and his yearning for sympathy was almost feminine." Had he not written in his own defense to his brother Charles, "You like the strife of the world. I detest it and despise it. . . . You like roughness and strength; I like taste and dexterity." Though informal in manner, Jefferson lived discriminatingly aloof preferring to receive "his friends and visitors" at his "chateau" at Monticello protected from "contact with man." The words, written while Adams was planning his own Romanesque citadel for Lafayette Square, must have engendered a sense of fellow feeling. Like Jefferson an aristocrat in his tastes, Adams had always felt drawn intellectually as had Jefferson, to "democracy and radicalism," but democracy purified by Alexis de Tocqueville; and radicalism enlightened by John Stuart Mill.[3]

The eminent pro-Federalist historian and Boston journalist Richard Hildreth, whom Adams had known in pre-War days as a political ally, had set the tone of criticism a generation before in his pioneer history of the period and the early impression on Adams seems to have been ineffaceable. The "great object" of Jefferson's ambition, Hildreth had written, was "to sail before the wind as a popular favorite." Hildreth had also fostered the myth that the early national period marked the disappearance of the hero in American history. To pass from the "mythical and heroic times" of the Revolution was to drop "suddenly from the golden to the brazen and iron ages of the poets." The alloy of those baser metals seemed all too visible in Jefferson. Adams's inventory of his sins curiously mixes the venial and the mortal. He harped on trifles as one who knew what it meant to be vulnerable to them, remembering perhaps the "seed-cakes" which had pursued him in the London *Times* or the accusatory begonia of Senator Timothy Howe. Jefferson's venture in Jacobin manners, the rule of *pêle-mêle* instead of diplomatic precedence, produced one serio-comic contretemps after another among place-conscious envoys. Adams worried *pêle-mêle* through his pages like a terrier. Jefferson's "heelless slippers" suffered a similar fate. Charles, baffled by the satiric reprises about them, queried in the margin, "Why?" Henry retorted, "Because Jefferson fought the British minister with them. See Vol. I." Himself the object of his brother's strictures on a similar score, Adams satirized Jefferson's proneness to mix metaphors in his annual messages to Congress. But these were only satirical flourishes among the main counts of the indictment. He censured his compromises with the New York spoilsmen on patronage, his inexplicable weakness in protecting Burr's accomplice, General Wilkinson, his moral responsibility for General Hull's surrender at Detroit, and his sordid attempt to acquire the Florida territory. Not only had he committed blunders of judgment and policy; he had even compromised his integrity as in his Machiavellian scheme to induce the Indians to cede their tribal lands and settle down as farmers. Adams saw a similar moral obtuseness at work in Jefferson's management of the abortive Florida Purchase.[4]

Instance after instance like these show that Adams spoke grim truth when he once wrote to young Judge Holmes that he had "settled down for the winter and Mr. Jefferson is feeling the knife." Yet not all of the animus against Jefferson was his own. Indeed, there exists a tell-tale discrepancy between the introductory characterization of Jefferson and the treatment of his character in the ensuing narrative. Adams started out conceiving of Jefferson's "contradictions" as worthy of the light touch of Beaumarchais, needing "the lightest of touches," but in the sequel applied more of the harsh satire of Swift. Jefferson did have an inspiring vision of the future of democracy; he did have popular support; his "innate kindliness" was undeniable. He did have an "extraordinary success" in the acquisition of the Louisiana territory; "never had so much been acquired for so little." But the compassionate feelings toward Jefferson which went into the original private edition were largely edited out under the merciless prodding of his elder brother Charles, the process clearly visible in the two volumes of the private edition which still exist.[5]

In his role as chief private critic, Charles impatiently scored almost every sign of praise of Jefferson. The effect of Charles's criticism is strikingly shown in what happened to Henry's original commentary on Jefferson's great public welfare message of 1806 on the use of the Treasury surplus. Henry had written as follows: "In meeting this issue, on which the future character of the Union seemed to depend, Mr. Jefferson rose to an elevation such as he never elsewhere reached. Through most of his writings, both before and after, it is easy to feel the pulsations of a genial temper, a pure patriotism, a liberal and active mind; but very rarely indeed are these high qualities to be seen except in company with some trace of pure Virginian prejudice or fantastic or half-developed thought which he took for philosophy. The Annual Message of 1806 rose above all these mental limitations, and reached a level such as lifted its author among statesmen of the highest order, whose minds developed with experience, have by natural good sense overcome their own innate prejudices." "This seems to me all stuff!" Charles scoffed. "So far from rising to a higher level, J[efferson] descended to the commonplace in thus abandoning the correct principle of local government. He showed that he was not really a great man by thus yielding to the allurement of favor. . . . Before this J. was a doctrinaire; he now became a wobbling doctrinaire . . . devoid of executive ability and had no real convictions." So reprimanded, Henry expunged the whole passage. His allusion a few pages later to Jefferson's scheme as one "to which he had devoted the energies of his ripened mind" fell similarly before Charles's fire: "In other words, the plan of an Augustus or a Richelieu was to be worked out through a political machinery set in motion by the average voter and resulting in the American Congress. The thought was puerile." [6]

Try as he might to be scientific in his treatment of Jefferson and Madison, Adams could hardly escape the effect of family

tradition and where he faltered Charles stood ready to hold
him to the mark. When Henry showed that by an ironic mis-
chance America declared war twenty-four hours *after* England
abandoned the hated Orders in Council, Charles jotted down
the bitter comment: "Madison and Monroe bungled the country unprepared into war in 1812; under almost precisely
similar circumstances John Adams by a masterly stroke of
policy, extricated the country, when prepared for it. Madison's administration was approved; that of John Adams condemned." In the end Henry achieved the desired effect, for
another of his private critics, Abram Hewitt, made a point
of congratulating him on his success, "whether conscious or
unconscious, I know not, in having redressed the grievances
of the Adams family." [7]

Sometimes Henry rebelled as for example in the chapter
called "Monroe's Diplomacy." He exhibited Monroe trapped
by the tortuous interplay of diplomacy first of Spain, then of
France, and finally of England and involved in a series of
personal disasters which proved the futility of further negotiation. Charles scored the chapter as "long, obscure, and
dull. Verbose and inconclusive diplomacy can be spared in
history. It will bear boiling down." Henry protested, "Nonsense! This is the most important chapter in the book and
readers must not only read but study it." He contented himself with rewriting the opening page of the chapter, dropping
some witty satire of Jefferson and Monroe, and replacing
it with an explanation of the Southern stake in the Florida
negotiation. Here as elsewhere he resisted the exhortations
to condense the complex narrative. [8]

Charles's comments show that he too had the Adams instinct for the jugular and an almost unerring sense of Henry's
weaknesses and extravagances, his addiction to picturesque
epithets and high-colored figures of speech, the "Macaulay
flowers of literature," in Dr. Holmes's famous pun. An allusion

to the judgment of posterity as "never long satisfactory to itself," brought the reminder that "it is 'almost never,' or 'hardly ever' since *Pinafore*." When Henry asserted that the fall of Detroit was the "greatest military disaster" in American history, Charles, drawing on his authority as a Civil War colonel, brusquely cited the first Bull Run and McClelland before Richmond, obliging Henry to settle for "the greatest loss of territory." Again and again the comment read, "Why not strike out words underlined?" and out the words would come. Searching for a cliché, Henry unwarily wrote at one point that Perceval could be extricated "only by the aid of Divine Providence." Said Charles, "Isn't 'Divine Providence' a little out of place in agnostic historical composition?" Henry bowed to the impeachment. The *fortissimo* emphasis of the comment "statesmen can sleep in peace amidst the wreck of worlds" was reduced to mere *forte,* by changing "worlds" to "nations," when Charles argued from ancient history that only philosophers had that cosmic privilege. Similarly the Philippic scorn of "convulsions that shook the very stars in the skies never stirred the composure of these men" provoked Charles to ask, "What stars and what convulsions?" Reluctantly Henry lowered his rhetoric from the "stars in the skies" to "the world," though his instinct ran to planetary catastrophes. "To me the crumbling of worlds is always fun," he once remarked.[9]

Henry's political epigrams sometimes provoked an impatient query. "What does this mean?" asked Charles: "In politics nothing surprises. Whatever is most respected becomes respectable." Replied Henry, "It seems clear to me. H. A." Charles defended Madison's theory that war would create the patriotic means to wage it; Henry held his ground and saved a glittering epigram: "The debate threw light upon the scheme by which the youthful nation was to reverse the process of Medea, and pass through the caldron of war in confidence of gaining the vigor of age." Thanks to his censor, he curbed the too-frequent use of the prize-fighter comparison. Occasionally Charles warned him against "the covert tone of sarcasm at the English." Henry grudgingly consented to soften here and there "the light touch of cynicism." George Bancroft, whose comments were far less frequent than Charles's, objected chiefly to Adams's tendency to make sweeping generalizations, both "broad" and "strong." He too balked at theatrics and overblown rhetoric. Thus was lost the following piece of thunderous sarcasm: Pitt would have been "amused to see Mr. Gregg thrust up his Pennsylvania head, in the crack of artillery and the wreck of empires to tell giants who were flinging chaos at each other, that if they should by accident touch Mr. Gregg he would no longer buy his woollen hose of them." [10]

All this pruning and suppressing of his rhetorical exuberance cost him something of a pang. "If you compare the tone of my first volume," he suggested to Elizabeth Cameron, "even toned down, as it is from the original — with that of the ninth when it appears, you will feel that the light has gone out." Something had been lost in the revision, but his explanation for the long prosaic stretches of the volumes seems in part a rationalization. "I am not to blame. As long as I could make life work, I stood by it, and swore by it as though it was my God, as indeed it was." Had he been quite honest with himself he would have had to concede that the summary chapters of the ninth volume contain some of the most powerful writing of the *History* and these were written after his life had been broken in halves. Moreover, the battle scenes and naval engagements often have the hard, etched reality of a Goya sketch, exhibiting his sinewy prose at its best. Undoubtedly in this more "scientific" portion of the history there are far fewer purple passages. Literary and epic allusions almost disappear, but the colloquial directness of statement brings the writing much closer to the disciplined restraint which he constantly preached. [11]

It was inevitable that the long-sustained effort should have palled on him, even granting "the different frame of mind from that in which the work was begun," the change wrought by his wife's death; but he also realized that American history itself had to share some of the blame, as the following isolated draft passage shows: "Deep weariness oppresses the mind in following the thread of national spirit through the labyrinth of national helplessness. Such moments in history are full of danger. Restless impatience is their outcome. At all times men in such emergencies have cried for a dictator; they have rebelled against their own incompetence, and have implored the tyrants of history, — the Caesars, Cromwells and Napoleons — to supply the brain and the will which the people lacked." [12]

Charles continued to have his doubts about the basic method of the *History*. "The plan of telling the story by extracts from contemporaneous documents is carried to excess in these chapters," went one of his marginal warnings, in substance repeating the complaint of his anonymous review of the *Gallatin*. In another place he said, "You are writing for historians, but only indirectly writing history." Henry had himself deprecated his summer's work in 1885 as "a mere mechanical fitting together of quotations," but on this point he did not yield. Though he had admitted his excess in the biography, he felt sure of the validity of the method. More than a decade later he advised Sarah Hewitt, "Your task is only to give a running commentary on the documents in order to explain their relation." If the past were to be recreated as it truly was, and yet with the ironic perspective of subsequent knowledge, nothing could surpass this method of interweaving contemporary accounts to give the illusion that neither the wear of time nor the preconceptions of the historian stand between historical reality and the reader. Perfected in the *History*, the device became in his hands an extraordinarily supple instrument especially in dealing with debates in Congress or the complexities of diplomatic interchanges.[13]

If for the most part the documents are not obtrusive, there are many passages that celebrate the scholar's triumphs. The English archives in particular were virgin soil. Dwight carefully impressed on Charles Scribner that "the larger part of the foreign documents has never before been consulted, or even opened for consultation by any historical writer." Even when the first two volumes were out, Adams pressed his friend Cunliffe to continue the hunt at the British Records Office. "I shall still have time to use new material." That already sent, he was rapidly working into the text. "The more, the better, if it is not in print." When a hitch developed, he successfully played his trump card, the "special privilege granted in 1880 by Lord Salisbury and his colleagues." With justifiable complacence, he exclaimed, "The fool who comes after me will find small gleanings." Cunliffe's new materials made him expansively grateful. "You have shed lustre on your times." He burrowed on almost to the last moment. Knowing that an important part of the secret history of the War of 1812 lay hidden in the Canadian archives, he got special permission for a search and journeyed to Ottawa in the latter part of August, 1889, to rummage seven hours a day in virgin documents. As a result he missed his brother Brooks's spur-of-the-moment wedding. Long years afterward, when the glow of scholarly discovery was considerably diminished and only the drudgery of his research remained in memory, he entertained a more cynical view of the value of manuscript sources. Hearing of the disastrous fire at the Albany capitol, he remarked that it was "one of the greatest steps ever taken by historical studies." [14]

Adams frankly demanded a place for his history alongside of the works of Gibbon and Macaulay, Froude and Green, Parkman and Bancroft, and the rest of the masters of the craft, and in the eyes of one critic, Yvor Winters, he belongs in the very forefront of their ranks. "The greatest historical work in English, with the possible exception of the *Decline and Fall*." Adams presented his work without preface or acknowledgments. What debts he owed to fellow scholars and readers, librarians and copyists, the great debt to his wife, were the private affair of a gentleman, to be paid privately. The attitude had its touch of arrogance perhaps, but it was part of the armor of disdain which he now wore against the world. Intent on disencumbering the text, he managed to give the impression of citing few sources in his footnotes, but the impression is misleading. In Volume VIII, for example, some fifty works are credited, besides manuscript and newspaper sources. Even more revealing of the breadth of his study are the hundreds of volumes of memoirs, letters, biographies, special histories, and reports with which he surrounded himself in his study. Scores of volumes show the stigmata of his aggressive and restless reading, annotations of his agreement, or disbelief, qualifications and frequent cross-references. When he spoke of the small fortune he had spent on the whole project, no least part of it went into the library of materials which he collected.[15]

Taking to heart the criticisms made of the *Gallatin*, Adams resolutely translated every foreign diplomatic dispatch, often suggesting its special flavor and giving his warrant of linguistic tact by quoting a word or two of the original in the body of the translation. One of many instances occurs in a letter from Napoleon to Talleyrand: "You will declare to him [the American Minister] that it is time for this thing to stop (*que cela finisse*); that it is shameful (*indigne*) in the Americans to provide supplies for brigands and to take part in a commerce so scandalous . . ." Adams doubtless ran certain risks in thus threading his way through the verbal mazes of diplomatic language, where so much turns on nuance and implication, and one critic has charged that as a result of Adams's "appalling mistranslation" of a report by the French envoy Turreau, Madison's character was seriously blackened. "The picture of Madison as a half-fainting, shifty-eyed weakling comes entirely from Adams and not from Turreau." In the light of the available evidence, the charge seems a considerable exaggeration. Subsequent historians, in their search for picturesque touches for their own portraits of Madison, may have wrenched Adams's words out of context, but that reflects on their literary acumen rather than on Adams's.[16]

As a matter of fact, Adams on occasion was ready to concede, if not praise, Madison's courage. Speaking of the War of 1812, he wrote, "President Madison's war was the boldest and most successful of all experiments in American statesmanship, though it was also among the most reckless." There is, of course, evidence enough in the *History* that Adams had a low opinion of Madison's abilities, but he was not the first historian to depreciate, and perhaps, underrate Madison, as well as Jefferson. Richard Hildreth's important history had set the pattern a generation earlier. Hildreth admitted that Madison "possessed remarkable acuteness, and an ingenuity sufficient to invest with the most persuasive plausibility whichsoever side of a question he espoused. But he wanted the decision, the energy, the commanding firmness necessary in a leader. More a rhetorician than a ruler, he was made only for second places, and therefore never was but second, even when he seemed first." On occasion he was capable of fright, as when he learned of the Hartford Convention. Hildreth quoted a letter by Wirt who had called on Madison at the time. "He looks miserably shattered and woebegone. In short, he looks heart-broken. His mind is full of the New England sedition. . . ." Madison was admittedly a far less attractive personality than Jefferson and by no means as great a historical figure. Jefferson preoccupied Adams's attention so much that he had little to spare for Madison. He ascribed to Madison a sense of humor in conversation that Jefferson lacked but the precise, quiet little man whose somewhat wizened face was marked by "the demure cast of his flexile lips" remained to the end, in Adams's reading, a curiously self-effacing personage, a diminutive shadow of his chief, even in the Presidency. As a member of the despised Virginia school, whose States' rights fantasies had left a blight on Constitutional law, Madison fell under the general ban to be dealt with without pity.[17]

When the circumstances warranted, Adams showed himself capable of the deepest compassion. His treatment of the unfortunate Toussaint L'Ouverture, who was cynically betrayed by Napoleon, his condemnation of the attempt to restore slavery in Haiti, his sympathy for the democratic rising in Madrid and elsewhere, his pity for the lot of frontier women, and especially his sympathy for the Indian tribes and for Tecumthe, Benjamin Harrison's noble adversary, all these show that there was considerable truth in Saint Gaudens's humorous medallion of him as "Porcupinus Angelicus," the angelical hidden beneath the quills. Where political or moral principle was involved, whether in the case of Burr and Pickering or Jefferson and Madison, he was unforgiving. The higher the station of the person involved, the more exacting the standard of morality.

2 Drama and Paradox

The literary artist in Adams neglected no opportunity to exploit a dramatic *mise en scène* ushered in with such phrases as the "actors in the drama assembled to play another act in a tragi-comedy of increasing interest"; the "plot of the culminating drama"; "a scene in some respects new in the drama of history"; or "the curtain was about to rise upon a new tragedy." Society itself looks down from the historian's box upon the crucial figures and events of history: At the dramatic moment of the closing of New Orleans, "all eyes were bent on the President"; again, "from that moment all eyes turned toward the embargo"; and once again, Europe "watched with breathless interest the deaththroes of Spain." Jefferson's personality made him a dramatic focus, "all eyes fixing themselves upon the desperate malice with which his ancient enemies strove to drive him from his cover." When Spencer Perceval was assassinated, "he vanished in the flash of a pistol from the stage where he seemed to fill the most considerable part." [18]

If history was a drama, sometimes tragic, tragi-comic, and melodramatic, it was a comedy as well. Some have felt the comic muse to be omnipresent because of Adams's many references to Sheridan and Beaumarchais, but the tone is far more often somber and the ironies are more commonly pathetic rather than comic. Beaumarchais's comedies did run much in his mind in these years, but they too were part of the drama of history as Napoleon's famous epigram acknowledged: The comedies were the "revolution already in action." [19]

Only a few incidents lent themselves to high comedy, most notably perhaps the superbly farcical scene of Napoleon in his bath, quarrelsomely disposing of kingdoms while a terrified lackey faints in the background. In the immense context of the *History* these moments are rare and suggest a certain straining for effect, a shrillness of tone. Laski's remark to Holmes comes close to the truth. "It's no use trying to be superior to men like Hamilton, Jefferson, and Burr." This trait, which deepened with the years, provoked Lord Morley to say, after reading *The Education*, "If Adams had ever looked at himself naked in a glass, he would have rated other men a little more gently." [20]

Though comedy is a rare visitant, satiric wit is always within

easy reach of Adams's inkwell, and mocking understatement
plays a lively counterpoint to the narrative. At the news of
the Louisiana cession, "Federalist orators of July 4, 1803, set
about their annual task of foreboding the ruin of society amid
the cheers and congratulations of the happiest society the
world then knew." When Godoy, "the Prince of Peace," finished
with Monroe at Madrid he had gained every point "except
that of proving the defeat of the United States by publishing
it to the world. For this, he could trust Monroe." The Federalists were incredulous at Madison's war-like policies: "They
could not believe that a government would fling itself head-
long out of the window in order to oblige the people to save
it from breaking its neck." Had Talleyrand supported Moreau
instead of Napoleon "some millions of men would have gone
more quietly to their graves." "Although in logic the *tu quoque*
was an argument hardly deserving notice, in politics it was
only less decisive than cannon." The epigrams sometimes have
the salt of La Rochefoucauld. "In conspiracies, men who
knew what they wanted commonly ended by controlling the
men who did not." The Majority in Congress had "little
energy except for debate, and no genius except for obedience."
"The House twisted and turned like a martyr on his bed of
steel, but its torture was of painful doubt, not of passion."
In the main, Adams held to his self-denying resolution to
economize his style. He never forgot the ordeal. "I think I
never have written a chapter less than five times over unless
it were from sheer collapse," was his rather exaggerated recollection.[21]

The fourth volume, the concluding years of Jefferson's
administration, is the richest in literary metaphors and allusions; the eighth, where diplomacy and Congressional politics
give way to military campaigns, is the leanest. A speech in
Congress elicits the comment: "Only some demon of bad taste
could have inspired an orator at such a moment to use the

language of Falstaff." Canning's innuendos are likened to Iago's.
A certain "piece of dissimulation" is deemed "worthy of Shakespeare's tragic invention." Monroe was insensitive to "the
arrows of his outrageous fortune." Here and there the pages
are also marked by allusions to Chateaubriand, Le Sage, and
Smollett. Randolph, among the mass of mediocrity in Congress,
shone "like the water-snakes in Coleridge's silent ocean" whose
"every track was a flash of golden fire." Milton supplies his
finest epic image. Napoleon comes on the stage as "the most
picturesque of all figures of modern history" who "like Milton's
Satan on his throne of state . . . sat unapproachable on his
bad eminence; or when he moved, the dusky air felt an unusual weight." His most graphic figure describing the effect of
the Chesapeake outrage he owed to Homer. "The brand
seethed and hissed like the glowing olive-stake of Ulysses in
the Cyclops' eye, until the whole American people, like
Cyclops, roared with pain and stood frantic on the shore,
hurling abuse at their enemy, who taunted them from his safe
ships." [22]

Adams diligently collected anecdotes as the key to private
character, citing in the opening volume Cardinal de Retz's
maxim, "I have often observed that the smallest things are
sometimes better marks than the greatest." In the throes of his
final revision he was still mining de Retz for an anecdote and
Bolingbroke "in search of style." How pathetically revealing of
slighted talent, for example, was Grétry's famous retort to
the absent-minded Napoleon, "Sire, toujours Grétry." And
how true in spirit was the far more notorious ejaculation of
Alexander Hamilton, "Your people, sir, — your people is a
great beast," though it hovered on the edge of legend. A
macabre anecdote buried in the War Department archives
grimly helped document the white man's barbarism. "The
Kentuckians . . . cut long strips of skin from the thighs [of

Tecumthe], to keep, as was said, for razor-straps, in memory of the River Raisin." [23]

What stands out most vividly in the long marches of the narrative are the many brilliant portraits and flashing vignettes. Jefferson strides on to the stage as a kind of Figaro. "For eight years this tall, loosely built, somewhat stiff figure, in red waistcoat and yarn stockings, slippers down at the heel, and clothes that seemed too small for him may be imagined as Senator Maclay described him, sitting on one hip, with one shoulder high above the other, talking almost without ceasing to his visitors at the White House. His skin was thin, peeling from his face on exposure to the sun, and giving it a tettered appearance. This sandy face, with hazel eyes and sunny aspect; this loose shambling person; this rambling and often brilliant conversation, belonged to the controlling influences of American history." Toussaint looms etched against the sky for a moment alongside of Napoleon, two who "should have known how to die when their lives were ended." Godoy the Spanish premier comes to life like a character out of Saint Simon. Talleyrand, as evilly predacious as Napoleon, stems the current of history as "incarnate conservatism." [24]

In the analytic portrait of George Canning, the ruthless foreign minister who taught three generations of Americans to hate England, Adams rose to his devastating and eloquent best, almost as if aware that his would be the swan song of the grand style in American historiography. "Of George Canning, who passed so rapidly across the scene, and yet left so sharp an impression on the memory of America, something must be said, if only to explain how a man so gifted, and in later life so different in influence, should have thought it worth his while to challenge the hatred of a people whose future he, unlike his colleague Perceval, had imagination to foresee. . . . In the hotbed of Pitt's personal favor Canning's natural faults were stimulated, until the irritation caused by his sarcastic wit and by what the stolid gentry thought his flippancy roused a sort of insurrection against him. Few men were more admired, and none was more feared and hated; for it was impossible to say what time-honored monument he might overthrow in defending." Obeying the impulses of his passionate contempt for liberal principles, "he lost whatever political morality he had possessed," and applauded Napoleon's usurpations with "paroxysms of delight." His evil genius was forged in the same infernal fire. On him rested the blame for the bombardment of defenseless Copenhagen. At the news of "the awful tragedy at Copenhagen, Europe, gorged as for fifteen years she had been with varied horrors, shuddered from St. Petersburg to Cadiz." "The attack upon the 'Chesapeake' was a caress of affection compared with this bloody and brutal deed. As in 1804 Bonaparte — then only First Consul, but about to make himself a bastard Emperor — flung before the feet of Europe the bloody corpse of the Duc d'Enghien, so George Canning in 1807, about to meet Bonaparte on his own field with his own weapons, called the world to gaze at his handiwork in Copenhagen." [25]

At the literary level Adams's theory of scientific determinism had been translated into an all-enveloping structure of irony and paradox. The story opened with Jefferson and his party the captives of their "passion for peace." It closed with a great war fought under the leadership of the "peace party," the United States the chief loser on paper, but destined to win in fact. The two administrations had proved the truth of the Faustian sentence,

> While Man's desires and aspirations stir,
> He cannot choose but err.

A higher law than politics governed the nation's destiny and salvation lay not in political dogmas but in knowledge of the true laws of history. An even deeper and more tragic irony might yet attend the nation. The struggle for existence had brought it into being and fixed it on the path of material progress and power; unless the laws of moral and spiritual progress could be discovered, that very success would have set the stage for ultimate failure of the republican experiment.[26]

3 Changed Perspectives

The collection of *Historical Essays,* printed uniform with the *History,* gave symmetry to the set by adding a tenth volume. All but two of the nine essays were reprints more or less revised of articles previously published; four of them had first been collected in *Chapters of Erie.* One of the new ones, "Primitive Rights of Women," revised his Lowell lecture, given fifteen years before. The other, "The Declaration of Paris, 1861," returned to one of the most puzzling diplomatic episodes of his days as private secretary in London. To the scientific historian the implications of that episode in Anglo-American relations grew more ominous with the passing of the years for it seemed to undermine the foundations of rational diplomacy. Shortly after his arrival in London in 1861, Henry's father had offered to Russell "the adhesion of the United States to the four articles of the Treaty of Paris," expecting that the pacific gesture would be welcome. To his surprise the British Foreign Secretary temporized and hesitated so long that the project died.

Why or when Henry Adams returned to the problem of Lord Russell's motives cannot be fixed with any precision. His exhaustive study of British diplomacy leading up to the War of 1812, especially of the theory of belligerency on which Canning and Erskine acted, may possibly have led him to review the tortuous negotiation of 1861 in the light of the earlier experience. The publication of Spencer Walpole's biography of Russell in 1889 may also have challenged him to throw this sidelight upon Russell's character. The article demonstrated with great circumstantiality that Lord Russell "had intended to mislead" the American Minister. If so much was clear, what still remained tantalizingly unclear was "the unavowed motive," "the true intentions" of the British government at that time. Adams felt that his article, so far as it went, was conclusive and when his brother Charles took up the question in 1896 for his biography of their father, he offered the article as "a sort of guidepost," incidentally declaring it was the only worthwhile article in the collection. By this time another biography of Russell had appeared which confirmed Adams's suspicion of "the double-dyed rascality and duplicity of Lord Russell, which our father did not and could not believe." In *The Education* he would return again to what seemed Russell's motiveless malignity because "he was wholly upset by the idea that Russell should think himself true." Whatever may have been Lord Russell's protestations or private wishes, his actions aimed at the overthrow of the Union. Only afterwards as a moral philosopher did Adams rise above the pragmatic aspect to consider the metaphysical one of the sinfulness of the thought, applying to Lord Russell one of the tests he had imposed upon Jefferson. Adams, as the *Nation* reviewer of the *History* detected, had censured Jefferson for the Kentucky Resolutions of 1798 even though Jefferson's draft had never been published. The secret draft sufficiently evidenced moral turpitude. Lord Russell, like Jefferson, responded to inner impulsions which the conscious mind refused to acknowledge.[27]

Of the original group of articles, the "Captaine John Smith" stood most in need of revision since it had provoked the most indignant counterattacks. Years of association with Southern friends like Lamar, Lowndes, General Richard Taylor, and

William Wirt Henry inevitably made some of the aggressive and sensation-mongering language seem provincial and jejeune. At the time of the first reprint in *Chapters of Erie,* he still thought of the article as subverting the foundations of colonial Virginian history and aiming "at nothing less than the entire erasure of one of the most attractive portions of American history." Now the tone of literary vendetta against the "rare effrontery" of Smith's "falsehoods" and "the tyrannical sway still exercised by Smith over the intelligence of the country" gave way to calm understatement. Smith's account of his rescue by Pocahontas still had to be rejected as "spurious," but more sophisticated now as an ironist, Adams was content to let the unadorned facts speak for themselves. Only two aspects of the story any longer deserved stress; first, that Smith's veracity was questionable; second, that the genesis and growth of the Pocahontas legend was "as interesting as the question of its truth," for it offered material for the laws of history.[28]

One of the essays, "Napoleon at St. Domingo," a revision of the one he had written for Monod's *Revue Historique,* stands apart from the rest. Adams had graciously supplied his friend a thirty-eight page contribution in French on "Napoleon Ier et Saint-Domingue," made up chiefly of archival materials relating to Napoleon's destruction of the black republic established by Toussaint L'Ouverture. Three-fifths of it consisted of excerpts from the secret correspondence of Napoleon and General Leclerc, the rest being sufficient commentary to make the sequence of documents intelligible.[29]

Adams had included a chapter on Toussaint L'Ouverture in the *History* on the ground that Toussaint exercised on United States history "an influence as decisive as that of any European ruler." At stake in the struggle for power was the control of the Caribbean trade and access to the vast and vaguely defined hinterland of the Floridas. A victim of Napoleon's treachery, Toussaint died miserably in solitary confinement, not knowing that his fanatical successors, Christophe and Dessalines, "had successfully resisted the whole power of France." That resistance blocked Napoleon's colonial schemes in the Caribbean and destroyed for him the value of Louisiana. "The prejudice of race alone," according to Adams, "blinded the American people to the debt they owed to the desperate courage of five hundred thousand Haytian negroes who would not be enslaved." Particularly struck by the tragic irony of the situation, he imagined how Toussaint in his last moments "shivering in the frosts of the Jura . . . would have glowed with gratified revenge had he known that at the same instant Bonaparte was turning into a path . . . which was to lead him to parallel at St. Helena the fate of Toussaint himself at the Chateau de Joux." Napoleon too was at the mercy of forces which he could not control and it was his destiny to struggle helplessly and ignorantly against them.[30]

For his scholarly French readers Adams had approached the episode not from the side of its relation to American history but its significance in the collapse of Napoleon's imperial schemes. Thiers had argued that Napoleon turned toward Louisiana to compensate for the loss of St. Domingo; Adams contended that Louisiana on the contrary was "subsidiary to the purpose of recovering St. Domingo from the blacks" as a key colonial base. Napoleon at St. Helena had blamed his brother-in-law Leclerc and the intrigues of the British for the disastrous failure of the French expedition. What the secret archives revealed was that Napoleon was himself to blame. He had foolishly destroyed the black leadership on the mistaken theory that they were the cause of the revolt and he himself had basely connived at the restoration of slavery. Not only were the English not involved in the revolt, they had every reason to avoid embroilment in the West Indies. Having failed in his enterprise Napoleon tried to blot out his blunder by a new and dramatic adventure, the scheme for an invasion of

England, for which he recklessly sacrificed the enormous domain west of the Mississippi, a domain that the Americans had no designs upon at all. In St. Domingo as in Egypt, Spain, Russia, and Germany, Napoleon had blindly thrown himself across the path of the historical movement toward democracy and had been swept away.[31]

Adams indicated in a footnote that the article was "originally published in the *Revue Historique*," but gave no hint that it had been very extensively revised. In the translation he purged away the florid eloquence into which the French had occasionally tempted him. He slashed away most of the historical asides and reshuffled sentences to give a terse, almost scientific precision to his recital. For instance, Napoleon had praised Leclerc's delivery of Toussaint to France as an "honorable" achievement. Adams jettisoned the sarcastic addition: "*Honorable* is not the word which posterity has chosen to characterize Leclerc's act." The archives themselves bristled with self-satire as in the disingenuous report of the autopsy on Toussaint, so like the cynical reports of the Third Reich; the cause of death, "apoplexy-pleuro-peripneumonia." Adams saw that the true value of the documents was the light they threw on Napoleon's character and he added fresh excerpts and deleted others to emphasize the point. The array of documents formed a classical illustration of the insignificance of heroes in history. Where he had written that the cause of Napoleon's failures was his habit of treating free people as slaves, he now advanced the more philosophical conception: "The idea that leaders were everything and masses without leaders were nothing, was a military view of society which led Napoleon into all his worst miscalculations." [32]

A glance at the alterations made in the other essays indicates how rigorously he applied to his own writing the Spartan advice he gave to others. The historical present which had annoyed him in Nicolay's sections of the *Lincoln* was regularly

changed to the simple past tense. The editorial *we* similarly
went by the board. So also vanished the vague moralizing at
the end of "The Legal Tender Act." Relentlessly he hunted
down adjectives and intensives whose force was already
implicit in the narrative. Why "a series of disasters"? Why not
simply "disasters"? He slashed away at "which" clauses and
verbal crutches like "but," "however," "It seems," and all the
parenthetical reservations of the scholar. One result of this
zeal for a completely functional style, void of adornment like
a runner or prize fighter, impersonal as fate — or science, was
to give to some reviewers of the *History* an impression of cold-
ness and inhuman detachment. He was called a "brilliant and
somewhat cold-blooded truth teller . . . [whose writing] approaches nearer the standard of science than any extended
historical work yet written on this side of the Atlantic." [33]

Adams had effectively armored himself against a lack of
critical attention, so much so that the enthusiastic reception of
the early volumes must have a little disconcerted his pose of
indifference. He gave no sign that he was mollified by the
evidence of public taste and steadily avoided any mention
of the reviews or let slip any sign of anxiety. The New York
Times noticed the first two volumes on October 27, 1889, in
two and a half columns of appreciative comment that reflected
the general attitude. He had achieved a "historical work of
great importance," although rather "cold and grudging" in its
treatment of Jefferson. The diplomatic sections, as was to be
expected, were particularly able. In view of the importance
of the archival materials, it would have been "nothing less
than a public misfortune if this work should have been done
by a vulgar or pretentious writer or by a dull and confused
one. But it is in perfect taste. The style is admirable; combines
clearness with elegance and simplicity with dignity and a
gravity worthy of the greatness of the subject." The New York
Critic assured its readers that the work fulfilled "the expec-

tation of a brilliant narrative," and drew particular attention
to the opening panorama; "no American writer has given so
true a picture of American life and ideas." Hewitt, one of his
staff of private readers, wrote to him that the volumes had
"all the charms of a romance," the chapters being like "successive scenes of a drama." He was quick to see the "irony of
fate" that Jefferson's "real history should have been written
by a descendant of the great man whose administration he
thwarted."

The chorus of public and private praise greatly pleased
Adams's publisher. "I did not at first intend to send these
volumes over," Scribner wrote to a business associate in
London, "as the author is a peculiar man and don't care
whether his book sells or not and I should not like to insist
upon any less royalty (as is usually the case) on copies going
abroad; but the exceptional success here has led us to expect
some market abroad."

Adams's idea of success hardly squared with Scribner's. As
he had commiserated with Parkman, they had come too late
into the world. It was pleasant to have "solid butter laid on
with a trowel" by the New York press, but it would have been
pleasanter to have the public besiege the booksellers for his
History. No American could hope for the acclaim and fortune
that had greeted Gibbon and Macaulay. Besides, there ran
beneath the columns of praise a disagreeable undertone of
qualification and captiousness. The New York *Times* thought
his style not up to Parkman's and even questioned whether as
political history it was as good as von Holst. The *Atlantic* be-
grudged the "nearly a score of years . . . since it was first
whispered abroad that this work was in creation," although the
reviewer conceded that "the anticipation [of a great produc-
tion] is very nearly fulfilled." He was repelled by the "carping,
critical spirit" against New England and the contradictions in
the appraisal of Jefferson, which made the author's own atti-

tude toward Jefferson "almost a psychological study." With so much open to controversy and traditional loyalties still keen, it was a foregone conclusion that Adams's interpretations would be challenged as often as they were approved. As the *Atlantic* put it, Adams threw himself "very uncomfortably across the stream of received belief and universal opinion." [34]

Perhaps least gratifying was the series of long reviews in the *Nation,* which almost parodied the judicial manner of the *History* by carefully balancing praise and censure in the manner of a critical Polonius. Godkin, it would appear, once again cast himself in the role of literary Dutch uncle, a fact which may partly explain the disappearance of his name from Adams's later correspondence. The anonymous reviewer, James Clarke Welling, president of Columbia College in Washington, thought that Adams's style and grasp of materials and the "striking" and "philosophical" introduction warranted the highest praise. On the other hand he argued that Adams had so lost himself in contradictions in Jefferson's character as to overlook the "key" to it in party history. Like others he noted the absence of any preface or recital of obligations, but he conceded that Adams's qualifications were already plainly manifest from his earlier work. Thus he went, back and forth, cautiously turning the pages of the volumes as they came out until he left at last the impression of a great forest somehow lost among the trees. [35]

The outcry which Adams anticipated from English readers did not develop. The *Times* did not condescend to take notice of the book or of Adams's obnoxious criticism of the Tory tradition, but the few reviews that greeted the work were disarmingly friendly. Like its American counterparts, the *Spectator* singled out the admirable opening chapters and the skill with which the fearfully complicated diplomatic skeins were unwound. With perfect good humor, it praised the fairness of the treatment of English statesmen, even suggesting that Canning was dealt with "very leniently." After all, if not for the blunders of these men, America might have been an ally in the war against Napoleon. The London *Athenaeum,* in one of its brief notices, remarked that "Mr. Adams has had Macaulay's ideal in view as an historian, and his success in making his pages as attractive as those of a novel deserve recognition." When the war volumes arrived, the critic added that "while patriotic, Mr. Adams is not unduly partisan." [36]

In this benevolent climate of measured praise and qualification, one significant fact emerged. Obliged to read the work piecemeal, critics did not perceive the extraordinary novelty of its approach or the grandeur of its "scientific" architecture. They contented themselves with appreciative nibbling at the overwhelming mass of details, rode their particular hobbies and historical favorites, relished the picturesque and dramatic moments, and missed the philosophical point of the work. It was Brooks Adams's experience with his *Emancipation of Massachusetts* over again. In effect he too was being read merely for the story. Less sanguine than his brother, Henry Adams stoically resigned himself to missing his aim among his own generation. He could afford to wait as he had assured Holt and Scribner in turn. He too had his secret depths of self-trust, even though he could not bring himself to say as Macaulay had that "posterity will not willingly let my book die."

4 A Belated Ulysses

For the second time in a dozen years, Adams felt the keen relief of casting off harness that had begun to gall him unbearably. Six years of classroom teaching at Harvard had sent him to Washington railing at education. The incubus of the *History* had ridden him like the Old Man of the Sea for nearly twice as long and had inspired a similar satiety. All through the harried months that succeeded the publication of the first two volumes he chafed impatiently to get away. The "gigantic index" and the "revises" that remained to be done were no more than busy work. He distracted himself with a few brief visits to the Donald Camerons in their Blue Mountain retreat. He seemed no longer to fit anywhere. Periods of boredom with life and civilization came and went. Once he had been "ashamed to seem restless" and thought it "ludicrous to play Ulysses"; now no other role was conceivable. Eagerly he looked westward again to distant China and the tantalizing "Asiatic mystery," to which his more adventurous friends had gravitated. William W. Rockhill, former secretary of the Legation at Peking and now on the staff of the Smithsonian, had recently returned from Mongolia and was planning a second expedition to Tibet. Adams besought him for "a Chinese education." Rockhill gave him a copy of his scholarly *Life of the Buddha* and "the accidental presence" of the orientalist, H. Shugio, helped him "to understand a little of it." Hay, watching the bustle of preparation, saw a cheerless vista ahead. "That pleasant gang, which made all the joy of life in easy irresponsible Washington will fall to pieces in your absence. You were the only principle of cohesion." [37]

He planned to approach the mystery by way of the South Seas and India, for he was taken with the adventurous notion of tracing out the medieval trade route explored by Marco Polo from the upper reaches of the Oxus across Sinkiang and the Gobi to Peking. He would see for himself the elements of the problems that were exciting ethnologists and anthropologists in Washington and elsewhere. Perhaps he might be the first to deduce the true laws of the origin and transit of civilizations. Such was his ultimate scheme. More immediately, he planned to re-ascend the trail of history in the South Pacific in the manner once suggested by Lewis Henry Morgan. He began to fit himself out for "two years in the South Seas," reserving the right to retreat the moment boredom set in. He talked facetiously of imitating Stevenson whose expedition to the Marquesas and Tahiti had created a world-wide stir two years before.

In July, 1890, his one-time classmate, Judge Alfred S. Hartwell, now Special Agent for the Republic of Hawaii, spent a few weeks with him, while trying to protect Hawaiian sugar from McKinley's already notorious tariff bill then on its way to passage. Hartwell had gone out to Hawaii shortly after the Civil War and had become a leading figure there, first as an associate justice and then as attorney general. He offered Adams the use of a house in Honolulu.[38]

A thousand details needed to be attended to and all contingencies provided for with his customary thoroughness. To his family co-trustees he could conveniently leave the management of his substantial fortune. His eldest brother John Quincy and Edward Hooper could attend to Boston affairs. In Washington, Dwight would be left in charge of the house on the Square with a budget of $3000 a year. Amidst the bustle, intervals came as he sat at his desk putting his house in order when he somberly brooded over the spent years. "In anticipation of a long voyage," he wrote Gaskell, "I have gone through all my papers lately and destroyed everything that I should have wished an executor to destroy." He bundled up his friend's letters, "going back five-and-twenty years," not daring, as he said, to look at them again, and promised to send them over by Brooks. Echoing Adams's mood, Gaskell replied, "Your letter is full of sad thoughts to me, and I shall feel deeply the sight of all my old letters. . . . I have as you know all yours, and value them deeply." [39]

These were characteristic moments of the ebb tide of his feelings. Faced with the Fate-like visits of pompous old Evarts and the faithful Lowndes, he sometimes recoiled into gaiety

and avuncular whimsicality. And across the Square, Mrs.
Cameron presided over a gracious oasis. More and more he fell
into the habit of taking his daily mint julep there and to bask
with his fellow courtiers in the candid, melting glance that
still charms the eye in Anders Zorn's matchless portrait. With
extraordinary tact she humored him in his brilliant self-drama-
tizing talk and his incessant Hamlet-izing. Sometimes, in a
mood of painful self-analysis, he would bewail "that other
self," bitter and cynical, hoping that she might help him overcome it.[40]

As the time for his departure began to fix itself as a fact
upon the horizon, Adams became almost wholly dependent
on her for "feminine society." Every few days, and often daily,
letters passed between them on a hundred topics of common
interest, on friends and family, on grave matters and trifles,
and trifles of trifles, their manner faultlessly correct; only
rarely, almost inadvertently, did Adams reveal the depth of his
feeling. In the autumn of 1887 Mrs. Cameron had returned to
the Square with the infant Martha, her trio of cavaliers bound
ever more closely to her. The sonneteering began again.
Adams made his playful vaunt to her, "I too was in Arcadia
born — or in Hancock Place, beneath the shadow of the State
House dome, — much the same thing I presume." [41]

Strolling in the moonlight on the Mall in Washington he
sang his melancholy to her in accents dreamily reminiscent of
Arnold and Swinburne.

> Infinite Peace! The calm of moon and midnight! Where
> The marble terrace gleams in silvery light,
> Peace broods. Drugged by the brooding night
> The crowded tree-tops sleep in passionless air.
> Look up, where like a God, strong, serene, fair,
> The pale dome soars and slumbers, shadowy white,
> Endymion, dreaming still that on his Latmian height
> He feels Helene's breath warm on his eyes and hair.
> Infinite Peace! Yet, bending from the West,
> Flash out the fierceness and the fire of Mars,

While there beneath, straining to touch the stars,
The obelisk mocks us with its sweet unrest,
And even this soft air of the terrace throbs
With some low moan — sigh of a heart that sobs.

More often the note was that of a faithful Petrarch. Love
had come unbidden and unforeseen and now had made him an
idolator at her shrine.

As a musician who, in absent thought,
    Touching a viol that he chanced upon,
    Pleased with the sweetness of some happy tone,
Some liquid note coming like love unsought,
Some virgin purity, like love untaught,
    Should make the vocal instrument his own
    And slowly ask its secrets, one by one,
Careless at first, deeming the task his sport,
Till, as its notes grow deeper and more sure;
    Its scope more ample with each ripening year,
    He joys to touch its chords, strong, sweet, and clear,
And strives to make its purity more pure,
    So I, who, all these years, my mistress task,
    Find more and richer charm, the more I ask.

Gallantly he protested that "poetic merit must be given" his
lines "by you." Gracefully accepting her role, his Laura gently
chided him for his diffidence. He was indeed a poet, "one of
very high order," she said. "I have suspected it, and *Esther*,
if not my own sonnets, have convinced me." [42]

But these two romantics soon had to acknowledge to themselves that courtly love masked deeper and less tractable
emotions. Formal salutations and conventional "Yours truly's"
could not hide the intensity of their feelings. His incessant
attentions, no matter how scrupulously correct, could hardly
escape censorious comment. He discovered the truth of what
he had himself written in *Esther*: "Every man who has at last
succeeded, after long effort, in calling up the divinity which
lies hidden in a woman's heart, is startled to find that he must
obey the God he summoned." No choice longer remained
except flight. His fair lady of the sonnets had no alternative but

to send him away. For her part she decided to find distraction in Europe. Adams bowed to her wishes though he foresaw that flight would be useless. He distracted himself with errands for her voyage. Up to the moment of his departure he continued to grasp at straws. From Nahant on August 15, 1890, he wrote posthaste, "The mere hope of seeing you again made me try the experiment, but it was foolish, for the disappointment is worse than the regret. I start in twenty minutes, and go straight away to New York, leaving Hay here. Tomorrow evening, at six o'clock, we start for San Francisco. I feel that the devil has got me, for I have said to the passing moment 'Stay,' but the devil gave a splendid price for a very poor article." [43]

He had angled first for the elusive King, jesting that they would "drink our enemies' blood from their empty skulls"; then he settled briefly on young George Agassiz, but in the end had had to fall back on La Farge. La Farge had his usual unrealistic qualms about finances. He thought a second visit to Japan might be feasible, but their friend Gilder of the Century had cooled to a new series of articles on Japan, for Harper's planned to pre-empt the field. Adams talked him out of his scruples against traveling once again as his guest, listening with indulgent amusement to La Farge's threats to pay his own way. On a budget of $1000 a month they could travel in lordly fashion. He lashed him into a frenzy of work to try to finish his painting and stained glass commissions, and finally carried him and his Japanese boy Awoki triumphantly off with him, leaving a trail of unfinished windows behind. [44]

Aboard the train with the irrepressible La Farge Adams regained his equanimity. In lieu of a diary he made a daily entry in a long travel letter to Elizabeth Cameron. La Farge's enthusiasm for the play of color on the Western desert echoed his own. "To me it has always seemed pure purple joy." La Farge fairly danced about trying to "catch the shadows

and colors." He quieted down sufficiently to give Adams his
first water color lesson and the pupil "dabbled all day in cobalt,
indigo and chrome." Full of his new hobby he hurried to share
it in his affectionate "Uncle Henry" fashion with his young
niece, Mabel Hooper, herself a talented watercolorist. Knowing
La Farge, she could relish his uninhibited exclamations: *"By
Jove* and *Adams, look at that!,* and *Just see the color of that
pig-stye,* or *Now we're getting into yellow again,* or *What is
the color of that sky,* just when I think it's pure cobalt, and he
sees sixteen different shades of red in it." [45]

He beguiled some of the vacant hours across the plains
with more sonnets, sending off one to Elizabeth called "Eagle
Head," the name of a sea-girt promontory near Beverly Farms.

> Here was the eagles' nest! The flashing sea,
>   Sunny and blue, fades in the distant gray,
> Or flickers green on reefs, or throws white spray
>   On granite cliffs, as a heart restlessly
> Beats against fate, and sobs unceasingly,
>   Most beautiful flinging itself away,
> Clasping the rock by which it must not stay,
>   Sublimest in revolt at destiny
> Here where of old the eagles soared and screamed
>   Answering the ocean's restless, longing roar,
> While in their nest the hungry eaglets dreamed
>   — Here let us lie and watch the wave-vexed shore,
> Repeating, heart to heart, the eagles' strain,
> The ocean's cry of passion and of pain.

"The octave," he deprecated, "is faulty in too much similarity of rhyme, but I think I like it notwithstanding its defects." [46]

In San Francisco he felt a moment of panic as his mind
winged back to Elizabeth Cameron and her little daughter on
the seashore at his beloved Beverly Farms. "A sudden spasm
came over me," he said, "just at the foot of the hotel stairs,
that I must see Martha." He tried to skirt that perilous shoal;
"I got over it with the help of a bottle of champagne and a

marvellous dinner at the Club." Yet he could not dissemble. Not willing to trust his own pen, he urged her to look at Clough's poem, the one "beginning 'Come back. Come back,'" for, as she might see, he like the poet could only ask

> . . . and whither and for what?
> To finger idly some old Gordian knot,
> Unskilled to sunder, and too weak to cleave.

"Poor Clough was another wanderer who could not make his world run on four wheels" he sighed. The golden era that had opened with such promise in Washington nearly thirteen years before was closing with strangely unforeseen anguish. Too late now for regrets. He almost visibly straightened up: "Here goes, then, for Polynesia." [47]

Appendix
Notes
Bibliography

The Writings of Henry Adams

1878–1891

This list is a continuation of that which appears in *The Young Henry Adams*. Like that list it is based on "A Bibliography of the Writings of Henry Adams," prepared by William A. Jackson for James Truslow Adams, *Henry Adams* (New York, 1933), pp. 213–229. The few items that can authoritatively be added to that list are marked by a star. Recourse has also been had to Jacob Blanck, *Bibliography of American Literature* (New Haven, 1955), vol. I, for details of publication.

1879

*Review of Clarence King's *Systematic Geology*, in *Nation*, 28: 73–74 (January 23, 1879). See Haskell, *The Nation: Index of Titles*, vol. II.

The Life of Albert Gallatin. Philadelphia: Lippincott & Company, 1879. Deposited for copyright, June 19, 1879. London edition, same publisher, first advertisement, August 2, 1879.

The Writings of Albert Gallatin. Edited by Henry Adams. 3 vols. Philadelphia: Lippincott & Company. Listed in *Publishers' Weekly*, June 28, 1879. London edition, same publisher, advertised July 2, 1879.

1880

Democracy An American Novel. (Anonymous.) New York: Henry Holt & Company, 1880. Leisure Hour Series, No. 112. Deposited for copyright, March 26, 1880. London edition, Macmillan, first advertised, May 27, 1882. French translation, *Démocratie, roman Américain*. Paris: Plon & Co., 1883, in print by November 28, 1882.

*"Albert Gallatin," in *Memorial Biographies of the New England*

Historic Genealogical Society. Vol. I. Boston, published for the Society, 1880. Pages 203–212.

1882

John Randolph. Boston: Houghton Mifflin Company, 1882. American Statesmen Series. Advertised in *Publishers' Weekly,* October 14, 1882. Very slightly revised edition published in 1883, used in subsequent reprintings.

Manuscript of biography of Aaron Burr prepared for publication. Publication abandoned. Final disposition of the manuscript unknown.

1884

"Napoléon Ier et Saint-Domingue," *La Revue Historique,* Paris, April, 1884, vol. XXIV, pp. 92–130. (In French.) English version, much revised, published in *Historical Essays,* 1891.

Esther A Novel. Pseudonym, Frances Snow Compton. American Novel Series. No. 3. New York: Henry Holt & Company, 1884. Deposited for copyright, March 22, 1884. Listed in *Publishers' Weekly,* May 10, 1884. English edition, London: Richard Bentley & Son, 1885. Advertised July 4, 1884.

*History of the United States of America During the First Administration of Thomas Jefferson. Cambridge: John Wilson & Son, 1884. Privately printed. Six copies. (See Ford I, pp. 356, 357 and Cater, p. 134. Printing was completed before February 3, 1884. No copies of this private edition appear to be extant. The volume contained 584 pages. Referred to in Dwight to Scribner, July 12, 1888. Scribner Files.)

1885

History of the United States of America During the Second Administration of Thomas Jefferson. Cambridge: John Wilson & Son, 1885. Privately printed. Six copies. The printing was evidently completed before December 21, 1884. See Cater, p. 133. Cited in Notes, below, as "Draft Volume II."

1888

History of the United States of America During the First Administration of James Madison. 1809–1813. Cambridge: John

Wilson & Son, 1888. Privately printed. Six copies. The volume was probably printed in August, 1888. See Cater, p. 180. Cited in Notes, below, as "Draft Volume III."

1889

History of the United States of America During the First Administration of Thomas Jefferson. 2 vols. New York: Charles Scribner's Sons, 1889. First trade edition. Corrected and revised version of the privately printed volume. Deposited for copyright, October 23, 1889.

1890

History of the United States of America During the Second Administration of Thomas Jefferson. 2 vols. New York: Charles Scribner's Sons, 1890. Deposited for copyright, February 11, 1890. Corrected and revised version of the privately printed volume. A "Ladies Edition" of twelve sets on thin paper of the four Jefferson volumes was also printed for Adams's private use. Scribner Files. Cf. also Blanck, *Bibliography*.

History of the United States of America During the First Administration of James Madison. 2 vols. New York: Charles Scribner's Sons, 1890. Deposited for copyright September 27, 1890. Corrected and revised version of the privately printed volume.

1891

History of the United States of America During the Second Administration of James Madison. 3 vols. New York: Charles Scribner's Sons, 1891. Printed directly from the manuscript, there being no privately printed edition of this portion of the work. Deposited for copyright, January 12, 1891. Minor revisions of portions of the history were subsequently made in the reprinting of the volumes but without change of the copyright notice.

Historical Essays. New York: Charles Scribner's Sons, 1891. Deposited for copyright September 15, 1891. London edition listed December 19, 1891. Contains nine essays, two of which had not previously been published: "Primitive Rights of Women" (revision of Lowell Institute lecture of December 9, 1876), "The Declaration of Paris." Four had been previously reprinted in *Chapters of Erie* and were again corrected and revised for this publication; "Captain John Smith," "The Bank of England Restriction," "The Legal-Tender Act," "The New York Gold Conspiracy." Three of the essays were here reprinted for the first time: "Harvard College, 1786–1787," "The Session, 1869–70," "Napoleon at St. Domingo" see *supra*, 1884).

History of the United States of America. 9 vols. London: G. P. Putnam's Sons, 1891–1892.

Notes

To keep these notes within reasonable compass, the following expedients have been employed. Ordinarily only the surname of the author and the short title of the work referred to is cited, the full description being given in the Bibliography. The documentation for an entire paragraph is generally grouped into a single note, arranged in the order of quotation or reference.

The titles of the chief published collections of Adams letters have been abbreviated as follows: *Letters of Henry Adams* (1858–1891), (1892–1918), both collections edited by Worthington Chauncey Ford, as Ford I and Ford II; *Henry Adams and His Friends*, edited by Harold Dean Cater, as Cater; *Letters of Mrs. Henry Adams*, edited by Ward Thoron, as Thoron.

Unless otherwise indicated, Adams Papers refers to the large collection of family papers at the Massachusetts Historical Society (hereafter cited as MHS). The several groups of unpublished letters of Marian Adams (Mrs. Henry Adams) to her father, Dr. Robert W. Hooper, and to other correspondents are cited as MA to RWH or MA to the particular correspondent. Similar abbreviations are used for frequently cited members of the Adams family; thus, HA for Henry Adams, BA for Brooks Adams; CFA Jr. for Charles Francis Adams, Jr.

Chapter One. The Return of the Native

1. For summary treatments of this confused epoch in American history see Cochran and Miller, *Age of Enterprise*, p. 164 ff.; Morison and Commager, *Growth of the American Republic*, II, 214 ff. ("no drearier chapter in American political history"); Barnard, *Hayes;* Rhodes, *Historical Essays*, p. 245 ff. *Congressional Record*, March 2, 1877; Rhodes, *History*, VII, *passim*. By 1881, with the inauguration of Garfield, Adams conceded, "Grantism, which drove us to rebellion, is dead" (Ford I, p. 329). See also Woodward, *Meet General Grant*. For the chorus of criticism see Rhodes, *History*, VII, 191–193. For the arrival of Adams, see Cater, p. 85.

2. Gurney to Godkin, August 27, 1870, Godkin Papers; Ford I, p. 268. Dislike of New England winters was a family tradition and so was rheumatism. As an old man, Charles Francis Adams, Jr. wrote to Henry, "I hate the winters here. Their inclemency and harshness so far as out-of-doors life is concerned weighs upon me more heavily every season. I am always thinking of poor old John Adams and his wish that he was a dormouse so that he could go to sleep in the autumn and not wake up till spring" (January 15, 1908, Adams Papers). For the magnolias, see Federal Writers' Project, *Washington*, "Lafayette Square," p. 650 ff.

3. Charles Francis Adams, Diary, October 17, 1877, Adams Papers. Henry Adams to his mother, February 18, 1860, Adams Papers: "People can be lead by their stomachs as well as by their understandings, and the opening is now a magnificent one. I don't see why you can't make your drawing-rooms as necessary and as famous as you please and hatch all the Presidents for the next twenty years there. . . . It's all infernal nonsense you and papa sacrificing yourselves for the good of your country; I tell you, you're doing nothing of the sort, at least if I can help it; you must take just as many honors as you can get and what's more, you must work to get them and be glad that the paths of duty and of ambition combine for you; for most people they lie in contrary directions."

4. "The Club," John T. Morse, *Thomas Sergeant Perry* (Boston, 1929), p. 63.

5. Ogden, *Godkin*, II, 61; Cater, p. 80; Ford I, p. 300.

6. The "new departure" in history was an outgrowth of President Gilman's conference with Adams (*U. S. Circulars of Information*, Bureau of Education, 1887, p. 173). HA to Robert Cunliffe, August 31, 1875, Adams Papers. Scudder, *Lowell*, II, p. 218. For Adams's dealings with Gilman see W. S. Holt, "Henry Adams and Johns Hopkins University," *New England Quarterly*, XI (1938), 633.

7. Charles Francis Adams, Diary, November 7, 1877, Adams Papers: "Both of my sons failed of an election, Brooks losing it by two votes. I regret the failure in the case of John far the most, but all elections are such a lottery that it is folly to put confidence in any result. I am rejoiced that I am out of the scrape."

8. Winsor, *Memorial History of Boston*, III, 546.

9. *Nation*, November 8, 1877, p. 277; Parkman to Pierre Margry, December 15, 1875, quoted by Kraus, *A History*, p. 289. On the "race-pride or race-prejudice" of Bostonians against the

"foreign infusion," see Henry Cabot Lodge, Boston (London, 1892), p. 204.

10. Federal Writers' Project, *Washington, passim*. Of Rock Creek, a favorite haunt of the Adamses, Lord Bryce remarked, "There is nothing comparable in any capital city of Europe" *ibid.*, p. 581). On his return from his tour Grant said, "It is the finest national capital in the world" (Chapin, *American Court Gossip*, p. 8).

11. Ford I, p. 302; *Nation*, December 6, 1877, p. 350. For an indication of Adams's delight in the Maryland spring and his interest in nature study see Cater, p. 147, and *Education*, pp. 8, 44, 268, and 402. For a memorable echo of "the dogwood and the judas-tree" of the *Education* (p. 268) see T. S. Eliot's "Gerontion," discussed in Grover Smith, *T. S. Eliot's Poetry and Plays* (Chicago, 1956), p. 62.

12. Federal Writers' Project, *Washington*, p. 650.

13. MA to RWH, November 18, 1877, Adams Papers. The incautious remark circulated swiftly and raised a few eyebrows, returning to Washington "as a long sharp *pin*," as Mrs. Adams wrote; "and one would suppose Henry was a fool from the new interpretation put on it. If we are fools, we are and too old to reform" (MA to RWH, January 6, 1878, Adams Papers).

14. Federal Writers' Project, *Washington*, p. 651; *Education*, p. 253. The Washington guide reports that when the architect Charles F. McKim was asked his opinion, he "called for an ax."

15. At the local level the revolution in political morality had made small progress. Boss Tweed's self-righteous lectures on the art of buying legislatures horrified the *Nation* but not his constituents who, on his death in 1878, regarded him as the victim of "rich men's malice" (*Nation*, October 4, 1877, p. 237; April 18, 1878, p. 257).

16. Dodge, *Gail Hamilton's Life in Letters*, May 27, 1880. Lodge and Brooks Adams once dined with her, "athirst for political talk." Impressed by their "almost amusing enthusiasm," she wrote, "It is a great deal for an Adams to be enthusiastic about anything" (*ibid.*, 758; cf. also pages 265, 271, 759). Marian Adams encountered her and Blaine at a reception at General Beale's home, the old Decatur House. She passed judgment in these words: "Gail looks like a caricature of a scarecrow, both eyes squinting madly, mouth like a dying sculpin, hair like Medusa" (MA to RWH, January 28, 1878). With some excuse, Blaine was to suspect Mrs. Adams of having written *Democracy* (Ford I, p. 345). The monkey image became more and more for Adams a symbol of universal simianity, a satire on Darwin's

Descent of Man, and he collected monkey emblems with great relish. Cf. Thoron, pp. 380 and 430.

17. Ford I, pp. 305, 306, 307.

18. February 17, 1878, Munroe, *Walker,* p. 188; Rhodes, *History,* VII, 94 ff.

19. *Nation,* May 2, 1878; Brooks Adams, "Supreme Court and the Currency Question," *International Review,* 6:635–649 (June 1879).

20. While Henry kept silent, his brother Charles, as a railway expert, proposed the adoption of the French welfare scheme with its stake-in-the-job theory ("The Prevention of Railroad Strikes," *Nation,* August 30, 1877). In the privacy of his diary, President Hayes voiced his humane misgivings: "The strikes have been put down by *force;* but now for the *real* remedy. Can't something [be] done by education of the strikers, by judicious control of the capitalists?" Barnard, *Hayes,* p. 446.

21. *Nation,* June 27, 1878, August 8, 1877. May, *Protestant Churches,* p. 96 and *passim.*

22. Munroe, *Walker,* p. 188; Ford I, pp. 305, 309; *Nation,* October 11, 1877.

23. From J. S. Mill, *Three Essays on Religion* (1874). Henry Holt's estimate of the "positivist" John Fiske might equally well apply to Adams: "Fiske was never absorbingly interested in the specific problem of the elevation of the less fortunate portion of mankind, but the wider philosophic and historic problems to which he was devoted include these specific ones" (*Garrulities,* p. 331). Cf. John Hay's avowal as a young man, "I am not suited for a reformer. I do not like to meddle with moral ills. I love comfortable people" (Hay, *A Poet in Exile,* January 2, 1859).

24. From portion of letter to Gaskell, November 25, 1877 (Adams Papers) omitted in Ford I, p. 302. His concern about their childlessness evidently led him to acquire a copy of J. Marion Sims, M.D., *Clinical Notes on Uterine Surgery with special reference to the management of sterile conditions* (New York, 1873).

25. Information supplied by Mrs. Frank Harris, one-time secretary of Brooks Adams; Charles Francis Adams, Diary, March 2, 1872, January 19, 1878, Adams Papers.

26. See Hooper and Sturgis genealogies in Thoron, p. 463 ff.

27. MA to RWH, January 13, 1878; March 24, 1878; November 25, 1877; December 9, 1877, Adams Papers.

28. The practice of five o'clock tea was a recent importation; see John H. Young, A.M., *Our Deportment or the Manners, Conduct and Dress of the Most Refined Society,* Chicago, 1881, p. 129.

MA to RWH, November 18, November 25, December 2, 1877, Adams Papers.

29. Thoron, p. 170; MA to RWH, December 25, 1877, January 27, 1878, Adams Papers.

30. Quoted in Chanler, *Roman Spring*, p. 303.

31. The Washington *Star* editorialized, December 16, 1876, that something needed to be done about the calling card burden on public officials. MA to RWH, December 30, 1877, January 13, 1878, Adams Papers. Cater, p. 88. MA to RWH, December 2, 1877, February 10, 1878, December 30, 1877, January 13, 1878, Adams Papers.

32. MA to RWH, January 13, 1878, April 7, 1878, January 6, 1878, Adams Papers.

33. MA to RWH, November 18, 1877; March 9, 1878, Adams Papers. *Portable Mark Twain*, p. 761.

34. MA to RWH, March 3, 1878, January 6, 1878, Adams Papers. For a fine self-portrait of General Taylor see his *Destruction and Reconstruction: Personal Experiences of the Late War* (1879; reprinted, 1956).

35. MA to RWH, January 6, 1878; Thoron, pp. 30, 443.

36. Thoron, p. 399; MA to RWH, March 24, 1878, November 25, 1877, Adams Papers.

37. MA to RWH, December 23, 1877; February 10, 1878; January 27, 1878; February 3, 1878, Adams Papers. A new litter of puppies had not yet been distributed to friends.

38. The figure (the equivalent of sixty to seventy-five thousand dollars after taxes today) is suggested by the income which Adams was soon to attribute to the heroine of *Democracy*, by the estimate given in Cater, p. xcii, and the fragmentary data reported by executors in various probate court proceedings.

39. Thoron, p. 430, for dodging of columnists. Adams reportedly did give one interview at this period (Cater, p. xlix). MA to RWH, March 3, 1878, Adams Papers. Anderson, *Letters*, p. 195; Thayer, *Hay*, II, 20. MA to RWH, January 27, 1878, Adams Papers. This was apparently their first acquaintance with Clara Stone Hay whom Hay had married in 1874 (Dennett, *Hay*, p. 97). Clara Louise Hay (December 28, 1848–April 25, 1914), married John Hay, February 4, 1874 (J. Gardner Bartlett, *Simon Stone Genealogy*, Boston, 1926).

40. MA to RWH, January 6, 1878, Adams Papers; Howells, in *Clarence King Memoirs*, p. 136; MA to RWH, February 17, 1878, Adams Papers.

41. MA to RWH, February 17, February 24, March 3, 1878;

January 13, March 3, 1878, December 30, 1877, Adams Papers.

42. MA to RWH, February 2, 1879, Adams Papers. Henry Adams's version is in Cater, p. 89.

43. MA to Charles Gaskell, March 29, 1875, Adams Papers.

44. MA to RWH, March 24, April 28, 1878, March 30, 1879, April 28, 1884, Adams Papers.

45. The president of the Biological Society of Washington, G. Browne Goode, in a lengthy address on "The Beginnings of American Science," delivered in 1887, boasted that in Washington there was "one scientific man to every 500 inhabitants," whereas the proportion in Cambridge was "one to 850," and in New Haven "one to 1,100" (*Proceedings*, Biological Society of Washington, IV, 1886–1888, p. 90). Introduction to King, *Systematic Geology; Clarence King Memoirs*, p. 255 ff.

46. Geike, *Founders of Geology*, p. 178; King, *Systematic Geology*, Introduction. Ford I, p. 215.

47. King's achievement as a scientist has been variously estimated. The biographers of his associate, Powell, think him overrated as a geologist and incline to minimize his role in the consolidation of the Surveys. See Darrah, *Powell*, p. 251 and *passim*, and Stegner, *Beyond the Hundredth Meridian*. His career is exhaustively reviewed in Wilkins, *King* (1958). A chapter from Harry Crosby's doctoral dissertation, *So Deep a Trail*, a biography of Clarence King, has appeared in *American Heritage*, February 2, 1956, p. 58 ff., but it deals only with his famous exposure of the notorious "Diamond Swindle" of 1872. The Century Association symposium, *Clarence King Memoirs*, by eleven of King's friends, including pieces by Adams, Hay, Howells, La Farge, Stedman, Gilman, Brownell, Cary, Emmons, Raymond, and Hague, remains the indispensable source of information about the enigmatic King. King's prowess as a raconteur of Western yarns is exhibited in Bronson, *Reminiscences of a Ranchman*. Excellent accounts of the early fortunes of the Survey and the scientific renaissance in Washington appear in Darrah, *Powell*, and Stegner, *Beyond the Hundredth Meridian*. The famous Reports consisted of the following volumes: I. *Systematic Geology* (1878); II. *Descriptive Geology* (1877); III. *Mining Industry* by James D. Hague, with geological contributions by King (1870); IV. Pt. 1. and 2. *Paleontology*, Pt. 3, *Ornithology* (1877); V. *Botany* (1871); VI. *Microscopical Petrography* (1876); VII. *Odontornithes, Extinct Toothed Birds of North America* (1880).

48. Minutes of the Cosmos Club in the Club archives in Washington, used through the courtesy of Mr. Frank B. Sheets. Spauld-

ing, *The Cosmos Club on Lafayette Square; Documentary History of the Cosmos Club.*

49. Darrah, *Powell*, p. 251; Crosby, *So Deep a Trail*, p. 239; MA to RWH, April 6, 1879.

50. Adams became a member of the Washington Philosophical Society in 1881, a forum for discussions of every branch of science but especially of mathematical and physical sciences, and of the Anthropological Society, presumably about the same time. In 1894 he was one of the founders of the Columbian Society, established to study Washington history. His social club in Washington was the Metropolitan, which he helped found in 1882. His New York clubs were the Century and the Knickerbocker, the former from 1892 and the latter from 1886 or earlier (Cater, p. 162, but cf. Cater, p. lxviii). See *Bulletin,* Philosophical Society of Washington, XI, 1888–1891, p. xviii.

51. For King's place in geology see Merrill, *The First Hundred Years of American Geology.* Adams's review of his lecture appeared in the *Nation,* August 30, 1877, p. 137; its authorship and that of the succeeding review is identified in Haskell, *Nation.* King attacked uniformitarianism from one side and Alexander Agassiz, another of Adams's intimates, attacked it from another, with respect to the "coral reef theory" of Darwin and Dana. Both heresies greatly affected Adams's own "Darwinism"; see for example Ford I, pp. 448, 470, 499. The debate over Darwinism divided Washington scientific opinion into a number of militant camps. The great prominence of the issue was reflected in part in the *Proceedings* of the Washington Biological Society; see, for example, the Darwin memorial addresses, May 12, 1882, William H. Dall's "On Dynamic Influences in Evolution," March 8, 1890, and Lester Ward's presidential address dealing with the great controversy over the inheritance of acquired characteristics, "Neo-Darwinism and Neo-Lamarckism," January 24, 1891. Ward rejected the Neo-Darwinian heresies of Weismann and argued for the "law of the transmissibility of acquired qualities." Cf. also George E. Pond in *Galaxy,* 15:695 (May 1873): "Not only does all physical research take color from the new theory [Darwinism], but the doctrine sends its pervasive lines through poetry, novels, history."

52. *Nation,* January 23, 1879, pp. 73, 74. Stegner, *Beyond the Hundredth Meridian,* p. 153. Adams's friend, Samuel F. Emmons, alluded to the anonymous reviewer as the "most competent critic" of the work and quoted a portion of the review in one of his memoirs of King (National Academy of Sciences, *Biographical Memoirs,* vol. VI, 1909, pp. 27–55). Emmons also made the char-

acterization in his article in the *American Journal of Science,*
March 1902, which was partially reprinted in the *Clarence King
Memoirs.*

53. The article in the *Star* (December 22, 1877) had its counterpart in the learned discussions of the Washington Philosophical
Society; cf. for example a paper on the evil effects of high-heeled
shoes, *Proceedings,* 1880. Adams's reservations about woman's
suffrage may be deduced from his lecture "The Primitive Rights
of Women," discussed in *The Young Henry Adams,* p. 260 ff. The
Adams family attitude was probably reflected by Henry's eldest
brother, John Quincy, who wrote that woman's suffrage contra-
vened the "division of activities and functions which . . . lie at
the foundations of society" (Letter to the New York *Times,* October 28, 1871). Tolstoy, *War and Peace* (Modern Library edition), p. 1283; De Tocqueville, *Democracy in America* (London,
1889), II, 194.

Chapter Two. *The Admirable Alien*

1. Albert Gallatin to Henry Adams, May 27, 1879, pasted into
Adams's copy of *Gallatin,* MHS. For his high opinion of Gallatin
see his letter to Lodge, October 6, 1879 (Ford I, p. 314), and
to Tilden, January 24, 1883 (Cater, p. 125), cited in Jordy, *Henry
Adams,* pp. 47, 48. [The reference to an L. Lawrence Gallatin
in *The Young Henry Adams,* p. 293, as Gallatin's son and executor, is incorrect, having been suggested by a misreading of
Adams's index to his manuscript Date Book.] Adams's out-of-
pocket expenses for copying, stationery, and supplies, conscientiously billed in full detail to "Albert R. Gallatin, Dr.," amounted
to $237.80. The total cost of publication of the small edition of
the four volumes was $5,115.85. Gallatin Papers, New York His-
torical Society.

2. Adams thought well enough of the article to reprint it in
Chapters of Erie; cf. *Young Henry Adams,* p. 192 ff. and 318.
James Gallatin retired from the presidency of the Gallatin National Bank in 1868 and moved to France where he died in 1876;
see obituary, New York *Herald,* May 30, 1876. Albert Rolaz Gallatin died in New York, February 25, 1890, at the age of ninety.
Gallatin's Treasury Report on the eve of the War of 1812 had
said of open market borrowing in event of war, "In that case the
most simple and direct is also the cheapest and safest mode"
(Adams, *Gallatin,* p. 447). Cf. Adams's remark in "The Legal
Tender Act": "The simplest bargain is the best for the public"

North American Review, 110:312. On JQA's relations with Gallatin, see Adams, *Gallatin*, pp. 522, 527, 576, 599, especially p. 676, and Walters, *Gallatin*, p. 281. On resumption, Adams, *Gallatin*, p. 662; Walters, *Gallatin*, p. 365.

3. From Beverly Farms he reported on October 14, 1877: "By the time I go from here, I hope to have all the important papers in my possession ready for the press. This leaves only the State Department, and the letters to Dallas, Crawford, Joseph H. Nicholson, Lafayette, and some few others, to be sought for." HA to A. R. Gallatin, unpublished letter in the Albert Gallatin Collection, New York Historical Society. Frequent allusions to Adams's researches crop up from time to time in his letters. Cf. Cater, pp. 81, 82, 87. Ford I, pp. 303, 305. MA to RWH, December 16, 1877; cf. Adams, *Gallatin*, pp. 6–8.

4. Henry Adams to A. R. Gallatin, December 24, 1877, Gallatin Papers, New York Historical Society. Adams also justified his "off-hand" treatment of Gallatin's ancestors: "I understand this to be your wish."

5. Cf. Eugène L. Didier, ed. *Life and Letters of Madame Bonaparte* (New York, 1879) and Mrs. Adams's caustic comments on the book, Thoron, p. 163. Madame Bonaparte's grandson, Jerome Napoleon Bonaparte-Patterson, joined the Adams circle in 1880; see many entries in index of Thoron, p. 566. For Adams's impression of the old lady, MA to RWH, January 27, 1878, Adams Papers.

6. On the visit to Mount Vernon, MA to RWH, April 7, 1878, Adams Papers. HA to Bancroft, Cater, p. 87.

7. His unnoted obligations to Lewis Henry Morgan are suggested in Cater, p. 87. HA to Bancroft, April 19, 1879, MHS: "I send you another batch of proof. Whenever you are done with the last batch (which I stuck in the Fisher Ames), the printers will be glad to have it."

8. Cater, p. 89. Cf. Adams, *Gallatin*, p. 377. HA to Mrs. Samuel Parkman, Parkman Papers, Houghton Library.

9. Adams, *Gallatin*, p. 154. See p. 496 for the "curious parallelism in the lives and characters" of Gallatin and John Quincy Adams. Adams challenged a slurring reference by the Federalist historian Richard Hildreth, *ibid.*, p. 456.

10. *Ibid.*, p. 137; Bryant, "The Embargo." Defenses of Jefferson in Malone, *Jefferson, the Virginian*, xi, xvii, 358, 367, and Padover, *Jefferson*, 186 and note. Ford I, p. 286, Ford II, p. 319. Adams, *Gallatin*, p. 343.

11. Adams, *Gallatin*, pp. 279, 372, 353, 349, 350.

12. *Ibid.*, pp. 378, 379, 380.

13. *Ibid.*, pp. 379, 559, 560.

14. *Ibid.*, p. 639.

15. *Ibid.*, pp. 639, 432. One of the leaders whom Adams most despised, Roscoe Conkling, was soon to be the chief instrument in persuading the Supreme Court to give corporations the status of persons within the meaning of the due process clause. Cf. Hacker, *Triumph of American Capitalism*, pp. 387 ff.

16. Adams, *Gallatin*, p. 267. At a recent convention of the Social Science Association, Perry Belmont, a former student of Adams and son of August Belmont, the Rothschild agent in New York, argued for adoption of the British practice. For his friendship with Adams, see index to Thoron, and Perry Belmont, *An American Democrat* (New York, 1940), pp. 132, 133.

17. Adams, *Gallatin*, pp. 354, 355.

18. *Ibid.*, pp. 355, 391.

19. Cater, p. 125. Adams also prepared at this period a brief and carefully judicial summary of Gallatin's career for inclusion in the first volume of *Memorial Biographies of the New England Historic Genealogical Society* (Boston, 1880), pp. 203–212. From it he scrupulously excluded all unfavorable comment on Gallatin's associates and suppressed all his historical generalizations, limiting himself to a formal eulogy of Gallatin's character. "As a practical statesman he had no equal in his day, and his scattered writings show him to have had no superior as a man of science and study." The same volume contained a similar memorial of John Quincy Adams written by Henry Adams's father.

20. Adams, *Gallatin*, p. 81. Jefferson to William Stephen Smith, November 13, 1787 (*Papers of Thomas Jefferson*, XII, 356).

21. Adams, *Gallatin*, p. 269; Parrington, *Main Currents*, III, 217; Adams, *Gallatin*, pp. 269, 270, 175. Cf. HA to CFA Jr., February 20, 1863, Ford I, p. 95: "Peace and small armaments will be our salvation as a united and solvent nation."

22. Adams, *Gallatin*, p. 159. Adams's thesis translated into economic terms received its fullest development in Parrington's great work, but his resolution of the American historical process into the struggle between the two great factions has been severely criticized for its oversimplifications. See, for example, Jones, *Theory of American Literature*, p. 141 ff.

23. Adams, *Gallatin*, pp. 68, 302. For an indication of the substantial amount of manuscript materials unused by Adams, see "Notes" of Walters, *Gallatin*, p. 381 ff. On the vogue of "Life and Letters," see Nicolson, *Development of English Biography*, pp. 77, 79.

24. Lodge's further *caveat* that he had "not deemed it neces-

sary, in a work of this nature, to give elaborate authorities" would seem to reflect Adams's instruction — and practice. Adams regarded political biographies like Lodge's and his as part of the history of Federalism and anti-Federalism. Cf., for example, Adams's review of Lodge, *Nation*, 25:12 (July 5, 1877). In his prefatory acknowledgments Lodge expressed his thanks to Adams for "many suggestions and for much valuable aid."

25. Adams, *Gallatin*, p. 635.

26. In review of Stubbs, *North American Review*, 119: 233 ff. (July 1874). On Adams's concern with style see Samuels, *The Young Henry Adams*, p. 232 ff., and its index for references to Gibbon and Macaulay. HA to Lodge, Ford I, p. 318. Adams, *Gallatin*, pp. 415, 492. For an especially elaborate period, see the same book, p. 443.

27. A. K. Fiske in a running review on recent history and biography, *North American Review*, 129:410–411 (October 1879). Part III of the mysterious "Diary of a Public Man" appeared in the same issue. The misguided effort to attribute its authorship to Adams ignores this evidence of Rice's hostility or indifference to Adams's achievement. For further discussion of the question see Chapter III, p. 126 and note 59.

28. *Saturday Review*, 47:123 (July 26, 1879). London *Athenaeum*, September 6, 1879, p. 295. Ford I, pp. 312, 313. Lodge in *International Review*, 7:250–266 (1879). HA to Lodge, Ford I, 314.

29. *Ibid.*

30. *Nation*, August 21 and 28, 1879, pp. 128, 144. Haskell, *Nation*, incorrectly attributes the article to A. R. Macdonough.

31. MA to E. L. Godkin, December 25, 1879, Godkin Papers, Houghton Library. Cater, pp. 101–105. Cf. Evelyn Page, "The Man around the Corner," *New England Quarterly*, 23:401–403 (September 1950).

32. HA to CFA Jr., April 29, 1869, Adams Papers. CFA Jr. to E. L. Godkin, October 30, 1880, Godkin Papers, Houghton Library.

33. Gwynn, *Spring Rice*, I, 68.

34. *Atlantic*, October 1879, pp. 513–521. Thoron, p. 186. Boston *Literary World*, August 30, 1879, and July 5, 1879. *Magazine of American History*, 3:697–703 (November 1879). According to Mrs. Adams, the Boston *Daily Advertiser* naturally was not attracted by "the anti-Federalist tendencies" of the biography (Thoron, p. 165). A full column notice appreciatively reviewed the Life in the New York *Times*, July 26, 1879 (p. 6): ". . . the best piece of work we have in its line." The New York *Tribune*,

July 4, 1879 (p. 3), acknowledged the scholarship and good sense but objected that the book showed "no extraordinary skill or practice in the arts of literary composition."

35. Fäy, *Proceedings*, American Antiquarian Society, New Series, XL (1930), 280. Morison and Commager, *Growth of the American Republic*, I, 770. Other representative estimates are to be found in Edward H. O'Neill, *A History of American Biography, 1800–1935* (Philadelphia, 1935), p. 63: "We are more than thankful to come upon this finished biographical work in the midst of a host of unorganized, undigested, uninteresting books miscalled biographies," and in Dana K. Merrill, *American Biography: Its Theory and Practice* (Portland, 1957), pp. 68, 175: "A great political biography of the last century . . . has never been superseded. . . . It has earned the status of being definitive." Kraus, *A History of American History* (New York, 1937), p. 323: ". . . not yet superseded." *American Historical Review*, 49:543 (1944) on the occasion of the A. L. A. reprint: "It is still standard, if not definitive, and indispensable to the special student of the man, the period, or public finance." On the perfections of Gallatin's character cf. Walters, *Gallatin*, p. vii.

Chapter Three. The Great American Mystery

1. HA to Cunliffe, August 7, 1878, Adams Papers; HA to C. M. Gaskell, November 28, 1878, Ford I, p. 309. The novel was published by Henry Holt in The Leisure Hour Series, April 1, 1880; see *Publisher's Weekly* for that date. A curious typographical error persists through the reprintings of the 1908 edition; the chapter numbering omits XII, going from XI to XIII without any sign of omitted text. The error is unnoticed in Blanck, *Bibliography of American Literature*.

2. Holt, "Foreword," *Democracy* (New York, 1925). The date of Hay's oath of office was November 1, 1879, but that document was evidently dated back a week or two. The Hays took a house at 1400 Massachusetts Avenue, within short walking distance of Lafayette Square (Dennett, *Hay*, p. 129). Thayer, *Hay*, II, 59, 75. Holt, *Literary Review*, December 24, 1920, and *Unpartizan Review*, January-March 1921. Theodore Stanton, ed., *Manual of American Literature* (New York, 1909), p. 212. Hay is also there correctly identified as the author of *Breadwinners*. Holt turned over to Stanton, Adams's jocose evasion (HA to Holt, December 13, 1906, Adams Papers). Stanton, then in Paris, wrote directly to Adams explaining that "Mrs. Hay authorized me to announce

her husband as the author of 'The Breadwinners' " and he pleaded for help to "make my catalogue perfect." Adams evidently gave in without further ado. Stanton to HA, January 17, 1907, Adams Papers.

3. Holt, "Foreword," *Democracy.*

4. Adams, *Democracy,* pp. 10, 75. Adams echoes *Hamlet,* III, iii, line 382. Ford I, pp. 12, 164.

5. HA to C. M. Gaskell, January 13, 1870, Ford I, pp. 177, 178. On Feuillet, see Ford I, p. 101. Adams's set of Feuillet is at MHS; for his interest in George Eliot as a novelist see Ford I, pp. 273, 354, 323.

6. Disraeli, *Sybil* (New York, n.d.), p. 38; *Coningsby* (London, 1870), p. 236; *Tancred* (New York, n.d.), p. 128. Cf. Adams, *Democracy,* p. 10.

7. *Ibid.,* p. 177, for Madeleine's conclusion.

8. Mrs. Ward in the *Fortnightly,* July 1882. On Gladstone's opinion, Crosby, *So Deep a Trail,* p. 314.

9. For Adams's highly individual arrangements for the republication of the novel, see Cater, pp. 122–125. To insure having his own way he offered to guarantee the cost. For the publication data see [William Jackson], "A Bibliography," in James T. Adams, *Henry Adams,* pp. 213–229; Cater, p. 104, and Hume, *Runaway Star,* p. 246. For the 1952 reprint, see comment in *Saturday Review,* October 25, 1952, p. 37. On the offer to make a play of it, Ford II, p. 342. Holt approached him in 1907 proposing to syndicate the novel for newspaper publication, again with complete lack of success, though Adams's reply was so playfully cryptic (see Cater, p. 594) that Holt at first thought Adams had approved. Holt to HA, April 15 and 17, 1907, Adams Papers: "Wise men are very apt to speak in parables. From the edifying and entertaining ones in yours of the 15th, I infer that you have no objection to having the matter syndicated, and unless I hear to the contrary this week, I shall proceed on that assumption. . . . P.S. I know such considerations are far beneath you, but it can do no harm to mention that there would be shekels proceeding from the before-suggested syndication." Adams was willing to be pirated but refused to surrender his anonymity (HA to BA, July 11, 1905, Ford II, p. 452 n.). *Publishers' Weekly,* April 24, 1880, reported that *Democracy* was "having a good sale, and promises to be one of the 'hits' of the spring." According to Holt the novel had sold 14,000 copies up to the time of Adams's death. Thayer, *Letters,* p. 355. David Garnett in the *New Statesman and Nation,* November 11, 1933, p. 584, reported the English sale at 14,000 copies, an extraordinary coincidence with Holt's figure, if correct.

10. Adams, *Democracy*, p. 224. The Lucretian passion for first principles with which he endowed his heroine Adams owed in part to Grandfather John Quincy Adams. Cf. J. Q. Adams's oration at the dedication of the Cincinnati observatory, quoting Lucretius, "Happy the man who has been able to ascertain the causes of things," cited in Rukeyser, *Gibbs*, p. 77. On Henry Adams's intellectual likeness to his grandfather see Brooks Adams, "The Heritage of Henry Adams," in Henry Adams, *Degradation of the Democratic Dogma*, pp. 66, 102, 103.

11. Adams, *Democracy*, pp. 2, 83, 3, 4, 178, 6, 7. On current vogue of pessimism see also James, *The Siege of London*, "The Point of View," p. 239: "It will not help a young person to be sought in marriage that she can give an account of the last German theory of Pessimism." For echoes of ideas in Schopenhauer, cf. *Philosophy of Schopenhauer* (Modern Library), pp. 269, 312.

12. *Democracy*, p. 12. The following analysis of the novel is based on the able and well-documented Master's essay (unpublished) of Agnes Mary Hyde (Mrs. E. T. Gough), University of Chicago, 1938.

13. *Democracy*, pp. 38, 62, 71, 88, 82.

14. *Ibid.*, pp. 171, 141, 136, 135.

15. *Ibid.*, p. 126.

16. *Ibid.*, pp. 144, 128.

17. *Ibid.*, p. 145.

18. *Ibid.*, pp. 189, 190.

19. *Ibid.*, pp. 218, 219.

20. *Ibid.*, pp. 261, 268, 286.

21. *Ibid.*, pp. 279, 282. For a superb recent illustration see *Time, Life,* and other American periodicals on the occasion of the visit of Queen Elizabeth and Prince Consort Philip to the United States, October 16 to 22, 1957.

22. Adams, *Democracy*, p. 290. Holt declared, "Part of the portraits of the women were attributed to Mrs. Adams, but her husband told me that he really had not depended upon her for anything but an occasional description of a costume for a woman" (Holt, "Publisher's Foreword," *Democracy*, 1925 edition). Spring Rice erroneously declared that Adams wrote the novel with his wife (Gwynn, *Spring Rice*, I, 68). On Adams's meeting with Worth, Thoron, p. 180. It is probable, however, that Mrs. Adams did exercise her editorial privileges. Cf. HA to Hay, October 31, 1883, Ford I, p. 355: "I make it a rule to strike out ruthlessly in my writings whatever my wife criticises, on the theory that she is the average reader, and that her decisions are, in fact if not in reason, absolute."

23. Adams, *Democracy*, pp. 307, 308. For many allusions to

Blaine see Thoron, p. 252, "Mulligan letters," and index. See also index to Ford I. A detailed account of the scandal appears in Rhodes, *History*, VII, 194–206.

24. *Democracy*, p. 336.

25. *Democracy*, p. 351. Rhodes, *History*, VII, 219.

26. *Democracy*, pp. 353, 354, 361. For an explicit reference to *Vanity Fair* see *Democracy*, p. 217.

27. *Ibid.*, pp. 370, 374, 7.

28. *Ibid.*, p. 196. Mrs. Green's letter is given in full in Thoron, p. 357 n. 2.

29. King to Hay, from Paris (1882), Cater Transcripts, MHS.

30. Adams, *Democracy*, pp. 195, 77 ff.

31. The following list of reviews and most of the quotations from them in the text are taken from the unpublished Master's essay of Mrs. E. T. Gough (Agnes Mary Hyde):

Academy, July 1, 1882; *Appleton's*, June 1880; *Athenaeum*, June 24, 1882; *Atlantic*, September 1880; *Blackwoods*, June 1882; *Dial*, May 1880; *Edinburgh Review*, July 1882; *Fortnightly Review*, July 1882; *Graphic*, July 15, 1882; *Harper's*, July 1880; *Lippincott's*, June 1880; *Literary Review*, July 15, 1882; *Literary World*, May 8, 1880, July 15, 1882; *Nation*, April 22, 1880; *Saturday Review*, July 8, 1882, February 2, 1884; *Scribner's*, July 1880; *Spectator*, November 19, 1881; *Westminster*, October 1882; Boston *Transcript*, April 4, 1880, December 12, 1882; *Louisville Courier Journal*, April 22, 1880; *Manchester Guardian*, May 10, 1881, June 7, 1882; *National Republican* (Washington), December 28, 1882; New York *Times*, April 11, 1880; New York *Semi-Weekly Tribune*, July 14, 1882, August 1, 1882, August 18, 1882, October 20, 1882; *The Times* (London), June 27, 1882. On the occasion of the 1952 reprint the *New Yorker* (August 23, 1952) contrived to say of it, "A strutting, graciously phrased little novel of Washington society in the eighteen-seventies."

32. Whitman, *Democratic Vistas*, a work begun as a retort to Carlyle's "Shooting Niagara" (1867); Lowell, "The Place of the Independent in Politics" (1888), *Writings*, VI, 199; Ward, *Dynamic Sociology*, II, 227–252; James Bryce, "Some Aspects of American Public Life," *Fortnightly Review*, 38:634 ff. (November 1882); commented on in the *American*, December 30, 1882, pp. 183, 184. *Young Henry Adams*, p. 183. HA to BA, Ford II, p. 392, n. 1. On the political apathy of cultivated and wealthy Americans see J. L. Diman, "The Alienation of the Educated Classes from Politics," Phi Beta Kappa oration at Harvard, June 29, 1876, reviewed in NAR, 124:156 (1877), and also Bryce, *The American Commonwealth* (1888). Dennett suggests (*Hay*, p. 165 n.) that Bryce may well have had his friends Adams and Hay in mind. The

young activist Theodore Roosevelt, soon to become one of Adams's incongruous friends, wrote to Bryce, "I was especially pleased at the way in which you pricked certain hoary bubbles, notably the 'tyranny of the majority' theory" (Fisher, *Bryce*, I, 235, 236). Madeleine's horror of practical politics recalls that of John Quincy Adams, who remarked to George Bancroft that the democracy of Paine and his like is a "government for wild beasts and not for men" (JQA to Bancroft, March 31, 1838, *Bulletin* of the New York Public Library, X, 1906). See Lippincott, *Victorian Critics of Democracy*, and Jacobson, *Development of American Political Thought*, for materials on the great continuing debate.

33. Thoron, p. 247; Cater, pp. 49, 50, 115; Ford I, p. 286; Thoron, p. 252 and n. 2.

34. Bradford, *American Portraits*, p. 125. Ingersoll's seconding speech at the Republican convention, 1876. Rhodes, *History*, VII, 209. Thoron, p. 252 and notes 1 and 2, p. 359. Adams, *Democracy*, p. 150.

35. Dennett, *Hay*, p. 130. The first impression made by Emily Beale on the Adamses — "rather pretty and uncommonly lively" — appears in MA to RWH, January 6, 1878, Adams Papers.

36. Thoron, p. 263 and "Conkling" in index. Adams, *Democracy*, pp. 30, 182. *Education*, p. 261.

37. Rhodes, *History*, VIII, 5, 92.

38. Adams, *Democracy*, p. 198; *Education*, p. 276. Nevins, *Fish*, p. 379. For Motley's account see Holmes, *Motley* (1879 [1878]).

39. Adams, *Democracy*, p. 162; Kraus, *A History*, p. 235; Thoron, pp. 240, 253, 266, 284, 339; Ford II, p. 342.

40. Cf. probable portrait of Emily Beale in Frances Burnett, *Fair Barbarian* (1881). See references to Emily Beale (Mrs. John Roll McLean) in Ford II, index. See her daughter-in-law's reminiscences, Evalyn Walsh McLean, *Father Struck It Rich*, p. 195.

41. Ford I, p. 349; Adams, *Democracy*, p. 73, 342.

42. *Ibid.*, pp. 1-12 *passim*, 102, 216. The Howe anecdote is given in Marquis Childs's editor's introduction to Brooks Adams, *America's Economic Supremacy*.

43. Adams, *Democracy*, p. 179, 334.

44. *Ibid.*, pp. 194, 322, 323. Ogden, *Godkin*, II, 43.

45. See above, note 31: *Dial, Fortnightly, Saturday Review; Graphic, Scribner's, Academy, Saturday Review; Athenaeum, Blackwoods.*

46. Ford I, p. 348. Adams apparently did not read or was unimpressed by Mark Twain's (and C. D. Warner's) *Gilded Age*, published in 1873, for he makes no allusion to that hilarious and savage satire of political corruption in Washington and the workings of the lobbies. His sole allusion to John W. DeForest, another

well known political novelist of the time (*Playing the Mischief*, 1875; *Honest John Vane*, 1875), occurs in 1882 (Ford I, p. 340). For a useful review of the genre see Morris Speare, *The Political Novel: Its Development in England and America* (New York, 1924).

47. Matthiessen, *James*, p. 51. Cf. reviews in *Atlantic, Nation,* Boston *Literary World,* New York *Times, Blackwood's.* Cf. Ford I, pp. 337, 338.

48. Ford I, pp. 336, 345. Thoron, pp. 247, 284, 285, 306, 307. Chapin, *American Court Gossip,* p. 62.

49. Cater, p. 103, 105. But cf. the humorously cryptic allusions of HA to Hay, April 20, 1883, Ford I, p. 350. A source of the legend appears in Thayer, *Letters,* Thayer to HA, July 17, 1915, p. 250: "When I was in Washington your brother Charles told me that you had an intimate coterie, consisting of yourself and Mrs. Adams, of Mr. & Mrs. Hay, and of Clarence King — and that this was called the Five of Hearts. From it, he said, issued 'Democracy,' Hay being the writer and you others the critics. Was he right in the name — Five of Hearts?" Obviously Charles still was ignorant of Henry's authorship and the circumstances of its publication. Thayer evidently had not seen Stanton's *Manual of American Literature,* but was pretty certain of Adams's authorship, having been working on a biography of Hay for two years, though he prudently based his attribution on internal evidence. "You alone," he told Adams, "were up to the level of its substance, vocabulary and style" (*ibid.*). Henry also kept the secret from Lodge, a fact which led to a curiously interesting exchange between Theodore Roosevelt and Lodge. Roosevelt to Lodge, Sept. 2, 1905: "The other day I was reading *Democracy,* that novel which made a great furore among the educated incompetents and the pessimists generally about twenty-five years ago. It had a superficial and rotten cleverness, but it was essentially false, essentially mean and base, and it is amusing to read it now and see how completely events have given it the lie." Lodge to Roosevelt, September 7, 1905: "I have not read *Democracy* for years, but I remember when it came out it impressed me as very clever, probably more clever than I should think it today, and also extremely sordid in the view which it took." *Correspondence of Theodore Roosevelt and Henry Cabot Lodge,* II, 189, 191, quoted in Ford II, p. 480, n. 3.

50. See Note 48. CFA Jr. to HA, June 4, 1880, Adams Papers.

51. CFA, Jr. to Godkin, January 31, 1884; the excerpt in the following paragraph is taken from HA to Hay, February 2, 1884, Adams Papers. *The Breadwinners* was serialized in the *Century,*

August, 1883 to January, 1884, and published in book form January 5, 1884.

52. *Nation*, February 21, 1884.

53. MA to RWH, November 10, 19, 24, 1878. Adams, *Democracy*, pp. 214, 215.

54. Cater, p. 88. HA to Dr. Hooper, December 27, 1878; MA to RWH, December 29, 1878, Adams Papers.

55. MA to RWH, December 22, 1878; January 5, 1879; December 29, 1878, Adams Papers.

56. Thayer, *Hay*, II, 23, 24; MA to RWH, January 26, 1879, December 10, 1878, December 29, 1878, Adams Papers.

57. MA to RWH, January 15, February 23, March 27, 1879, Adams Papers. Ford I, p. 309. Appendix V in Thoron.

58. Ford I, p. 311.

59. According to Jacob Blanck, *Bibliography of American Literature*, I, the "Diary" is "sometimes attributed" to Henry Adams, citing Evelyn Page, "The Diary of a Public Man," *New England Quarterly*, 22:147-172 (June 1949) and Benjamin M. Price, "Who Wrote 'The Diary of a Public Man'?" *American Bar Association Journal*, August 1951, elaborated in *South Atlantic Quarterly*, 54:56–64 (January 1955). The second article is, if anything, more speculative and inconclusive than the first, offering a few conjectural "additional reasons" to support the attribution in the form of highly dubious single word parallels. The major investigation of the problem is Frank Maloy Anderson, *The Mystery of "A Public Man": A Historical Detective Story* (Minneapolis, 1948), discussed in Barzun and Graff, *The Modern Researcher* (New York, 1957), pp. 107–113, as a model of exhaustive and painstaking research. See their note, *ibid.*, p. 113, for additional citations continuing the fruitless debate. The only fact which may safely be asserted is that the "Diary" is a mixture of fact and fiction if any due regard is paid to the standard principles of verification of authorship through external and internal evidence. Cf., for example, Chauncy Sanders, *An Introduction to Research in English Literary History* (New York, 1952), chapter iii, and R. S. Crane, *New Essays of Oliver Goldsmith*, p. xx and *passim*, for analysis of internal evidence. If any inference may be drawn from the *North American Review* treatment of Adams's *Gallatin* and the fact that there occurs only one allusion to its editor, Allen Thorndike Rice, in the entire correspondence of Adams and his wife, published and unpublished, it is that their relationship was not cordial and that Adams would have had no special reason to befriend or trust him. (HA to Marian Adams, April 9, 1885, Adams Papers: "I went up to Scott Circle, and rather to my dis-

appointment found that Allan (*sic*) Rice and Sally Loring had been added to the family. . . . Allan Rice's presence and that of Sally Loring prevented all confidential talk.")

60. Ford I, p. 89. "The Great Secession Winter 1860–1861," printed in *Proceedings,* Massachusetts Historical Society, vol. 43 (1909–1910), pp. 666, 668. Cf. Charles Francis Adams's report of Douglas's midnight visit to the campaign train in 1860, "half-drunk . . . whiskey bottle in hand," *An Autobiography* (Boston, 1916), p. 65 and see also p. 47. There is no indication that either Henry or his brother ever wished to moderate their condemnation of Douglas. Reviewing "The Great Secession Winter" in 1910, Charles remarked, "It revealed a maturity and an insight which I had not at all appreciated on the previous reading" (*Proceedings,* MHS, 43:657). Though Henry's philosophical interpretation in the *Education* (chapter vii) of the experience of 1860 was to give it a darker color, it did not alter his earlier analysis of the facts or personalities. Cf. *The Young Henry Adams,* pp. 81–93.

61. HA to Gaskell, April 9, 1879; MA to RWH, April 6, 1879, Adams Papers. Gallatin to Adams, May 27, 1879, in Adams's copy of his *Life of Gallatin,* MHS. Codicil dated May 24, 1879, Probate Court, Suffolk County (Boston), Massachusetts.

Chapter Four. European Orbit

1. Ford I, pp. 308, 314. Cater, p. 101.
2. Ford I, p. 307. HA to Cunliffe, August 7, 1878, Adams Papers. Nye, *Bancroft,* pp. 121, 168.
3. Cater, p. 92; Ford I, p. 298.
4. Thoron, p. 140; Ford I, p. 340; Thoron, p. 151. HA to Salisbury, July 3, 1879, HA to Philip Currie, July 11, 1879, British Foreign Office archives. Thoron, pp. 155, 157.
5. Thoron, pp. 171, 177, 187, 163; Cater, p. 91.
6. Thoron, p. 198; Ford I, p. 315.
7. Thoron, pp. 200, 216, 201, 205.
8. HA to Cunliffe, December 21, 1879, Adams Papers.
9. Thoron, p. 216. Cater, p. 100 n.
10. Ford I, p. 318. The phrase from Gambetta's famous speech of May 4, 1877, was quoted by Laugel in his attack on Gambetta's "Kulturkampf" to free French education from the control of the Catholic clergy (*Nation,* 29:172, September 11, 1879). For a full account of the involved struggle see Hanotaux, *Contemporary France* (1877–1882), vols. III and IV.
11. Thoron, pp. 106, 113, 182, 173. MA to RWH, January 4,

1880, Adams Papers. Reviewed in the *Nation*, 25:244, 245 (October 18, 1877). J. M. Hart's review of Vetault's *Charlemagne*, *Nation*, 25:301 (November 15, 1877), attribution in Haskell. The idea of French degeneracy became one of the clichés of the explanation of the French defeat in 1870 and a characteristic self-recrimination of the French Conservatives. Cf. Arnold, *Discourses in America* (1885): "France did not go with the Reformation; the Germanic qualities in her were not strong enough to make her go with it"; cited in Faverty, *Arnold*, p. 107. Cf. also Raymond, *British Policy and Opinion*, pp. 145, 373. For a favorable American estimate of the French character, see Barrett Wendell, *The France of Today* (New York, 1908).

12. MA to RWH, January 4, 1880; Thoron, pp. 185, 220, 222. For Adams and Monod, see Cater, pp. 95, 96. R. R. Hitt to Jauréguiberry, October 29, 1879, in Baym, *French Education of Henry Adams*, p. 36. Correspondence with Vignaud published in Baym, *French Education*, pp. 36–40, and Baym, "Henry Adams and Henry Vignaud," *New England Quarterly*, 17:442–449 (September 1944). Ford I, p. 319, MA to RWH, January 25, 1880, Adams Papers.

13. On worth, Thoron, pp. 180, 183, 224, 330, (Calumet copper) 184. Adams's sensitivity about his wife's bluestocking indifference to dress was of long standing. Cf. his humorous exaggeration just before his marriage in a letter to Gaskell. "She is very open to instruction. We shall improve her. She dresses badly" (Ford I, p. 223). Thoron, p. 178 and *passim* (see index under James, for many meetings with him). On Amiens, HA to Cunliffe, September 13, 1879, Adams Papers.

14. *Nation*, 26:257 (April 18, 1878). Cf. Waddington, *My First Years as a Frenchwoman*, pp. 160, 161, on American gaucheries. Disgust with Paris, Ford I, p. 319; Thoron, p. 221; Ford I, pp. 143, 144.

15. Thoron, p. 218, and Waddington, pp. 160, 161. MA to RWH, January 4, 1880, for the rigors of that winter, Adams Papers. Political troubles, in Hanotaux, *Contemporary France*, IV, 77–82, 469 *passim*.

16. Wright, *Background of Modern French Literature*, pp. 227 ff. and 233 ff. for literary situation; Brogan, *Development of Modern France*, for political background. Thoron, pp. 185, 224 for Mrs. Adams's comments. *Nation*, 26:273 (April 25, 1878).

17. Watterson, 'Marse Henry,' II, 34. Thoron, pp. 165, 197. MA to Godkin, December 25, 1879, Godkin Papers. Ford I, p. 313.

18. Thoron, p. 145.

19. HA to Cunliffe, July 13, 1879, Adams Papers. Trevelyan to HA, December 13, 1880; letter inserted in Adams's copy of Trevelyan's *Macaulay*.

20. For Empire politics, Slosson, *Europe Since 1870*, and contemporary articles on European affairs in the *Nation*, June 1877 *et seq.*

21. MA to RWH, March 28, 1880, April 4, 1880. Ford I, p. 322. Since John Cross had American connections they were "beset with inquiries. . . . We declare that a woman of genius is above criticism" (May 9, 1880, Adams Papers).

22. Thoron, p. 145. Ford I, pp. 313, 325.

23. Quoted in Roe, *Victorian Prose*, "The Victorian Age," pp. xv, xvii.

24. On James, see Aldrich, *Crowding Memories*, p. 185. MA to RWH, April 4, May 2, February 15, 1880, Adams Papers.

25. MA to RWH, March 21, May 2, June 27, 1880, Adams Papers. For an earlier after-dinner speech in London, see Thoron, p. 124.

26. Ford I, p. 321. MA to RWH, January 21, March 14, April 4, 1880, Adams Papers. Cf. William James's satirical greeting to his brother Henry on arriving in England: "My! how cramped and inferior England seems" (W. James, *Letters*, I, 209). Bret Harte meeting Henry James that winter for the first time noted that he "looks, acts, thinks like an Englishman and writes like an Englishman" (Harte, *Letters*, January 7, 1880). On Adams's "delightfully English" manner, see Watterson, 'Marse Henry,' II, 33, 34: "In manners, tone, and cast of thought he was English."

27. James, *Hawthorne*, chap. i; HA to Lodge, Ford I, p. 328. MA to RWH, April 18, August 29, July 4, 1880, Adams Papers.

28. MA to RWH, June 27, 1880, Adams Papers. Thoron, pp. 141, 156, 159, (Cuban diplomat) 219.

29. Grant-Duff, *Notes from a Diary*, July 16, 1880. Thoron, pp. 151, 154. For Becky Sharp and the baronet, MA to RWH, February 15, 1880, Adams Papers.

30. Thoron, pp. 147, 416, 159, 148. Chanler, *Roman Spring*, p. 303. H. James, *Letters*, I, p. 26: "Clover Hooper has it — intellectual grace — Minny Temple has it — moral spontaneity." Cf. also Matthiessen, *James*, p. 46.

31. MA to RWH, April 11, February 22, March 21, 1880, Adams Papers.

32. Ford I, pp. 313, 323. Green's remark passed on by his wife, Thoron, p. 360 n.

33. On his "score," Ford I, p. 325. MA to RWH, April 11, 1880, Adams Papers. On Renan and Taine, Wright, *Background*

of Modern French Literature, p. 238 and *passim;* also Baym, *French Education of Henry Adams*, pp. 62–107, *passim*, although the wide array of conjectures in that exhaustive work must be taken with considerable reserve.

34. Adams's opinion of Spencer appears in his review of Maine in *NAR*, 120:432. Thoron, p. 157 (meeting Spencer). On Spencer's influence, Holt, *Garrulities*, pp. 130, 299, 317, 332, 341, and Curti, *Growth of American Thought*, p. 567. Opinion of Huxley and Tyndall, *Education*, p. 225.

35. Fiske to Hale, Fiske, *Letters*, April 16, 1879. Other notable guests at the "tremendous spree" of July 14, 1879, were James Bryce, Henry Holt, Thomas Hughes, and Henry James. *Ibid.*, pp. 414, 415; Fiske "lionized," *ibid.*, p. 398. Langley in *Documentary History of the Cosmos Club*.

36. Fiske to Darwin, October 23, 1871, Houghton Library. Holt, *Garrulities*, pp. 136, 299, 317. *Democracy*, pp. 2, 83. For Fiske's changing attitude see his *Destiny of Man* (1884) and *Idea of God* (1885).

37. Ford I, pp. 320, 322, 323.

38. Ford I, p. 323.

39. *Ibid.*, p. 325. A partial record of his researches appears in one of Adams's notebooks: "July, 1879, Foreign Office: Diplomatic Correspondence: America 1800–1815," and in a pocket notebook summarizing articles in British newspapers of the period 1800–1815; both notebooks are in the Adams Papers. See also Henry Adams, *Transcripts* [British-Canadian (10 vols.), Spanish (1 vol.), and French State Papers (9 vols.), War of 1812 (1 vol.)], Manuscripts Division, Library of Congress. Adams, *History*, VI, 182.

40. Correspondence relating to British archives: HA to Lord Salisbury, July 3, 1879; Foreign Office to HA, July 11, 1889; Foreign Office to Record Office, July 11, 1879; HA to Foreign Office, July 11, 1879; Record Office to Foreign Office, July 26, 1880 [enclosing transcripts]; Foreign Office to Master of the Rolls, August 11, 1880 [approving transcripts], British Foreign Office archives. For a reappraisal of the Henry Papers, see Morison, *Proceedings*, MHS, vol. 69 (1947–1950), pp. 207 ff.

41. Ford I, pp. 318, 324.

42. *Ibid.*, p. 325. On Lecky and Lowell, MA to RWH, July 4, 18, 25, May 24, 1880, Adams Papers.

43. Meeting Harte, MA to RWH, August 22, 1880, Adams Papers. Harte, *Letters*, pp. 169, 170.

44. MA to RWH, September 12, August 29, 1880, Adams Papers.

45. On selling the house, MA to RWH, May 30, 1880, Adams

Papers; Thoron, pp. 203, 219, 220. On the Corcoran "White House," Ford I, pp. 325, 328. HA to Cunliffe, October 26, 1873; "For this small paradise we give about £ 10,000, including furniture," Adams Papers. For negotiations with Corcoran, see correspondence, W. W. Corcoran Papers, volume 51 (January 1–July 1, 1880), Manuscripts Division, Library of Congress, April 25, May 15, June 23, July 9. Corcoran wrote on June 11, "I am so desirous to have you for my neighbor and tenant that I am willing to let the house remain vacant until you return about the first of October next." The "cheery tomb," Ford I, p. 325.

46. HA to Gaskell, September 26, 1880. Absence of regrets, MA to RWH, July 25, 1880, Adams Papers. HA to Lodge, Ford I, p. 326.

Chapter Five. The Golden Age of Lafayette Square

1. Additional details on lease and renovation, Thoron, p. 227. On visit to Boston, HA to Gaskell, January 1, 1881, portion of letter omitted in Ford I, p. 328, Adams Papers. Thoron, pp. 237, 238. *Washington Square*, ed. Edel, p. 80.

2. Typical entry, Thoron, p. 358. On Mrs. Adams's photography, MA to RWH, September 7, 1883, Adams Papers; Thoron, p. 452. Hay portrait reproduced in Dennett, *Hay*, p. 108. When the artist Francis Millet visited the Adamses, Mrs. Adams spent a few hours photographing while the artist draped Mrs. Millet and a Miss Dodge (probably Rebecca Dodge; cf. Cater, p. 145) "in different poses, as statuary, he having some stuffs in his trunk" (MA to RWH, February 10, 1884, Adams Papers). In a systematically kept notebook, Mrs. Adams carefully entered data on photographic processes and formulas, names of sitters, etc. The photograph of Henry, reproduced in Thoron, facing p. 260, was made August 13, 1883. The last entry is dated January 22, 1884, Adams Papers.

3. Thoron, pp. 321, 411. Details concerning furnishings are in Chanler, *Roman Spring*, pp. 300, 301.

4. Thoron, pp. 341, 351, 246, 321. Woolner also sent a copy of his book, *Silenus*, hoping that Adams would "find the work carefully studied so that every word has its proper weight towards developing the main idea; but as to the ideas I must leave others to judge of them as best they may" (Woolner to HA, July 13, 1884, letter pasted in Adams's copy of Woolner's *Teresias*).

5. Cater, pp. lxiii, lxiv. Inventory, Estate of Henry Adams, Docket 24633, Probate Court, Washington, D. C.

6. Cf. Larkin, *Art and Life in America*, p. 204. Cf. Ford II, p. 273, and Thoron, pp. 23, 141, 159. *Education*, p. 213.

7. On the 1883 exhibition, Thoron, p. 438; *Nation*, 36:327 (April 12, 1883).

8. Thoron, p. 227 and n. Ford I, pp. 327, 324. See Rhodes, *History*, vol. VIII, chaps. iv and v. Garfield had entered the war from civilian life as a lieutenant colonel of the 42nd Ohio Volunteers. Hancock's brilliant war record surpassed Garfield's, but in spite of his popularity, he could not defeat the entrenched organization supporting Garfield. Hancock lost the popular vote by only 7,000 votes out of 9,000,000 votes cast for the two major parties.

9. Dennett, *Hay*, p. 129. On the Adams's quarrel with Blaine, Thoron, pp. 252, 281, 334; Ford I, p. 333. Allusion to Mrs. Blaine, HA to Gaskell, January 29, 1882, portion of letter silently omitted in Ford I, p. 333. One of Adams's friends and former students, Congressman Perry Belmont, a member of the committee investigating Secretary Blaine's activities, joined the "rat hunt" and touched off a violent quarrel. See excerpts from the *Nation* in Thoron, Appendix XIII.

10. Ford I, p. 333. Diary quoted in Williams, *Hayes* (February 11, 1881), p. 643. Legislative breakdown, HA to Gaskell, February 10, 1881, Adams Papers.

11. Ford I, p. 329. Hay's remark in Rhodes, *History*, VIII, 141. On the assassination, Cater, pp. 108, 115.

12. Thoron, pp. 307–309. HA to MacVeagh, July 18, 1881. "Henry Adams and Wayne MacVeagh," *Pennsylvania Magazine of History and Biography*, 80:493–512 (1956).

13. Godkin hopefully suggested $50,000. Adams said, "I am not Vanderbilt." On his investment in the *Post*, Cater, pp. 109–113, 114–116, 117. He was still listed as one of the nine principal stockholders in the "Statement of Ownership," *Nation*, 104:444 (April 12, 1917), but the stock did not appear in the inventory of his estate.

14. Cater, p. 112. On Schurz's resignation, Fuess, *Schurz*, p. 279.

15. Thoron, p. 259. Ford I, p. 345 (cf. Thoron, p. 414). Cater, p. 117.

16. Cater, p. 118. Thoron, p. 419.

17. Ford I, p. 331; Cater, p. 113. Cf. the similar appraisal by Lowell in his paper "The Independent in Politics," April 13, 1888, *Writings* (Boston, 1892), VI, 213: "What to me is the saddest feature of our present methods is the pitfalls which they dig in the path of ambitious and able men who feel that they are fitted for a political career, that by character or training they could be

of service to their country, yet who find every avenue closed to them unless at the sacrifice of the very independence which gives them a claim to what they seek. . . . with our political methods the hand is of necessity subdued to what it works in."
18. Fuess, *Schurz*, p. 282.
19. Lamar's speech, Thoron, p. 423. Adams to Schurz, Ford I, p. 351.
20. Ford I, pp. 359, 358. Adams to Hewitt, Cater, p. 131. On "socialist rubbish," HA to Gaskell, October 30, 1887, Adams Papers.
21. Ford I, pp. 358, 360. For Brooks Adams's support of Cleveland's candidacy, see Anderson, *Brooks Adams*, p. 36, and Beringause, *Brooks Adams*, pp. 78–79.
22. MA to RWH, March 5, 1885, Adams Papers. Ford I, p. 362.
23. Charles Francis Adams quoted in Rhodes, *History*, VIII, 254.
24. Cater, pp. 138, 140.
25. Ford I, p. 362. On the offer of the Costa Rica mission, Thoron, p. 364; MA to RWH, February 16, 1883, Adams Papers. Ford I, p. 362. Cf. Adams's later interpretation of the experience in the *Education*, p. 322, and his letter to Lodge, November, 1915, in which he remarked that his elder brother Charles "was a man of action, with strong love of power. I for that reason, was almost compelled to become a man of contemplation, a critic and a writer" (Cater, p. 772).
26. HA to Cunliffe, November 12, 1882, Adams Papers.
27. HA to Cunliffe, July 25, 1872. Ford II, p. 333 n.
28. On Mrs. Adams's "nervous collapse" in 1872, see Cater, p. 1. On Henry's concern for her and the state of her health, Thoron, pp. 274–275, 437, 441, 418. Her mother's death of "consumption" at the age of thirty-six (Death Records, 1848, Boston Registry Department) for a long time seems to have cast a shadow of concern over Mrs. Adams, especially whenever she developed a persistent cough. Cf. Ford I, p. 283.
29. "But as Mrs. Adams was inclined to be a bit exacting, pouring without reserve the vials of her wrath upon nearly everybody with whom she came in contact, the egregious Don Cameron being one of the few exceptions, it is possible that her criticisms should be accepted with some reserve" (Richardson, *Chandler*, p. 356). Cf. Mrs. Adams on Chandler, Thoron, p. 436. See *ante*, Chapter I, ii, "The Social Vortex."
30. *The Titan* (New York, 1914), p. 63. On a street car episode, see Chicago *Daily News*, June 4, 1886. Earnest, *Mitchell*,

pp. 135, 178. HA to Hay, January 18, 1885 (HA to Hay, May 20, 1883: "Man delights me not, woman is my only solace"), Adams Papers. See also the extended analysis of attitudes toward women and sex in Wecter, *Sam Clemens of Hannibal*. Another ingredient in the pedestalization of women was provided many years earlier by De Tocqueville, *Democracy in America*, II (1889 edition), 194: "If I were asked . . . to what the singular prosperity and growing strength of that people ought mainly to be attributed, I should reply, — to the superiority of their women."

31. Thoron, p. 352. Omitted portion of letter, HA to Hay, January 7, 1883, Adams Papers. HA to Lowell, May 15, 1883, Cater, p. 127. HA to Hay, April 4, 1883, Adams Papers. On Mrs. Cameron [1857–1944], Gwynn, *Spring Rice*, I, 51 ff. and *passim*. She married Senator Cameron [1833–1918], a widower with six children, in 1878, Thoron, p. 256 n. 4 and p. 257 n. 1. Chapin, *American Court Gossip*, p. 248. "Considered by many the most beautiful person in society" (Washington *Critic*, December 19, 1885). The Adamses first met Mrs. Cameron in January, 1881 (Thoron, pp. 256–257) shortly after Henry met her husband: "Don Cameron scintillates as you once did. His wit is of a different quality than yours — more subtle and veiled" (HA to Hay, November 29, 1880, Adams Papers).

32. MA to Mrs. Cameron, January 11, 1884; HA to Mrs. Cameron, Christmas, 1883; MA to RWH, May 25, 1884; Adams Papers.

33. Thoron, pp. 363–364, 377. On Wilde, *ibid.*, pp. 328, 333, 338, 329. See Thoron, p. 352 n., for Julia Ward Howe's defense of Wilde and the *Nation's* satirical comment thereon.

34. Thoron, pp. 239, 282. Dodge, *Gail Hamilton*, November 11, 1881, II, 818. Anderson, *Letters and Journals*, p. 265.

35. HA to Cunliffe, November 12, 1882, Adams Papers. The extraordinary squeamishness of polite society was so fully echoed in the *Century* and the *Atlantic* that Dr. S. Weir Mitchell remarked after visiting the offices of the *Century* in 1895, "The monthly magazines are getting so lady-like that naturally they will soon menstruate" (Earnest, *Mitchell*, p. 174). Cf. remark of Henry James, "The stuff that is sent me [from America] seems to me written by eunuchs and sempstresses" (Harlow, *Perry*, p. 309).

36. Ford I, p. 334; Thoron, p. 330 ff. Immediately after the review appeared in the *North American Review*, 114:110–147 (January 1872), Freeman wrote a long letter to the magazine, objecting to the carping criticisms of his style and "laboured attempts at wit" (Freeman to [Adams], February 17, 1872, Adams Papers). See Preface to Vol. I, *Norman Conquest*, 3rd ed. (Ox-

ford, 1877): "It would almost seem as if 'H.A.' had written this [review] without either looking at the Chronicles themselves or at the examination of their witness in my Appendix. . . ."

37. MA to RWH, November 4, 1883, December 23, 1883; HA to Hay, January 6, 13, 1884; MA to RWH, February 16, 1884, Adams Papers. On the "real" reason for Arnold's tour, see R. L. Lowe, "A Note on Arnold in America," *American Literature*, 23: 250–254 (May 1951); the explanation is questioned in W. E. Buckler, "Matthew Arnold in America," *ibid.*, 29:464 (January 1958). Adams's tribute to Arnold occurs in his letter to Mrs. Cameron, September 22, 1892, Adams Papers. On Arnold's blundering during his American tour, see Howard Mumford Jones, "Arnold, Aristocracy, and America," *American Historical Review*, 49:393–409 (April 1944), and references there cited. On Mrs. Leiter's famous "mots," Griscom, *Diplomatically Speaking*, p. 16.

38. Thoron, pp. 327, 320. James's comment on Washington in Harlow, *Perry*, January 23, 1882; on Marian Adams, Thoron, p. 384. Plan for "Pandora," James, *Notebooks*, see index. "Pandora" in James, *Novels and Tales*, New York Edition, XVIII, p. 128; cf. also, "The couple had taken upon themselves the responsibilities of an active patriotism" (ibid., p. 131). HA to Cunliffe, December 3, 1882, Adams Papers.

39. For allusions to James's books see HA to Gaskell, June 22, 1877, May 30, 1878, August 28, 1878 (opinion of *Daisy Miller*), Adams Papers. Ford I, pp. 323 (avoids James's books), 333 (broke down on *Portrait*). Thoron, p. 306 (" 'Ann Eliza' "). MA to RWH ("alienated Americans") November 29, 1880, Adams Papers. Marian's defense in Thoron, p. 403. Reprinted in James's *Siege of London;* for verbal echoes see especially p. 287.

40. Thoron, p. 404.

41. *Siege of London, the Pension Beaurepas, and the Point of View* (Boston, 1883), pp. 284, 285, presentation copy to "Marian Adams from the author" dated February 16, 1883.

42. James, Siege of London, p. 286. Concerning *The Sacred Fount*, Ford II, p. 333. James later recorded in his notebook a story which Adams told him in London and the "dim little germ of an anecdote" tantalized him for years as "The Henry Adams story" (James, *Notebooks*, pp. 113, 119, 135–136, 297, 298).

43. Perhaps inspired by the "Five of Clubs" of Longfellow's inner circle (Jones, et al., *Major American Writers*, New York, 1945, p. 561). For the "Five of Hearts" see Thoron, p. 238 n., Ford I, p. 335 n., Dennett, *Hay*, p. 156 ff. Reputedly they also had a special tea set, Cater, xliv. Holt, *Garrulities*, p. 135. On Mrs. Hay, Dennett, *Hay*, p. 148 and Mark Twain's *Auto-*

biography (New York, 1924), I, 34, 232 ff. On the printing of "1601," Hay to Alexander Gunn, June 21, 1880: "I cannot properly consent to it, and I am afraid the great man [Clemens] would think I was taking an unfair advantage. . . . If, in spite of my prohibition you take these proofs, save me one" (Hay Papers, Library of Congress).

44. Dennett, *Hay* (leapfrog play), p. 93. Holt, *Garrulities,* p. 136. For King's puns, Thoron, pp. 271, 277. On Boston icebergs, HA to Gaskell, February 15, 1875, Adams Papers. For King's dislike of the laboratory, Bronson, *Reminiscences of a Ranchman,* pp. 3–4.

45. "Old Man Tison" in Bronson, *Reminiscences of a Ranchman.* On his intimacy with Hay, see Dennett, *Hay,* p. 156 ff. Howells in *Clarence King Memoirs,* p. 141.

46. HA to Cunliffe, July 9, 1882, Adams Papers. Eagerness of Hay and King to quit, Thoron, p. 286. HA to Holmes, January 4, 1883, Adams Papers. On Hay's liking for King, MA to RWH, March 30, 1884, Adams Papers. On King's attire, *King Memoirs,* p. 345; also Edgar B. Bronson, "A Man of East and West," *Century,* 80:376–382 (July 10, 1910). King's common law marriage, Cater, lxviii; the full account drawn from court files, Crosby, *So Deep a Trail* and Wilkins, *King,* 320 ff., 355, 356. See New York *Times,* January 24, 1934, for lawsuit by Mrs. Ida King seeking to establish existence of a trust fund for her and her children. The suit was dismissed on the ground that King's letters to her failed to create a trust. Cater Transcripts, MHS.

47. W. James's famous epithet on success, quoted by Aldous Huxley, *Proper Studies,* p. 318. On the extraordinary dividends of Calumet and Hecla, see Agassiz, *Letters and Recollections of Alexander Agassiz,* p. 226. King's speculations, Cater, p. 213. Hay's financial acumen, Dennett, *Hay,* p. 144; Ford I, p. 361. Hay on King, Dennett, p. 160. Adams as investor, Cater, p. 111, 114.

48. Hay to Miss Perry, January 2, 1859, Hay, *A Poet in Exile.* Dennett, pp. 103, 104, 110–118.

49. Quoted in Dennett, pp. 114–115. Ford I, pp. 353–356.

50. For Adams's usefulness to Hay, Dennett, p. 167. HA to Cunliffe, November 12, 1882. Adams Papers. Henry Loomis Nelson in *Atlantic,* 52:821 (December 1883).

51. Thoron, pp. 277, 295, 442. Anderson, *Letters and Journals,* p. 25. Thoron, p. 449.

52. Thoron, p. 368, for Brooks's visit. On Brooks Adams and Holmes, see Beringause, *Brooks Adams,* pp. 68–69, and Anderson, *Brooks Adams,* p. 33.

53. Holmes, *The Common Law* (1881), p. 1.
54. Quoted in Anderson, *Brooks Adams*, pp. 34, 36.
55. Ford, I, p. 364. Cf. *post*, Chapter X, note 60.

Chapter Six. Portraits in Acid

1. The transcripts are now in the Manuscripts Division, Library of Congress. Cf. *ante*, Chap. 6, n. 39.
2. Letters to Winsor, June 6, 1881, September 27, 1881, Cater, pp. 106–107, Ford I, p. 329. A manuscript notebook in the Henry Adams library at the MHS, bearing the date August, 1877, is headed "Manners and Customs." Apparently he had begun to look ahead to the *History* when he was beginning to work on the manuscript of the *Gallatin*.
3. Ledgers in the Henry Adams library at MHS. De Tocqueville, *Democracy*, II, 75, 79.
4. Ford I, pp. 328, 329. Lodge dedicated the book to Adams.
5. In a letter dated March 10, 1881, Morse invited Von Holst to do the life of Calhoun for the American Statesmen series, listed other contributors, and added, "I intend also to invite Mr. Henry Adams" (Von Holst Collection, University of Chicago). "I think only one real blunder was made [in recruiting biographers], and that was in allotting Randolph to Henry Adams. I fancied that I should evoke something quite different from what I got, and I admit that the error was wholly my own fault. In justice it should be said that he accepted the proposal with much doubt and little ardor" (Morse, "Incidents Connected with the American Statesmen Series," *Proceedings*, MHS, 64:374). Cf. also J. T. Adams, *Adams Family*, pp. 328–329, on Morse's recollection.
6. HA to Morse, April 9, 1881, April 27, 1881, Morse Papers, MHS. In another letter (March 2, 1882) Adams wrote, "I wish I could help you about Webster. [Morse gave it to Lodge.] Did you ever think of applying to John C. Hurd; whose late book on "The Theory of Our National Existence" [Boston, 1881] is so remarkably strong a piece of criticism? . . ." Hurd's book explored the question of the true locus of national sovereignty, "To whom is allegiance due by each natural person" (p. 536), and he predicted that the ultimate struggle for power in the United States would be a civil war between those who supported a national government and those who supported the sovereignty of the states. Apparently, Stevens for his part was not attracted to Adams. His professional and workmanlike biography obviously

relied heavily upon Adams, but he refrained from any but the most trifling acknowledgment and, without citing the *Writings*, pointedly stated that the "mass of documents and letters" had already been "collected and partially arranged by [Gallatin] himself, with a view to posthumous publication." Stevens, *Gallatin*, p. 46 and p. 335, which briefly quotes Adams's praise of Gallatin's part in the Treaty of Ghent and alludes to Adams as "his biographer," p. 336. The uncertainty of his spelling of Carlyle's name was habitual. A few other names including Bryce and Trevelyan also troubled him.

7. Adams, *Randolph*, p. 26.
8. Cater, p. 109. On the completion of two volumes, HA to Gaskell, July 9, 1881, Adams Papers. HA to Morse, March 2, 1882, Morse Papers, MHS. On September 2 he was in the midst of "correcting the proofs" (Ford I, 338).
9. Garland, *Randolph*, p. 375. Also accessible to Adams were two other works, Lemuel Sawyer, *John Randolph* (New York, 1844) and Powhatan Bouldin, *Home Reminiscences of John Randolph* (Richmond, 1878).
10. Adams, *Randolph*, pp. 33, 34.
11. *Ibid.*, pp. 38, 18.
12. *Ibid.*, p. 32. Note Clarence King's use of the phrase in "The Helmet of Mambrino," *Century*, May 1886.
13. Cf. Craven, *The Repressible Conflict*, and the "revisionist" literature considered in Arthur Schlesinger, Jr., "The Causes of the Civil War: A Note on Historical Sentimentalism," *Partisan Review*, October 1949.
14. Bradford, *Letters*, p. 137. "Spent the morning absorbed in Henry Adams's John Randolph, the last preparation for writing the portrait. . . . And the Adams is really a profound and brilliant book" (Bradford, *Journal*, p. 323).
15. Ford I, pp. 352, 338. John Quincy Adams and Gretry's opera, allusion in Henry Adams, *New England Federalism*, vi, Ford I, p. 314.
16. On Trollope, Ford I, p. 347. A "shield of protection," Ford II, p. 495.
17. Cater, pp. 135, 649.
18. Ford II, p. 413.
19. *Randolph*, p. 24.
20. *Ibid.*, pp. 44, 247.
21. *Ibid.*, pp. 271, 304. Gallatin's estimate, Adams, *Gallatin*, p. 55.
22. *Randolph*, p. 12.

23. *Ibid.*, pp. 253, 254, 171, 286. In the same speech he is supposed to have attacked Clay with a figure of speech that became a cliché of political oratory. Clay was a "being, so brilliant yet so corrupt, which, like a rotten mackerel by moonlight, shined and stunk" (*ibid.*, p. 286). Randolph also applied the figure to Livingston (Bruce, *Randolph*, II, 197).

24. Adams, *Randolph*, p. 128.

25. *Ibid.*, pp. 68, 66.

26. *Ibid.*, pp. 121, 50, 73, 84, 142.

27. *Ibid.*, pp. 265, 14, 15.

28. *Ibid.*, p. 234.

29. *Ibid.*, pp. 303, 304. Cf. Bruce, *Randolph*, p. 711, "a morbidly high-strung nature and tragic intervals of mental aberration."

30. Ford I, pp. 338, 341, 342.

31. HA to Morse, November 19, 1882, Morse Papers, MHS. "Instinct for the jugular," quoted in *Young Henry Adams*, p. 194. On public taste, HA to CFA, Jr., December 24, 1867, Adams Papers. By 1918, 22,000 copies had been sold (Hazen, *Thayer*, p. 355). Blanck, *Bibliography of American Literature*, "Henry Adams," gives an admittedly incomplete listing, but does indicate frequent reprinting of the "revised" edition of 1883. The 1883 issue dropped the covertly satirical opening phrase, "William, first American ancestor of the innumerable Randolphs of Virginia," and replaced it with, " 'William Randolph, gentleman, of Turkey Island,' born in 1650, was a native of Warwickshire in England, as his tombstone declares." Another phrase, similarly questionable in taste, eliminated from the opening page, read: "whose descendants swarmed like bees in the Virginia hive." In 1911 Adams carefully tabulated the year-by-year sales and royalties, the aggregate sales then amounting to 19,000 copies and the royalties to $2,000, in round figures (Adams Papers).

32. Smith's review appeared in the *Dial* (Chicago), March 1883, p. 247. Mrs. Adams's report in Thoron, p. 396. Adams to Lodge in Ford I, p. 341. Lodge in *Atlantic*, 51:131 ff. (January 1883), alluded to in Ford I, p. 344. The *Gallatin* and the *Randolph* together constituted "a preliminary essay" (HA to Cunliffe, November 12, 1882, Adams Papers). *Nation*, 35:514 (December 14, 1882). Tyler's diary, in Austen, *Tyler*, October 2, 1882, p. 175. Tyler quoted in "Estimates of the Press," in the back pages of the 1888 reprint (eleventh edition) of the *Randolph*, as given in Edward Chalfant's doctoral dissertation, p. 128. Chalfant, pp. 151, 152, cites an interesting illustration of the "Virginian attacks" in the address of Daniel B. Lucas given June 13, 1883, and printed

as a pamphlet, *John Randolph of Roanoke* (New York, 1884), a copy of which was owned by Adams. *The American* (Philadelphia), December 2, 1882, p. 120.

33. Bruce, *Randolph*, p. 218; for his violent attacks on Adams see pp. 731, 740, 741, 743, 749. Bruce appears to have used the 1882 edition rather than the corrected edition of 1898. On Randolph as a disciple of Burke, Kirk, *Randolph*, p. 163.

34. The allusions to the manuscript are gathered together in Thoron, p. 405 and n. 1.

35. Thoron, p. 405. HA to Hay, June 25, 1882, Ford I, p. 337, collated with the original in the Adams Papers. Ford I, p. 341.

36. HA to Morse, October 6, 1882, Morse Papers, MHS; cf. Ford I, p. 341. Thoron, p. 405. HA to Hay, Ford I, pp. 344, 345.

37. HA to Morse, September 26, 1883, Morse Papers, MHS.

38. Morse, "Incidents Connected with the American Statesmen Series." Cf. *ante*, n. 5.

39. Adams, *History*, II, 191.

40. "Denationalizing forces," *ibid.*, III, 217. Burr sections, *ibid.*, III, chapters 10–14, 19. On Mephistopheles, *ibid.*, II, 171. Lodge's *Hamilton*, p. 245, argues that the epithet is inappropriate. "A mere episode," Adams, *History*, III, 328.

41. Adams, *Randolph*, pp. 153, 172.

42. Adams, *History*, III, 155, 157, 158.

43. Ford, "Some Papers of Aaron Burr," *Proceedings*, American Antiquarian Society, 29 (NS): 43. Adams, *History*, III, 233, 442.

44. Ford II, p. 201.

45. Ford I, p. 336. For a brief review of the controversy over Burr, see Julius W. Pratt, "Aaron Burr and the Historians," *New York History*, XXVI (1945), 447–470. Adams was the first to use the evidence in foreign archives which confirmed Burr's guilt.

46. Ford I, pp. 330, 332, 333, 334.

47. *Ibid.*, p. 333.

48. HA to Cunliffe, May 2, 1882; HA to Gaskell, December 3, 1882, Adams Papers.

49. Ford I, p. 346. HA to Hay, January 13, 1883, Adams Papers. Cater, p. 125. On two trade volumes, Ford I, p. 346.

50. MA to Mrs. Cameron, July 26, 1883, Adams Papers. Ford I, p. 353. HA to Hay, September 26, 1883; HA to Gaskell, September 9, 1883, Adams Papers. On success, Ford I, p. 349.

51. HA to O. W. Holmes, Jr., September 26, 1883, Holmes Papers. HA to Parkman, Cater, p. 132. HA to Hay, Ford I (January 8, 1884), p. 346, misdated in Ford, cf. Dennett, *Hay*, p. 110.

Chapter Seven. The Warfare Between Science and Religion

1. MA to RWH, January 13, 1883, February 3, 10, 1884, Adams Papers.
2. MA to RWH, January 6, 1884; HA to Hay, January 6, 1884, Adams Papers.
3. MA to RWH, December 2, December 16, December 26, 1883; March 23, April 2, May 5, 1884; MA to Mrs. Cameron (on her sudden change of mind) January 11, 1884, Adams Papers. Conveyance by John Hay and Clara Stone Hay to Henry Brooks Adams, January 14, 1884 (Deed Records, District of Columbia, Liber 1066, p. 163, recorded February 5, 1884). All the actual negotiations were carried on by Adams, acting as undisclosed agent for Hay ("I have not lisped your name") and the preliminaries for the purchase were well along by November 11, 1883. The agreement called for the sale of the whole corner lot (of which Adams was to take one third, the west 44 feet) "on payment of $12,606 and assumption of the deed of trust for $59,394" (HA to Hay, November 11, 1883, Adams Papers). Mrs. Hay's father left $6,000,000 to her and her sister and a bequest of $500,000 to Hay personally (MA to RWH, May 13, 1883, Thoron, p. 450). On Hay's share, HA to Gaskell, June 10, 1883, Adams Papers.
4. Richardson's extravagance was reflected in the Anderson house. The original contract called for an outlay of $37,000, but the addition of exquisite carved mahogany and oak and other refinements brought the cost to $60,000. For the Anderson experience with their friend Richardson, see Anderson, *Letters*, index, under Richardson. The plans came by June 1, 1884 (MA to RWH, June 1, 1884, HA to Hay on Richardson's plans, January 18, 1884, Adams Papers). For details concerning Richardson, see Saint-Gaudens, *Reminiscences*, p. 328. HA to Hay, April 6, 1884 ("leave your 'spare heart' authority to sign contracts"), Adams Papers. To finance the building Adams sold all his Calumet Copper holdings, netting "beside income some $30,000 from original cost. . . . We miss it tho; it has been so good a friend" (MA to RWH, March 30, 1884, Adams Papers). Fortunately for their finances, Adams's mother decided at this time to divide her share of the Peter Chardon Brooks estate among her five children and thus relieved them of any need of borrowing from their own trust estates. Evidently Adams was also able to buy back into Calumet Copper (MA to RWH, May 4, 1884,

Adams Papers). There was much good-humored perplexity and debate in the unpublished letters over the relative value of the corner lot compared with Adams's "inside" lot.

5. No copy of the first privately printed volume appears to have survived. HA to Gaskell, February 3, 1884. Ford I, p. 356.

6. King, *Catastrophism and the Evolution of Environment* (Sheffield Scientific School, Yale, 1877), p. 4. Symptomatic of the debate was the remark of Frederic Harrison: "To oppose or contrast science and religion would be, for a positivist, as irrational as it would be to a Christian to oppose the creeds and gospels of Christianity. . . . With us science is religion, so far as it is the intellectual aspect of religion." NAR, 129:340 (1879).

7. HA to Holt, Cater, pp. 128, 137 and notes 2 and 3, p. 130 and n. 2. On the disclosure of Adams's authorship, see Spiller's Introduction to *Esther* (New York, 1938), p. iii, n. 1 and Thayer, *Letters*, pp. 351–355. In 1918 Lodge passed on to Brooks Adams, Holt's proposal to republish *Esther*. Brooks replied characteristically, "I agree with you . . . that it would neither be agreeable to Henry, nor would it be for his reputation, for either 'Democracy,' or 'Esther,' whatever that may be, to be republished. I know nothing of Esther, nor do I wish to. Henry's strong point did not lie in fiction, and I should, for his sake, wish to suppress all he wrote" (BA to Lodge, April 11, 1918, Lodge Papers, MHS). Marian Adams's niece, Mrs. Ward Thoron, who came to know Adams very intimately, is confident that her aunt read the novel (personal interview, April 21, 1954).

8. *Publishers Weekly*, May 10, 1884. HA to Holt, Cater, pp. 130, 136.

9. Publication data in Spiller, Introduction to *Esther*, pp. xxiv, xxv. On February 14, 1898, Holt wrote Adams:

"Most potent, grave, and reverend Signor:

"Bentley writes us that the last copy of *Esther* sold was in 1893, and wants to know if the stock that he has on hand shall go to the paper-mill.

"If you are ready now to have us make a little flourish of trumpets over a second edition of the book, announcing that it is by the author of the book which made your anonymous fame, I shall tell Bentley to hold on to what he has. If, on the other hand, you think that contingency will never arise, I will tell him to appease the appetite of the paper-maker. . . ." (Adams Papers).

Adams bought up the unsold stock in 1899 and arranged to have the copies destroyed (Cater, p. 456).

10. Cater, pp. 130, n. 2, 136, 137, 138. The advertisement appeared in the *Athenaeum* on July 4, 1885, and the book was

reviewed, *ibid.*, July 25, 1885, pp. 107–108. It was published in England by Bentley and Son. Cf. Blanck, *Bibliography of American Literature*, I, p. 4.

11. Cater, pp. 130, 137.

12. Ford I, pp. 377, 468.

13. HA to Hay, *ibid.*, p. 354. For his "one superstition" ("never move into a new house,") see Cater, p. 172, n. 2. A marked characteristic was his half-serious belief in premonitions of evil, increasingly frequent as he grew older, a trait inherited from his mother. Cf. *Young Henry Adams*, p. 93. He seems also to have shared the widespread interest of his time in occult phenomena. Bernard Berenson has kindly called my attention to Barrett Wendell's report of having seen Adams coming out of the house of Mrs. Piper, "the famous medium that fascinated Boston" (Letter from Berenson, December 17, 1957). King to Hay, June 20, 1886, Cater Transcripts, MHS.

14. Comte, *Positive Philosophy*, p. 36. The best account of this development is given by Hofstadter, *Social Darwinism in American Thought*. See also Merle Curti, "The Delimitation of Supernaturalism" in *Growth of American Thought*.

15. *Bulletin*, Washington Philosophical Society, V (1883), 49, 78, 105, 169. Cf., also, James McCosh, *Christianity and Positivism* (1871); John Stuart Mill, *Three Essays on Religion* (1874); Arthur Balfour, *Defence of Philosophical Doubt* (1879); Robert Ingersoll, *Some Mistakes of Moses* (1879); William Mallock, *Is Life Worth Living* (1879); Sir John Seeley, *Natural Religion* (1882); Lester Ward, *Dynamic Sociology* (1883), which declares, for example, that the doctrine of immortality "has exerted an exceedingly pernicious influence upon progress of thought" (p. 697); Joseph Henry Allen, *Our Liberal Movement in Theology* (1883). Cf. also Matthew Arnold's many essays on the question of religion, science, and culture, for example, *Last Essays on Church and Religion* (1877).

16. James, "The Sentiment of Rationality" (1879), in *Essays on Faith and Morals*. Note that Dr. Oliver Wendell Holmes's Phi Beta Kappa address of 1870, *Mechanism in Thought and Morals*, had just been reprinted. The old "Autocrat," one of Adams's Beverly Farms circle of neighbors, adopted evolutionary principles, but, admitting "certain residual convictions," he rejected "the mechanical doctrine which makes me the slave of outside influences, whether it work with the logic of Edward, or the averages of Buckle." In effect this was the pragmatic position of William James, who studied under Dr. Holmes in the 60's. (The "Mechanism" essay reprinted in *Pages from an Old Volume of*

Life, Boston, 1883, p. 302.) Cf. also the Rhode Island business-man and philosopher, Rowland G. Hazard, *Man a Creative First Cause* (1883), whose attitude toward freedom of the will was analogous to that of James. His earlier work, *Letters on Causation and Willing,* was highly praised by Mill. Note also George Henry Lewes, *The Physical Basis of Mind* (1877), which, though strongly opposed to traditional metaphysics, acknowledged, as James did, that subjective introspection was a legitimate tool even for the scientific materialist (William James, "Rationality, Activity and Faith," *Princeton Review,* July 1882, p. 71). For a striking Russian illustration of this intellectual ferment see Tolstoy's *Anna Karenina* (1878), especially in the spiritual di-lemmas of Levin.

17. W. James, the article cited above, and *post,* n. 19. His remark on the free will controversy was made in his address "The Dilemma of Determinism" to divinity students in 1884 (*Essays on Faith and Morals,* p. 184). His review of Renan's *Dialogues* (quoted in the next paragraph) appeared in the *Nation,* 23: 78–79 (1876).

18. Cater, p. 121. Fiske, *Outlines of Cosmic Philosophy,* II, 173 n.

19. William James, "Great Men, Great Thoughts, and the En-vironment," *Atlantic,* October, 1880.

20. HA to W. James, Cater, p. 122. Their friend Fiske con-tested James's article in "Sociology and Hero Worship," *Atlantic,* January, 1881, reprinted in *Excursions of an Evolutionist,* p. 158 ff.

21. James's reconstruction of the grounds of religious belief was but one symptom of the almost panicky flight of many intellectuals from the odium which the Papacy and fundamentalist Protestant churches had succeeded in fastening upon "vulgar positivism" and "materialism" ever since Pius IX issued his militant *Syllabus of Errors* in 1864. Fiske early disassociated himself from the dangerous label of Comtism as did Spencer, Tyndall, and Huxley. Spencer admitted to Fiske that he had postulated the Unknowable "simply for the purpose of guarding myself against charges of atheism and materialism." Fiske praised the "positivist" W. K. Clifford for overturning the "crude notion of the materialists . . . that changes of consciousness are *caused* by physical changes on or within the organism." Even so James attacked Fiske for his ideas of the "Spencerian or evolutionist school" (Fiske, *Cosmic Philosophy,* I, 144, 145; Spencer, *Illustra-tions of Universal Progress;* Huxley, *Essays,* IX, 130). On Spencer's "Unknowable," see Holt, *Garrulities,* p. 332; Fiske, *Excursions of an Evolutionist,* p. 303.

22. HA to Gaskell, Ford I, pp. 339, 349, 357. Reference to Henry George in HA to Cunliffe, November 12, 1882, Adams Papers. Henry Gannett, "The Wealth of the United States and the Rate of Increase," *International Review*, 12:497–504 (May 1882), alluded to in Ford I, p. 339.

23. George P. Fisher, *Princeton Review*, July 1882.

24. *Ibid.*, pp. 16, 17, 34.

25. *North American Review*, vol. 131, (1880). CFA to HA, October 25, 1858, Adams Papers. Nordhoff's pious text acknowledged another practical purpose: "If you could persuade the tenement house population of New York that there is no future life beyond the grave, they would sack Fifth Avenue overnight" (*God and the Future Life*, New York, 1883, p. 56). Cf. Harold Frederic, *Damnation of Theron Ware* (Chicago, 1896) p. 359: "There must always be a church. If one did not exist, it would be necessary to invent it. It is needed, first and foremost, as a police force. It is needed, secondly, so to speak, as a fire insurance."

26. *Esther*, pp. 1, 7–9. The "Cogito" had become one of the great philosophical commonplaces of the time; cf., for example, Francis Bowen, under whom Adams studied at Harvard, whose *Modern Philosophy*, according to the *Nation*, 25:335 (November 29, 1877), traced all modern philosophy to Descartes and *Cogito ergo sum*.

27. Thayer, *Letters*, p. 353.

28. On the grave risks in marriage, MA to RWH, November 11, 1884, Adams Papers. Cf. *Esther*, p. 41, Esther's aunt speaking of her own marriage: "Nothing on earth would induce me to begin over again and take such a risk a second time, with life before me. As for bringing about a marriage, I would almost rather bring about a murder."

29. *Esther*, p. 41. Cf. Adams's description of his wife in 1872, Ford I, p. 223. For Marian Adams's genealogy see Thoron, p. 466 *passim*. On the best age for marriage, HA to Elizabeth Cameron, July 2, 1908, Adams Papers.

30. *Esther*, pp. 58, 21. Marsh, a member of the Geological Survey, presented the Adamses with a copy of his book on extinct toothed birds, December 25, 1880.

31. *Esther*, pp. 69, 26, 27, 36. Cortissoz, *La Farge*, p. 212 and *passim*. See also John La Farge, S.J., *The Manner Is Ordinary*, for reminiscences of his father, the artist John La Farge, and Waern, *La Farge*.

32. Allen, *Brooks*, II, p. 437. *Esther*, p. 72.

33. See Mrs. Schuyler Van Rensselaer, *Richardson*. Adams's

debt to Richardson, Ford II, p. 240. For Hazard's "thirteenth-century ideas," *Esther*, p. 104. On Adams's familiarity with Viollet-le-Duc, see La Farge, *An Artist's Letters*, p. 105. For rebellion against Viollet-le-Duc, see Cortissoz, *La Farge*, p. 153. See Richardson's account of the building and decoration of Trinity in *Trinity Church in the City of Boston*, p. 196 ff. La Farge did the murals and the lancet windows in the west end. The church was consecrated February 8, 1877. For the Pre-Raphaelite interests of such members of Adams's circle as Clarence King, John La Farge, and Russell Sturgis, see David H. Dickason, *The Daring Young Men* (Bloomington, 1953).

34. *Esther*, pp. 45, 46.

35. *Ibid.*, p. 85.

36. *Ibid.*, pp. 61, 60.

37. *Ibid.*, pp. 76, 77, 74, 101, 28.

38. *Ibid.*, pp. 29, 129, 98, 79. Wharton's mariolatry, echoed elsewhere in the novel (cf. p. 74), reflects the remarkable growth of the cult in Protestant as well as Roman Catholic circles, especially with the revival of interest in Gothic cathedral architecture. To La Farge, reared a Catholic, the cult was second nature. The dogma of the immaculate conception of the Virgin Mary proclaimed in 1854 initiated the modern phase of the cult. The famous debate between Pusey and Newman over the worship of Mary and other points of dogma was still relatively recent. Cf. Newman, *Certain Difficulties Felt by Anglicans in Catholic Teaching* (1876) replying to Pusey's *Eirenicon* of 1864. Cf. allusion in *Esther*, p. 193, to Newman.

39. Pumpelly, *Across America and Asia*, 1869 edition. Cf. allusions to Buddha and the Orient in *Esther*, e.g., pp. 79, 175, 211, 270. Note the highly perceptive comment on the cultist aspect of enthusiasm for Buddhism by Lafcadio Hearn in Bisland, *Hearn*, I, p. 265. He objected that Sinnett's *Esoteric Buddhism* and Olcott's *Buddhist Catechism* represented "a sort of neo-gnosticism which repels by its resemblance to Spiritualistic humbug. But the higher Buddhism, — that suggested by men like Emerson, John Weiss, etc., will yet have an apostle." For the best treatment of the subject see the essays in Arthur Christy, ed., *The Asian Legacy and American Life*.

40. Thoron (on Emily Beale), p. 369; *Esther*, p. 143. On W. S. Bigelow, see article in *DAB* and Thoron, p. 183 n.

41. Adams on Emerson, Cater, p. 135.

42. *Esther*, pp. 108, 115, 287, 288. Cf. R. P. Blackmur's perceptive analysis of Strong's inactivity in this episode of the novel ("The Novels of Henry Adams," *Sewanee Review*, 51:281–304,

April 1943). Note that Hazard selected novels for Catherine "with the idea of carrying her into the life of the past" (*Esther,* p. 100).

43. *Ibid.,* pp. 117, 157.

44. *Ibid.,* p. 293.

45. *Ibid.,* p. 158 ff.

46. *Ibid.,* pp. 158, 180, 191. Cf. Phillips Brooks, *The Influence of Jesus* (1879), Lecture III, and Allen, *Brooks,* II, p. 533.

47. *Esther,* pp. 18, 186.

48. *Esther,* pp. 198, 199, 191. Balfour, *Defence of Philosophical Doubt* (London, 1879), p. 325. Huxley, *Essays,* IX.

49. *Esther,* pp. 201, 202, 204. Cf. Brooks's habitual appeal to "those deeper instincts of the human constitution which do not originate so much in the mind as in the heart." Reason had been unduly exaggerated, obscuring the "mighty functions of the human will" (Allen, *Brooks,* II, p. 345). William James would, of course, supply the scientific rationale for the opinion put into Strong's mouth, but whereas Hazard professes like William James that the will is free, Strong acts on the contrary hypothesis.

50. *Esther,* p. 22. "King" Robert Hooper was the brother of Marian's great-grandfather (*Hooper Genealogy*). I am indebted to R. P. Blackmur for kindly calling my attention to Hawthorne's story as a clue to the reading of *Esther.* On the tyranny of ancestral associations, see "The Custom House," introductory to *The Scarlet Letter,* in *Novels and Tales of Hawthorne* (Modern Library), p. 90. For a few significant allusions to Hawthorne, see Ford I, pp. 168, 219.

51. *Esther,* pp. 28, 29.

52. *Novels and Tales of Hawthorne,* p. 620. Father John La Farge, S.J., narrates that "though he was a Unitarian by profession, Edward Hooper [Marian Adams's brother] entertained a deep devotion to the Blessed Virgin. . . . Every night, before they went to bed, Mr. Hooper gathered his five daughters around him and said a prayer to Our Lady" (*The Manner Is Ordinary,* p. 74). The prayer aroused in one of the girls the curious wish that "everybody will sleep well, *except the Jews.*" A wish devoutly concurred in by the English historian Edward Augustus Freeman, who recorded the anecdote, after a visit to the Gurneys, in a letter to his wife, October 30, 1881 (quoted in Malcolm Hay, *The Foot of Pride,* p. 213).

53. *Esther,* p. 291. Further on Pascal's wager, see Ford II, p. 295. On tyranny of the self, *Esther,* p. 297 ff.

54. *Esther,* p. 297 ff. Adams quoted in King to Hay, 1886. Cater Transcripts, MHS. Cf. Ward, *Dynamic Sociology* I, p. 697,

on "the exceedingly pernicious influence" of the "doctrine of immortality."

55. *Esther,* p. 41.
56. *Ibid.,* p. 259.
57. *Ibid.,* p. 269 ff.

Chapter Eight. The Forsaken Garden

1. Shackleton, *Book of Washington,* p. 124. For a view of the house see Dennett, *Hay,* p. 162.

2. Anderson, *Letters,* p. 250; Larkin, *Art and Life in America,* p. 285; Van Rensselaer, *Richardson,* pp. 106–108; Hitchcock, *Architecture of H. H. Richardson,* pp. 121–123 ("relative failures"). Cf. also Jordy, *Adams,* pp. 43–44, and notes 2, 3.

3. Ford I, p. 361; La Farge, *Letters from Japan,* p. 106; Ford I, p. 363.

4. Cater, pp. 146, 152, 154, 156.

5. HA to Parkman, December 21, 1884, Cater, p. 134.

6. Imprint date of the volume, 1885; HA to Bancroft, January 10, 1885, Cater, p. 129.

7. Ford I, p. 362.

8. MA to RWH, March 8, 1885, Adams Papers; Thoron, p. 7; Cater, p. xiv and n. 108.

9. HA to Marian Adams, March 14, 1885, from the collection of twelve letters in the possession of Mrs. Robert W. Homans. Three have been published in Cater, pp. 141, 143, 146. Cater, p. 147. Cf. Adams's sympathy for George Eliot's "isolation," Ford I, p. 322, and his remark to Rebecca [Dodge] Rae, "I have told you again and again that life is not worth having unless one is attached to some one" (September 7, 1889, Cater, p. 188).

10. HA to Marian Adams, March 22, March 28, April 11, 1885, Mrs. Homans' collection.

11. Cater, pp. 147, 144.

12. HA to Hay, Ford I, p. 363. MA to Clara Hay [May? 1885]; on reading Mrs. Carlyle's letters, HA to Gaskell, September 9, 1883, Adams Papers. Record of Deaths, Cambridge, Massachusetts, volume 9, folio 87. Will of Robert William Hooper [1810–1885], appointing Henry Adams one of three trustees of the half-million dollar estate, dated March 4, 1875, and codicil dated April 28, 1882, Records of the Probate Court, Suffolk County, Massachusetts. The remarkable affinity between Marian and her father inspired a friend to remark that "it's ridiculous that any man and woman should be so like one another" (Thoron, p. 371).

Obituary notices appeared in the Boston *Transcript*, April 17, 1885, and the Boston *Herald*, April 17, 1885. One of Dr. Hooper's most notable benefactions was the gift of Washington Allston's painting of "St. Peter and the Angel in Prison" to the Worcester Insane Asylum, of which he was a trustee. Boston *Daily Advertiser*, December 29, 1877.

13. Cater, pp. 149, 145, 151. "On reflection I decided not to venture with my wife on any rough or long work at first; but to try a six weeks' excursion in the Yellowstone; and if it succeeded do the bigger thing next year. So I got Arnold Hague to write off to the Yellowstone to inquire what the cost (hire) of a dozen animals, and the necessary outfit for six weeks would come to. . . . At any rate, please let Logan know that the Canadian journey will not be made this summer, and that we will give him longer notice if we make it next year." HA to Pumpelly, May 21, 1885, Adams Papers.

14. Cater, pp. 151, 152. HA to Field, September 20, 1885, Adams Papers. Treasurer's Book, American Historical Association Papers, Library of Congress.

15. American Historical Association, *Proceedings* (September 8–10), 1885. Cater, p. 153.

16. HA to Dwight, November 4, 1885, Cater, p. 156. Anderson, *Letters and Journals,* November 4, 1885, p. 250. HA to Holt, November 13, 1885, Cater, p. 157.

17. HA to Cunliffe, November 29, 1885, Adams Papers.

18. MA to RWH, January 26, 1879, Adams Papers. On her "taste for horrors," MA to RWH, Christmas Sunday, 1881, Thoron, p. 315. Marian Adams's unsent letter was quoted in part by Ellen Hooper Gurney to E. L. Godkin, December 30, 1885, Godkin Papers, Houghton Library. The scientific evidence for Marian Adams's remark about the prevalence of mental illness in Boston may be found in A. Myerson and R. Boyle, "The Incidence of Manic-Depressive Psychosis in Certain Socially Important Families," *American Journal of Psychiatry,* 1941. Boston "eccentricity" meant as often as not a pathological or a psychotic personality. As one of the authors, Mrs. Boyle, has kindly pointed out to me (letter of July 2, 1954), "Neurotics have an irresistible fascination for one another and patients will marry time and again with unhappy consequences." The in-bred character of Boston society tended to greatly accelerate this process. This situation explains in part the large number of "spend-thrift trusts" established by testators. By way of compensation there has been a correspondingly large number of geniuses and highly endowed individuals. Cf. the tragic suicide of one of Henry Adams's paternal uncles,

George Washington Adams, whose mental aberration was one of the most painful trials of his father, John Quincy Adams (Bemis, *John Quincy Adams and the Union*, pp. 179–181). Francis Galton in his *Hereditary Genius* (1869) noted in his Preface the "painfully close relation" between genius and insanity. See generally, John D. Campbell, *Manic-Depressive Disease*, for a conservative analysis of the disease. It is clear from his discussion that the "dynamic" or "Freudian" school would probably seek the cause of Marian's illness in the traumatic childhood experience resulting from the death of her mother and the resulting profound alteration of her relation to her father.

19. Washington *Critic*, December 7, 1885; Washington *Post*, December 7, 1885; Washington *Evening Star*, December 8, 1885. Notices also appeared in the New York *Times*, December 7, 1885, and the Boston *Transcript* and the Boston *Post*, December 7, 1885, and a friendly obituary in the New York *World*, December 10, 1885. The Boston *Herald*, December 9, 1885, carried a notice that the funeral services would be held that day, Wednesday, at the house in Washington and that the burial would be private. Friends were asked not to send flowers. In accordance with their long-standing resolve (MA to RWH, March 24, 1878, Adams Papers), burial was in Washington, Rock Creek Cemetery. Rev. E. H. Hall of Cambridge traveled to Washington to conduct the services. A very modest headstone marked the grave. See Executor's First Account, Estate of Marian Adams, No. 74682. Probate Court, Suffolk County, Massachusetts.

20. Washington *Critic*, December 9, 1885. Mrs. Whiteside, entry in Miscellaneous Papers, volume 33, p. 34, Shattuck Collection, MHS. New York *Sun*, December 9, 1885.

21. Washington *Critic*, December 12, 1885. New York *World*, December 13, 1885. Chapin, *American Court Gossip*, p. 247. Mrs. Adams once sent a sample of the ill-natured gossip to Mrs. Hay: "Godkin with us a week ago, told of Blaine's remark at a dinner that I had acknowledged the authorship of that mistresspiece [*Democracy*] and then W. W. Phelps added 'The reason of Mrs. Adams's bitterness is that there are refined circles in Washington into which she cannot gain admittance'" (MA to Clara Hay, February 16, 1883, Adams Papers).

22. Boston *Transcript*, December 8, 1885.

23. New York *World*, December 10, 1885; Boston *Herald*, December 9, 1885.

24. *Esther*, p. 38; Thoron, p. 418. Adams's father's loss of memory became so severe by the end of 1882, at the age of seventy-five, that Mrs. Charles Francis Adams, Henry's mother,

became head of the family with an annual income of about $73,000 to manage (HA to Gaskell, December 3, 1882). Marian's "silent prayer," MA to RWH, April 28, 1884, Adams Papers. On Hunt, Thoron, p. 181. On futility of prolonging life, MA to RWH, September 12, 1880, Adams Papers. Jane Carlyle's wish, in Carlyle, *Reminiscences*, p. 505.

25. Simonds, "The Tragedy of Mrs. Henry Adams," *New England Quarterly*, 9:564–582 (1936). James, *Washington Square* (ed. Edel), p. 119.

26. *Esther*, p. 14. Dr. Hooper owned Pew 45 in King's Chapel (H. W. Foote, *Annals of King's Chapel*) Edward Hooper in *Harvard University Memoirs of the Class of 1830*. On Pius IX, MA to RWH, February 10, 1878; on the Comédie Française, MA to RWH, January 18, 1880; on Nordhoff's *God and Future Life*, MA to RWH, November 18, 1883; on Sturgis's advertisement, MA to RWH, July 26, 1883 (Adams Papers).

27. MA to RWH, May 4, 1884, Adams Papers. Note her remark to her father, April 28, 1884, after a four-and-a-half-hour cross-country jaunt with Henry, "No one knows a tenth part of the beauty of this neighborhood unless they explore it on horseback. . . . Our daily rides are a joy" (MA to RWH, May 4, 1884). "Last week, as Clarence King says, I met up with an accident. I wished to go through a marsh, Powhatan [her horse, named after the father of Pocahontas] did not, so he jumped over a white birch which swept me gently into a foot of water where I sat in my best new London habit. . . . It was very comical and very moist" (MA to Elizabeth Cameron, July 26, 1883, Adams Papers).

28. MA to RWH, Karnak, February 16, 1873, Thoron, p. 75.

29. *Esther*, pp. 38, 39.

30. HA to Miss Dodge, as paraphrased in Cater, p. li; Anderson, *Letters and Journals*, December 9, 1885, p. 252.

31. HA to Mrs. John Hay, quoted in Cater, li. Elliott, *Three Generations*, p. 338.

32. The mourning band incident was reported by Adams's niece, Mrs. Robert Homans, in an interview with the author in March 1954. Cf. Thoron, p. 272 n. on the stoical custom of the Sturgises of discouraging "conventional outward signs of mourning." Diary of Charles Francis Adams, Jr., December 8, 1885, Adams Papers. On his nieces, HA to John Chipman Gray, January 25, 1885 [1886] (Houghton Library). Trust Indenture dated January 30, 1886, executed by Henry Adams, naming himself, Edward W. Hooper, and John C. Gray, as trustees, recorded in Book 1168, p. 4, Essex County, Registry of Deeds. Mrs. Adams was the benefici-

470 NOTES: CHAPTER EIGHT

ary of three trusts, in addition to the one created by her father (Executors Inventory, March 26, 1886, Recorded vol. 579, p. 192, Probate Court, Suffolk County). The Beverly Farms house and 22 acre tract on which it stood was valued in the Inventory of Marian Adams's Estate at $25,000, in effect what it had cost (HA to Cunliffe, September 8, 1876, Adams Papers). His equal provision for his wife's nieces is indicated in the Executors Reports on the distribution of his own large estate (over $800,000) after his death in 1918 (Estate of Henry Adams, Docket No. 24633, Probate Court records, Washington, D. C.

33. Hay to Adams, December 9, 1885, Thayer, *Hay*, II, 59, 60. King to HA, December 10, 1885, Cater Transcripts at MHS. HA to Hay, December 8, 1885, Adams Papers.

34. Gurney to Godkin, December 11, 1885, Godkin Papers. HA to Hay, December 17, 1885, Adams Papers.

35. Ellen Gurney to Godkin, December 30, 1885, Godkin Papers. Washington *Critic*, December 19, 1885.

36. "The Heritage of Henry Adams," *Degradation of the Democratic Dogma*, p. 102; Chanler, *Roman Spring*, p. 299.

37. One of the games he whimsically played through the years with his girl nieces was to pretend to be their little boy and he wrote them winsome letters as their little "Dear Dordy," a pet name which they gave him. On his self-mortification and death to the world, "Heritage of Henry Adams," pp. 12, 2. His twelve years of happiness, HA to Godkin, December 16, 1885, Cater, p. 157. Life a theatre, HA to John Chipman Gray, January 25, 1886, Houghton Library. Life with Marian, HA to Holt, March 8 [1886], Cater, p. 158. Johnson, *Remembered Yesterdays*, p. 447 (c. 1905). Thenceforth he appeared to adopt the maxim of his favorite philosopher, Marcus Aurelius: "Consider thyself to be dead, and to have completed thy life up to the present time; and live according to nature the remainder which is allowed thee" (Meditation 56). He afterwards recalled Gurney's ("our old teacher in wisdom") saying to him at this time that "of all moral supports in trial only one was nearly sufficient. That was the Stoic" (HA to H. O. Taylor, February 15, 1915, Cater, p. 768).

38. On "notice to quit" see Ford II, p. 55. Keats, "Ode to a Nightingale"; Tennyson, "Prefatory Sonnet" (March, 1877). On the death of Lowell's wife, quoted in Spiller, ed., *Literary History*, I, 602. Carlyle, *Reminiscences*, p. 505. Agassiz, *Letters and Recollections*, p. 125. On Queen Victoria, *Time Magazine*, January 2, 1950. Mrs. Adams's anecdote, Thoron, p. 452.

39. Anderson, *Letters and Journals*, pp. 309, 310. For a penetrating analysis of these compulsion neuroses see Freud, *Totem*

and Taboo in *Basic Works of Freud* (Modern Library), p. 827.
40. HA to Elizabeth Cameron, December 25, 1885, Adams
Papers. ". . . As examples of Sir Joshua's work, they have a certain value; and if the Museum should think them worth its acceptance, I shall be happy to present them to it in the name of
my wife, who bought them from Mrs. Hughes" (HA to W. W.
Corcoran, May 27, 1886, Corcoran Gallery archives). These por-
traits were listed in *Catalogue of The Corcoran Gallery of Art*
(Washington, 1887). Mrs. Hughes afterwards prevailed upon
Adams to help her reacquire them, since they were family pic-
tures. The trustees acquiesced and the portraits were returned
February 1, 1895, to W. Hallett Phillips acting as Adam's agent
(Phillips to Charles G. Glover, January 28, 1895, Records of
Corcoran Gallery).
41. *Sonnets and Poems of Petrarch,* trans. Joseph Auslander
(New York, 1932), pp. 309, 254, 236. Cf. also one of the passages
marked by Adams in his copy of the 1886 edition of Rousseau's
Confessions, p. 233 (Plon ed., p. 62), in which Rousseau recalled his despair at the loss of Mme. de Warens: "Ce moment
fut affreux: ceux qui le suivirent furent toujours sombres. J'étais
jeune encore, mais ce doux sentiment de jouissance et d'espérance
qui vivifie la jeunesse me quitta pour jamais. Dès lors, l'être sen-
sible fut mort à demi. Je ne vis plus devant moi que les tristes
restes d'une vie insipide" (cited in Baym, *French Education of
Henry Adams,* p. 142). Among his most treasured personal possessions were three volumes of the poems of Elizabeth Barrett
Browning (New York, 1857), Adams Papers, "Miscellaneous."
42. The concluding couplet of "Itylus" reads:

> Thou hast forgotten, O summer swallow,
> But the world shall end when I forget.

See Swinburne's *Poems and Ballads,* esp. pp. 57, 75, in Adams's
copy at MHS. Cf. also his scorings in 1866 edition, especially p.
203, "Too soon did I love it, and lost love's rose, / And I cared not
for glory's." On Swinburne, Ford I, pp. 352, 357. Sonnet translated in *Esther,* p. 114. HA to Elizabeth Cameron, March 1, 1916.
Ford I, p. 638. Cater, p. 394 (Rebecca Dodge married Charles
Rae in 1890, *ibid.,* p. 145 n). In his copy of Helen Hay Whitney's
Sonnets and Songs, inscribed "To Uncle Henry from his niece
Helen. 1905," Adams carefully scored the passage (p. 14), "Beg-
gared of all, I face the world forlorn." For a remarkable fictional
treatment of the romantic idealization of the dead, see Henry
James's story "The Altar of the Dead," with its ritual of the
"religion of the Dead."

Chapter Nine. The Season of Nirvana

1. *Esther,* p. 211.
2. HA to Hay, October 1, 1885, Adams Papers. On Pumpelly's visits, MA to RWH, April 2, May 4, 1884, January 7, 1885; and La Farge, January 7, 1885, Adams Papers. Agassiz, *Letters, passim.*
3. On the "Ascension" painting, Cortissoz, *La Farge,* p. 165. Adams as host, Cater, p. 161, n. Attitude toward women, La Farge, *The Manner Is Ordinary,* p. 29. Freedom from vice, Cortissoz, *La Farge,* p. 212.
4. La Farge to Adams, 1887, quoted in La Farge, *The Manner Is Ordinary,* p. 4. For Adams's estimates of La Farge, *Education,* p. 369 ff. Ford II, pp. 559, 567, 572. La Farge's reproach, *Education,* p. 370. Purpose of trip, La Farge, *An Artist's Letters,* p. 17. Adams owned the 1871 edition of Pumpelly's book.
5. Interest in *kakemonos* and things Japanese, cf. MA to RWH, October 23, 1883, Adams Papers; cf. also Thoron, p. 305. C. A. Dana asked for his expert opinion on Chinese porcelain (Dana to HA, April 2, 1889, Adams Papers). On an early Japanese visitor, MA to Gaskell, May 17, 1874; Holmes sent on a Japanese lawyer, MA to RWH, January 20, 1884, Adams Papers.
6. Plan to go to Pacific, Ford I, p. 167. Yoshida and archaic law, MA to RWH, November 19, 1878, Adams Papers.
7. On influence of Morse's lectures in Boston, Carter, *Gardner,* and "Morse" in *DAB.* Cf. Lafcadio Hearn, *Life and Letters,* p. 290 ff., on a new edition of Arnold's *Light of Asia,* in 1883: "After all Buddhism in some esoteric form may prove the religion of the future. . . . What are the heavens of all Christian fancies after all but Nirvana, — extinction of individuality in the eternal." Adams, of course, procured a copy of Murray [author: Basil Hall Chamberlain] (Cater, p. 164).
8. Condolence calls, Cater, pp. 158, 159. HA to Hay, January 22, 1886, Adams Papers.
9. HA to Ford and to Mrs. Ford, Cater, pp. 159, 160. Cf. his genealogical researches of the previous summer.
10. *Papers of American Historical Association,* II, 46 (meeting dates, April 27–29, 1886). Cf. Adams, *History,* I, 228, 234, on Jefferson and patronage.
11. HA to Gaskell, April 25, 1886, Adams Papers.
12. *Ibid.*
13. New York *Times,* April 29, 1886. Richardson's funeral, Anderson, *Letters and Journals,* p. 257. CFA, Jr. in Van Rens-

selaer, *Richardson*. Allusions to "Fez" Richardson, Ford I, p. 110, and *Education*, p. 213.

14. Richardson's "overflow of life," Ford I, p. 490; Cater, p. 755.

15. King to Hay, [1886]. He first allowed Hay to guess the authorship: "Of course you see it. *Esther* is by Henry"; also, King to Hay, [1886] (Cater Transcripts, MHS).

16. King to Hay, June 10, 1886, Cater Transcripts, MHS. Ford I, pp. 365 (probably reached Omaha June 6), 366. Cf. La Farge's allusion to the Omaha incident in his dedication to Adams of *An Artist's Letters from Japan* and in the chapter, "Nirvana."

17. Ford I, pp. 365, 366.

18. HA to Dwight, Cater, pp. 161, 163.

19. Cater, pp. 163, 165, 166; Ford I, pp. 366, 370.

20. Ford I, pp. 367, 372. On Ernest Fenollosa, see *DAB*. Born in 1853, he had gone to Japan in 1878 to teach political economy and philosophy at the Imperial University in Tokio and became a Buddhist convert, as did W. Sturgis Bigelow (*DAB*).

21. Journey to Nikko, Ford I, p. 371. Adams quoted in La Farge, *An Artist's Letters*, p. 81; the letters were first published in the *Century Magazine*, February 1890, *et seq.*, and in book form in 1897. *Chartres*, p. 97.

22. Ford I, pp. 367, 369, Loti, "Japanese Women," *Harpers Magazine*, 1890–91. On archaic society, Ford I, pp. 376, 377. La Farge, *An Artist's Letters*, p. 201.

23. HA to Hay, Ford I, p. 377. Morgan, *Ancient Society* (New York, 1877), pp. 454, 455. Ford I, p. 378 (bric-a-brac).

24. HA to Dwight on Huckleberry Finn, Cater, p. 167. Hirschfeld, *Men and Women*, p. 7, on "fetish." Ford I, pp. 369, 381. Cf. A. E. Jones, "Mark Twain and Sexuality," PMLA, 71:595–616 (1956).

25. Adams's "historical sense," La Farge, *An Artist's Letters*, p. 25. The Adams library at MHS contains a large album of photographic views taken by Adams of temples, gates, and scenery in Japan. He filled his small travel notebook with all the miscellany of a philosophic tourist: items to purchase, phonetic transcriptions of Japanese words, financial transactions, queries about places and customs, tiny sketches, etc., etc.

26. Adams's purchases, Cater, p. 170. La Farge, *An Artist's Letters*, p. 84.

27. *Ibid.*, pp. 175, 98, Dedication.

28. *Ibid.*, pp. 106, 107, 112.

29. On the androgynous nature of the Daibutsu of Kamakura, Hirschfeld, *Men and Women*, p. 32.

30. La Farge, *An Artist's Letters*, p. 175. On Kwannon, Pumpelly, *Travels*, p. 168. See Suzuki, *Essence of Buddhism*, for character of Kwannon.

31. Cater, pp. 168, 165.

32. Ford I, p. 377.

33. Alfred de Musset, *Poésies Nouvelles* (Paris, 1885), p. 149. Adams owned eight volumes of his works. The story of "Le Fils du Titien," was also told in prose by de Musset in *Pages Choisis* (Paris, 1902), p. 186.

34. *Paradiso*, XIII, XVII. Pocket notebooks, Adams Papers.

35. Proverb in Murray [Basil Hall Chamberlain], *Japan*, Fourth Edition, p. 191. Details of journeying, Ford I, pp. 373, 375, 379; Cater, p. 172.

36. Ford I, p. 379.

37. Cater, p. 171. On Fuji, La Farge, *An Artist's Letters*, p. 261.

38. Bishop, *Unbeaten Tracks in Japan* (New York, n.d.) p. ix.

39. HA to Hay, Cater, p. 174.

40. Death of Gurney, *ibid.*, p. 172. Decline of CFA, HA to Gaskell, June 14, 1876, Adams Papers.

41. Plan of travel, Cater, p. 174. On Gould's unscrupulous financiering see Cochran and Miller, *Age of Enterprise*, pp. 147–149. *Chapters of Erie* (1886 ed.), p. 1.

42. Charles Francis Adams, Jr., 1889, *Memorabilia*, Adams Papers.

43. Quoted in Lodge, *Early Memories*, p. 301.

44. CFA, Jr., *Memorabilia*, April 21, 1889. HA to Cunliffe, December 16, 1888, Adams Papers.

45. Henry's maxim, HA to Cunliffe, January 17, 1887; on character of John, HA to Elizabeth Cameron, September 7, 1887, Adams Papers.

46. Abigail Brooks Adams to HA, October 4, 1858. On ethics, CFA to HA, October 25, 1858. The old man, devoutly religious, continued to attend church services practically to the end of his life (CFA manuscript diary, *passim*). Early ambition, HA to Abigail Brooks Adams, February 18, 1860, Adams Papers. HA to Gaskell, May 24, 1875, Cater, p. 67. William Everett, *Address in Commemoration of the Life and Services of Charles Francis Adams* (Cambridge, 1887).

47. Last Will of Charles Francis Adams, executed September 12, 1871, filed December 6, 1886 (No. 25276, Probate Office Norfolk County, Massachusetts). Executors First and Final Account, Estate of Charles Francis Adams, March 2, 1887. The coin collection, considerably added to by Henry Adams who

himself became an expert numismatist, was bequeathed by him to the Massachusetts Historical Society. Henry's father also left to him, "my gold sleeve buttons with the hair of my parents and grandparents, given to me by my father in 1826. Also the gold seal of my father with the motto 'Libertas, Amicitia Fides.'" For estimates of Henry Adams's income see Cater, pp. xcii ("not less than twenty-five thousand dollars"), cxviii, n. 196; Berkelman, "Clarence King," *American Quarterly*, 5:324 ("inherited an annual income of $50,000").

48. On problems of a trustee, HA to Gaskell, May 8, 1887. HA to CFA, Jr., April 30, 1867, Adams Papers.

49. CFA, Jr., *Memorabilia*, June 30, June 18, 1889, Adams Papers.

50. Francis Child of Harvard helped with the phrasing, HA to Child, July 25, 1887; HA to Cunliffe on Tennyson, January 17, 1887, Adams Papers.

51. Hay, "Israel," *Century*, 34:127–128. HA to Hay, Ford I, p. 383. Lowell, *Atlantic Monthly*, February 1887.

52. HA to Cunliffe, July 15, 1888, Adams Papers. On the same day he wrote Gaskell: "The process of growing old is infernal torture. One is conscious of dying with one's friends." Adams Papers.

53. HA to Cunliffe, January 17, 1887; HA to Hay, August 4, 1887; HA to Hay, May 23, 1887, Adams Papers. For allusions to his intention to visit China, see also Ford I, pp. 382, 392, 398; Cater, p. 174. Among the books in his collection at MHS are William Wells, *The Middle Kingdom* (1883), and Robert Morison, *Dialogues and Detached Sentences in the Chinese Language*. After twenty years of globe-trotting he was still planning that ultimate exploration that he was never to make. Cf. Cater, p. 614.

54. China "nearer," HA to Hay, May 15, 1887, Adams Papers. Two draft volumes, Cater, p. 176. Opinion of the *History*, Hay to Clark, May 14, 1887, Hay, *Letters* (1908), II, 113.

55. HA to Parkman, December 21, 1884, Cater, p. 134. Ford I, p. 397 (his "eternal history"). Elizabeth Cameron to HA, September 2, 1888, Adams Papers.

56. Ford I, p. 384. Cater, p. 179. Ford I, p. 385.

57. Cf. Dennett, *Hay*, p. 138. HA to Hay, Ford I, p. 385. Progress of *History*, HA to Elizabeth Cameron, September 7, 1887; HA to Dwight, August 4, August 31, September 2, September 22, 1887; HA to Hay, September 20, October 16, 1887, Adams Papers. The new greenhouse, Ford I, p. 386.

58. King to Mrs. Hay, December 30. 1887. Cater Transcripts,

MHS. Quieting effect of marriage, Cater, p. 66. HA to Gaskell, May 8, 1887, Adams Papers.

59. HA to Hay, May 15, 1887, Adams Papers.

60. Opinion of Spring Rice, Ford I, p. 383. Gwynn, *Letters and Friendships of Sir Cecil Spring Rice,* I, 64.

61. *Ibid.,* pp. 68, 78, 102.

62. HA to Elizabeth Cameron, "Wednesday" [1887]; October 10, 1887, Adams Papers. Washington, birth certificate 43514.

63. HA to Elizabeth Cameron, August 8, September 14, October 6, 1887, Adams Papers. Cf. HA to Elizabeth Cameron, March 20, 1904. "Now that my nervous system has gone to wreck, I take again to babies as I did to Martha seventeen years ago. If I only had you to fall back on."

64. The details of Ellen Gurney's death were reported in the Boston *Transcript,* November 22, 1887. Cater, pp. 179, 180.

65. Henry Adams Diary [February 12, 1888–July 7, 1889], Adams Papers. On the jaunt to Cuba, Ford I, p. 388.

66. HA to Elizabeth Cameron, March 7, 1888. Diary, March 20, 1888, Adams Papers. Cf. his report to Hay, HA to Hay, March 4 [1888], Cater, p. 311 [misdated 1894].

67. The doll's house which delighted the little girls who were brought to visit him is described in Chanler, *Roman Spring,* p. 300. HA to O. W. Holmes, Jr., November 3, 1887, Holmes Papers. HA to Cunliffe, May 27, 1888, Adams Papers.

68. The "happy stock of the Mathers," HA to Elizabeth Cameron, December 20, 1914, Ford II, p. 628.

69. HA to Hay, Quincy, September 23, 1888, Adams Papers. Cf. allusion to Gibbon in Ford I, p. 392. Cf. Gibbon's famous account of his deliverance in his *Autobiography:* "After laying down my pen, I took several turns in a berceau, or covered walk of acacias, which commands a prospect of the country, the lake, and the mountains. The air was temperate, the sky was serene, the silver orb of the moon was reflected from the waters, and all nature was silent. I will not dissemble the first emotions of joy on the recovery of my freedom, and perhaps the establishment of my fame. . . ." On the last page of the *Decline,* Gibbon entered the date of its completion: June 27, 1787.

70. Passage in brackets omitted in published letter, Ford I, p. 395.

71. HA to Martha Cameron, September 9, 1888; HA to Elizabeth Cameron, September 8, 1888, Adams Papers. To help pass the time at Beverly, Mrs. Cameron took up photography, the darkroom facilities being available as Marian Adams had left them.

72. La Farge dedicated his *An Artist's Letters from Japan* to Okakura also. See the note prefixed to that volume: ". . . these notes, written at the time when I first met you . . ." See also La Farge, *The Manner is Ordinary*, p. 12 ff., for a few details concerning Okakura [Kakuzo] and his relations with the artist's family. On the first pose, Saint-Gaudens, *Reminiscences*, I, 148. On Okakura see also *Bulletin*, Boston Museum of Fine Arts, XI (1913), pp. 72–75; Okakura dedicated his *Book of Tea* (1906) to La Farge.

73. Saint-Gaudens to HA, July 8, 1888. Stanford White to HA, August 9 and 13, 1888. Records of negotiations are in Saint-Gaudens Papers, Library of Congress.

74. Saint-Gaudens to HA, January 25, October 11, November 5, 1888, January 3, 1889, March 21, 1889; Adams, *Diary*, Sunday, December 10, 1888, on visit to Saint-Gaudens' studio, Adams Papers. Saint-Gaudens, *Reminiscences*, I, 359 ff. Saint-Gaudens' memorandum, in letter of Homer Saint-Gaudens to HA, January 27, 1908. The first model of the cowl-shaded face did not have the right hand raised to the face, but the drapery dropped down along the side of the cheek. See the fine illustration in Leslie, *American Wonderland*, facing p. 54. The cost of the memorial did not exceed $25,000 (Ford II, p. 285).

75. On the "Silence," Saint-Gaudens, *Reminiscences*, I, 140. On the fold of drapery, Homer Saint-Gaudens to HA, January 27, 1908. Saint-Gaudens to HA, May 6, May 16, 1889, February 21, 1890. Adams Papers.

76. HA to Hay, Ford I, p. 389. Departure for China, HA to Hay, September 12, 1888, Adams Papers. The extensive series of letters from Dwight and from Adams to Scribner are in the files of Charles Scribner's Sons, New York.

77. Dwight to Scribner, July 12, 1888 enclosing Adams's memorandum. HA to Scribner, August 1, 1888, Scribner files. Cf. Bancroft's outlay of $50,000 to $70,000 on source materials (Howe, *Life and Letters of George Bancroft*, II, 261).

78. HA to Scribner, August 1, 1888, Scribner files; Scribner to HA, August 7, 1888. Adams, *Diary*, September 16, 1888, Adams Papers. Gilder, *Letters*, p. 201. Sales and royalty figures kindly supplied by Charles Scribner's Sons. On Macaulay's *History*, cf. H. V. Routh, *Towards the Twentieth Century*, p. 19.

79. Scribner to HA, December 13, 1888, Adams Papers.

80. HA to Scribner, November 26, 1888, January 8, September 20, 1889. Adams apparently decided not to print a "Ladies Edition" of the Madison volumes, and seems to have directed that the gifts be completed from the trade edition. His list to Scribner

included seventeen names: Elizabeth Adams, Lucy Baxter, Elizabeth Cameron, Mrs. Archibald Campbell, Catholic University of America, Miss Frelinghuysen, Arnold Hague, Col. John Hay, Eunice Cooper, Clarence King, Constance Lodge, James Lowndes, William H. Phillips, Mrs. Charles Rae, Mrs. Theodore Roosevelt, Prof. Charles W. Stoddard, Ward Thoron (Scribner files).

81. HA to Scribner, December 19, 1888, Scribner files. Scribner to HA, December 20, 1888, Adams Papers.

82. On his original intentions, Ford I, pp. 346, 357. On the Epilogue, HA to Scribner, January 12, 1890, Scribner files.

83. BA to HA, March 7, 1887, Houghton Library. Beringause, *Brooks Adams*, p. 92. Henry's testy reply that silence was really best elicited from Brooks a quieting, "My dear fellow — don't get mad" (BA to HA, March 8, 1887).

84. The North Carolina expedition, Ford I, p. 397; Cater, pp. 182, 183.

85. HA to Burlingame, May 3, 1890, published in Burlingame, *Of Making Many Books* (New York, 1946).

86. Ford I, p. 398.

87. JQA, 2d, to HA, May 18, 1889. Fate of presidential ancestors, HA to Elizabeth Cameron, June 8, 1889, Adams Papers. Ford I, p. 399. HA to Mrs. E. W. Lippitt: "I do not doubt but that I have inherited her disposition, for I cannot see anything in life worth having, except the things one wants to have. When one has reached this stage, life is over" (Cater, p. 185).

88. HA to Scribner, August 19, 1888, Scribner files. HA to Paul Hamilton, quoted in Paul Hamilton to HA, April 9, 1887, Adams Papers. See on Hamilton, Adams, *History*, V, 9; VI, 290, 395, 398, 425.

89. Wheeler to HA, April 3, 1890, supplemented by a letter from a family connection, Eliot C. Clark, dated April 30, 1890, Adams Papers. One sentence especially objected to, read: "His army became mutinous from disgust at his vacillation and at their own idleness." This became, "His army lost respect for him in consequence of his failure to attack Malden." *History*, VI, 314, also VI, 417. T. Peyton Giles to HA, January 12, February 5, February 21, 1910 (Adams Papers), all challenging the assertion in Adams's *Randolph*, p. 141, "Giles of Virginia, whom no man ever trusted without regret," and other derogatory characterizations of Giles's grandfather. Adams's defense left him quite unconvinced. See also Gabriel E. Manigault, "General George Izard's Military Career: A Reply to Mr. Henry Adams," *Magazine of American History*, 26:457–462 (December, 1891), defending Izard's reputation.

90. HA to Cunliffe, March 11, 1890, Adams Papers. On La Farge, HA to Hay, July 9, 1890. Cater, pp. 190, 191. Proof sheets, Ford I, p. 404. Stock-room records, Scribner files.

Chapter Ten. Decline and Fall of the Hero

1. De Tocqueville, *Democracy in America* (New York, 1946), ed. H. S. Commager, p. 242.

2. Adams's copy of *La Guerre et la Pais* (3 vols., Paris, 1884) is at MHS. Cf. on American destiny as the leader of Christian Anglo-Saxon civilization, Josiah Strong, *Our Country* (1885). On the mission of Russia see Dostoyevsky, *Diary of a Writer* (New York, 1949), *passim*.

3. HA to Tilden, January 24, 1883, Cater, p. 126. *History*, VI, 69, 75. *War and Peace* (Modern Library), pp. 669, 670, 671, 917, 1095, 1321; cf. also pp. 792, 1317, 1330, 1336, 1349, 1351, 1359; note especially p. 1318: "To find component forces equal to the composite or resultant force, the sum of the components must equal the resultant," and p. 1351: "In history the new view says: 'It is true we are not conscious of our dependence, but by admitting our free will we arrive at absurdity, while by admitting our dependence on the external world, on time, and cause, we arrive at laws."

4. *History*, I, 31. Gibbon, *Autobiography* (Everyman's Library), p. 124. "It was at Rome, on the 15th of October, 1764, as I sat musing amidst the ruins of the Capitol, while the barefooted friars were singing vespers in the Temple of Jupiter, that the idea of writing the Decline and Fall of the City first started to my mind." Cf. also concluding sentence of the *Decline and Fall*.

5. Buffon cited by Jefferson in *Notes on Virginia*, answer to the sixth query of the Marquis de Barbé-Marbois; Comte, *Positive Philosophy*, p. 666. Arnold, *Discourses in America*, especially "Numbers; or the Majority and the Remnant." See also Lippincott, *Victorian Critics of Democracy*. For one species of refutation see Lowell, "On a Certain Condescension in Foreigners" (1864).

6. *History*, IX, 173; allusion to his friend Gannett's article, "The Wealth of the United States," *International Review*, May 1882, an article Adams had "caused . . . to be written" (Ford I, p. 339). The open-end theory, *History*, IX, 241. Cf. Brooks Adams's later version of it, Anderson, *Brooks Adams*, pp. 66, 78–79, and *passim*.

7. *History,* I, 184; HA to W. James, Cater, p. 122; *History,* IX, 241. The perspective is suggestively treated in William R. Taylor, "Historical Bifocals on the year 1800," *New England Quarterly,* 23:172–186 (1950). Comte, p. 483.

8. Bancroft, *History,* II, chapter xix. Adams, *History,* IX, 219, IV, 289.

9. *Ibid.,* IX, 224.

10. Buckle, *History of Civilization in England,* I, 3; Fiske, *Outlines of Cosmic Philosophy,* II, 195, 228. Cf. postulate of a "theory of the progress of civilization" in HA to Lodge, February 1, 1878 (Ford I, p. 305). Cf. also Henry George, *Progress and Poverty* (Modern Library), p. 478 ff., for a critique of "the vulgar explanation of progress."

11. Adams, *History,* IX, 222. HA to Parkman, December 21, 1884, Cater, p. 134.

12. Comte, p. 466; De Tocqueville, *Democracy in America,* p. 29; Adams, *History,* IX, 224.

13. HA to Tilden, January 24, 1883; Cater, p. 126. *History,* IX, 225.

14. Comte, pp. 465, 471, 472. On Spencer, Fiske, *Excursions,* p. 172. For replies to W. James, "Great Men, Great Thoughts, and the Environment," *Princeton Review,* October 1880, see Fiske, "Sociology and Hero Worship," *Atlantic,* January 1881, and Grant Allen, *Atlantic,* March 1881; Ward, *Dynamic Sociology,* II, 4. Cf. Lincoln's remark, "Events have controlled me," quoted in A. Nevins, "Is History Made by Heroes?" *Saturday Review,* November 5, 1955; Galton, *Hereditary Genius,* p. 35.

15. Morison, *Macaulay,* p. 143 and *passim;* see allusion to this biography in Ford I, 346. HA to Gaskell, December 12, 1886, Ford I, 383; *History,* IX, 224; Ford I, p. 357. Cf. HA to Parkman, December 21, 1884, "a new school of history will rise which will leave us antiquated" (Cater, p. 134).

16. Fiske, *Outlines,* II, 209, 372; Comte, pp. 457, 467. Cf. Oliver Wendell Holmes, Jr., to Pollock, *Holmes-Pollock Letters,* p. 58, July 2, 1895, on Spencer: "I doubt if any writer of English except Darwin has done so much to affect our whole way of thinking about the universe."

17. *History,* IX, 225. Cater, p. 126. For Adams's re-use of the metaphor, see Jordy, *Adams,* pp. 127, 128. Cf. entry in Adams's notebook, "Manners and Customs": "In degree as the historian grows old he sees in the world less personality and more generalisation: less chance and more fate" (Adams library, MHS).

18. Spencer, *First Principles,* p. 230; Fiske, I, 296; Spencer, p. 482. Adams owned the 1882 edition of Spencer's *First Principles.*

The widely scattered scorings and queries, pages 5, 196, and 215, suggest an attentive reading of the work.

19. Spencer, pp. 488, 517; Adams, *History*, IX, 225.

20. Comte, p. 467; Fiske, II, 193; Ward, *Dynamic Sociology*, pp. 166, 167.

21. Fiske, II, 227.

22. Quoted in Fiske, II, 213; Morgan, *Ancient Society*, pp. vi, 30.

23. Spencer, *Education*, p. 54 ff.; Comte, p. 483.

24. *History*, I, 73. "Ideas govern the world, or throw it into chaos" (Comte, p. 36); "Ideas do not govern or overthrow the world; the world is governed or overthrown by feelings, to which ideas serve only as guides" (Spencer in "The Classification of the Sciences," pp. 37–38, quoted in Mill, *Auguste Comte and Positivism*, p. 102). Adams's library at MHS includes also the Harriet Martineau translation of Comte, published in 1853, and the Littré edition in French of 1863. The annotations·of the law of phases and of fetishism (pages 157 to 279, Martineau ed., vol. II) probably date back, at least initially, to the early 1870's. Cf. allusion in Adams's *Syllabus: History II*, Harvard Library. Cf. discussion of Comtism in Jordy, p. 113 and *passim*.

25. Adams, *History*, I, 16, 29, 30, 17. Adams's method of organizing his materials seems much like that used in Macaulay's famous third chapter, being roughly parallel in the topics considered. To Macaulay, England, like the America of Adams's analysis, was also exempt from the evils of the Continent, thanks to her geographical isolation and moral superiority, and she too underwent "portentously rapid" change at an "accelerated velocity" (Macaulay, *History*, I, 258, 306). For an admirable analysis of the parallels, see Jordy, *Adams*, p. 76 ff.

26. Adams, *History*, I, 60, 65, 73, 59, 57, 62, 73, 74.

27. *Ibid.*, 66, 41, 42.

28. *Ibid.*, 157.

29. *Ibid.*, 159, 161. Cf. an earlier use of this striking figure of speech in HA to Lodge, May 21, 1881, Ford I, p. 328.

30. Adams, *History*, I, 163, 181. See article by Edward Atkinson, "Relative Strength and Weakness of Nations," *Century*, 33: 423 (1886).

31. Adams, *History*, I, 168.

32. *Ibid.*, VII, 403; V, 190.

33. *Ibid.*, I, 115; III, 367, 366; I, 143, 113, 112.

34. *Ibid.*, II, 65, 61, 13. On "Chaos," *ibid.*, II, 315, IV, 301, 370, V, 212, VI, 231, VII, 69. Cf. also vol. III, pp. 102, 124, 397.

35. HA to BA, October 7, 1900, Cater, p. 499.

36. Adams, *History*, VI, 379.
37. *Ibid.*, VI, 374, VIII, 362, 365.
38. *Ibid.*, IV, 289, 211.
39. *Ibid.*, V, 196, IV, 277.
40. Cater, p. 645.
41. Adams, *History*, VII, 402; IV, 277; III, 421. For the figure of the precocious child, VI, 123. A favorite figure, it had occurred earlier in IV, 302.
42. *Ibid.*, IV, 300, 302.
43. *Ibid.*, VI, 67. Cf. also another critical nexus of power in the Baltic, *ibid.*, V, 408.
44. *Ibid.*, I, 176, III, 370, II, 320.
45. *Ibid.*, IV, 300, 301, II, 95, 90, 115, III, 77. Cf. other lesser steps toward centralization: *ibid.*, II, 244, 153.
46. *Ibid.*, IV, 27, 79, VI, 375, VII, 319, 320.
47. *Ibid.*, IV, 135.
48. *Ibid.*, IV, 161. Cf. *ibid.*, I, 403, III, 80, VI, 282; IV, 161. Besides the forces of inertia there were such active "denationalizing forces" as the Essex Junto and the Burr Conspiracy, III, 217, and the Hartford Convention, III, 328.
49. Adams's use of both these analogies suggests that he did not, any more than Spencer or Fiske, distinguish between organic and inorganic "evolution" (HA to Parkman, December 21, 1884, Cater, p. 134). On the crystal, *History*, IX, 224. Cf. Henry George, *Progress and Poverty* (Modern Library), p. 487, which partially adopts the Spencerian formula.
50. *History*, III, 208, 211, 197, 196. Cf. De Tocqueville, "If those nations whose social condition is democratic could remain free only while they inhabit uncultivated regions, we must despair of the future destiny of the human race" (*Democracy in America*, p. 418). *History*, III, 212, in spirit a reflection of Carlyle's *Past and Present* and its anxieties about democracy.
51. Adams, *History*, IV, 411, 441, 184, I, 179.
52. *Ibid.*, I, 184.
53. *Ibid.*, IX, 80, 52, 46, 45.
54. *Ibid.*, IX, 80, 81.
55. *Ibid.*, IX, 105, 119, 132, 158, 104, 135.
56. *Ibid.*, IX, 172, 174.
57. *Ibid.*, IX, 175.
58. *Ibid.*, IX, 175, 180, 183, 185, 186.
59. *Ibid.*, IX, 187, 192, II, 243, IX, 188.
60. *Ibid.*, IX, 194, V, 354. HA to Bancroft, February 11, 1886. Ford I, p. 364. Note Marian Adams's exclamation "Judge Gray had better never been born than back up Ben Butler in this

shameful fashion" (MA to RWH, March 9, 1884, Adams Papers). The case was *Juilliard* vs. *Greenman*, 110 U.S. 421 (1884). Cf. George Bancroft, *Plea for the Constitution of the United States, Wounded in the House of Its Guardians* (New York, 1886).
61. Adams, *History*, IX, 221, 227.
62. *Ibid.*, 236, 238.
63. *Ibid.*, 241; cf. *Young Henry Adams*, p. 271. Charles annotation, Draft Volume III (1811), p. 287, MHS. The *History* "intended only to serve the future historian with a fixed and documented starting-point" (Cater, p. 480).

Chapter Eleven. Art and Scholarship

1. Adams, *History*, IV, 29; Draft Volume II (privately printed), p. 324, Adams Library, MHS.
2. Ford I, pp. 284, 323.
3. Adams, *History*, I, 277, 144. Ford I, p. 160. HA to C. W. Eliot, March 3, 1877, Cater, p. 81. Cf. HA to CFA, Jr., May 1, 1863, *A Cycle*, I, 281, 282.
4. Allusions to Hildreth in Ford I, pp. 65, 73. Hildreth, *History of the United States*, IV, 293, VI, 617, 618, and as cited in Kraus, *A History*, p. 247. Jefferson's sins, Adams, *History*, II, 258, 365, 367, 373, 375, III, 203. Marginal comment, Draft Volume II, p. 42. On weaknesses of Jefferson, Adams, *History*, II, 207, III, 115, 456, 457, VI, 336, 337. Jefferson "deliberately ordered his Indian agents to tempt the tribal chiefs into debt in order to oblige them to sell the tribal lands" (*History*, VI, 74, 75).
5. HA to O. W. Holmes, Jr., November 3, 1887, Holmes Papers. Ford I, 338. *History*, II, 49.
6. Draft Volume II, p. 227.
7. Draft Volume III, p. 436; Cf. *History*, VI, 288. Hewitt to HA, December 27, 1889, Adams Papers.
8. *History*, III, 22; Draft Volume II, p. 15.
9. Cf. *History*, VI, 336. Draft Volume III, pp. 2, 7 ff., and *History*, VI, 2. On "crumbling of worlds," Ford II, p. 627.
10. Draft Volume II, pp. 51, 115, 340. *History*, VI, 212; Draft Volume III (Bancroft copy), pp. 221, 399, MHS.
11. Ford I, p. 458.
12. *Ibid.*; draft passage in ledger, MHS.
13. Draft Volume II, p. 460 (cf. *History*, IV, 248); Draft Volume III, p. 251. HA to Field, September 20, 1885, Adams Papers. Draft Volume III, p. 251. HA to Hewitt, January 7, 1904, Cater, p. 548.

14. Dwight to Scribner, September 22, 1889, Scribner files. HA to Cunliffe, November 10, 1889, March 11, 1890, July 14, 1889, January 4, 1890, Adams Papers. Adams also made a holiday trip of the expedition to Ottawa, taking three of his nieces with him. Details given in HA to Hay, September 14, 1889, and HA to Elizabeth Cameron, September 5, 1889, Adams Papers, and in Cater, pp. 187, 189. Chagrined by the stir caused by his absence from Brooks's wedding, he defended himself to Mrs. Cameron: "No, I was not at the wedding. The fault was not mine, for my journey had been fixed long before the engagement took place; but I was sorry, for I always like to do the correct conventional thing and I ought to have been there. The refinement of satire in being conventional would not have been my inducement in this case, as in some conceivable weddings. Rather I should have enjoyed seeing Brooks submit to the conventionalities which he has hitherto made a business of swearing at" (HA to Elizabeth Cameron, September 15, 1889). Brooks's earlier unsuccessful and romantic courtship of a young woman had caused some talk. This time, with characteristic impulsiveness, he chose to waive romantic overtures (cf. Cleveland Amory, *The Proper Bostonians,* p. 166). On the Albany fire, alluded to in J. F. Jameson to HA, December 17, 1912, Adams Papers.

Sixty years of intensive historical research into almost every aspect of the period have not materially weakened Adams's claim, although his interpretations of particular figures and events have been challenged by a large number of scholars and partisans of special causes. See the admirably annotated bibliography, "Some Reviews and Corrections of the *History,*" in Jordy, pp. 298–302. A few further corrections of details are to be found in Brant, *Madison,* an exhaustive and definitive review of the sources. In a few instances Brant shows that Adams's handling of his materials gives a mistaken reading of the facts at the expense of Madison's character as a resolute statesman. Cf. Brant, V, 54, 63, 284, and notes on pages 492, 497–498, 510. Apparently he did not avail himself of all of the materials unearthed by Adams for the *History* or for the article identifying Crillon in the *American Historical Review,* 1:50–69 (1895). Cf. Brant, notes to the Henry-Crillon affair, V, Index. Cf. also S. E. Morison, "The Henry-Crillon Affair of 1812," *Proceedings,* MHS, 1947–1950 (published 1956), 69:207–231.

15. Winters, *The Anatomy of Nonsense,* p. 69. See the large Adams collection at MHS and at Western Reserve University. Cf. Bixler, "A Note on Henry Adams," *Colophon,* Vol. 5, part 17 (1934). On Adams's notebooks, see Jordy, p. 77.

16. It is difficult to agree with Brant (*Madison*, IV, 330) that the mistranslation is an "appalling" error, putting aside Adams's general competence in the language (cf. Baym, *French Education of Henry Adams* and Bixler, in *Colophon*). Turreau reported his interview concerning Miranda's filibustering activities to his Spanish confrere, Yrujo, in part as follows (all spellings are as they appear in a photostat of the official records):

"J'etais ce matin avec [code number cancelled] (Madison) Jé lui ai fait part de mes soupçons et des vôtres[.]

"J'ai cherché ses yeux et ce qui est assez rare jé le ai rencontrés: *jé crois y avoir saisi la conviction du sujét de nos craintes.* Il etait dans un abattement extraordinaire pendant que jé lui demandais une explication positive sur les demarches en question.

"Je a eu peine á rompre lo silence, et enfin il m'a repondu que déja [code number cancelled] (le President) avait anticipé sur mes representations en ordonnant des mesures contra les complices restés au continent, et contra les coupables qui y reviendrairont. . . .

Adams translated this as follows, omitting, apparently through oversight, to translate the italicized passage (*History*, III, 194, 195):

"I was this morning with Madison. I imparted to him my suspicions and yours. I sought his eyes, and, what is rather rare, I met them. He was in a state of extraordinary prostration while I was demanding from him a positive explanation on the proceedings in question. It was with an effort that he broke silence, and at length answered me that the President had already anticipated my representations by ordering measures to be taken against the accomplices who remained in the country and against the culprits who should return. . . .

Brant translates the omitted sentence as, "I think that I found strong evidence to support the subject of our fears." The omission was an obvious blunder, although it makes no radical alteration in the total effect of the letter. If anything, it supports the implication that the look in Madison's eyes involuntarily gave him away. Brant would render the second sentence, "I looked into his eyes, and what is rather unusual, I caught the meaning in them." One can agree with Brant that Adams's rendering of "abattement" as "prostration" is clearly too strong. "A state of extraordinary dejection" would perhaps have been more accurate; although Brant prefers to change the syntax with the rendering,

"He was very dejected while I was requesting. . . ." The differences do not seem crucial in any comprehensive estimate of Madison's character. Even the boldest Secretary of State would, at that moment, have had reason to avoid looking a hostile inquirer squarely in the eye. As Adams says on the page immediately following, "Madison might well have shown disturbance." Adams's "disturbance" so far as it is not ironic, suggests that "prostration" was employed in a figurative sense. He "had in his desk the parting letter of Miranda which if published would have proved the truth of these charges to the mind of every diplomatist and political authority in Europe."

The omitted sentence is included in the transcript made for Adams. Turreau to Yrujo, February 7, 1806 (should be "February 8" according to Brant), Spanish State Papers (Adams Transcripts), Manuscripts Division, Library of Congress. Photostats of the official records in Legajo 5544, Sección de Estado, Archivo Histórico Nacional, Madrid. See brief excerpts in Brant, *Madison*, IV, 509, and text, pp. 330–331. Also Brant in *American Historical Review*, 57:866.

17. Adams, *History*, VI, 418. Hildreth, *History*, VI, 618, 537.

18. Adams, *History*, III, 123, IV, 384, VI, 133, IV, 105, I, 422, IV, 290, 359, VI, 285.

19. On the comic muse, see Yvor Winters, "Henry Adams, or the Creation of Confusion," in *The Anatomy of Nonsense*. "In Mr. Adams's nine volumes, if my young friends the historical novelists of today only knew it, there is material for endless comedies which are not yet written" (Edward Everett Hale, *Memories of a Hundred Years*, p. 183). Cf. Ford I, pp. 338, 365.

20. Napoleon in his bath, Adams, *History*, II, 34 ff. *Holmes-Laski Letters*, II, 1431; for remark of Lord Morley, *ibid.*, September 26, 1924.

21. *History*, II, 83; III, 37; V, 356; I, 335; VI, 37; VIII, 4; IV, 424. Ford II, p. 501.

22. *History*, IV, 437, 333, 120, 379, 27. Cf. also I, 335, V, 122.

23. *History*, I, 186, 187. HA to Hay, August 6, 1888, Adams Papers. *History*, V, 235; I, 85; VII, 140.

24. *History*, I, 187, 395, 346; II, 310.

25. *History*, IV, 57, 59, 66.

26. Cf. for the pattern of paradox, *History*, I, 217; IV, 464; V, 321; VI, 69.

27. *A Cycle*, I, 40; *Historical Essays*, pp. 266, 270; Ford II, p. 95; cf. also CFA Jr., *Charles Francis Adams*, p. 208. *Nation*, 49:505. On HA's earlier suspicions of Russell, see *A Cycle*, I, 280; II, 13, 83; Ford, I, p. 122; cf. also *Education*, p. 163 ff.

28. *Chapters of Erie,* pp. 193, 206; *Historical Essays,* pp. 55, 62.
29. *Revue Historique,* January–February 1884.
30. *History,* I, chapter xv and II, chapter i. *History,* II, 21, 20.
31. *Historical Essays,* p. 122.
32. *Historical Essays,* pp. 155, 175. *"Honorable* n'est pas le mot que la postérité a choisi pour qualifier l'acte de Leclerc" (*Revue Historique,* 1884, p. 110).
33. New York *Critic,* December 7, 1889. For Hewitt's opinion, in the succeeding paragraph, Hewitt to HA, December 27, 1889, Adams Papers.
34. Scribner to Bangs, February 28, 1890 [pp. 181–182], Scribner files. The English edition was published by Putnam in 1891–92. *Atlantic,* 65:274–278 (February 1890). Notice in New York *Tribune,* February 23, 1890; commented on in HA to Dwight, March 6, 1890, Adams Papers.
35. *Nation,* 49:480–483, 504–506 (December 12, 1889). For reviews of succeeding volumes see, *Nation,* 50:376, 395, 51:405, 424, 52:322, 344. For other contemporary American reviews, see *Dial* (Chicago), 11:33; *Overland,* 16:336, 395, 547; *Harpers,* 80:968 ff.; New York *Times,* February 9, 1890, March 1, 1891; New York *Tribune,* December 8, 1889, February 23, 1890, October 5, 1890, January 25, 1891; W. C. Ford, in *Political Science Review,* 5:541, 697. See also the extensive list in Jordy, p. 298 ff., for contemporary and later reviews. For a unique personal attack, see "Housatonic" [William Henry Smith]. *A Case of Hereditary Bias* (New York, 1891), reprinted from the New York *Tribune,* September 15, December 15, 1890.
36. *Spectator,* 66:726; 68:126; *Athenaeum,* 64:253; 66:669; 67:507; cf. also London *Critic,* 13:164; 14:229; 15:106. But cf. J. A. Doyle, *English Historical Review,* 8:802–806: ". . . too earnest and convinced a patriot to maintain an attitude of severe impartiality in all questions." Macaulay's remark in the following paragraph appears in Trevelyan, *Macaulay,* II, 38.
37. Ford I, pp. 403, 404, 308; Cater, pp. 189, 193. Hay to HA, July 12, 1890, Adams Papers.
38. Cater, pp. 193, 194.
39. HA to Gaskell, April 13, 1890; Gaskell to HA, May 8, 1890, Adams Papers.
40. Cater, p. 192. HA to Elizabeth Cameron, August 16, 1890 (a portion omitted in Ford I, p. 404), December 6, 1891, Adams Papers.
41. HA to Elizabeth Cameron, November 10, 1889, "Wednesday" (Spring? 1890), Adams Papers.

42. Unpublished poems of Henry Adams; Elizabeth Cameron to HA, September 2, 1888, Adams Papers.

43. *Esther,* p. 168. HA to Elizabeth Cameron, August 15, 1890, Adams Papers.

44. HA to Elizabeth Cameron, January 12, 1888, Ford I, p. 404; Cater, p. 195. King to Hay, August 12, 1888, Cater Transcripts, MHS. La Farge to HA, May 22, 1890, Adams Papers.

45. HA to Elizabeth Cameron, August 21, 1890, Adams Papers. Cater, p. 195.

46. HA to Elizabeth Cameron, August 22, 1890, Adams Papers.

47. *Ibid.; Poems of Arthur Hugh Clough* (Oxford, 1950), p. 98.

Selected Bibliography

Manuscript Collections

Archivo Histórico Nacional, Sección de Estado, Madrid
British Foreign Office Archives, London
Corcoran Gallery, Washington
Johns Hopkins University: Gilman Papers
Houghton Library, Harvard University
    Adams Papers, Correspondence of Brooks Adams and Henry
    Adams. Correspondence of Henry Adams and John Chipman
      Gray
    Godkin Papers
Library of Congress
    Henry Adams Transcripts
    American Historical Association Papers
    Corcoran Papers
    Saint-Gaudens Papers
New York Historical Society: Gallatin Papers
New York Public Library: Ford Papers
Massachusetts Historical Society
    Adams Papers: Charles Francis Adams. Charles Francis Adams,
      Jr. Henry Adams. Marian Adams. Clarence King Transcripts
      prepared by Harold Dean Cater.
    Henry Cabot Lodge Papers
    John T. Morse Papers
    Shattuck Papers
Private Collections
    Bernard Berenson, Florence
    Mrs. Robert Homans, Boston
    Mark DeWolfe Howe, Cambridge, for letters in the Holmes
      Papers
    Charles Scribner's Sons, New York
Public Records
    Registry Department, Death Records, Boston
    Records of Probate Court and registers of deeds in Essex County,
      Norfolk County, Suffolk County, Massachusetts
    Probate Court records and registry of deeds, District of Columbia
University of Chicago: Von Holst Papers

Biographical, Critical, and Historical Works Cited

(See footnotes *passim* for books owned and used by Henry Adams. Supplementary references in the notes are not included here, since the full citation appears in the note.)

Adams, Brooks. *America's Economic Supremacy.* Edited by Marquis Childs. New York, 1947.

———— "The Heritage of Henry Adams," *The Degradation of the Democratic Dogma.* New York, 1919.

Adams, Charles Francis, Jr. *An Autobiography.* Boston, 1916.

———— *Charles Francis Adams.* Boston, 1900.

Adams, Henry. See Appendix for List of Writings.

———— *The Education of Henry Adams.* Privately printed, 1907. Boston, 1918.

———— *A Cycle of Adams Letters.* Includes letters of Charles Francis Adams, Henry Adams, and Charles Francis Adams, Jr. Edited by Worthington C. Ford. Boston, 1920.

———— *Henry Adams and His Friends.* Compiled, with a Biographical Introduction, by Harold Dean Cater. Boston, 1947.

———— *Letters of Henry Adams,* 1858–1891; 1892–1918. Edited by Worthington C. Ford. Boston, 1930; 1938.

Adams, James Truslow. *Henry Adams.* New York, 1933.

Adams, Marian Hooper. *Letters of Mrs. Henry Adams,* 1865–1883. Edited by Ward Thoron. Boston, 1936.

Agassiz, George. *Letters and Recollections of Alexander Agassiz.* Boston, 1913.

Allen, Alexander. *Life and Letters of Phillips Brooks.* New York, 1900.

Aldrich, Mrs. Thomas Bailey. *Crowding Memories.* Boston, 1920.

American Historical Association. "Proceedings," in *Papers of the American Historical Association.* Vol. I. New York, 1886. Vol. II. New York, 1888.

Amory, Cleveland. *The Proper Bostonians.* New York, 1947.

Anderson, Frank Maloy. *The Mystery of "A Public Man."* Minneapolis, 1948.

Anderson, Nicholas L. *Letters and Journals.* Edited by Isabel Anderson. New York, 1942.

Anderson, Thornton. *Brooks Adams: Constructive Conservative.* Ithaca, 1951.

Austen, Jessica Tyler. *Moses Coit Tyler: Selections from His Letters and Diaries.* New York, 1911.

Barnard, Henry. *Rutherford B. Hayes and His America.* Indianapolis, 1954.

Bartlett, J. Gardner. *Simon Stone Genealogy*. Boston, 1926.

Baym, Max I. *The French Education of Henry Adams*. New York, 1951.

Bemis, Samuel F. *John Quincy Adams and the Union*. New York, 1956.

Beringause, Arthur F. *Brooks Adams*. New York, 1955.

Berthoff, Warner B., and D. A. Green. "Henry Adams and Wayne MacVeagh," *Pennsylvania Magazine of History and Biography*, LXXX, 1956.

Bixler, Paul H. "A Note on Henry Adams," *Colophon*, vol. 5, part 17.

Blackmur, Richard P. "The Novels of Henry Adams," *Sewanee Review*, LI, April 1943.

Blanck, Jacob. *Bibliography of American Literature*. New Haven, 1955.

Bradford, Gamaliel. *American Portraits*. Boston, 1931.

—————— *Letters of Gamaliel Bradford*. Edited by Van Wyck Brooks. Boston, 1934.

—————— *Journal of Gamaliel Bradford*. Edited by Van Wyck Brooks. Boston, 1933.

Brant, Irving. *James Madison*. Vol. IV: Secretary of State. Vol. V: The President. Indianapolis, 1953; 1956.

Brogan, Denis. The Development of Modern *France*. London, 1940.

Bronson, Edgar Beecher. *Reminiscences of a Ranchman*. New York, 1908.

Bruce, William Cabell. *John Randolph of Roanoke*. New York, 1922.

Buckle, Henry. *History of Civilization in England*. New York, 1878. From 2d London edition.

Buckler, William E. "Matthew Arnold in America. 'The Reason,'" *American Literature*, vol. 29, January 1958.

Campbell, John D. *Manic-Depressive Disease*. Philadelphia, 1953.

Carlyle, Thomas. *Reminiscences*. New York, 1881.

Carter, Morris. *Isabella Stewart Gardner and Fenway Court*. Boston, 1940.

Chalfant, Edward Allan. *Henry Adams and History*. University of Pennsylvania, 1954. Doctoral Dissertation Series, Publication Number 8539. University Microfilms, Ann Arbor, Michigan.

Chanler, Mrs. Winthrop. *Roman Spring*. Boston, 1934.

Chapin, Mrs. Elizabeth N. *American Court Gossip*. Marshalltown, Iowa, 1887.

Christy, Arthur, ed. *The Asian Legacy and American Life*. New York, 1945.

Clemens, Samuel L. *Mark Twain's Autobiography*. New York, 1924.

Cochran, Thomas C., and William Miller. *The Age of Enterprise*. New York, 1942.

Comte, Auguste. *The Positive Philosophy of Auguste Comte*. New York, 1855.

Cortissoz, Royal. *John La Farge*, Boston, 1911.

Craven, Avery. *The Coming of the Civil War*. 2d ed. Chicago, 1957.

Crosby, Harry Herbert. *So Deep a Trail: A Biography of Clarence King*. Stanford University, 1953. Doctoral Dissertation Series, Publication Number 5791. University Microfilms, Ann Arbor, Michigan.

Curti, Merle. *The Growth of American Thought*. New York, 1943.

Darrah, William C. *Powell of Colorado*. Princeton, 1951.

Dennett, Tyler. *John Hay: From Poetry to Politics*. New York, 1933.

De Tocqueville, Alexis. See Tocqueville.

Dickason, David H. *The Daring Young Men*. Bloomington, 1953.

Didier, Eugene L. *Life and Letters of Madame Bonaparte*. New York, 1879.

Documentary History of the Cosmos Club. Twenty-Fifth Anniversary. Washington, 1904.

Dodge, Mary Abigail. *Gail Hamilton's Life in Letters*. Edited by H. Augusta Dodge. Boston, 1901.

Duncan, David. *Life and Letters of Herbert Spencer*. New York, 1908.

Earnest, Ernest. *S. Weir Mitchell: Novelist and Physician*. Philadelphia, 1950.

Eggleston, George Cary. *Recollections of a Varied Life*. New York, 1910.

Elliott, Maud Howe. *Three Generations*. Boston, 1923.

Emmons, Samuel F. *Biographical Memoir of Clarence King*. Washington, 1907.

—————— "Clarence King," *Biographical Memoirs, National Academy of Sciences*, vol. VI. Washington, 1909.

—————— "Clarence King," *American Journal of Science*, March 1902.

Everett, William. *Address in Commemoration of the Life and Services of Charles Francis Adams*. Cambridge, 1887.

Faverty, Frederic E. *Matthew Arnold the Ethnologist*. Evanston, Illinois. 1951.

Federal Writers' Project. *Washington, City and Capital.* American Guide Series. Washington, 1937.

Fisher, H. A. L. *James Bryce.* New York, 1927.

Fiske, John. *Excursions of an Evolutionist.* Boston, 1884.

—— *Outlines of Cosmic Philosophy.* Boston, 1887 [1874]

—— *The Letters of John Fiske.* Edited by Ethel Fisk. New York, 1940.

Fleming, Donald. *John William Draper and the Religion of Science.* Philadelphia, 1950.

Foote, Henry Wilder. *Annals of King's Chapel.* Boston, 1900.

Freud, Sigmund. *Totem and Taboo.* New York, 1918.

Fuess, Claude M. *Carl Schurz: Reformer.* New York, 1932.

Gabriel, Ralph Henry. *The Course of American Democratic Thought.* New York, 1940.

Gannett, Henry, "The Wealth of the United States and the Rate of Increase," *International Review,* vol XII, May 1882.

Garland, Hugh A. *John Randolph.* New York, 1851.

Galton, Francis. *Hereditary Genius.* Rev. ed. New York, 1871.

Geike, Sir Archibald. *The Founders of Geology.* 2d ed. London, 1905.

Gibbon, Edward. *The Autobiographies of Edward Gibbon.* London, 1896.

Gilder, Richard Watson. *Letters of Richard Watson Gilder.* Edited by Rosamund Gilder. Boston, 1916.

Grant Duff, Sir Mountstuart E. *Notes from a Diary.* London, 1898.

Grattan, C. Hartley. *The Three Jameses.* London, 1932.

Gwynn, Stephen. *Letters and Friendships of Sir Cecil Spring Rice.* London, 1929.

Griscom, Lloyd C. *Diplomatically Speaking.* Boston, 1940.

Hacker, Louis M. *The Triumph of American Capitalism.* New York, 1940.

Hale, Edward Everett. *Memories of a Hundred Years.* New York, 1902.

Hanotaux, Gabriel. *Contemporary France.* Trans. by J. C. Tarver and E. Sparvel-Bayly. London, 1903–1909.

Harlow, Virginia. *Thomas Sergeant Perry.* Durham, N.C., 1950.

Harte, Bret. *The Letters of Bret Harte.* Edited by Geoffrey Bret Harte. Boston, 1926.

Haskell, Daniel C. *The Nation: Index of Titles and Contributors.* New York, 1953.

Hay, John. *A Poet in Exile: Early Letters of John Hay.* Edited by Mrs. Caroline Ticknor. Boston, 1910.

Hay, Malcolm. *The Foot of Pride: The Pressure of Christendom on the People of Israel for 1900 Years.* Boston, 1950.

Hearn, Lafcadio. *Life and Letters of Lafcadio Hearn.* Edited by Elizabeth Bisland. Boston, 1906.

Hewitt, Abram S. *Selected Writings of Abram S. Hewitt.* Edited by Allan Nevins. New York, 1937.

Hildreth, Richard. *History of the United States.* Rev. ed. New York, 1863.

Hirschfeld. Magnus. *Men and Women.* New York, 1935.

Hitchcock, Henry Russell. *Architecture of Henry Hobson Richardson and His Times.* New York, 1936.

Holmes, Oliver Wendell. *John Lothrop Motley.* Boston, 1879.

Holmes, Oliver Wendell, Jr. *The Common Law.* Boston 1881.

Hofstadter, Richard. *Social Darwinism in American Thought,* 1860–1915. Philadelphia, 1945.

Holt, Henry. *Garrulities of an Octogenarian Editor.* Boston, 1923.

Howe, Mark A. De Wolfe. *Life and Letters of George Bancroft.* New York, 1908.

——— *James Ford Rhodes:* American Historian. New York, 1929.

Howe, Mark DeWolfe, ed. *Holmes-Laski Letters: The Correspondence of Mr. Justice Holmes and Harold J. Laski.* Cambridge, 1953.

——— *Holmes-Pollock Letters. The Correspondence of Mr. Justice Holmes and Sir Frederick Pollock.* Cambridge, 1941.

Hume, Robert. *Runaway Star: An Appreciation of Henry Adams.* Ithaca, New York, 1951.

Huxley, Aldous. *Proper Studies.* London, 1927.

Huxley, Thomas H. *Essays.* Vol. IX. London, 1896–1902.

Hyde, Agnes Mary [Mrs. E. T. Gough]. "Henry Adams's Democracy." Unpublished M. A. dissertation. University of Chicago, 1938.

James, Henry. *The Letters of Henry James.* Edited by Percy Lubbock. New York, 1920.

——— *The Notebooks of Henry James.* Edited by F. O. Matthiessen and Kenneth B. Murdock. New York, 1947.

——— *Hawthorne.* English Men of Letters. New York, 1880.

James, William. *Collected Essays and Reviews.* New York, 1920.

——— *The Letters of William James.* Edited by his son, Henry James. Boston, 1920.

——— *Essays on Faith and Morals.* New York, 1943.

Johnson, Robert U. *Remembered Yesterdays.* Boston, 1923.

Jones, Howard Mumford. "Arnold, Aristocracy, and America," *American Historical Review,* vol. 39, April 1944.

——— *The Theory of American Literature.* Ithaca, New York, 1948.

Jordy, William H. *Henry Adams: Scientific Historian.* New Haven, 1952.

King, Clarence. *Clarence King Memoirs.* Century Association. New York, 1904.

—— *Systematic Geology.* Washington, 1878.

Kirk, Russell. *Randolph of Roanoke. A Study of Conservative Thought.* Chicago, 1951.

Kraus, Michael. *A History of American History.* New York, 1937.

—— *The Writing of American History.* Norman, Oklahoma, 1953.

La Farge, John. *An Artist's Letters from Japan.* New York, 1897.

La Farge, John. S.J. *The Manner Is Ordinary.* New York, 1954.

Larkin, Oliver. *Art and Life in America.* New York, 1949.

Leslie, Shane. *American Wonderland.* London. 1936.

Levenson, J. C. *The Mind and Art of Henry Adams.* Boston, 1957.

Lippincott, Benjamin. *Victorian Critics of Democracy.* Minneapolis, 1938.

Lodge, Henry Cabot. *Early Memories.* New York, 1913.

—— *Alexander Hamilton.* Boston, 1882.

Lowe, R. L. "A Note on Arnold in America," *American Literature,* vol. XXIII, May 1957.

McLean, Evalyn Walsh. *Father Struck It Rich.* Boston, 1936.

Malone, Dumas. *Jefferson, The Virginian.* Boston, 1948.

Matthiessen, Francis O. *Henry James: The Major Phase.* New York, 1944.

May, Henry F. *Protestant Churches and Industrial America.* New York, 1949.

Merrill, Dana K. *American Biography.* Portland, Maine, 1957.

Merrill, George P. *The First Hundred Years of American Geology.* New Haven, 1924.

Mill, John Stuart. *Auguste Comte and Positivism.* London, n.d.

Morison, James A. *Macaulay.* New York, 1883.

Morison, Samuel Eliot and Henry Steele Commager. *The Growth of the American Republic.* 3rd ed. New York, 1942.

Morison, Samuel Eliot. "The Henry-Crillon Affair of 1812," *Proceedings,* Massachusetts Historical Society, vol. 69, 1947–1950. Boston, 1956.

Morse, John T. "Incidents Connected with the American Statesmen Series," *Proceedings,* Massachusetts Historical Society, vol. 64.

Munroe, J. P. *A Life of Francis Amasa Walker.* New York, 1923.

Myerson, Dr. Abraham and Rosalie Boyle. "The Incidence of Manic-Depressive Disease in Certain Socially Prominent Families," *American Journal of Psychiatry,* 1941.

Nevins, Allan. *Abram S. Hewitt*. New York, 1935.
——— *Hamilton Fish*. New York, 1936.
Nicolson, Harold. *The Development of English Biography*. London, 1927.
Newman, John Henry. *Certain Difficulties Felt by Anglicans in Catholic Teaching*. London, 1876.
Nye, Russel. *George Bancroft: Brahmin Rebel*. New York, 1944.
Ogden, Rollo. *Life and Letters of Edwin Lawrence Godkin*. New York, 1907.
O'Neill, Edward H. *A History of American Biography, 1800–1935*. Philadelphia, 1935.
Padover, Saul K. *Thomas Jefferson*. New York, 1942.
Page, Evelyn. "The Man around the Corner," *New England Quarterly*, vol. XXIII, September 1950.
——— "The Diary of a Public Man," *New England Quarterly*, vol. XXII, June 1949.
Parrington, Vernon Louis. *Main Currents in American Thought*. New York, 1927, 1930.
Pemberton, T. Edgar. *The Life of Bret Harte*. London, 1903.
Pratt, Julius W. "Aaron Burr and the Historians," *New York History*, vol. XXVI, 1945.
Rhodes, James Ford. *History of the United States*. Vol. VII, 1872–1877. Vol. VIII, 1877–1896. New York, 1906, 1919.
——— *Historical Essays*. New York, 1909.
Pope, C. H. and T. Hooper, compilers. *Hooper Genealogy*. Boston, 1908.
Raymond, Dora. *British Policy and Opinion during the Franco-Prussian War*. New York, 1921.
Richardson, Leon Burr. *William E. Chandler: Republican*. New York, 1940.
Roe, Frederick William, ed. *Victorian Prose*. New York, 1947.
Routh, Harold V. *Towards the Twentieth Century*. New York, 1937.
Ruykeyser, Muriel. *Willard Gibbs*. New York, 1942.
Saint-Gaudens, Augustus. *The Reminiscences of Augustus Saint-Gaudens*. Edited by Homer Saint-Gaudens. London, 1913.
Schlesinger, Arthur, Jr. "The Causes of the Civil War: A Note on Historical Sentimentalism," *Partisan Review*, October 1949.
Scudder, Horace E. *James Russell Lowell*. Cambridge, 1901.
Shackleton, Robert. *The Book of Washington*. Philadelphia, 1922.
Simonds, Katherine. "The Tragedy of Mrs. Henry Adams," *New England Quarterly*, vol. IX, December 1936.
Slosson, Preston. *Europe Since 1870*. Boston, 1935.
Spaulding, Thomas M. *The Cosmos Club on Lafayette Square*. Washington, 1949.

Speare, Morris. *The Political Novel: Its Development in England and America*. New York, 1924.

Spencer, Herbert. *First Principles*. 2d edition. New York, 1872.

Spiller, Robert, *et al*. *Literary History of the United States*. New York, 1946, 1947, 1948.

Stanton, Theodore, ed. *Manual of American Literature*. New York, 1909.

Stegner, Wallace. *Beyond the Hundredth Meridian; John Wesley Powell and the Second Opening of the West*. Boston, 1954.

Stevens, John Austin. *Albert Gallatin*. Boston, 1884.

Stevenson, Elizabeth. *Henry Adams*. New York, 1955.

Streeter, M. E. *Books from the Library of Henry Adams at Western Reserve University*. Typescript, Western Reserve University, Cleveland, n.d.

Taylor, W. R. "Historical Bifocals on the Year 1800," *New England Quarterly*, vol. XXIII, 1950.

Thayer, William Roscoe. *Life and Letters of John Hay*. Boston, 1915.

―――― *Letters of William Roscoe Thayer*. Edited by Charles D. Hazen. Boston, 1926.

Tocqueville, Alexis de. *Democracy in America*. Translated by Henry Reeve. 2 vols. London, 1889.

Trevelyan, Sir George Otto. *Life and Letters of Lord Macaulay*. (London, 1876) New York, 1909.

Trinity Church in the City of Boston. Boston, 1933.

Van Rensselaer, Mrs. Schuyler [Mrs. Mariana Griswold]. *Henry Hobson Richardson and His Works*. Boston, 1888.

Waddington, Mary King. *My First Years as a Frenchwoman, 1876–1879*. New York, 1914.

Waern, Cecilia. *John La Farge*. London, 1896.

Ward, Lester. *Dynamic Sociology*. New York, 1883.

Walters, Raymond, Jr. *Albert Gallatin*. New York, 1957.

Watterson, Henry. '*Marse Henry*' *An Autobiography*. New York, 1919.

Wecter, Dixon. *Sam Clemens of Hannibal*. Boston, 1952.

White, Edward A. *Science and Religion in American Thought*. Stanford, 1952.

Wilkins, Thurman. *Clarence King*. New York, 1958.

Williams, Charles Richard. *Life of Rutherford Birchard Hayes*. Boston, 1914.

Winsor, Justin, ed. *The Memorial History of Boston*. Boston, 1881.

Woodward, William E. *Meet General Grant*. New York, 1928.

Wright, Charles H. *Background of Modern French Literature*. Boston, 1926.

Winters, Yvor. *The Anatomy of Nonsense*. Norfolk, Conn., 1943.

Index

torian, 263; first letters to his wife, 265; calls on Cleveland, 266; named trustee, 267; onset of Marian's depression, 269; at meetings of Historical Association, 269, 295, 296; attitude toward Marian, 279; plans trip to Japan, 282, 291; trust fund for nieces, 282; moves to new house, 283; turns to women, 283 ff., *see also* Women; La Farge on Adams, 292; plans memorial, 298; arrives in Japan, 300; effect of nudity on, 302; mourning, 308; reading Dante, 309; photography, 310, 473; leaves Japan, 311; path blocked by family, 316; prepares father's epitaph, 318; learning Chinese, 321, 330, 475; taboos talk of *History,* 322; "nieces-in-residence," 324; characterized by Spring Rice, 325; love for Mrs. Cameron, 326, 416 ff.; keeps Diary, 327 ff.; fits of depression, 329, 331; completes *History,* 331; destroys Diary and papers, 331, 415; travel plans, 414, 415; leaves for South Seas, 348, 418; sonnets to Mrs. Cameron, 416 ff.; first painting lessons, 419; deflected to life of contemplation, 451; uses stenographer, 323; misses Brooks's wedding, 484

Traits: contempt for Harvard teaching, 5; love of luxury, 11; fond of dancing, 26; aloofness and exclusiveness, 17, 20, 26, 27, 171; optimism, 19, 233; detachment, 19, 96; childlessness, 21, 22, 96, 160; pride in Marian, 25, 26; anti-clerical, 27, 257; contentment, 33, 107, 214; like Jefferson, 49, 388 ff.; like Casaubon, 71; like Randolph, 198, 200; restlessness and ambition, 64; anonymity, 69; sense of guilt, 82; dislike of strife of

world, 89, 388; seasickness, 111, 296, 310, 311; self-depreciation, 111; prudery, 120, 121; homesickness, 121; distaste for politics, 122; anglicized, 127; facetiousness, 129, 184, 185; contradictoriness, 139, 200, 231; violent temper, 143; liberal proclivities, 153; domesticity, 160; stoicism, 200; detests own books, 201; health, 215; preference for small dinners, 218; feminism, 226, 284 ff.; pessimistic, 71, 230, 233, 315, 323, 330, 345; interest in genealogy, 269, 295; fear of age and mental decay, 215, 279, 297; indifference to fame, 216, 411; fear of criticism, 217; scepticism, 230; agnosticism, 257, 393; insomnia, 265; love of nature, 266, 267; guilt-complex, 279; deceptive memory, 281; pose of posthumous existence, 284 ff.; connoisseur, 293; bystander, 297; historical sense, 304; business acumen, 317; sense of mutability, 320; love of archaic, 293, 328; passion for statistics, 369; Puritan morality, 378; inherited political feelings, 388; love of form, 388; effect of family tradition, 391, 392; tendency to sweeping generalizations, 394; "Porcupinus Angelicus," 399; Hamlet-izing, 416; love of nature, 429; misspells names, 456; love of babies, 476; inherited mother's disposition, 478

General: Literary style and theory, 60, 61, 62, 66, 191, 201, 207 ff., 263, 295, 372, 401, 403, 407; literary revision, 211, 212, 213, 393 ff., 406 ff., 409, 410; graphic images, 367; prize ring image, 366, 380, 394; monkey image, 429; eloquence, 386; mixing metaphors, 390; travel letters, 328, 333; debt to Haw-